Banishment and Belonging

Lanka, Ceylon, Sarandib: merely three disparate names for a single island? Perhaps. Yet the three diverge in the historical echoes, literary cultures, maps and memories they evoke. Names that have intersected and overlapped – in a treatise, a poem, a document – only to go their own ways. But despite different trajectories, all three are tied to narratives of banishment and exile. Ronit Ricci suggests that the island served as a concrete exilic site as well as a metaphor for imagining exile across religions, languages, space and time: Sarandib, where Adam was banished from Paradise; Lanka, where Sita languished in captivity; and Ceylon, faraway island of exile for Indonesian royalty under colonialism. Utilizing Malay manuscripts and documents from Sri Lanka, Javanese chronicles, and Dutch and British sources, Ricci explores histories and imaginings of displacement related to the island through a study of the Sri Lankan Malays and their connections to an exilic past.

RONIT RICCI is Sternberg-Tamir Chair in Comparative Cultures at Hebrew University of Jerusalem and Associate Professor of Asian Studies at Australian National University. She is the author of the multiple-prize-winning *Islam Translated: Literature, Conversion, and the Arab Cosmopolis of South and Southeast Asia* (2011).

Asian Connections

Series Editors

Sunil Amrith, *Harvard University*

Tim Harper, *University of Cambridge*

Engseng Ho, *Duke University*

Asian Connections is a major series of ambitious works that look beyond the traditional templates of area, regional or national studies to consider the trans-regional phenomena which have connected and influenced various parts of Asia through time. The series will focus on empirically grounded work exploring circulations, connections, convergences and comparisons within and beyond Asia. Themes of particular interest include transport and communication, mercantile networks and trade, migration, religious connections, urban history, environmental history, oceanic history, the spread of language and ideas, and political alliances. The series aims to build new ways of understanding fundamental concepts, such as modernity, pluralism or capitalism, from the experience of Asian societies. It is hoped that this conceptual framework will facilitate connections across fields of knowledge and bridge historical perspectives with contemporary concerns.

Banishment and Belonging

Exile and Diaspora in Sarandib, Lanka and Ceylon

Ronit Ricci

Hebrew University of Jerusalem and Australian National University

CAMBRIDGE
UNIVERSITY PRESS

CAMBRIDGE
UNIVERSITY PRESS

University Printing House, Cambridge CB2 8BS, United Kingdom

One Liberty Plaza, 20th Floor, New York, NY 10006, USA

477 Williamstown Road, Port Melbourne, VIC 3207, Australia

314–321, 3rd Floor, Plot 3, Splendor Forum, Jasola District Centre, New Delhi – 110025, India

79 Anson Road, #06–04/06, Singapore 079906

Cambridge University Press is part of the University of Cambridge.

It furthers the University's mission by disseminating knowledge in the pursuit of education, learning, and research at the highest international levels of excellence.

www.cambridge.org
Information on this title: www.cambridge.org/9781108480277
DOI: 10.1017/9781108648189

© Ronit Ricci 2019

First published 2019

Printed in the United Kingdom by TJ International Ltd, Padstow Cornwall

A catalogue record for this publication is available from the British Library.

ISBN 978-1-108-48027-7 Hardback
ISBN 978-1-108-72724-2 Paperback

Contents

Figures

Maps

A Note on Orthography and Manuscripts

The sources cited and discussed in this book span several places, periods and languages. In addition, orthographic variation was very much the norm for much of the period covered, and it is not unusual to find the same word or name spelled differently even in a single document or manuscript. Variation typically also occurs when spelling the same words across scripts. This raises the question of whether standardization is a technical move or an imposition as, for example, when Arabic diacritics or long vowels are added to Malay words to "correct" them.

I have attempted to retain the original spelling as much as possible and therefore the same word may be spelled differently depending on language or source (i.e. *Pangéran* in Javanese, *Pangeran* in Malay, in Ceylon sometimes spelled *Pangeeran* or *Pangerang*).

When citing manuscripts, the available information, often incomplete, is given in the first citation. For Javanese sources it is sometimes known who the author was, as well as who inscribed the particular exemplar cited. For the Sri Lankan materials that is not the case and therefore, when known, I have included the name of the person who created the exemplar available at present.

Non-English terminology is italicized on first appearance. Capitalization and punctuation have sometimes been added to Javanese and Malay citations and their translations in order to make them more legible to the reader.

Acknowledgments

Many individuals and institutions have assisted and supported me during the course of researching and writing this book, and it is my pleasure to offer my heartfelt thanks.

My greatest debt is to the members of the Malay community in Sri Lanka. I arrived in Colombo in late 2009 as a complete newcomer to the country. In 2003, while conducting dissertation research in Madras, I had read Tayka Shuʿayb ʿĀlim's *Arabic, Arwi and Persian in Sarandib and Tamil Nadu* and had been intrigued by a footnote that mentioned a group of Javanese princes exiled to Ceylon. It took several years until I was able to follow in the footsteps of that footnote, embarking on a journey that took me to Sri Lanka and allowed me the privilege of meeting a remarkable and resilient community. Many Malay families around the country opened their homes to me and offered me kind and generous hospitality in the form of meals, tea, sweets and above all conversation. They shared their childhood stories, precious family heirlooms and documents, jokes, reflections and a warmth that has touched me deeply. I was especially moved by meeting the older generation, quite a few of them in their eighties and nineties, who despite ailments and the challenges of old age gracefully answered my questions and helped me imagine their, and their community's, past in a vivid and honest manner. I wish to express my sincere gratitude to Muzni Ameer, Iqram Cuttilan, Warnesia Dole, Muhaj Hamin, T. S. Jamalon, Thalip and Jayarine Iyne, Kartini Mohamed, Naleera Rahim, Noor Rahim, Romola Rassool, B. A. Sadar, the late B. D. K. Saldin, M. J. (Joe) Weerabangsa and M. M. K. Weerabangsa. Although I can, regretfully, only offer a very partial list of names here due to the constraints of space, I take this opportunity to thank everyone in the community whom I had the good fortune to meet.

As I was a newcomer to the country, so I was to the field of Sri Lankan studies. I am deeply grateful to Dennis McGilvray, Charlie Hallisey, John Rogers, Jonathan Spencer and Alicia Schrikker for offering invaluable help and advice, answering my novice's questions with endless patience, and generously sharing with me the fruits of their years of study and experience and their love of Sri Lanka.

Others offered invaluable support in a range of ways: I am most grateful to B. A. Hussainmiya for his encouraging response when I first contacted him about my research, for introducing me to central figures in the community and for giving me photocopies of several Sri Lankan Malay manuscripts; I wholeheartedly thank Muhammad Endy Saputro and Sri Ratna Saktimulya for assisting me in locating, translating and reading several of the Javanese manuscripts mentioned below and for insightful discussions of their content and context; I thank Nadeera Rupasinghe for her invaluable assistance at the Department of National Archives, Sri Lanka, most importantly with access to eighteenth-century Dutch sources; at the Department of National Archives I also thank K. D. Paranavitana, former director Saroja Wettasinghe, and the very helpful staff. I am grateful to Tinaz Ameeth, Mona Ismail, Romola Rassool and Megara Tegal for significant research assistance that included travel across the country, digitalization work and accessing their networks of relatives, neighbors and friends in pursuit of Malay documents. My thanks to Merle C. Ricklefs for sharing his expertise on Javanese history, to Mahmood Kooriah for providing me with a scan of Sheikh Yusuf's *al-Nafḥat al-Sailāniyyah,* and to Udaya Prasanta Meddegama for allowing me to cite his English translation of the Sinhala poem *Ingrīsi Haṭana.* Conversations with Craig Reynolds in Canberra while we were both writing our respective books were always stimulating and enjoyable.

I also wish to express my gratitude and *utang budi* ("indebtness for kindness") to colleagues and friends who assisted me in myriad ways, such as translating difficult passages, deciphering idiosyncratic handwriting in manuscripts, suggesting readings, commenting on drafts and offering priceless support, encouragement and friendship: Ruth Barraclough, Assi and Minnie Doron, Greg Fealy, Nancy Florida, Annabel Teh Gallop, Ken George, Priya Hart, Mulaika Hijjas, George Hoffmann, Virginia Hooker, Tony Johns, Ann Kumar, Sumit Mandal, Farina Mir, Kirin Narayan, Inez Nimpuno, Gananath Obeyesekere, Jan van der Putten, Tony Reid, Laurie Sears, Anton Shammas, David Shulman, Monica Smith, Mirjana Vajic and Amrih Widodo. At Colombo's American Institute for Sri Lankan Studies on Sulaiman Terrace, I thank Deepthi Guneratne, Heevi Rodrigo and the late Ira Unamboowe for offering me a home away from home.

Some sections of this book were presented at conferences and talks at the University of Michigan, University of Toronto, Australian National University, SOAS, University of London, Hebrew University of

Jerusalem, University of Washington, Leiden University, University of Hamburg and Tokyo University of Foreign Studies. I thank the audiences in all these places for their questions and constructive criticism.

I offer my gratitude to all those who helped me prepare this book for publication: the two anonymous reviewers for their many useful comments and suggestions; Leigh Chipman for her editorial assistance; and Lucy Rhymer, Natasha Whelan, Karen Anderson, Lisa Carter and Lauren Simpson – the excellent editorial team at Cambridge University Press – for their never-failing guidance. Any remaining errors are my own.

I am deeply appreciative for the generous support I have received over the years from the Asia Research Institute in Singapore, the American Institute for Sri Lankan Studies, the British Library's Endangered Archives Programme (EAP450 and EAP609), the Australian Research Council (Distinguished Early Career Research Award 120102604) and the Israel Science Foundation (grant no. 484/14).

I dedicate this book to the memory of four individuals who, through the inspiration they provided, made studying Java, the Malay world and Sri Lanka a fascinating and personally rewarding experience: Pete Becker (1930–2011), teacher and friend, whose attunement to language and stories was profound; Ian Proudfoot (1946–2011), meticulous and original scholar of the Malay world whom I knew only briefly but whose kindness will remain with me always; B. D. K. (Baba) Saldin (1928–2017), a pillar of the Sri Lankan Malay community, who welcomed me time and again to his home in Dehiwala and shared his knowledge with generosity, patience and insight; and Ira Unamboowe (1939–2015), Executive Director of the American Institute for Sri Lankan Studies in Colombo from 2004 to 2015, whose sense of humor, wisdom and resourcefulness are greatly missed.

Saying "thank you" to my family members feels completely inadequate. They have shared this journey, in its multiple dimensions, with me from the start. I hope that my parents, my sisters and Tamir, Tom, Yasmin and Adam know how much their love and support sustain me.

★★★

Several sections of this book first appeared elsewhere: parts of Chapter 2 draw on "Asian and Islamic Crossings: Malay Writing in Nineteenth-Century Sri Lanka," *South Asian History and Culture* 5.2 (April 2014): 179–194, "Reading between the Lines: A World of Interlinear Translation," *Journal of World Literature* 1.1 (March 2016): 68–80, and "The Discovery of Javanese Writing in a Sri Lankan Malay Manuscript," *Bijdragen tot de Taal-, Land- en Volkenkunde* 168. 4 (December 2012):

511–518; sections of Chapter 3 were included in "Remembering Java's Islamization: A View from Sri Lanka," in *Global Muslims in the Age of Steam and Print* edited by Nile Green and James Gelvin (Los Angeles: University of California Press, 2013), 185–203; sections of Chapters 4 and 5 appeared in "From Java to Jaffna: Exile and Return in Dutch Asia in the Eighteenth Century," in *Exile in Colonial Asia: Kings, Convicts, Commemoration*, edited by Ronit Ricci (Honolulu: University of Hawai'i Press, 2016), 94–116; a portion of Chapter 9 was first published in "Along the Frontiers of Religion, Language and War: Baba Ounus Saldin's *Syair Faid al-Abad*," in *The Routledge Companion to World Literature and World History*, edited by May Hawas (London: Routledge, 2018), 82–92; I thank these journals and publishers for kindly granting me permission to reprint these materials.

Abbreviations

Manuscript Collections, Archives, and Publishers

BL	British Library
BP	Bale Pustaka
BU	Budi Utama
DBP	Dewan Bahasa dan Pustaka, Kuala Lumpur, Malaysia
EAP450	British Library Endangered Archives Programme project #450, "Manuscripts of the Sri Lankan Malays," https://eap.bl.uk/project/EAP450
EAP609	British Library Endangered Archives Programme project #609, "Digitising Malay Writing in Sri Lanka," https://eap.bl.uk/project/EAP609. The site contains, in addition to digital copies of collected materials, available information on each item such as ownership history, current ownership, condition etc.
KS	Karaton Surakarta, Surakarta, Indonesia
LOr	University of Leiden Oriental Manuscripts, The Netherlands
MF	microfilm, in Hussainmiya Collection, Department of National Archives, Sri Lanka
MN	Reksa Pustaka Library, Kadipatèn Mangkunagaran, Surakarta, Indonesia
PNM	Perpustakaan Negara Malaysia, Kuala Lumpur, Malaysia
PNRI	Perpustakaan Nasional Republik Indonesia, Jakarta, Indonesia
PP	Kadipatèn Pura Pakualaman, Yogyakarta, Indonesia
RP	Redya Pustaka Museum, Surakarta, Indonesia
TT	typescript of manuscript

Archival Documents

SLNA/1   Department of National Archives, Sri Lanka
          Lot 1 (VOC Archive)

Journals

BKI   *Bijdragen tot de Taal-, Land- en Volkenkunde*
JRAS   *Journal of the Royal Asiatic Society*

Languages

A.   Arabic
D.   Dutch
J.   Javanese
M.   Malay
Sin.   Sinhala
Skt.   Sanskrit
T.   Tamil

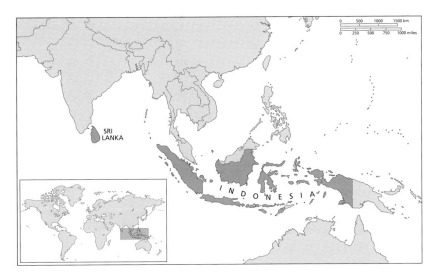

Map 1 Indonesia and Sri Lanka

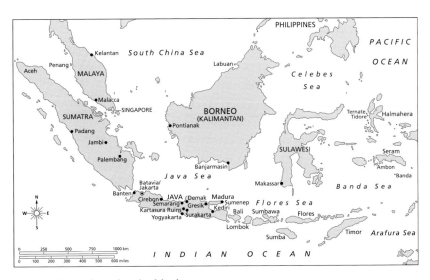

Map 2 The Indonesian Archipelago

Map 3 Sri Lanka

1   Introduction

Beginning in the late seventeenth century and throughout the eighteenth, the Dutch United East India Company (VOC) used the island of Ceylon as a site of banishment for those considered rebels in the regions under Company control in the Indonesian Archipelago, many of whom were members of royal lineages. Convicts and slaves from these territories were also sent to Ceylon, as were native troops who served in the Company's army. After their takeover of the island in 1796, the British, too, brought to Ceylon colonial subjects from the archipelago and the Malay Peninsula, primarily to serve in their military. It is from these early political exiles and the accompanying retinues, soldiers, servants, convicts and slaves that the community of the Sri Lankan Malays developed, with its cohesiveness based, above all, on an ongoing adherence to the Muslim faith and the Malay language.

The previous paragraph has briefly introduced a group now referred to as the "Sri Lankan Malays." And yet the history of this designation is neither simple nor straightforward, regarding both place ("Sri Lanka") and people ("Malay"), and as a result nomenclature has emerged as a methodological and theoretical theme in this book, its exploration bringing to the fore a set of questions about understandings of space, temporality, stories and belonging. I raise it here, at the very start, because it is impossible to refrain from naming the place, people and culture I write about, yet also untenable to qualify what is written at every turn. In considering exile, diaspora and the literary culture they fostered, place is clearly a central theme. But what constitutes "a place"?

The island to which Javanese princes, and many other members of royal families from across the Indonesian Archipelago, were sent by the VOC in the seventeenth and eighteenth centuries possessed several names: Sarandib, Lanka, Ceylon. How, I ask in this book, do the different – perhaps distinct, overlapping or competing – names of a place shape the ways in which that place is imagined, and the way its histories are told and retold across space, time and literary cultures? Furthermore, I consider how these different imaginings in turn come to shape experiences and affiliations. The island's names, I propose, were not mere interchangeable designations. Rather, they represented different traditions, histories and attachments that fostered understandings of, and approaches to, exile and diaspora in lived experience. I will suggest that nomenclature determines place and its imaginings no less than do its physical and spatial dimensions.

Different religious and literary traditions attached different names to the Indian Ocean island off India's southeastern coast. What exile-related echoes did these names – Sarandib, Lanka and Ceylon – carry, especially for a diasporic community? Sarandib, the old name employed by the Arabs for the island, was the spot where according to Muslim tradition Adam, the first man and first prophet, fell to earth upon his banishment from Paradise, a tradition that was known and retold across South and Southeast Asia. Exiles and their descendants engaged with this exilic geography, one that implied that they were not only banished individuals but also returnees to a primordial sacred site. Lanka, the fabulous demon kingdom in the Ramayana, was also a site of banishment, where Sita was forcibly taken by Ravana, far from her husband Rama, his kingdom and his subjects. The Ramayana was widely known in the archipelago, where its story was recast in stone, expressed through dance and theater, and written down in a range of genres, and it would have been intimately familiar to Javanese exiles. Ceylon, the name employed by successive European rulers of the island, was closely associated with exile in the colonial period. To consider if and how these nomenclatures were linked is to ask whether these were parallel, synonymous or perhaps competing nomenclatures for a single place or, possibly, names that were employed for what their users believed to be distinct sites rather than a shared location. Far from constituting a technicality or a marginal scholarly quibble, this is a query that can help assess whether the different exile narratives of Adam, Sita and the eighteenth-century banished were, or could have been, linked in people's imagination and lives.

The question of nomenclature extends beyond place also to the people whose history and writing traditions are at the heart of this study. The ancestors of today's Sri Lankan community came from diverse backgrounds with many being of Javanese or east Indonesian ancestry. A portion of the political exiles in the late seventeenth century, and especially throughout the eighteenth, were members of ruling families in their homelands. For example, the Javanese king Amangkurat III of Mataram was exiled along with his retinue in 1708 after a bitter struggle over the throne with his uncle, the future Pakubuwana I; the twenty-sixth king of Gowa in south Sulawesi, Sultan Fakhruddin, was exiled in

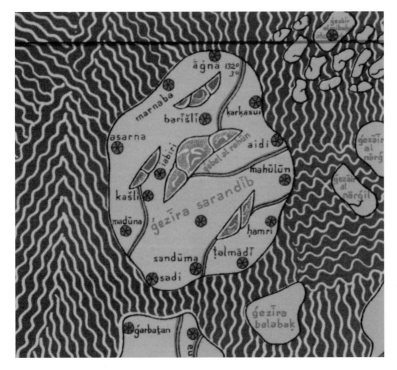

Figure 1.1 Detail showing Sarandib from al-Idrīsī's 1154 world map, as reconstructed by Konrad Miller in 1927.

1767 on charges of conspiring with the British to oppose the VOC trading monopoly in eastern Indonesia.[1] Also exiled during the eighteenth century were, among others, the prince of Bantam, the crown prince of Tidore and the king of Kupang. Another important figure exiled by the Dutch even earlier (1684) was Sheikh Yusuf of Makassar, a leader, religious scholar and "saint" from Sulawesi. Such prominent figures had followers who joined them in exile and often also established a local following in Ceylon. Some of the banished eventually returned to

---

[1] Mataram was the central Javanese dynasty that rose to power in the sixteenth century. It reached its heyday under Sultan Agung (r. 1613–1646), who established hegemony over central and east Java. Although in the eighteenth and early nineteenth centuries the Mataram kingdom increasingly lost power and territory to the Dutch East India Company and split gradually into several smaller courts, their rulers were all descended from a single family. On the sultan of Gowa and his family's life in Ceylon, see Suryadi, "Sepucuk Surat dari Seorang Bangsawan Gowa di Tanah Pembuangan (Ceylon)," *Wacana: Jurnal Ilmu Pengetahuan Budaya*, 10.2 (2008): 214–245.

their places of origin. Thus, for example, after the aforementioned King
Amangkurat III's death in Ceylon, following almost thirty years of exile,
his descendants and servants were repatriated in 1734 to Java, where the
king's body was reinterred in the royal cemetery at Imogiri. Many others,
however, stayed and lived out their lives in Ceylon, either by choice or
deprived of any alternative.

Not only did early arrivals from the archipelago to Ceylon come from
different islands and regions and, as a consequence, speak multiple
tongues: Their religious affiliation was also not monolithic, as can be
glimpsed occasionally in archival records. A Dutch document from
1691, for example, noted that "widows of Amboin soldiers would be
provided with small pensions provided they are Christians."[2] There is
evidence that certain exiles, convicts or soldiers, accepted Christianity
and that some later reverted to Islam.[3] The references to Balinese and
Ambonese soldiers in Dutch service, although not explicitly discussing
religion, suggest that there were Hindus and Christians among the
larger group.

How did a group possessing such diverse ethnic, linguistic, and religious pasts come to be masked by the unifying terms "Malay" and
(in Sinhala and Tamil) "Ja," the two most common appellations used
today? Both "Malay" and "Javanese" are, to a certain degree, misnomers
for a group with such varying ancestry. Using "Indonesian," a more
accurate term in today's context in terms of describing their country of
origin, would be anachronistic, and it is, consequently, a designation that
carries little attachment. My point, however, is not to assess the "cor-
rectness" of a particular name but to raise questions about this shifting
nomenclature, its imposition from without and adoption from within
during different periods, and its relationship to a sense of belonging
and place.

The appellations used to identify the Sri Lankan community have
changed over time. During the seventeenth and eighteenth centuries
the Dutch referred to the group as the "Easterners" (D. *Oosterlingen*),
another blanket term, like "Malay," that did not hint at the diversity of
their home regions.[4] This tendency may have reflected the fact that many
of the "Easterners" had lived in Batavia (to the east of Ceylon) before
coming to Ceylon and so may have developed a sense of community and

[2] SLNA 1/23, Political Council Minutes, July 18, 1691.
[3] *Jubilee Book of the Malay Cricket Club* (Colombo: Ceylon Malay Cricket Club, 1924),
158–159.
[4] See, for example, SLNA 1/73, Political Council Minutes, August 30, 1736.

shared identity that reflected that experience rather than their individual, geographically diverse backgrounds. However, the designation "Javanese" (D. *Javaans*) was also used in some Dutch sources and could suggest that Javanese people formed a majority within the community in its formative stages or again that, with many coming from Batavia (situated on Java), it indicated their site of departure to Ceylon.[5] Yet many sources contained a broader range of appellations for people originating in the Indonesian Archipelago, including "Balinese," "Makassarese," "Madurese," "Javanese," "Ambonese," "Buginese" and others. In his 1672 account of life in Ceylon, the Dutch reverend Philippus Baldaeus depicted in great detail many of the battles between the Portuguese and the Dutch, and repeatedly mentioned various categories of soldiers fighting on both sides, among them the Javanese and Bandanese.[6] In the customary document that Librecht Hooreman, outgoing commander of Jaffna, wrote in 1748 for his successor Jacob de Jong, outlining developments during his tenure and challenges for the future, he mentioned two particular individuals: "Lastly, I mention here that two persons are confined to this Castle as Prisoners of State viz. Bantams Pangerang [Prince] Diepa Coesoema and the Madura Prince Radin Tomogon Rana Diningrat. The followers of the former consist of three men and three women and that of the latter two men and two women."[7] Specific sites were indicated in this passage: Bantam (Banten) in west Java and the island of Madura.

Such depictions raise questions about the almost complete disappearance of languages of the Indonesian Archipelago other than Malay from the extant written records. It is true that Malay was a lingua franca of trade and Islamic culture, widely known in Southeast Asia for several centuries, certainly along the coasts. Yet the islands known as Indonesia today were, and still are, among the world's most linguistically diverse

[5] B. A. Hussainmiya, *Lost Cousins: The Malays of Sri Lanka* (Bangi: Universiti Kebangsaan Malaysia, 1987), 55–57.
[6] Phillipus [sic] Baldaeus (originally published 1672), translated from Dutch by Pieter Brohier, "Phillips Baldaeus: A True and Exact Description of the Great Island of Ceylon," *Ceylon Historical Journal* 8.1–4 (1958–1959): 1–403. For mention of Javanese soldiers see, for example, 147, 225, 226, 279; for soldiers from Banda see 147, 162, 225.
[7] For the Dutch original and an English translation, see *Memoir of Librecht Hooreman commander of Jaffna 1748 for his successor Jacob de Jong*, translated and edited by K. D. Paranavitana (Colombo: Department of National Archives, Sri Lanka, 2009), 74. The information contained in such passages has historical significance that goes beyond the nomenclature question. Ranadiningrat, the Madurese prince mentioned by Hooreman, was the son of Cakradiningrat IV, the king of Madura who was exiled to the Cape, while his sons Ranadiningrat and Sasradiningrat were exiled to Ceylon; see Zainalfattah, *Sedjarah Tjaranja Pemerintahan di Daerah-daerah di Kepulauan Madura dengan Hubungannja* (Pamekasan: Paragon, 1951), 154.

regions and the early arrivals to Ceylon must have spoken a wide range of tongues. As will be shown, some traces of the earlier diversity do remain, with the links to Java, although not immediately apparent, closer to the surface of Malay texts than those to other parts of the archipelago, perhaps because of the high percentage of Javanese among the early exiles, their elevated status and a long-standing written Javanese literary tradition whose products could be transmitted to new surroundings. The very term used for writing Malay in Sri Lanka, employing a modified form of the Arabic script that is known across Southeast Asia as *jawi*, is a Javanese one: *gundul*.[8] However, mention in Malay manuscripts of Makassar, Sumenep, Aceh and additional places shows clearly that sites beyond Java were significant as well.

Other sources, especially letters and petitions written in exile, point to additional, far-flung places across the Indonesian–Malay world to which those classified as Malays felt a connection and allegiance, and to which they often wished to return. For example, a letter written in 1792 by two brothers, descendants of Sultan Bacan Muhammad Sah al-Din from the island of Bacan in eastern Indonesia, beseeched the Dutch governor and Council in Batavia to allow them to leave Ceylon after having lived there for twelve years.[9]

Based on evidence found in Malay writings and colonial documents preserved in Sri Lanka, it is therefore not obvious that the community would develop an exclusively Malay affiliation. Along with its varied roots and adding to its internal diversity were the Malays' close contacts and frequent intermarriages with the Tamil-Muslim community, the Moors, traces of which are found in many manuscripts.[10] It seems,

---

[8] The term *gundhul* ("bald") is used in Java to refer to the Javanese language written in an unvocalized form of the Arabic script (whereas the more common, and vocalized, Arabic script used to write Javanese is known as *pégon*). For an excellent survey of jawi across the Malay world, see Annabel Teh Gallop et al., "A Jawi Sourcebook for the Study of Malay Palaeography and Orthography," *Indonesia and the Malay World* 43.125 (2015): 13–171. An example from Ceylon is on 116–117.

[9] Letter, Ceylon to Batavia, 1792, Leiden University Library, MS Cod. Or. 2241-Ia (11).

[10] In this context it is of note that, to the best of my knowledge, no term corresponding to *peranakan* is used at present in Sri Lanka to describe the children born of such marriages. The term, however, was used occasionally in the past to refer to individuals from the archipelago who were of Chinese descent, as evident from Dutch records. See, for example, the request made by Pernakan Sinees Jan Lochsien to the court in Galle, to return to Batavia (SLNA 1/173, Political Council Minutes, December 5, 1776). For an example from a Malay text, see Chapter 8. The Moors, like the Malays, have traditionally written their language in the Arabic script (known as Arabu-Tamil or *arwi*). I consider the Arabic script, in some ways, as another standardizing cloak, like Malay, that has acted as a unifier that obscures a diversity of languages and backgrounds. On the Moors, see Asiff Hussein, *Sarandib: An Ethnological Study of the Muslims of Sri Lanka* (Dehiwala: Asiff Hussein, 2007), 1–400.

however, that with time a gradual process of moving toward a unifying appellation (as well as an almost complete dominance of the Malay language and a more religiously homogeneous group) took place. If during Dutch times the categories of Easterners and Javanese were dominant (with occasional references to additional subgroups, including Bandanese, Malays and Balinese, among others), under the British the term "Malay" gained prominence, certainly in colonial records. The British categorized the group based first and foremost on their collective language, Malay, but also on the physical similarities they identified between them and the local inhabitants in the newly founded British settlements in Malaya (Penang, 1786) and, later, Singapore (1819). Malays were perceived as possessing features unique unto themselves, as Robert Percival concluded in 1803: "The religion, law, manners and customs of the Malays, as well as their dress, colour and persons, differ very much from those of *all the other inhabitants of Asia.* The Malays of the various islands and settlements also differ among themselves, according to the habits and appearance of the nations among whom they are dispersed. Yet still they are all easily distinguished to be of the Malay race."[11]

The use of "Malay" certainly became more entrenched with the founding by Governor Frederick North of the Ceylon Rifle Regiment, also known as the Malay Regiment in the early nineteenth century, in which many Malays served and which provided not only employment but also a shared sense of commitment and community.[12] A significant relationship existed between life in the Regiment and Malay literary culture: Members of the Regiment copied classical Malay works and also wrote their own stories and poems, especially in the form of *pantun*s and *syair*s;[13] the literature's principal promoters and audiences were

---

[11] Robert Percival, *An Account of the Island of Ceylon: containing its history, geography, natural history, with the manner and customs of its various inhabitants: to which is added, the journal of an embassy to the court of Kandy* (London: C. and R. Baldwin, 1803), 147 (my emphasis).

[12] On the history of the Regiment, see B. A. Hussainmiya, *Orang Rejimen: The Malays of the Ceylon Rifle Regiment* (Bangi: Universiti Kebangsaan Malaysia, 1990).

[13] The relationship between the Regiment and Malay literary culture was first pointed out by Hussainmiya, *Lost Cousins*, 92–94. Pantuns were popular throughout the archipelago, in Malay, Minangkabau, Achenese, Batak, Sunda and Javanese (in which they were known as *parikan* or *wangsalan*). The Malay pantun is a quatrain, with a rhyme scheme of ABAB, and meant to be sung. The genre has been oft-studied, including inquiries about whether there was a semantic connection between the first and second couplets; see Liaw Yock Fang, *A History of Classical Malay Literature*, trans. Razif Bahari and Harry Aveling (Singapore: ISEAS, 2013), 442–445. The syair, among the most popular of genres across Muslim Southeast Asia, is a form of traditional Malay verse, consisting of four-line verses with each line containing four words, i.e. eight to twelve syllables. Its rhyme scheme is AAAA and internal rhyme is common. Heated debates raged among

related, in one way or another, to the Regiment; members of the Regiment conducted lessons for Malay children, ensuring they were literate in Malay written in the jawi script; soldiers who traveled to Malaya and Singapore on assignment served as a bridge between the community in Ceylon and the large Malay centers to the east by guaranteeing a circulation of ideas, texts and people among them.[14] In addition to these significant dimensions of the community's life that came to bear also on language dominance and nomenclature, especially pertinent to further understanding of the adoption of the designation "Malay" is the question of how interactions among colonial administrators and scholars categorizing the peoples of Ceylon and those peoples', in this case the Malays', self-definitions shaped the nomenclature over time. In other words, how did "insider" and "outsider" perceptions interact and impact shifting naming practices and, with them, shifting identities and understandings of the past and the present?[15]

Throughout this book, I have tried to consistently use the "appropriate" place and group names in context so as to convey the force and different memories they carried. For example, Chapter 6 is an investigation of the island and its exilic histories through the prism of "Sarandib." Because "Sri Lanka" (replacing Ceylon) was adopted as the name of the nation state only in 1972, it is used for the most part when recent references are made, yet the designation "Lanka" is ancient and resonates deeply, as elaborated in Chapter 7 with its focus on the Ramayana. The terminologies used for the wider region can often be anachronistic when considering earlier centuries, or otherwise vague or constructed, and I employ them – the Indian Ocean world, Indonesian Archipelago,

scholars in the twentieth century over the dating of the syair's early appearance as a poetic form in Malay literature with claims ranging from the fourteenth to the eighteenth century; see ibid., 447–449. The most famous syairs are likely those composed by Hamzah Fansuri (c. sixteenth century) on mystical themes, but as the genre gained ever wider popularity in the Malay-speaking world it was employed also for writing about nonreligious subjects, including romance and history; see Ismail Hamid, *The Malay Islamic Hikayat* (Bangi: Universiti Kebangsaan Malaysia, 1983), 39. Syairs were recited and performed on various occasions and served didactic, religious and political purposes. They became, like the more story-like Malay hikayats, almost all-encompassing in the breadth of their themes and perspectives.

[14] See Hussainmiya, *Lost Cousins*, 93–94.
[15] The question of Malay identity has been the topic of heated debates and important scholarship in recent years, although the Sri Lankan Malays often remain unmentioned or are mentioned only briefly in these writings. For critical scholarship on Malayness, see, for example, the contributions in Maznah Mohamad and Syed Muhd Khairudin Aljunied (eds.), *Melayu: The Politics, Poetics and Paradoxes of Malayness* (Singapore: NUS Press, 2011); also Timothy P. Barnard (ed.), *Contesting Malayness: Malay Identity across Boundaries* (Singapore: NUS Press, 2014); Joel Kahn, *Other Malays: Nationalism and Cosmopolitanism in the Modern Malay World* (Singapore: NUS Press, 2006).

Indonesian–Malay world, South Asia and Southeast Asia – at different points where fitting for the sake of clarity and approximation. Ultimately, my underlying assumption, following Doreen Massey's seminal work, is that space (however it is divided and marked) is the product of interrelations, constituted through interaction, a sphere of "coexisting heterogeneity" that is always in the process of being made and remade.[16] Exploring names – their histories and imaginings – provides one key to understanding this phenomenon.

As the book considers space or place in their varied meanings, so it considers time. Stories can operate in a range of ways, and their alternative forms of temporality have in part guided this endeavor, for which linear chronology seldom provided the model. What this means in practice is that the book's chapters explore texts from different periods and places to show how a particular exile- or place-related story or trope was imbued with different temporal dimensions, from the cosmic to the contemporary, collapsing time to allow multiple temporalities to coexist, making the story, or its germ, relevant across eras. Integrating sources from different periods in Malay, Arabic and Javanese from Ceylon, Java and elsewhere in single chapters not only challenges the linearity of time and literary transmission but also provides a further example of multiplicity, of open-endedness and continuity, across what are usually seen as distinct spatial categories, opening up "time-spaces" for exploration.[17]

There are several continuums that weave their way through the book which I wish to highlight. One is the continuum between exile and return. If, as I suggest, Adam's exile from heaven to earth foreshadowed the Malays' arrival in Sarandib, which constituted for them a form of return to the original site of human banishment, Adam's plight can offer a paradigm to think about both exiles and returns and how they connect and are intertwined in much of what follows. Sita's case is relevant, too, as her return from banishment in Lanka turned out ultimately to offer her another form, perhaps more agonizing, of exile. Several prominent eighteenth-century exiles to Ceylon also experienced returns, whether in life or in death. The latter, posthumous homecomings suggest another continuum, that of mobility, which took various forms – some literal, some more imaginative – within diasporic life, including the movement of exiles, soldiers, texts, sacred objects and familiar food. In some cases, not even death, burial and the construction of tombs, often considered places of "final rest," were indeed conclusive, precluding mobility. Finally, and further in the background, is the broader continuum of exile

---

[16] Doreen Massey, *For Space* (London: Sage, 2005), 9.   [17] Ibid., 177–195.

and forced migration as it took shape in colonial Dutch Asia, for which
we must consider a vast domain and the movements within it, a domain
that now traverses nation-states and continents but was contained within
a single imperial realm: exile from one's home region to a city such as
Batavia on Java, to Indonesian islands such as Sulawesi or Ternate,
across the Indian Ocean to Ceylon, or half a world away to South
Africa.[18]

Following stories and imaginings produced in relation to place, time
and movement through the prisms of Sarandib, Lanka and Ceylon
guides this book. For this purpose I employ a comparative approach
which seeks to explore the Sri Lankan Malays' history, literature and
perspectives on exile through multiple lenses and from different shores,
integrating sources in Malay, Javanese, Arabic, Dutch and English to
present the views of colonized and colonizer in the Dutch and British
periods, poetic and prose depictions of exile, single texts that move
between and across languages, religious traditions relating to Ceylon
and documents ranging from letters to family diaries to theological
manuals and charms. In this endeavor I build on, and extend, earlier
scholarship in which the nomenclatures of the island and the particular
textual and imaginative worlds they evoked did not play a major role.

To date, the Sri Lankan Malays have been studied first and foremost
by linguists who have found the local variety of Malay to constitute
a highly interesting contact language that combines Austronesian,
Dravidian and Indo-European elements, due to long-standing ties
among speakers of Malay, Tamil and Sinhala.[19] In several other academic fields the Sri Lankan Malays have remained on the margins of
scholarship, including in area studies, focusing on both South Asia and
Southeast Asia. Sri Lankan Malay writing was produced in a region now
referred to as "South Asia." The carriers of Malay to this region converted it, by way of their linguistic, religious and literary practices, into a
frontier of Southeast Asian, or Malay-world, Islam. Across the Indian
Ocean from the Indonesian Archipelago and on the path to Mecca,
Ceylon was not an entirely unknown site, yet still distant and foreign
and certainly not part of a (however loosely connected or imagined)
shared world of Malay writing practices and literary production. To this
day, this physical distance and frontier-like quality are reflected in the

[18] For an introduction to the topic, see Ronit Ricci, "Introduction," in Ronit Ricci (ed.),
Exile in Colonial Asia: Kings, Convicts, Commemoration (Honolulu: University of Hawai'i
Press, 2016), 1–19.
[19] See, for example, the contributions in Sebastian Nordhoff (ed.), *The Genesis of Sri Lanka
Malay: A Case of Extreme Language Contact* (Leiden: Brill, 2012).

Figure 1.2 Lanka as Ravana's golden palace, c. 1610, artist unknown.
The Picture Art Collection/Alamy Stock Photos

almost complete absence of Malay writing produced in Ceylon/Sri Lanka from the foundational books of Malay literary studies that survey Malay literature from a chronological, generic or thematic perspective.[20] More generally, the Malays' literature and community have, to a large extent, been excluded from discussions of the "Malay world" or been mentioned only in passing.[21] In a mirror image of this lack, and reflecting the Malays' peripheral position as a minority with distant roots, local Malays seldom appear significantly in mainstream accounts of Sri Lanka's history.[22]

Interestingly, the near silence surrounding the Sri Lankan Malays extends to historical scholarship produced in Indonesia, whence came the ancestors of today's Malays, and where exilic histories of the colonial period have received little attention in the era of the nation-state. A notable exception is the figure of Sheikh Yusuf of Makassar, the renowned religious and anti-Dutch leader who was exiled to Ceylon in 1684 and then, a decade later, further afield to South Africa. Besides being revered as a powerful saint, he has also received posthumous recognition from both the Indonesian and South African governments.[23] Still, in broader terms, there has been little work produced in Indonesia about the lives and afterlives of colonial exiles, including the royals among them.

Studies of the Sri Lankan Malays' history and culture have thus hitherto been few. Two of them must be acknowledged as foundational, laying the groundwork for further study: B. A. Hussainmiya's *Lost Cousins: The Malays of Sri Lanka*, which introduced the Malays' history and literature on the island, and the same author's *Orang Rejimen: The Malays of the Ceylon Rifle Regiment*, which presented a history of the Malays' service in the British army. These books, based on pioneering research into several private manuscript collections shown to the author in the 1970s, as well as Dutch and British sources, were the first

---

[20] Examples include Richard O. Windstedt, *A History of Classical Malay Literature* (Oxford: Oxford University Press, 1969); Ismail Hamid, *Kesusasteraan Melayu Lama dari Warisan Peradaban Islam* (Kuala Lumpur: Penerbit Fajar Bakti, 1983); Hendrik M. J. Maier, *We Are Playing Relatives: A Survey of Malay Writing* (Leiden: KITLV Press, 2004).

[21] Anthony Milner, *The Malays* (Oxford: Wiley-Blackwell, 2008), x, 87–88, 148–149.

[22] See, for example, K. M. de Silva, *A History of Sri Lanka* (Berkeley: University of California Press, 1981), who mentions the Malays once (p. 225) in his 603 pages; John Clifford Holt (ed.), *The Sri Lanka Reader: History, Culture, Politics* (Durham and London: Duke University Press, 2011); Nira Wickramasinghe, *Sri Lanka in the Modern Age: A History* (London: Hurst, 2014). According to the 2012 census the Malays make up approximately 0.2 percent of the population of just over 20 million.

[23] Kerry Ward, *Networks of Empire: Forced Migration in the Dutch East India Company* (Cambridge: Cambridge University Press, 2009), 1–5.

to raise awareness of a Malay populace in Sri Lanka and its ongoing linguistic and cultural vitality. Several books have been written by members of the Malay community in recent decades, largely drawing on family documents and personal recollections, but also on archival research, among them M. A. Sourjah's *The Sri Lankan Malay Heritage in Brief*;[24] B. G. N. Sariffo'deen's *The Story of My Life*;[25] and Noor Rahim's "Reminiscence of Our Proud Malay Heritage," and his cookbook *Malay Culinary Delights* which states on its cover that it is about "the culinary prowess and expertise of our Malay ancestry, and the types of food they brought along with them from the motherland."[26] Most recently, Tuan M. Zameer Careem's *Persaudaraan: Malay Life in Sri Lanka*, offers an encyclopedic and glorifying account of local Malay history.[27] Occasional articles in the Sri Lankan media have revealed intriguing aspects of Malay history.[28] Several scholarly articles have also appeared outside Sri Lanka, including those by Hamid and Harun Mat Piah, which examined Sri Lanka's Malay literature in the context of the wider world of Malay writing.[29]

Like the island's different names, the diverse archives available for the study of Malay life in colonial Ceylon evoke different voices, images and memories. None is complete, and each offers particular perspectives on events, containing its own revelations and silences. The Department of National Archives of Sri Lanka in Colombo holds a vast collection of Dutch documents, including Lot 1, an archive created by the VOC of the coastal districts of Ceylon from 1640 to 1796, a time when Company possessions in Ceylon were the second-largest territory administered by the Dutch in Asia.[30] The documents offer a mapping of exiles

---

[24] M. A. Sourjah, *The Sri Lankan Malay Heritage in Brief* (Battaramulla: M. Wazir Sourjah, 2005).

[25] B. G. N. Sariffo'deen, *The Story of My Life* (B. G. N. Sariffo'deen, n.d.). The author's ancestors went to Ceylon from Kuching, in Sarawak, presently in Malaysia.

[26] Noor R. Rahim, "Reminiscence of Our Proud Malay Heritage" (unpublished manuscript, June 2015); Noor R. Rahim, *Malay Culinary Delights* (Kotikawatta: Kumpulan Melayu Kotikawatta, 2015).

[27] Tuan M. Zameer Careem, *Persaudaraan: Malay Life in Sri Lanka* (Colombo: S. Godage and Brothers, 2016).

[28] See, for example, the following articles by M. D. Saldin, "Constable Tuan Saban's Shootout with Saradiel," *Sunday Island*, March 16, 2003; "The Keris – Malay Weapon, Social Symbol and Talisman," *The Sunday Times*, August 7, 2011.

[29] Ismail Hamid, "Islam dalam Sejarah dan Masyarakat Melayu Sri Lanka," *Sari* 9 (1991): 25–41; Harun Mat Piah, "Tradisi Kesusasteraan Melayu Sri Lanka dalam Konteks Kesusasteraan Melayu Tradisional Nusantara: Satu Tinjauan Ringkas," *Sari* 4.2 (1986): 63–82; B. A. Hussainmiya, "'Melayu Bahasa': Some Preliminary Observations on the Malay Creole of Sri Lanka," *Sari* 4.1(1986): 19–30.

[30] For a detailed introduction to this archive, see K. D. Paranavitana, "Dutch Political Council Minutes: An Introduction," in R. G. Anthonisz, *Digest of Resolutions of the Dutch*

sent to Ceylon via lists of names, dates of banishment and arrival, reasons for exile, details of living arrangements, of the status and of the treatment of royals, soldiers and slaves, allowances given in cash and provisions, requests for their increase and petitions of those wishing to return.[31] For example, information can be found about royal exiles living in Jaffna, Colombo, Trincomalee and Galle in the early eighteenth century, such as a note from 1717 reporting that Prince Aroetekoe was granted leave to live in town instead of inside the Galle Fort where he had been previously kept.[32]

The records of the British period are also voluminous, and they too contain information on the Malays, with a focus on their military role. In addition to the official archive, many memoirs and works sketching life in Ceylon in its myriad aspects were written in the nineteenth century by scholars, administrators, military personnel and visitors, and these included occasional depictions of Malays and their perceived way of life, sometimes in minute detail. Percival described the dress of the Malay slaves, contrasting it with the attire of the Malays of noble descent: "While Malays of a higher rank wear a wide Moorish coat or gown which they call Badjour ... most of the slaves in the service of Europeans, instead of the piece of cloth, have breeches of some coarse stuff given to them by their masters."[33] Such colonial-era sources, both Dutch and British, offer many interesting details. These are often precisely the kind of details missing from local Malay writings whose major concerns lay elsewhere. The European sources are important and revealing yet circumscribed, and with their external gaze tell only part of the story. One way to gain better insight into the exilic experience – for those exiled and those left behind – is to move beyond the colonial archive and explore indigenous chronicles.

The Malays' history between the seventeenth and early twentieth centuries reflects connectivities, interactions and movement across the

Political Council Colombo: 1644–1796 (Colombo: Department of National Archives, Sri Lanka, 2012), 9–20.

[31] A few examples will suffice here: Eight state exiles from Tidore were given an allowance increase (SLNA 1/183, Political Council Minutes, November 30, 1781); the allowances of state exiles from across the archipelago were increased or decreased based on careful surveillance of their family size, including among others the widow of the prince of Bantam, the king of Gowa, the family of Pangéran Buminata, the prince of Bacan, the former king of Kupang, and the emperor of Padang (SLNA 1/200, Political Council Minutes, March 8, 1788); eighteen slaves of the Company were taken into service as soldiers, among them Bugis, Balinese, Makassarese, Batak and Sumbawanese individuals (SLNA 1/176, Political Council Minutes, June 19, 1778).

[32] On Aroetekoe, see SLNA 1/51, January 1717 (no day noted).

[33] Percival, *An Account*, 148.

Indian Ocean in a range of ways: the Malays' religious, cultural and linguistic ties to the lands to the southeast and further west in Arabia; the entanglements of colonized and colonizers in South and Southeast Asia; and the ways cultural survival and diasporic imagination played out in the community's writing practices in its new home. A primary gateway to understanding these processes is offered by surviving Sri Lankan Malay texts, fragments of a tradition that allow us to recover the Malays' own voices.

Sri Lankan Malay manuscripts written and copied between the eighteenth and early twentieth centuries and early print books have survived almost exclusively in private family collections with several small, and challenging-to-access, collections kept at libraries in Kuala Lumpur, Colombo and Brunei. Such manuscripts and books testify to an impressive and ongoing engagement by previous generations of Malays with a range of texts, written primarily in Malay and Arabic with occasional sections in Tamil, pointing to the links between the Malays and their Tamil co-religionists. The linguistic multiplicity of many manuscripts is contrasted by orthographic unity, with all languages – Malay, Arabic, Tamil, Javanese – almost always written in forms of the Arabic script.[34]

The majority of extant Malay manuscripts and books possess an "Islamic character" in that they include theological treatises, manuals on prayer and ritual, well-known hadith, tales written in the Malay genres of *hikayat* (prose) and syair (poetry) on the battles of early Islam, heroic figures and adventures, musings on Arabic letters and mystical tracts. A striking feature of these writings, at least to one approaching from the perspective of Indonesian or Malay studies, is how similar many of them are to those found in manuscripts now housed in Jakarta, Kuala Lumpur or Leiden. In addition, however, there are works that represent very local agendas, depict events that unfolded in colonial Ceylon, or are otherwise not known from the broader eighteenth- and nineteenth-century Malay literature from elsewhere. The vast majority of these materials have not been read by scholars, let alone been scrutinized for their religious, cultural and social significance.

Two major repositories formed the data base for this study. The first was the Hussainmiya Collection at the Department of National Archives in Colombo, a set of a dozen or so microfilm reels containing manuscripts and various documents collected in the 1970s by Hussainmiya and microfilmed at the time. The condition of many of the microfilms

---

[34] In some cases (and increasingly so in the twentieth century) Romanized Malay was used, as were the Tamil and Sinhala scripts.

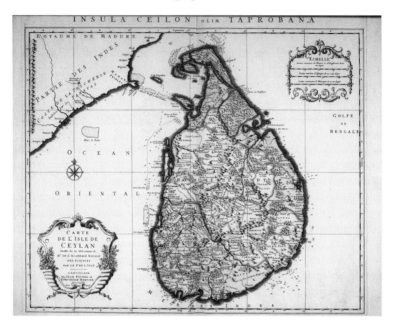

Figure 1.3 Map of the Island of Ceylon, Covens and Mortier, 1721.
Bern University Library, ZB Ryh 7401 10

is poor, and several reels are no longer readable. Many of the texts were microfilmed backwards (from left to right, rather than right to left as appropriate for works in the Arabic script), some texts are missing pages or merge abruptly into another work, and there is no catalogue or even basic list that guides one through the materials. The location of the original and very precious manuscripts which were microfilmed remains unclear, but they are now classified as "missing" from the archives.

The second repository on which this study is based was created by the present author. There are no publicly accessible Malay collections in Sri Lanka in libraries or museums, and Malay materials can be located only via personal connections and the visiting of private homes. From 2011 to 2016, with funding from the British Library's Endangered Archives Programme, I surveyed and documented surviving Malay writings across Sri Lanka, ultimately creating a digital archive through which the approximately 130 documented items can be viewed. These include manuscripts, family diaries, letters, booklets, mosque deeds, marriage records and more from the greater Colombo area, Kandy, Trincomalee, Kiniya, Hambantota, Matale, Badulla, Kurunegala, Kalpitiya, Puttalam and elsewhere, some of which are discussed in the pages to follow.[35] Having spent several years in attempts to locate Malay materials and witnessing the serendipitous nature of this search, it is my conviction that the materials found very likely form but a component of a larger, fragmented and significant archive.

The available Malay sources date almost exclusively from the early nineteenth century onward and are often silent on many of the details provided by earlier Dutch documents pertaining to living arrangements, ships carrying exiles or precise dates on which events related to banishment took place. They reveal much about religious and literary traditions passed down through generations, links to ancestral places in the archipelago, genealogies, local affiliations and agendas. The prism now available is not only temporally circumscribed but is also almost entirely Muslim in character. In considering the silences of this archive, in addition to absences of religious and language variation which loom large, we might also wonder what types of literature may have been taken to Ceylon but left no knowable trace. For example, Old Javanese literature was very important at the central Javanese Kartasura court, home to many of the early eighteenth-century exiles, prior to the Chinese War. However, the court's plundering by the Chinese and Madurese in 1742 signaled a watershed: a disaster after which that literature never regained its role in the court's literary life.[36] Might have Old Javanese works been taken from Kartasura to Ceylon, perhaps to survive there after their decline in Java?

As this book explores banishment to Ceylon and Malay diasporic life, it would have been incomplete without including views from the "other shore," that of the Indonesian Archipelago and in particular Java. I begin by asking what people in the courts of central Java, whence came many of the royal exiles, knew about Lanka, Sarandib and Ceylon and whether the names of the island echoed familiarly, evoking figures and episodes well known to them. I wonder what it might have been like to read, or listen to, tales of earlier exiles to the same island once exiled courtiers had arrived at their destination. These are questions that are important to understanding the Malays' experiences but also resonate

---

[35] Although due to space constraints I could not include as many passages in the original and translation from these sources as I had wished, all documents are freely available online on the British Library website at https://eap.bl.uk/project/EAP450 and https://eap.bl.uk/project/EAP609. Whenever available the site also contains information on each document including ownership history, current ownership, physical condition etc.

[36] Merle C. Ricklefs, *The Seen and Unseen Worlds in Java, 1726–1749: History, Literature and Islam in the Court of Pakubuwana II* (Honolulu: University of Hawai'i Press, 1998), 336.

with the broader history of exile by the VOC within and beyond the Dutch East Indies.

Studying exilic experiences in the colonial period poses many methodological challenges. Secondary sources that touch on exile while basing themselves on indigenous sources are few and, even in existing ones, exile does not typically constitute the main focus of attention. Regarding Indonesia, notable exceptions include Merle C. Ricklefs' prolific scholarship on eighteenth-century Javanese history and especially his research on the "missing *pusakas*" of Kartasura; Nancy Florida's study of the *Babad Jaka Tingkir*, inscribed by the ruler of Surakarta Pakubuwana VI, exiled to Ambon after the Java War; Peter Carey's monumental work on Prince Dipanagara, who was exiled to Manado and then Makassar; and Muridan Widjojo's book on Prince Nuku of Tidore which discusses cases of exile from the islands of eastern Indonesia in the late eighteenth century.[37] While all these studies, and several others, have contributed significantly to an understanding of the history of exile from the islands of today's Indonesia, attempts to reconstruct the map and legend of exilic movement under the VOC, however partially, still pose considerable difficulties, among them access to primary sources, including the vast number of potentially relevant manuscripts in Javanese and additional languages, many but not all catalogued, housed in archival collections across the world. Even for those catalogued, to researchers' great advantage, information needed to assess content in depth is often lacking. Javanese historical chronicles – *babad*s – can be hundreds of pages long and contain a wealth of details that cannot be easily summarized in a catalogue entry. For example, in the twenty-one volumes of the *Babad Giyanti*, a mere few pages are dedicated to a rare and highly significant passage about exilic life in Ceylon.[38]

---

[37] See Merle C. Ricklefs, *Jogjakarta under Sultan Mangkubumi 1749–1792: A History of the Division of Java* (London: Oxford University Press, 1974); Merle C. Ricklefs, *Modern Javanese Historical Tradition: A Study of an Original Kartasura Chronicle and Related Materials* (London: SOAS, 1978); Merle C. Ricklefs, "The Missing *Pusaka*s of Kartasura, 1705–1737," in *Bahasa- Sastra-Budaya: Ratna Manikam Untaian Persembahan kepada Prof. Dr. P. J. Zoetmulder*, ed. Sutrisno Sulastin et al. (Yogyakarta: Gadjah Mada University Press, 1985), 601–630; Ricklefs, *Seen and Unseen*; Nancy K. Florida, *Writing the Past, Inscribing the Future: History as Prophecy in Colonial Java* (Durham: Duke University Press, 1995); Peter Carey, *The Power of Prophecy: Prince Dipanagara and the End of an Old Order in Java, 1785–1855* (Leiden: KITLV, 2008); Muridan Widjojo, *The Revolt of Prince Nuku: Cross-Cultural Alliance-making in Maluku, c. 1780–1810* (Leiden: Brill, 2008).

[38] Yasadipura I, *Babad Giyanti*, 21 vols. (Betawi Sentrum: Bale Pustaka, 1937–1939), XXI: 83–87. On this episode, see Chapter 5. The published edition contains no information about its source manuscript. However, there are grounds to believe it was the Ned. Bijbel. Genootschap MS 29–33; see Theodore G. T. Pigeaud, *Literature of Java*, 3 vols. (The Hague: Martinus Nijhoff, 1967–1970), III: 719–720. On the *Babad Giyanti* as a historical

The Javanese sources for this book include the aforementioned *babad* genre, historical chronicles composed in the courts of central Java, primarily in Surakarta, in the eighteenth and nineteenth centuries and recounting events such as wars, internal conflicts and intrigues at court, evolving relations with the Dutch, and details of the nobility's personal lives. Some *babads* contain many inconsistencies; some were inscribed several years or decades after the events they depict or were copied anew much later. Like all historical documents, they represent a particular perspective, a moment in time, a surviving voice from a largely unknown past. Some bewilderment can arise from several *babads* possessing the same title and following the lives of particular figures, due to the confusing Javanese tradition of name-changing at important points during a person's life, such as when one was saved from calamity, received a new role at court or returned from exile. Other Javanese works cited are more literary and poetic in nature. Especially important to this study are the works composed or attributed to the court poet Radèn Ngabèhi Yasadipura I. Written in the eighteenth century, the century *par excellence* of banishment from the Dutch Indies to Ceylon, his works engage with the island's various nomenclatures and offer a glimpse of what may have been known about the site of exile, and the lived conditions and experiences of those banished and those returned.

One gap in the Javanese sources is the seemingly relative paucity of references within them to exile. This may be a mistaken perception, the result of the meager prior scholarly inquiry into the topic. But in the available sources, if exile to Ceylon was acknowledged, this was often done briefly and laconically. Statements such as *amikut bupati telu, linajengken manca layar, binucal Sélong nagari* ("the three *bupati* were captured, then sailed overseas, banished to Ceylon"), *kabucal dhateng Sélong, jalaran ngaturi dedamel perang, dhateng Sinuhun Sunan Kabanaran* ("he was banished to Ceylon because of waging war against Sunan Kabanaran," referring to the bupati of Semarang) or (writing of Mustapa, the sultan of Banten) *kakendhangaken dhateng Sélong, nanging lajeng kawangsulaken mulih kalenggahanipun lami* ("he was banished to Ceylon, only to be brought back again to his place of old") offer a justification for exile – typically framed in terms of revolts, treachery, suspicions in the political realm – but no word or close to none on the experience.[39] The time that elapsed between the affairs depicted and their narration

source, see Merle C. Ricklefs, "*Babad Giyanti*: sumber sejarah dan karya agung sastra Jawa," *Jumantara: Jurnal Manuskrip Nusantara* 5.2 (2014): 11–25.

[39] The quotes are from Yasadipura I, *Babad Giyanti* (Surakarta: Budi Utama, 1917), 3.1: 110; Yasadipura I, *Babad Giyanti* (BP), 7: 9, 9: 42.

could have dulled the force of dramatic events and raw emotions but, if so, the same should have been true for many other events depicted in the babads, which are portrayed with greater detail and nuance. A lack of information available to authors and scribes about what became of those exiled on their journeys and of the circumstances under which they lived in Ceylon could have also been an obstacle to detailed descriptions. There may have been very little contact, or none at all, between those exiled and their families and officials who remained behind, although letters to the governor-general and Council in Batavia have survived, proving that at least some contacts were maintained.

The reasons for the brevity of depiction could have been less straightforward, relating to the exiles' position on the "losing side" of history yet capable of concerning the powerful, in episodes discussed throughout this book. This was evident in the case of Amangkurat III, the exiled king of Mataram whose uncle Pangéran Puger received Dutch support and ascended the throne, and yet clearly Amangkurat's descendants still had some claim to power and still posed a threat, evident in Pakubuwana II's rather anxious insistence, depicted in the *Babad Kartasura*, that he was legitimate heir to Amangkurat III, not the latter's two sons who had returned from exile; and even though Pangéran Arya Mangkunagara, another member of the Javanese royal family whose life will be discussed later, was not allowed to return from Ceylon alive, prophecies and historical developments alike bestowed royal authority on his nearest of kin.[40]

The stories of early exile and later diasporic life of the Malays in Ceylon have thus been on the periphery of various forms of historical writing and of scholarship. As mentioned, the carriers of Malay to this region converted it, by means of their religious practices and textual culture, into a frontier of Malay-world Islam. Ceylon was also, more specifically, a frontier of the Malay language as well as of additional vernacular languages of the Indonesian Archipelago, the latter apparently gradually disappearing but leaving tantalizing hints, in several manuscripts and letters, of their past usage in the early period of exile and enlistment. In fact, spoken varieties of these languages may have survived to a much later date than assumed so far. The employment of Javanese, the Indonesian language for which some evidence exists in Sri Lankan

---

[40] These events will be discussed in Chapter 4. The diverse repository of Javanese historical materials also contains examples contrasting with those examined here, as in the case of the *Babad Mangkudiningrat*, a memoir that depicts in great detail the exilic experiences of Sultan Hamengkubuwana II and his two sons in Penang, Batavia and Ambon in 1813–1826. See Sri Margana, "Caught between Empires: *Babad Mangkudiningratan* and the Exile of Sultan Hamengkubuwana II of Yogyakarta, 1813–1826," in Ricci (ed.), *Exile in Colonial Asia*, 117–138.

Malay texts, included the use of poetic meters (*tembang*) and the preservation of certain literary-historical traditions like the tales of the *wali*s who are said to have taken Islam to Java (see Chapter 3). In the much more prevalent case of Malay, the use of the syair genre as well as the genres of hikayat, pantun, *kitab* and *maulud* in their Malay varieties in Ceylon testifies to the expansion of Islamic writing of the archipelago toward new frontiers. This expansion was neither initiated nor led by Muslim armies, itinerant teachers or religious travelers, but originated with forced migration through exile and recruitment to colonial armies. With time, and with subsequent locally born generations in Ceylon, an exilic experience transformed into a diasporic one, with the Ceylon diaspora living at a distant edge-point of its "home" culture, a condition that invited and reinforced the use of the imagination.

The study of diaspora has expanded greatly in recent years.[41] No longer referring exclusively to the post-exilic dispersion of the Jews, as it did for many years, the word "diaspora" has been employed so widely that some claim it has lost its analytic efficacy. In this book the Malays are understood as a diasporic community due to their ongoing connections, real and imaginary, to their lands of origin, their continuous use of the Malay language over many generations and the cultural and religious identity they have maintained in a Buddhist-majority society where Sinhala and Tamil have been dominant. Recent theorization by Ato Quayson on diaspora and literature – a theme central to this book – has called attention to the need to "generate a supple model for interpreting literary texts in full view of their grounding in the recursive mobilities of the past and present time, including the vast voluntary and coerced population movements of colonial times and their impact on the imagination."[42] This certainly rings true for understanding Sri Lankan Malay writing, which has its earliest roots in the forced migration of princes and kings, as well as in the mobility of soldiers, slaves, texts, ideas and material objects that circulated along with people. Quayson views literature as a privileged site for the study of a diasporic imaginary because of the manner by which it binds affect to questions of ontology in both the content and the form of narration.[43] Three elements are central to the

---

[41] For a comprehensive and regionally relevant introduction, see Sunil S. Amrith, *Migration and Diaspora in Modern Asia* (Cambridge: Cambridge University Press, 2011).

[42] Ato Quayson, "Postcolonialism and the Diasporic Imaginary," in Ato Quayson and Girish Daswani (eds.), *A Companion to Diaspora and Transnationalism* (Oxford: Wiley-Blackwell, 2013), 140.

[43] The term "diasporic imaginary" was employed earlier, in a slightly different manner, by Brian Keith Axel, "The Diasporic Imaginary," *Public Culture* 14.2 (2002): 411–428.

diasporic imaginary in literature according to this formulation: place, nostalgia and genealogical accounting. The question of identity – who am I – within the diasporic imaginary is viewed as necessarily entangled with that of place. The reference is to a place of origin, but can also apply, I suggest, to the diasporic's new home. Returning to the question of nomenclature, in the Malays' case this formulation also raises the question of which is the relevant "place" to speak of, and how the identity question shifts, if it does shift, when the place is Ceylon, Sarandib or Lanka. Nostalgia, in this model, overlaps markedly with the concept of place as it is intimately tied to a sense of displacement, foundational to the constitution of diasporic identity (even when the place has never been encountered in person).[44] Genealogical accounting, central to defining the diasporic imaginary, involves questions of "ancestry, ethnicity, tradition and culture and provides a distinguishing past to the person or community," often including stories of the "how we got here" variety, producing a nexus of affiliations such that the fate of the individual is seen to be inextricably tied to the fate of all others in the group.[45] In terms of nostalgia and also genealogy, many of the details of the Malays' homelands – diverse to begin with – faded with time, but an ongoing connection to places across the archipelago, as known or imagined, and to central components of literary and religious culture, well-known heroes and textual traditions, lived on.[46]

It is to these diasporic connections, sensibilities and imaginings, and their textual representations as gleaned from multiple perspectives, that the following pages are dedicated. What emerges are fragments of a history, of a literary culture, of lives lived individually and as a community, the ways in which they were documented, retold, imagined, remembered and forgotten in different places and moments, embedded in stories from the cosmic to the mundane. In view of this group's diverse origins, the time that has elapsed since its forefathers arrived in Ceylon as exiles, soldiers or slaves, its minority status within the population, and the fact that it still speaks Malay in the twenty-first century, its story is no less than remarkable.

---

[44] The desire for a lost or unknown place generates both possibilities and constraints for the imaginary: Quayson, "Postcolonialism and the Diasporic Imaginary," 148–149.

[45] Ibid., 151.

[46] Religion has been central to Malay diasporic identity, as well as to that of other diasporic groups, yet religion has received much less theoretical attention in diaspora studies than the notions of race, ethnicity and nation. See Sean McLoughlin, "Religion, Religions, and Diaspora," in Quayson and Daswani (eds.), *A Companion to Diaspora and Transnationalism*, 125–138.

2   Diasporic Crossings: Malay Writing in Nineteenth-Century Ceylon

This chapter explores how the small diasporic Malay community in Ceylon maintained its culture through the preservation of language, the transmission of literary and religious texts, and the maintenance of genres and of a script. Such an exploration evokes the world of the Indian Ocean in the seventeenth and eighteenth centuries: the contours of Dutch Asia, which at the time encompassed both the island of Ceylon and parts of present-day Indonesia, most predominantly the island of Java; contemporary routes of trade and travel, central among them the pilgrimage path from Southeast Asia to Mecca, traversing Ceylon; and the wide-ranging, active networks of Muslim scholars teaching and studying across these regions. Within this broad grid of geography, mobility and everyday life in the Indian Ocean world, Ceylon's location, its ancient religious significance and contemporary importance as a site of banishment and colonial profit make it an important node for considering histories of connectivity and crossings. However, until very recently it was marginalized, if not virtually ignored, in the scholarship on forms of interconnectedness in the region.[1] Considering Malay history and writing practices in Ceylon shows the extent of the island's centrality to processes and practices of connectivity and circulation and the particular ways in which these played out in the life of a diasporic community.

A close reading of sections of a single manuscript from early nineteenth-century Colombo and a discussion of its composition provide the backbone for this exploration. Consisting of a collection of various texts and dubbed the *Malay Compendium*, this untitled and seemingly unassuming manuscript is analyzed in particular via two of its key

---

[1] As Zoltan Biedermann and Alan Strathern state in their discussion of Sri Lanka's absence from debates in world history: "Sri Lanka sits exactly at the centre of the Indian Ocean: an excellent laboratory, one might think, in which to test any ideas about the connected and the cosmopolitan. But it has barely been visible in the resurgence of world history." See Biedermann and Strathern, "Introduction," in Zoltan Biedermann and Alan Strathern (eds.), *Sri Lanka at the Crossroads of History* (London: University College London, 2017), 2.

dimensions: the referencing of titles and names, and its multilingual character, highlighting intellectual and religious currents of contact and memory. Paramount among the crossings and connecting links revealed through this analysis is translation in its diverse manifestations, most prominently from Arabic into Malay. Because translation constituted a major component of Malay writing, the Malays possessing what Maria Rosa Menocal – writing of another time and place to which Arabic was central – has called "a culture of translation," the chapter considers translation's prevalence also beyond the *Compendium*.[2] Special attention is devoted to the interlinear form of translation, which offers a model for understanding connectivity across lines and languages but also serves as a metaphor for Malay life and writings in Ceylon.

From the close reading of the *Compendium* flows another goal: to look beyond the common generalizing and flattening terminology of "Sri Lankan Malays" in order to bring into view the diversity of those sent into exile and those enlisted in terms of language, place of origin, class and additional forms of affiliation. Although the ancestors of the Malays came from a range of places and linguistic and ethnic backgrounds in the Indonesian Archipelago and, to a lesser degree, the Malay Peninsula, the Malay language was the single most important tongue in which they wrote their literary and religious works. While there is no doubt that they spoke a variety of languages, at least initially, it is difficult to trace the history of their oral culture. More is known about their writing practices, but in this realm too many questions remain about the process by which Malay came to be employed so prominently. The examination of the *Compendium*, while not providing definitive answers, shows that beneath the cloak of Malay lie hints and traces of a more variegated linguistic and cultural past.

The manuscript, a 270-page-long compendium of texts of different lengths and authorship, was inherited by the late Mr. B. D. K. Saldin (1928–2017) of Dehiwala, from his father Tuan Junaideen Saldin, upon

---

[2] In her essay Menocal employs this term to depict the rich culture of translation of the middle ages that runs the gamut from the scientific and technological materials with which the translation movement from Arabic to Latin began in the early twelfth century to the translations of so much of the imperial culture of *Adab* (the vast "genre" in Arabic traditionally translated as "belles lettres" but perhaps better understood as "humanistic study") into Castilian at the end of the thirteenth century – and which ended up including works like a version of the *mi'raj*, the apocryphal narrative of the Prophet's ascent to Heaven and descent to Hell whose connection to Dante is still bitterly disputed. See Maria Rosa Menocal, "The Culture of Translation," *Words without Borders* (October 2003), www.wordswithoutborders.org/article/the-culture-of-translation (accessed August 7, 2018).

the latter's death in 1955.[3] The manuscript includes several dates and was written over the course of almost three decades and by several hands, a common practice in compendiums of its kind. The earliest date noted is 1803 while the latest, appearing on the inner back flap of the cover, is 1831. The years 1820 and 1824 are noted as well. The dating used does not conform to a single time-reckoning system. The Hijri and the Gregorian calendars, and sometimes both, are invoked in different instances. Noting the year according to the Gregorian calendar, the scribe termed it either *hijra Nasara* ("Christian calendar") or *taun Welanda* ("Dutch year"), the latter a reminder that although the manuscript was written and certainly completed in British Ceylon, its inscription took place only shortly after the end of Dutch rule in 1796.

The name of the owner (M. *yang punya ini surat*) appears several times in the manuscript as Encik Sulaiman ibn ʿAbd al-Jalil or ibn ʿAbdullah Jalil.[4] Encik Sulaiman described himself as hailing from Ujung Pandang in the land of Makassar, currently in the province of South Sulawesi, Indonesia.[5] Makassar was also the homeland of Sheikh Yusuf, a religious scholar, an anti-Dutch leader and the most prominent person to be exiled to Ceylon by the Dutch.[6] Encik Sulaiman provided a further, significant detail about his ancestry: He was descended from Mas Haji ʿAbdullah of the Javanese kingdom of Mataram.[7]

Haji ʿAbdullah of Mataram is mentioned elsewhere in the manuscript as a renowned sheikh whose writing was being cited, although a title for his work was not provided.[8] Toward the end of the fifteen-page-long

---

[3] *Malay Compendium*, listed as a compendium of religious texts, BL, EAP450/1/2. Mr. Saldin did not know how the manuscript came to be in his father's possession nor whether it was part of a family collection or acquired from elsewhere. He and his family trace their roots to Encik Pantasih, who came to Ceylon from Sumenep in the eastern part of Madura, Indonesia. For a family history, see B. D. K. Saldin, *Portrait of a Sri Lankan Malay* (Dehiwala: B. D. K. Saldin, 2003). On Encik Pantasih, see Chapter 9.

[4] *Encik* (sometimes spelt enci or ence') is a title, defined in Wilkinson's dictionary (first published 1901) as "master; mistress": R. J. Wilkinson, *A Malay–English Dictionary*, 2 vols. (Singapore: Kelly and Walsh, 1901; repr. London: Macmillan & Co., 1959), I: 303. Interestingly, a Javanese dictionary defines enci as a title for a non-Javanese, especially one from Bawean, Bandar, Sumatra or Malacca, or a term of address for a "full-blooded Chinese" (*Cina singkèk*); see W. J. S. Poerwadarminta, *Kamus Baosastra Djawa* (Groningen and Batavia: J. B. Wolters, 1939), 123.

[5] *Orang dari nakarinya Maqashar di Hujung Pandan*, *Malay Compendium*, BL, EAP450/1/2, 238. Ujung Pandang was an old pre-colonial fort, captured and rebuilt by the Dutch in 1667 and renamed Fort Rotterdam. The well-known Prince Dipanagara, who led an uprising in Java against Dutch rule in 1825–1830, was exiled to Ujung Pandang and died there.

[6] On Sheikh Yusuf, see Chapter 6.

[7] *Turunan daripada Mas haji ʿAbdullah Jawi Mataram*, *Malay Compendium*, BL, EAP450/1/2, 238. On Mataram in the context of exile to Ceylon, see Chapters 3–5.

[8] *Inilah risala daripada shaikh kamal mukamal yaitu daripada haji ʿAbdullah nagari Mataram*, *Malay Compendium*, BL, EAP450/1/2, 136.

quotation, it is noted that the text (kitab) was transmitted from the realm of Mataram. A warning was added that this text should not be read to those disciples who have not yet engaged in *'ilmu nafas* and that the guidance of a guru was essential to a correct understanding of this "science of the breath."[9] Indeed, discussions of this form of knowledge were common in Javanese works yet not easily found within the Malay "classics," a fact that complements additional evidence pointing to this circulating text having drawn on Javanese sources.

Encik Sulaiman's familial history links the islands of Sulawesi and Java, and the once-powerful kingdoms of Makassar and Mataram, both of which exhibited strong resistance to Dutch advancement in the seventeenth century. The details of this history and the circumstances under which a descendant of a Javanese haji, who spent at least part of his life in Ujung Pandang, arrived in Ceylon remain unknown. And yet the names of places and lineages, reference to a pilgrim who returned home from Arabia, and the text illuminating an important and secretive form of knowledge allow a view of larger and richer pictures of movement and connection in which Ceylon was deeply embedded.

As a compendium, the manuscript offers a broad snapshot of the kinds of texts that Malays in Ceylon were engaging with in the early nineteenth century. It contains sections that are several dozen pages long alongside very brief treatises, diagrams and notes. There are sections on *zikir* (ceremonially reciting the name of God), the five daily prayers, the connection between the letters of the Arabic alphabet and prayer times, prophets, angels and colors; and on God's attributes, essence and names, the breath, the afterlife, the *shahāda*, the importance of studying with the proper guru who will not lead one astray; also discussed are Muhammad's light (*nūr*), the human body, Adam as first human and prophet, Muhammad's advice to 'Ali, Islamic slaughter, conception and pregnancy, forms of secret knowledge that should not be revealed to all (*'ilmu ghaib*) and correct conduct for women. The list could go on, but rather than focus on an in-depth analysis of content, the discussion draws attention to what referencing in the manuscript reveals of the physical and figurative location of the Malays in early nineteenth-century Ceylon.

Through the mention of texts, authors, religious teachers and *tarekat* affiliations, the manuscript allows a glimpse of the religious and literary world of the Ceylon Malays, one that was complex and, above all, interconnected. Evidence of contact, circulation and the movement of sources and individuals is abundant. That evidence, however, telling as it

---

[9] *Kitab turun daripada nagari Mataram kepada anaq muridnya jangan engkau berikan membaca kepada orang yang belum mengaji 'ilm nafas ini*, ibid., 151.

may be, is brief and fragmentary. The manner in which titles and authors are mentioned in passing, not mentioned at all, or evoked in a very general way (a text is said to be "from Arabia"; transmitted by a "great sheikh") is highly reminiscent of the practice of scribes writing in Malay and Javanese in the archipelago.

A majority of cited texts and authors mentioned in the manuscript originated in the Arab world – Cairo, Damascus, Mecca, Medina – and among them, importantly, were included many that were transmitted to the Indonesian–Malay region by those who traveled to perform the hajj, or went to Arabia – especially the Haramayn – for long periods of study and initiation. The particular works they brought back circulated in Arabic, in translation and with local interpretations, making them into pillars of Islam as it was practiced and followed in their home regions. Some texts were likely taken to Ceylon directly from Arabia – situated as it was on the Southeast Asia–Arabia route of the pilgrimage – while others were taken there by exiles and soldiers from Java, Sumatra, Madura and Sulawesi. The result was a textual sphere that was inextricably linked in both directions.

Let us begin with the most traditional sources: citations from the Qur'an and hadith. These appear occasionally, often without referencing their origin. For example, sura 112 of the Qur'an, *Sūrat al-Ikhlāṣ*, is cited in full within a longer untitled section that reads like a string of quotes from various people and texts. The sura and the longer section are written in Arabic, accompanied by an interlinear translation into Malay. The sura is prefaced by *qāla Allah ta'ālā* (A. "thus said Exalted God"), but there is no indication that this is a precise quote nor mention of its location within the sequence of Qur'anic suras. The famous hadith *man 'arafa nafsahu fa-qad 'arafa rabbahu* ("he who knows himself knows his Lord") is cited in Arabic three times, once with a translation into Tamil and twice rendered in Malay, but only once is it attributed to the Prophet Muhammad.

Other, less canonical sources are mentioned in passing as providing inspiration or content. Among these are the *Kitab Mukhtasar*, Kemas Fakhruddin of Palembang's mid to late eighteenth-century Malay translation of, and commentary on, Sheikh Raslān al-Dimashqī's twelfth-century *Risāla fī'l-tawḥīd* ("Epistle on Unity"). The latter work was widely known in the archipelago in its Arabic original (with interlinear translations into Malay, Javanese and Bugis) as well as via commentaries and adaptations in Malay and Javanese.[10]

---

[10] On the Arabic text and its circulation in the Indonesian Archipelago from the eighteenth century onward, its Malay and Javanese adaptations, and translations of the latter, see G. W. J. Drewes, *Directions for Travellers on the Mystic Path: Zakariyya Al-Ansari's Kitāb Fatḥ Al-Raḥmān and Its Indonesian Adaptations*, Verhandelingen van

The *Kitab Bayanullah* is mentioned twice. A work bearing the same title (literally, "Book of the Proclamation/Clarification of Allah") and discussing Sufi teachings through allegory and allusion, written in Sundanese, Javanese and Arabic in the Bandung region of west Java around the mid nineteenth century, is listed in a catalogue of west Javanese manuscripts.[11] If the two are related, which is highly probable, mention of the *Bayanullah* in the Ceylon compendium may hint at traces of a west Javanese heritage, possibly deriving from the "Banten connection" in local history, the exile of the prince Raja Bagus Abdullah of Banten to Ceylon in the mid eighteenth century.

A list consisting of book titles appears toward the end of the manuscript. These books are not cited, yet their mention indicates that they were known to the list's compiler. Listed, among others, are the *Kitāb Minhāj al-qawīm* ("Book of Guidance on the Straight [Path]"), a fiqh work deriving from ʿAbdallāh b. ʿAbd al-Karīm Ba-Fadl's fifteenth-century *al-Muqaddimah al-ḥaḍramiyyah* ("The Ḥaḍrami Introduction") and composed by Ibn Ḥajar al-Haytamī in the mid sixteenth century. L. W. C. van den Berg in his 1886 survey of texts taught in Islamic educational institutions in Java listed the *Kitāb Minhāj al-qawīm* as a popular work, and it is still well known today;[12] the sixteenth-century *Kitāb Minhāj al-ṭullāb* ("The Students' Progress"), a summary of al-Nawawī's thirteenth-century *Minhāj al-ṭālibīn* ("The Pupils' Path") by Zakariyyā al-Anṣārī, an Egyptian scholar whose works were highly popular across the Indonesian–Malay world;[13] al-Ghazālī's *Kitāb Minhāj al-ʿābidīn* ("The Path of the Worshippers," translated into Malay by Sheikh Dāʾūd al-Fatanī in the late eighteenth century); the *Kitāb Ṣirāṭ al-mustaqīm* ("The Book of the Straight Path"), considered the earliest fiqh work produced in Muslim Southeast Asia, written in 1634 by

---

het Koninklijk Instituut Voor Taal-, Land- en Volkenkunde, vol. 81 (The Hague: Martinus Nijhoff, 1977).

[11] Edi S. Ekadjati dan Undang A. Darsa (eds.), *Katalog Induk Naskah-Naskah Nusantara. Jawa Barat: Koleksi Lima Lembaga* (Jakarta: Yayasan Obor Indonesia, 1999), 474–475.

[12] ʿAbdallāh b. ʿAbd al-Karīm Ba-Fadl's work is known in Java as *Bapadal* (deriving from Ba-Fadl). The *Kitāb Minhāj al-qawīm* and its glosses deal with the prescriptions concerning worship (*fiqh al-ʿubudiyyah*); see Martin van Bruinessen, "Kitab Kuning: Books in Arabic Script Used in the Pesantren Milieu," *BKI* 146 (1990), 238.

[13] Zakariyyā al-Anṣārī also wrote the *Kitāb Fatḥ al-rahmān* ("The Victory of the Merciful God"), a commentary on the above-mentioned *Risāla fī 'l-tawḥīd*. He died in Cairo in 1520. See Drewes, *Directions for Travellers on the Mystic Path*, 26–38. Another of his works, the *Fatḥ al-wahhāb* ("The Victory of the Generous God"), a commentary on his own *Minhāj al-ṭullāb*, also appears in the manuscript's list of titles. An early Malay translation of the *Fatḥ al-wahhāb*, titled *Mirʾat al-ṭullāb* ("Mirror for Students"), was made by ʿAbd al-Raʾūf of Singkel; see van Bruinessen, "Kitab Kuning," 236.

Sheikh Nūr al-Dīn al-Rānīrī, the leading scholar of the Acehnese court at the time.

In addition to the titles of works, the mention of certain scholars and teachers strengthens the impression of a strong connection to the Indonesian Archipelago. For example, one section is claimed by the author to be based on the fatwas of Sheikh Muhammad al-Zayn, possibly referring to Muhammad Zayn al-Asyī who served at the Acehnese court under Sultan Mahmud Syah (1760–1781).[14] A scholar of utmost importance cited in a section on zikir is Sheikh Muhammad ibn ʿAbd al-Karīm al-Sammān al-Madanī, better known as al-Sammānī (1718–1775), the Medina-born founder of the Sammaniyah. His disciples from the Indonesian Archipelago, several of whom became renowned scholars in their homelands upon return from Arabia, introduced his teachings to their own followers, with the Sammaniyah as a result spreading widely, especially in Palembang and Aceh.[15]

The Sammaniyah is not the only Sufi order invoked in the manuscript. A chain of transmission (silsilah) covering seven pages begins with the Prophet Muhammad, continues with his family members and other prominent Muslim scholars and reaches the great "saint" ʿAbd al-Qādir al-Jīlānī (d. 1166), founder of the Qadiriyyah. Five more of those appearing after him in the list bear the nisbah Qādirī, testifying to their affiliation. The order was popular in Java and Sumatra, and even more so in neighboring south India, where devotion to Sheikh Muhideen (as Jīlānī was known) was widespread.[16] Finally, the owner of the manuscript, Encik Sulaiman ibn ʿAbd al-Jalil, describes himself as one who followed the path of the Shatariyyah (M. akan jalan tarekat lishtariyah), the order that with its strong speculative tendencies and association with wujūdiyyah teachings was the dominant Sufi order in the archipelago in the seventeenth and eighteenth centuries.[17]

The story emerging from this brief overview of the Malay Compendium manuscript from Ceylon corresponds closely with that told by Azyumardi Azra in his seminal study of the ulama networks between the

---

[14] On al-Asyī, see Azyumardi Azra, *Jaringan Ulama: Timur Tengah dan Kepulauan Nusantara Abad XVII dan XVIII* (Bandung: Mizan, 1999), 261.

[15] For a list of some of al-Sammānī's well known disciples from the archipelago, see ibid., 261–262. These disciples often introduced their fellow countrymen to the teachings while still in Arabia; see Drewes, *Directions for Travellers on the Mystic Path*, 36–37.

[16] See Susan Elizabeth Schomburg, "'Reviving Religion': The Qadiri Sufi Order, Popular Devotion to Sufi Saint Muhyiuddin ʿAbdul Qadir Al-Gilani, and Processes of 'Islamization' in Tamil," unpublished Ph.D. thesis, Harvard University (2003).

[17] Marshall G. Hodgson, *The Venture of Islam*, 3 vols. (Chicago: University of Chicago Press, 1974), I: 464.

Middle East and the Indonesian Archipelago in the seventeenth and eighteenth centuries. Ceylon's location in the Indian Ocean, on the maritime route between the two regions, meant that pilgrim ships traveling in both directions docked regularly on the island's shores. In the late seventeenth century and throughout the eighteenth, when both present-day Sri Lanka and Indonesia were partially ruled by the VOC, with Ceylon serving the Dutch as a site of exile, military service and servitude for people from the archipelago, ties between colonial subjects on both shores were forged and, intentionally or otherwise, encouraged the creation of new religious networks.[18]

Names of authors, titles of texts and their content are telling. No less important to understanding the religious and literary culture of the Malays through their writing is the prism of language. Malay manuscripts from Ceylon reflect the linguistic multiplicity that characterized the community that produced them. Like many Malay manuscripts from Southeast Asia they contain sections in Arabic, often accompanied by interlinear translation or by a more holistic form of translation that conveys single sentences or longer sections of the Arabic text in Malay.

In addition to Arabic, some Malay manuscripts contain writing in Arabu-Tamil, Tamil written in the Arabic script and infused with Arabic vocabulary, commonly used by Muslims in Ceylon and south India and also known as arwi.[19] The inclusion of Arabu-Tamil reflects the close contacts between Malay- and Tamil-speaking Muslims in Ceylon which formed through intermarriage, business endeavors, residence in adjoining or shared neighborhoods, prayer in the same mosques and the use of Tamil for everyday pursuits by native speakers of both Malay and Tamil.[20] The *Malay Compendium* contains a single example of the aforementioned popular Arabic hadith – *man 'arafa nafsahu fa-qad 'arafa rabbahu* – with a translation and brief commentary in Tamil (see Figure 2.1).[21]

---

[18] A Javanese perspective on circles of diasporic Islamic teachers and disciples appears in the eighteenth-century *Babad Giyanti*; see Chapter 5.

[19] Tayka Shu'ayb 'Ālim, *Arabic, Arwi and Persian in Sarandib and Tamil Nadu* (Madras: Imāmul 'Arūs Trust, 1993). For an introduction to Arabu-Tamil, see 84–126.

[20] 'Ālim mentions a conversation he had in 1966 with the then qadi of Eravur Ḥabīb Muḥammad Labbai 'Ālim who told him that his great-grandfather had been one of seventeen Javanese ulama brought to Sarandib by the Dutch. The qadi further noted that in keeping with the trend of that earlier time his family had switched to speaking and writing in arwi. See ibid., 485.

[21] In addition to the inclusion of Arabu-Tamil in this manuscript and elsewhere, several Malay manuscripts from Ceylon include sections written in the Tamil script.

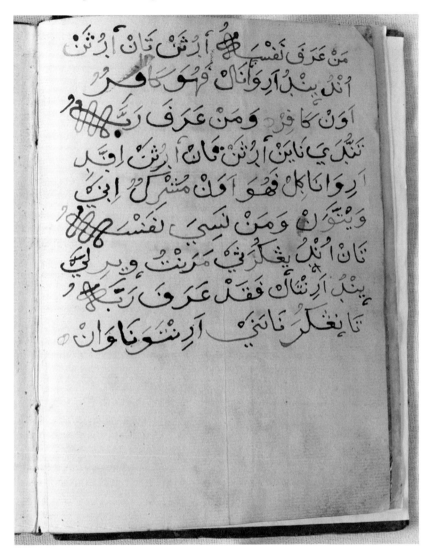

Figure 2.1 Arabic hadith with Tamil translation and interpretation. *Malay Compendium*, BL, EAP450/1/2.
Courtesy B. D. K. Saldin.

Considering the diasporic history of the Malays in Ceylon and their diverse ancestral roots in the Indonesian Archipelago, one might expect that writing in an Indonesian language other than Malay would emerge in Sri Lanka. However, Hussainmiya, in his two pioneering books on the Malays' past, in which he dedicated considerable attention to their writing practices and literary culture based on his access to a large number of manuscripts, mentioned no such finding.[22] Neither did others who wrote on the subject.[23] One may ask what happened to the multiple languages brought to Ceylon by exiles, soldiers and servants, among them Madurese, Buginese, Sundanese, Javanese, Balinese and others.[24] Were they entirely forgotten over time, or perhaps preserved in speech only, not leaving any written trace?

The *Compendium* offers a partial and suggestive answer to these questions. It contains several sections in Javanese, thus attesting to an Indonesian language other than Malay being preserved to some degree by the descendants of prior generations, perhaps going back to the early exiles, many of whom were members of Javanese royal families or served them in some capacity. The Javanese appearing in the manuscript can be described under several headings: three brief self-standing Javanese texts, a Javanese translation of an Arabic hadith, and single Javanese words scattered throughout the manuscript.[25]

The self-standing Javanese text discussed below is the most striking of these examples, not only for its completeness but also for its content and the associations it evokes. It is a poem titled *Kidung Rumeksa ing Wengi* ("A Song Guarding in the Night") that, as the title implies, offers its reciter protection from all dangers and evil lurking in the darkness, including jinn, devils, fire, water, thieves and others.[26] The poem is traditionally attributed to Sunan Kalijaga, the fifteenth-century leader of the Javanese *wali sanga*, the nine "saints" said to have converted Java to Islam and therefore resonates powerfully with foundational events of the Javanese past.[27]

The poem as it appears in the *Compendium* differs somewhat from the way it is conventionally written in Java, although variations are common

[22] Hussainmiya, *Lost Cousins*; Hussainmiya, *Orang Rejimen*.
[23] See, for example, Tuan Arifin Burah, *Saga of the Exiled Royal Javanese Unearthed* (Dehiwala: Tuan Arifin Burah, 2006); Hamid, "Islam dalam Sejarah dan Masyarakat Melayu Sri Lanka"; Harun Mat Piah, "Tradisi Kesusasteraan Melayu Sri Lanka."
[24] This diversity of origins is oft-documented in Dutch records. For its documentation in a Malay source, see the discussion of the *Syair Faiḍ al-Abād* in Chapter 9.
[25] Two of the three self-standing Javanese sections will be discussed in this chapter.
[26] *Malay Compendium*, BL, EAP450/1/2, 43.
[27] On the walis, see D. A. Rinkes, *Nine Saints of Java*, trans. H. M. Froger (Kuala Lumpur: Malaysian Sociological Research Institute, 1996; first published as an article series titled "De Heiligen van Java" in *Tijdschrift voor Indische Taal-, Land- en Volkenkunde* in 1910–1913). For an expanded discussion of the *Kidung*, see Chapter 3.

in Java as well. Several changes seem linked to a pronounced nasaliza-tion that occurs in Sri Lankan Malay that must have also found its way into what can be termed "Sri Lankan Javanese."[28] Thus *bilahing* for *bilahi* (disaster, bad luck) and *luputing* for *luput* (miss, escape). The sound "a" (similar to English "o" in orange) is sometimes replaced with "u": *adu* for *adoh* (far), *tirtu* for *tirta* (water). Some words are written incorrectly or are replaced altogether. This tendency suggests that the poem may have been copied and recopied by scribes who were not well acquainted with the language and could not identify and correct the errors. It may also be the case that the poem was written down from memory, with the scribe basing himself on aural memory rather than a written sample.

It is not only the questions of vocabulary and content that deserve attention. The poem is written in *macapat,* the poetic meters in which much of Javanese literature in the eighteenth and nineteenth centuries was composed, and which were not employed in Malay writing. The various *macapat* meters are differentiated by the number of lines per verse, the number of syllables in each line and the nature of the final syllable in each line. These meters dictated the way poets structured lines and selected words and, furthermore, were also closely associated with particular kinds of literary and performative scenes and with certain moods and atmospheres. The *Kidung* is written in *dhandhang-gula,* a meter which conveys a melodic mood that is lithe and flexible, "with didactic clarity and romantic allure."[29] The preservation of the poem's metrical properties suggests also a possible familiarity with, or perhaps distant memory of, Javanese prosody and literary conventions in nineteenth-century Ceylon (see Figure 2.2).

An additional example of self-standing Javanese writing appears in the form of a list of the numbers from one to forty that fills two pages of the manuscript. Whereas the *Kidung* suggests a certain acquaintance with Javanese literary tradition, the list of numbers signals a more mundane realm of knowledge in which the practical skills of counting and calculat-ing in Javanese may have remained significant or at least worthy of mention. After reaching forty with the numerals listed in the low register of Javanese (*ngoko*), the scribe went back to thirty-one and repeated the same numerals using a combination of low and high (*krama*) Javanese. This instance hints at the complex system of Javanese speech registers

[28] See B. D. K. Saldin, *The Sri Lankan Malays and Their Language/Orang Melayu Sri Lanka dan Bahasanya* (Kurunegala: B. D. K. Saldin, 1996), 51.
[29] Florida, *Writing the Past,* 90.

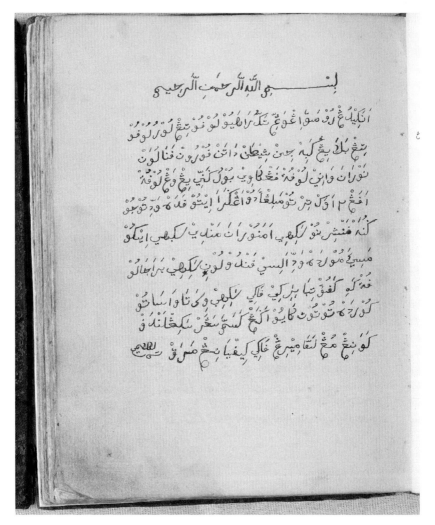

Figure 2.2 The Javanese poem *Kidung Rumeksa ing Wengi*. *Malay Compendium*, BL, EAP450/1/2, 43.
Courtesy B. D. K. Saldin

that lies at the heart of Javanese notions of power and societal hierarchies, albeit only a faint echo that does not constitute conclusive evidence for an in-depth understanding of that system.

The second form Javanese writing takes in the Malay manuscript is that of a brief hadith in Arabic that is translated, line by line, into

Javanese. Arabic and Javanese, both written in the Arabic script, alternate
on the page (Arabic in bold, in source and translation):

> **bism Allāh al-raḥmān al-raḥīm**
> *utawi pangandikaning Allah Taʾala*
> *ing ḥadīth qudsī* **al-insānu sirri**
> **wa-annā sirruhu** *tegesé manusa iki rasa*
> *nisun lan isun iku pawin rasané*[30]
>
> **In the name of God, the Compassionate, the Merciful,**
> The words of Exalted God
> In the sacred hadith **man is my secret**
> **And I am his secret;** this means man is my
> Secret and I am his secret.

The first Arabic phrase, the basmallah, is not translated into Javanese but
is left as is, perhaps because it was often included as an almost obligatory
opening line for texts and letters and was viewed more as a frame than an
integral element of the text. Also incorporated into the Javanese is the
term *ḥadīth qudsī* – a "sacred hadith" – referring not to traditions relating
the sayings and deeds of the Prophet that possess reliable chains of
transmission going back to Muhammad, called hadith, but to an utterance of God that is not part of the Qurʾan. Writing these Arabic words
within a Javanese text composed in the Arabic script is straightforward
and allowed the reader to recognize them immediately and pronounce
them correctly. The translation of the hadith itself is accurate and concise. There is however a possibility that the word *sirr* in Arabic, often
translated as "secret" or "hidden," was rendered here not as *rahsa*
(J. secret) but as *rasa*, a word that possesses a range of meanings including taste, meaning, sense, flavor, sensation, experience, inner feeling of
the heart. The latter translation – inner feeling, inner self – may in fact
correspond quite closely with the meaning of *sirr* in Sufi writings.
Whether the translator had *rasa* or *rahsa* decisively in mind is difficult
to determine because of spelling variations in these manuscripts, but it
may also be that he intentionally played on both possibilities. What is also
apparent in this passage is the adoption of an Arabic structure for the
Javanese sentence, indicated by the words *utawi* and *iku* that were
employed to show the position of words as subject and predicate in both
verbal and nominal Arabic sentences, a practice commonly used in the
Javanese *pesantren* system of Islamic education. This didactic measure,

---

[30] *Malay Compendium*, BL, EAP450/1/2, 181. The lines between Arabic and Javanese blur
here as elsewhere: *ḥadīth qudsī*, for example, apparently did not require translation.

known from Javanese manuscripts of the eighteenth century, was apparently also transmitted to Ceylon.[31]

Finally, the third manner in which Javanese was incorporated into the manuscript was in the form of single words that seem to appear occasionally throughout, used as part of local Malay vocabulary, perhaps interchangeably with corresponding words in that language. Examples include *tembung* (word), *sethithik* (a little, few), *tiyang* (person), *iki* (this), *saking* (because, on account of), *aja lali* (do not forget). Numbers in Javanese appear as well. A diagram that features the points of the compass lists them in Javanese: *lor, wétan, kidul* and *kulon* (north, east, south and west, respectively).

Exploring Encik Sulaiman's early nineteenth-century *Malay Compendium* along the axes of reference networks and language use, with brief forays into questions of content, prosody and genre, offers a glimpse of the religious and intellectual culture of the Malays in Ceylon. More than anything else, the manuscript shows how intertwined with Islamic life in the archipelago and the Middle East were the lives of these descendants of royal exiles, soldiers, servants and their families who as a community adhered both to Islam and to the Malay language.

The Javanese texts in Encik Sulaiman's manuscript go beyond testifying to the capacity to write in that language. The *Kidung Rumeksa ing Wengi* – evoking the period of Java's early Islamization, the walis and their powers of protection and guidance – indicates a certain sense of historical consciousness. The use of tembang and the Javanese speech registers, in however fragmentary a manner, represent additional ties to a cultural and literary world beyond Ceylon's shores. The multiple Arabic sections of the manuscript, almost always accompanied by detailed translation, cite the Qur'an, hadith and various works composed in Damascus, Cairo and Medina, then translated by men from Pattani, Palembang and Aceh, indicating the ties of local Malays to the historical heartlands of Islam and to the texts and ideas produced over generations of interactions – mutual processes of study, initiation and exchange – between those heartlands and the Indian subcontinent, Ceylon and the archipelago.

---

[31] On the use of *utawi* and *iku* in Javanese pesantren and manuscripts, see Saiful Umam, "God's Mercy Is Not Limited to Arabic Speakers: Reading Intellectual Biography of Muhammad Salih Darat and His Pegon Islamic Texts," *Studia Islamika* 20.2 (2013), 256–257. An additional noteworthy feature of the passage, not cited here, is the use of a "dotted dal" (with the dot above the letter) in the word *dhāt* (A. God's essence) to indicate the Javanese retroflex dh sound. On another variation of the dal indicating Bantenese (west Java) origin, see Edwin P. Wieringa, "Dotting the Dal and Penetrating the Letters: The Javanese Origin of the Syair Seribu Masalah and Its Bantenese Spelling," *BKI* 159.4 (2003), 511–514.

Encik Sulaiman's biography also reflects this history: Descended from a Javanese man who traveled on the hajj to Mecca and living across the Java Sea to the northeast in Ujung Pandang, he later – for reasons unknown – continued his life in British Ceylon, where he commissioned the writing of a manuscript encapsulating this tapestry of connections.

The networks of references, titles and quotes explored thus far were based to a large extent on processes of translation which formed the initial building blocks of non-Arabic Islamic literary cultures. Three broad translation paradigms common across the Malay world are also apparent in manuscripts from Ceylon: translation at the story, sentence and single-word levels. Although the three translation paradigms can be seen as occupying a continuum that goes from broad to narrow, general to detailed, paraphrased to literal, considering them only in this light would be far too simplistic. There was clearly overlap among the three, and they all contributed significantly to the translation of Islamic stories, ideas, expressions and vocabulary into a local Malay idiom.[32]

The first paradigm encompassed a form of holistic translation: entire works that were presented anew in Malay, maintaining – depending on the specifics of the particular text – a broad story line, a dialogic framework or a set of theological issues. Such works tended to display a high degree of creativity and flexibility, with local authors and translators finding ways to adapt the texts to their audiences' tastes and to their own agendas of propagating certain ideas and beliefs.

The second paradigm involved translation at sentence level with a brief section in Arabic followed immediately by a translation into Malay or Javanese. In this mode the original text appeared on the page and was there for all to see, accompanied by a translation which could be very literal, take the shape of a limited paraphrase or offer a rather broad interpretation. The type of translation provided, and its accuracy, was very much up to the individual who was rendering the text in Malay. Manuscripts following this translation paradigm contain pages that alternate between writing in two languages, obliging the reader or listener to move back and forth as well. A central and oft-used device employed in this form of translation of Islamic texts into Malay is the word *artinya*. *Arti*, deriving from the Sanskrit word for meaning, purpose or essence (*artha*), appears in various forms in Malay and Indonesian: *berarti*, has a

---

[32] On these paradigms, see Ronit Ricci, "Story, Sentence, Single Word: Translation Paradigms in Javanese and Malay Islamic Literature," in Sandra Bermann and Catherine Porter (eds.), *A Companion to Translation Studies* (Hoboken, NJ: Wiley-Blackwell, 2014), 543–556.

meaning; *mengerti*, get the meaning, understand; *mengertikan*, impart a meaning, explain. The Javanese equivalent is *tegesé* or *tegesipun*. "Artinya/ tegesé" in the context of translation can be rendered as "this means" or "this signifies," itself a translation of Arabic *ya'anī*. It appears very commonly as a bridge between an Arabic quote, idiom or single word and its Malay or Javanese translation, often with some elaboration of the Arabic, as in the passage citing the *ḥadīth qudsī* above. Another example from the *Compendium* is the *shahadat Fatimah* (Arabic and its translation in bold):

Ini bunyinya shahadat Fatimah
Ashhadu an lā ilāha illa Allāh wa ashhadu an Fāṭimah Zahrā bintī rasūl Allāh
Artinya bahwasanya aku mengetahui dan saksi tiada tuhan
hanya Allah dan aku mengetahui dan saksi bahwasanya Siti Fatimah
itu anaqnya perempuan rasulullah yang mengikuti dengan lakinya mengipuni
segala orang perempuan yang mengikuti dengan lakinya hari yang kemudian

This is the "Fatimah profession of faith":
I bear witness that there is no God but Allah and I bear witness that Fatimah Zahra ["The Radiant One"] is the daughter of God's Messenger.
This means that I acknowledge and bear witness that there is no God but Allah and I acknowledge and bear witness that Siti Fatimah is the daughter of God's Messenger who followed her husband and who [will] forgive all women who follow their husbands in the day to come.[33]

The frequency with which this "ultimate referent" of artinya/tegesé is featured is striking. Its presence allowed for Arabic to be included in the Malay or Javanese text while also remaining differentiated within it; it allowed the Arabic to form part of a Malay or Javanese text – giving it an authentic Islamic content and sound – but also guaranteed that the Arabic words would not remain foreign or unintelligible. For audiences of listeners rather than readers of the text, hearing this connecting, bridging word signaled that an Arabic quote had concluded and a translation and often an interpretation were imminent. Thus, Arabic quotations played an important aural role.

The third paradigm, the one to be highlighted, is that of interlinear translation. Whereas the first paradigm features outlines of stories and treatises, and the second conveys translations at the sentence level,

---

[33] *Malay Compendium*, BL, EAP450/1/2, 28. The main elaborations in the Malay rendering of this passage are the two Malay verbs (*mengetahui, saksi*) replacing the one (*ashhadu*) in Arabic and the mention of Fatimah's traditional role as intercessor on behalf of all pious women on the Day of Judgment. *Mengetahui*, translated as "acknowledge," can also be translated as "to know," "be aware, "to understand," "to perceive."

interlinear translation provided its audience with a word-for-word rendering of an Arabic text, with Malay "equivalents" appearing in between the Arabic lines on the page. This translation paradigm reveals more than any other the mechanics of translation as well as the unavoidable choices inherent in every translation act. The readings it offers across two languages and between the lines are a concrete manifestation of the larger crossings and relationships that characterized the Malays' Indian Ocean and Islamic links.

Before delving further into this translation strategy and its significance, the question of script usage deserves further mention. Tamil, Malay and Javanese were written in the *Compendium* and other manuscripts using modified forms of the Arabic script that accommodate sounds that do not appear in Arabic by adding diacritical marks to existing Arabic letters. The adoption of the Arabic script by speakers of these languages constituted an important dimension of Islamization and allowed for easier and more accurate rendering of Islamic terminology into Tamil, Malay and Javanese. A manuscript page that contains alternating lines of, for instance, Malay and Arabic embodies an orthographic continuity across languages and conveys the impression that the two flow from and into one another. That a single manuscript from Ceylon contains four languages all written in the same script offers one more testimony to the interconnectedness of local Malay Muslim communities with their co-religionists across geographical and linguistic boundaries.

The interlinear translation page offers a microcosm of the transmission of content, vocabulary and grammatical and syntactical structures from Arabic into Malay. Deriving from early traditions of translating the Qur'an into Persian and later spreading and gaining popularity across the Indonesian Archipelago, interlinear translations were composed in an attempt to replicate the Arabic with utmost care, at times to the detriment of semantic coherence. As Philippus Samuel van Ronkel noted in his 1899 study, such translations attempted to adhere to the features of tense, number and gender that were universally marked in Arabic but not at all so in Malay.[34]

---

[34] Ph. S. van Ronkel, *Mengenai Pengaruh Tatakalimat Arab Terhadap Tatakalimat Melayu*, trans. A. Ikram (Jakarta: Bhratara, 1977; first published as "Over de Invloed der Arabische Syntaxis op de Maleische," *Tijdschrift voor Indische Taal-, Land- en Volkenkunde* 41 (1899): 498–528. More recently the influence of Arabic on Malay was taken up by Cyril Skinner, "The Influence of Arabic on Modern Malay (with Particular Reference to Spoken Malay)," in Justin Corfield (ed.), *Cyril Skinner (1924–1986): Orientalist, Linguist,*

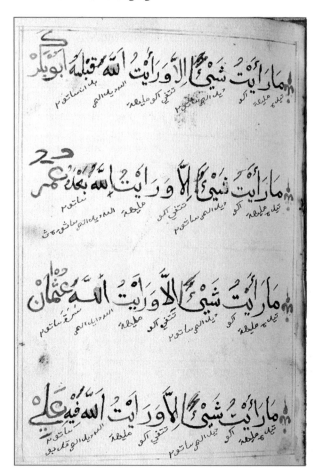

Figure 2.3 Arabic hadith with Malay interlinear translation.
Malay Compendium, BL, EAP450/1/2, 173.
Courtesy B. D. K. Saldin

Interlinear translation from Arabic into Malay in Ceylon followed the same pattern. The following example, from the *Compendium*, recorded the well-known replies offered by the Prophet Muhammad's four Companions and first four caliphs when asked about God's presence (Arabic in bold, with Malay beneath it (see Figure 2.3).

Historian, Scholar. A Collection of Essays and Reviews (Clayton: Monash Asia Institute, 1996), 3–20.

The Caliphs' Words: From Arabic to Malay

Mā ra'aytu   shay'an   illā wa-ra'aytu Allāh qablahu   Abu Bakar
Tiada melihat aku di dalam satu2 tetapi aku melihat Allah di dalam badan satu2
Mā ra'aytu   shay'an   illā wa-ra'aytu Allāh ba'dahu   'Umar
Tiada melihat aku di dalam satu2 tetapi aku melihat Allah di dalam seshudahnya
                                                                              satu2
Mā ra'aytu   shay'an   illā wa-ra'aytu Allāh   'Uthmān
Tiada melihat aku di dalam satu2   tetapi aku melihat Allah di dalam sarata satu2
Mā ra'aytu   shay'an   illā wa-ra'aytu Allāh fīhi   'Alī
Tiada melihat aku di dalam satu2   tetapi aku melihat Allah di dalam qalbu satu2

The Arabic may be translated into English as:

I see nothing without seeing God before it   Abu Bakar
I see nothing without seeing God behind it   'Umar
I see nothing without seeing God along with it   'Uthmān[35]
I see nothing without seeing God within it   'Alī[36]

The four caliphs, Abu Bakar, 'Umar, 'Uthmān and 'Alī, are listed in chronological order and their names appear in red at the end of the Arabic lines. Their identity is thus highlighted, and it is clear that their names stand apart from the quotations. The names appear only once and so can be understood as "belonging" to both languages concurrently. Taken together, the caliphs' definitions complement one another and map the physical world as entirely pervaded by God, who is palpable to His believers in and from all angles of any given object. The Malay translation is an attempt to conform as literally as possible to the Arabic. It also reflects a context of at least partial orality in which such texts were transmitted in person from teacher to disciple, a practice that could explain certain omissions and mistakes.

Here is the first line, presenting the words of Abu Bakar:

Mā ra'aytu   shay'an   illā wa-ra'aytu Allāh qablahu   Abu Bakar
Tiada melihat aku di dalam satu2 tetapi aku melihat Allah di dalam badan satu2

The Malay was rendered according to the verb–subject order of the Arabic verb form: *tiada melihat aku* rather than the anticipated *tiada kulihat* or, even more conventionally, *aku tidak melihat*. Malay *aku* ("I")

---

[35] An Arabic word (*ma'ahu* – with it, along with it) is missing in the original and I have filled it in based on the traditional citation of 'Uthmān's words.
[36] At the risk of stating the obvious, I will add here that the translation into English introduces an additional level of complexity and distance from the Arabic source. The translation here attempts to be idiomatic rather than literal (thus "I see nothing" rather than the more literal "I have not seen a thing") whereas the Malay interlinear translation tradition constitutes precisely the opposite: an attempt to record the Arabic as closely as possible, at times not just at the cost of being unidiomatic but also of being unclear.

here stands for the Arabic suffix -*tu* indicating the first-person singular in the past tense (*ra'aytu* – I saw; the past here used to indicate a constant state), even though Malay verbs remain uninflected (i.e. *melihat* can be used with any person, number or tense to indicate "see" or "look"); Arabic *shay'an* – a thing, here "anything" – is rendered by several words: *di dalam* means "in, inside," and *satu*, a variant of *suatu*, refers to "one, any, a single thing," with its repetition (*suatu-suatu*) indicating emphasis: "anything." Thus, the first part of the Malay sentence can be translated as "I do not see in anything," or "I do not look at anything."

Arabic *illā* – without – is translated by Malay *tetapi*: "but, however, nevertheless." Interestingly, the second appearance in Abu Bakar's words of Arabic *ra'aytu* – "I see"– includes a more idiomatic Malay phrase: *aku melihat*, following its typical subject–verb order. God's name is left as is. Finally, Arabic *qablahu* – "before it, in front of it, preceding it" – indicating both a temporal and spatial dimension when God is concerned, appeared in Malay as *di dalam badan satu-satu*: "in any body, or object" (*badan*). This could be an error, as the translator may have written *di dalam* ("in, inside") rather than *di depan* ("in front of") with *badan* translating Arabic -*hu*, indicating "it" ("in front of *it*"). However, since the phrase *di dalam* appears very consistently in all four lines, it may also be that the translator selected it – with its various meanings having to do with that which is inner, deep, profound – to emphasize God's all-pervading nature, the text's theme. In this more likely case, *depan* ("in front") may have been mistakenly replaced by *badan*, as the latter appears in the sentence where the positional term should be. The second part of the Malay sentence can be translated as "without seeing God in front of anything, that thing, it," and the full sentence as: "I do not look at anything without seeing God in front of it."

Such close readings show that even a very small text reveals both accurate translation strategies as well as misunderstandings and expansions of meaning, what A. L. (Pete) Becker called the "exuberances and deficiencies" inherent in all translations.[37] In the second line 'Umar is quoted as saying he sees nothing without seeing God behind or after it (*ba'dahu*), rendered in Malay as *sesudahnya* ("after it"), a temporal rather than a spatial designation indicating positionality; the third Arabic line, citing 'Uthman, is missing its positional term which, according to tradition should be *ma'ahu* ("with it"), yet the Malay fills in the gap with *sarata*: "all, all over," so that the sentence means "I do not see anything without seeing God all over it," a certain variation. Another variation, or

---

[37] A. L. Becker, "Silence across Languages," in A. L. Becker, *Beyond Translation: Essays toward a Modern Philology* (Ann Arbor: University of Michigan Press, 1995), 291.

rather expansion, likely based on a teacher's guiding words, appears in the final line where the Arabic *fīhi* ("in it") is rendered as *di dalam qalbu satu-satu*: "in that thing, [its] heart." These are the words of ʿAlī, the fourth caliph and one whose words and deeds provide special inspiration to the Sufis. And so, fittingly, it seems the Malay teacher or disciple understood the within-ness in his words as relating to the heart, God as residing in all hearts, God as the heart of everything.[38]

The example of the caliphs' Arabic words rendered in Malay highlights changes in word order, subject–verb position, tense and emphasis that transpired through the act of word-for-word translation, and it offers a sense of attempts made at precision and duplication of the Arabic that shaped Malay significantly in new ways. Van Ronkel, the pioneer of interlinear translation studies in the Malay world, concluded that such translations had a powerful influence not only in reshaping Malay vocabulary but also in recasting the more subtle realm of Malay syntax. For example, he found that the Arabic preposition *bi* was consistently translated as *dengan*, and so the phrase *bismillah* ("in the name of God") was translated into Malay as *dengan nama*, rather than the more conventional *atas nama*.[39] Such patterns were then gradually assimilated into texts that were not interlinear translations, generalized and incorporated into the Malay language, gaining a life of their own that was no longer dependent on a detailed translation strategy. Using Arabic syntax to write Malay became gradually more habitual, so much so that it is clearly visible in examples taken from the hikayat genre, often recounting tales of love, adventure and travel that have little to do with religion.[40] In the same vein, Saiful Umam in his study of the writings of the Javanese religious scholar Muhammad Salih Darat showed a similar tendency of Arabic syntactical influence in the context of nineteenth-century Java. Salih was well versed in the tradition of the Islamic pesantren schools, where Arabic-to-Javanese interlinear translations were used on a regular basis. And so, when he composed commentaries on Arabic texts, he used a form of Javanese highly influenced by that tradition of religious learning. Similar to van Ronkel's findings for Malay, Umam detected a clear Arabic structure to Salih's Javanese sentences, both nominal and verbal. For example, he often began a sentence with a verb as predicate followed

---

[38] The four lines of this brief Arabic text have been widely interpreted and are viewed as offering a profound truth, the explication of which is far beyond the scope of this discussion, limited as it is to the passage's linguistic and grammatical aspects and to its basic content.

[39] Van Ronkel, *Mengenai Pengaruh Tatakalimat Arab*, 23–25.

[40] Ibid., 20–31. Van Ronkel also showed how various irregular constructions in Malay can be understood if retranslated (i.e. "translated backwards") into Arabic.

by a noun in the subject position, rather than the idiomatic Javanese which tends to begin with a subject followed by a verb as predicate.[41]

What emerges from both studies and was relevant also for the tradition of interlinearity transmitted to Ceylon is how language worlds were irrevocably altered by this translation practice. Such changes encompassed grammatical and syntactical structures, sounds pronounced, vocabulary added and lost and the inclusion of hitherto unfamiliar idioms, images and concepts that shaped new ways of thinking. In this process movement can be detected in more than one direction: Translation moved the Arabic text away from its place of origin, the physical book (or memorized text) carried by travelers or traders across land and sea to a faraway site, to be reinscribed in very different natural and social environments that offered new frames of reference and interpretation; translation also "moved" the Austronesian and local Malay and Javanese languages closer to a Semitic and sanctified Arabic and pointed them in the direction of change, expansion and new possibilities, so that all these languages were more "out in the world" than they had previously been, exposed and influential concurrently.

The tropes of connectivity and movement apparent in the caliphs' passage in its interlinear form echo with local histories of literary and religious networks and human mobility. The Islamization of South and Southeast Asia in its early stages was a process intertwined with translation, but translation, and especially in its interlinear mode, also provided an ongoing form of connectivity that unfolded anew for each generation and individual living in Muslim, but non-Arab, environments. The inclusion of the Arabic text on the page made the authenticity and authority of the original visible and palpable, while the detailed translation made the content accessible and ripe for discussion; interlinear translations were, among other things, a primary means for teaching the Arabic language, in a broad sense that included vocabulary, grammar, syntax, idioms, Qur'anic quotes and poetic sensibilities; the learning often took place in educational contexts where the guru (or *kyai*/sheikh)–disciple relationship was central. In addition to the apparent practical and didactic advantages of interlinear translation it can also be considered from a more figurative standpoint, if local terminologies for the practice are explored. Whereas English "interlinear" is defined as that which is (1) inserted between lines already written or printed or (2) written or printed in different languages or texts in alternate lines,[42]

---

[41] Umam, "God's Mercy Is Not Limited to Arabic Speakers," 256–257.
[42] *Merriam-Webster Dictionary*, online at www.merriam-webster.com/dictionary/interlinear (accessed August 9, 2018).

in the Malay and Javanese traditions this definition typically referred to an Arabic text written on the page, often with wide spacing and in dark ink, with a word-for-word translation written between the Arabic lines. Malay and Javanese in such volumes can look identical to Arabic to the untrained eye although often unvocalized, with the script at times smaller and written in lighter ink. In such cases, the authority of the Arabic text is highlighted visually on the page through size and color. Its lines can be seen as framing each Malay line on both its sides or, depending on the eye of the beholder, the lines may be viewed as alternating between the two languages, flowing from and into each other by way of their shared script. The visual aspect of such interlinear translations is not marginal, but rather makes up one of several dimensions that take us beyond the initial tendency to consider, above all, the content-categories of text and translation.

The English word "interlinear" describes a central, yet particular aspect of the translation texts, while also shaping what one sees when approaching the page: a set of lines (dark, light, with writing of various sizes, with or without vocalization, straight or tilted) that can be viewed as separate, linked, merged, in dialogue or all of the above. Turning to other ways of naming the phenomenon offers additional perspectives. For example, Malay and Javanese manuscripts containing interlinear translations were often referred to as *kitab jenggotan*: "bearded books" in which the "beard" refers to the Malay or Javanese translation appearing between the Arabic lines and at times also spreading beyond them and onto the page's margins.[43] The image of the beard offers a visual metaphor but also a tactile one that can imply softness, smoothness, prickliness or roughness and invites one to imagine the stroking of the text while deep in thought, moving fingers across it as it was studied with a guru and recited repeatedly. In the educational and ritual contexts in which most religiously oriented kitabs were written, copied and read, the beard could also hint at the image of an old, knowledgeable and pious religious scholar. In the Malay-speaking regions, it may have also suggested the figure of a foreign teacher of Islam, likely an Arab.

In west Java, the verb *ngalogat* has been used for interlinear translations into Javanese and Sundanese. Deriving from Arabic *lughah* (language, speech, idiom, tongue), it suggests the Arabic text being "languaged" into the local idiom. Another Javanese term used was *makna gandhul*.

---

[43] The *Masā'il al-ta'līm* ("Questions for Teaching"), one of the oldest extant Javanese manuscripts now preserved in the British Library, is such a book; see Bernard Arps and Annabel Teh Gallop, *Golden Letters: Writing Traditions of Indonesia/Surat Emas: Budaya Tulis Di Indonesia* (London: British Library, 1991), 100.

Makna translates as "meaning" or "significance" and *gandhul* as "hanging on," "clinging or depending on something." This metaphor offers the image of the text's Javanese meaning hanging onto the Arabic lines, dependent on them: another visual and tactile metaphor of proximity and touch as the lines cling and connect, the Javanese leaning on the Arabic original for its explication and significance. Because of the active nature of the verb, the Javanese words hanging onto or between the Arabic lines also offer a less than static image of the writing in which the translation can be conceived as stretching toward the Arabic, holding on tightly, perhaps almost slipping at times. This image suggests dedication and determination but also the possibility of instability and risk.

The Javanese verb *ngesahi* is also employed to describe the act of translating between the lines. Deriving from the Arabic word *ṣaḥ* – its semantic field encompassing "valid, legitimate, legal, authoritative, genuine, real, true" – it refers to the traditional method of disciples studying the Arabic text with their teachers – word by word, line by line – and writing down the teacher's words of wisdom and truth as the lessons progressed. This metaphor is one hinting at the central relationship of any seeker of religious knowledge, as entry into the world of the Arabic language and, more broadly, Islamic knowledge, required an experienced, pious and learned teacher to guide the way. Thus, the connections, dependency and proximity found on the page are not between languages, scripts or teachings alone but also between teacher and disciple, knower and seeker, across generations in the long chain of transmission that moves slowly but consistently from past to present to future.

And so, metaphors of interlinear translation relate to various realms: visual, tactile, spatial, kinetic and relational. They point to engagement with languages, ideas, values and beliefs; and they imply an inbetweenness through which the translation can be understood as enclosed, enveloped, present in its own right, dependent and clingy or expanding. Different terms represent different perspectives on what such translation meant to individuals and communities and, together, they coalesce into a far more nuanced vision of the practice than that suggested by the English term "interlinearity" alone. Thinking of this practice and its associated meanings in the context of Malay writing in Ceylon, where multiple manuscripts attest to its prevalence, is pertinent. In addition to providing perspectives on translation per se it offers a paradigm for thinking about many of this chapter's themes. It broadly evokes Malay life in Ceylon and, more specifically, the makeup of the multilingual and multi-authored *Malay Compendium*, the Malays' bridging of languages and literary traditions, and their diasporic position of geographic, cultural and linguistic inbetween-ness that followed old ways as the Malay language replicated the Arabic yet, while leaning on and enveloped by those ways, expanded them to create new modes of speech, writing and meaning.

★★★

In maintaining their cultural world far from their places of origin and long after their ancestors had come to Ceylon, literary networks of references, titles, names and texts played key roles for the Malays, as did their particular use of language. There is no doubt that the ongoing use of Malay, both spoken and written, constituted the most pivotal connection to the wider Malay–Indonesian world to the southeast. It allowed for the preservation of texts, many of them in translation from Arabic, that were central to intellectual and spiritual trends in the lands whence came the Malays' forefathers, promising shared knowledge repositories and continuity. The insistence on transmitting the gundul script across generations meant that texts could be recopied when old books disintegrated and that familiarity with specifically Malay genres such as pantun and syair was perpetuated.[44] And, yet, possessing evidence as found in the *Compendium* of the ongoing use of another major language of the Indonesian Archipelago, especially one spoken by many of the early exiles – Javanese – along with hints of its poetic meters, didactic codes and echoes of its mythic-historical narratives, is an important reminder that this diasporic group possessed wide-ranging roots and was much more internally diverse than suggested by the category "Malay."

The references and texts found in the *Compendium* are clear indicators of intellectual and religious connections that the Malays maintained with the Islamic regions of the archipelago and Arabia. And this realization, in turn, suggests that, rather than considering the Malays in Ceylon/Sri Lanka as occupying a distant, marginal corner of a vast Malay sphere, their physical and figurative location between the Malay and Arab worlds signifies that crossroads, connections and movement are more appropriate conceptual categories for considering their case than is marginality. Within the *Compendium* and other nineteenth-century manuscripts, these connections are most concretely and minutely evident in sections containing passages translated from Arabic, paragraph by paragraph, sentence by sentence and even word by word, the latter taking the form of interlinear translation.

---

[44] On compulsory literacy lessons given to Malay children whose fathers served in the Ceylon Rifle Regiment of the British army, see Hussainmiya, *Lost Cousins*, 93.

Interlinearity is a form of continuity, an attempt at precise replication of one language into another that also binds the two in close proximity on the page, and beyond it in religious practice, speech and memory. In Malay writing from Ceylon, the shared script used for writing Arabic and Malay (as well as Javanese and Tamil) was a profound manifestation of the bonds linking these languages in a particular Islamic context. The Arabic text, often highlighted through size or darker ink, implied a standard, a stable point in time and space, as homelands are often imagined by those living in a diaspora: Arabic as representing a point of departure, a pre-exile and diaspora site that is close to the heart yet distant and filled with uncertainty. The Malay translation, in its following, clinging and taking inspiration from the Arabic yet also inevitably differing from it, represented the novel, the process of adaptation and change, the not-quite-authentic yet lithe, versatile stretching of the limits toward change and the accommodation of a diasporic textual culture that draws on multiple roots and routes.

3 Remembering Java

This chapter draws on materials from Ceylon to explore both personal and collective expressions of memory as they relate to the archipelago and especially to Java, and considers the shifts occurring in their construction and representation with the passage of time. In addressing textualized memories and links to the archipelago, the chapter expands the discussion of these themes presented in Chapter 2, differing in the genres, tone and atmosphere of the writing it explores. Whereas Chapter 2 focused on intellectual and religious currents of connectivity and memory, the present chapter engages with individual voices and traditions of storytelling and cultural heroes as transmitted to the Ceylon diaspora. There is often no clear boundary between forms of remembering here referred to as "personal" and "collective," yet the imposed distinction nonetheless highlights some distinguishing characteristics and textures. Recollections of home – places of origin, familial ties, social circles, politics, food, stories – were personal and private, certainly as experienced by individuals in the initial period following their banishment. As time passed and concrete images, events and people blurred or were transmitted in narrative form, spoken or written, to younger generations for whom exile was not a lived experience, memories were also formulated and reinforced in the public, collective sphere in paradigmatic, stylized ways.

The discussion of a personal realm of memory draws on a secret exchange of letters between Javanese exiles living in Trincomalee and in Jaffna in the 1720s. The letters, although brief and surviving only in translation, bear witness to private longings and misgivings. The realm of collective memory, as expressed through historical and literary writing, is considered by reading fragments of the Javanese wali sanga tradition preserved in Ceylon, including a poem, several loose manuscript pages and a hikayat recounting Java's Islamization. These sources invite a consideration of the role of the nine men, to whom tradition ascribes the conversion of Java, within a diasporic Malay imagination. The retelling of the walis' stories in the diaspora speaks to a transition from a personal to a more collective form of memory that, while still anchored in Java's history, geography and society, also forms part of a semi-mythic past to which none of the readers in Ceylon had an immediate connection. Ultimately the categories of memory blur at the edges to form a continuum of the distant and more recent past, of personal and political recollections.

Recovering the voices of those exiled and their personal recollections is challenging, as most left no written trace and many were subaltern subjects whose lives were not deemed worthy of recording. In the case of royal exiles in Ceylon, some documentation has survived but it, too, is very limited and often circumscribed by colonial agendas and anxieties. Nevertheless, such slivers of evidence can be revealing, and they often come in the form of letters, an important genre of personal and political writing in maritime Southeast Asia in the eighteenth and nineteenth centuries. Such letters from Ceylon, if read in tandem, can provide a kind of tapestry of experiences and historical memory expressed through details of royal genealogies, familial expansions, claims made in the name of exiled or enlisted forefathers that continued to play out in the present, complaints, blessings, requests and oaths.[1] One such letter exchange preserved in the Dutch archive provides evidence of Javanese royals in exile remembering their homeland and longing for it.

The letters were exchanged, covertly, between the banished Javanese king Amangkurat III and his sons in Jaffna (exiled in 1708), and Tumenggung Suradilaga, who was kept to the southeast in Trincomalee. The original letters, written in Javanese, were apparently discarded. What remains are dual translations of these documents into Dutch. Each letter was orally translated, separately, by two Javanese translators serving the Political Council in Colombo, in an effort to maximize the accuracy of the translation for the benefit of the Dutch administrators trying to understand the unfolding, forbidden contacts and to verify the translators' honesty. Each translation was then put into writing by the Dutch scribe Jan Carlier (see Figure 3.1).[2] Such a process entailed errors and

---

[1] Several such letters are discussed throughout; see for example the letters addressed to the governor-general and Council of the Indies in Batavia from Cucunda Prince Major Bacan Sadaralam and Gagugu Bacan Kecil Na'imuddin, Colombo, 1792, Leiden University Library, MS LOr 2241-Ia (11); from Pangéran Mas Adipati Mangkurat, Colombo, 1806, Leiden University Library, MS LOr 2241-I (23); from Cucunda Radèn Tumenggung Wira Kushuma ibn Mas Kreti, Colombo, 1806, Leiden University Library, MS LOr 2241-I(24).

[2] The translated letters appear in the Political Council Minutes of June 13, 1727. An attached note explains that the letters arrived from Jaffna already accompanied by a Dutch translation, but were retranslated twice more, as mentioned above, in order to assess to what extent the content of the more recent translations would accord with the translation from Jaffna (SLNA 1/61B). The 1727 Political Council Minutes of Jaffna, which may have preserved the originals, are no longer available.

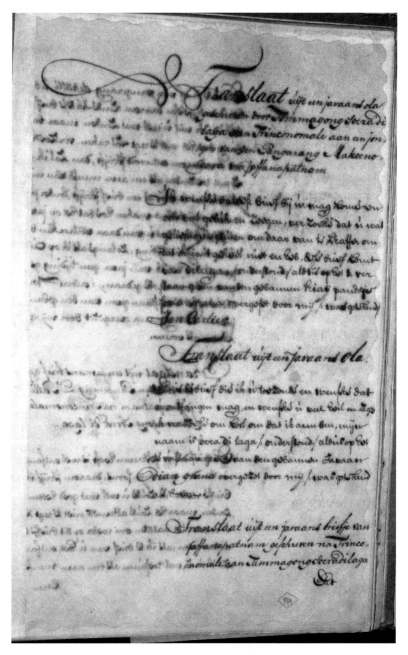

Figure 3.1 Dutch translation of a clandestine letter in Javanese exchanged between Jaffna and Trincomalee. SLNA 1/61B, 194.
Courtesy Department of National Archives, Sri Lanka

misunderstandings, no doubt: We cannot be certain how accurate the exiled translators' command of Dutch was nor how well they were able or willing to render the messages' intricacies as well as those of Javanese terminology and style in their translations. This matter was especially pertinent due to the pronounced hierarchical nature and linguistic subtlety of the Javanese language, all the more so when considering the status of those writing and receiving the letters, the elaborate conventions of contemporary letter writing, the use of greetings and blessings grounded in Islamic culture, and the letters' subject matter and tone carrying emotional urgency and a potential for meaning that remained hidden between the lines.

The two Javanese translators were themselves exiles (D. *gebannen*). The Political Council Minutes of June 13, 1727, give their names as Dian Grana and Kyai Panji Soereengrana, the latter's title (kyai) indicating that he was a religious scholar and teacher. Beyond these basic facts nothing is known of them, and it is also not clear whether the entire set of letters that were part of the aforementioned exchange were reported by Jaffna to Colombo and recorded in the Council's Minutes. Some are implied in the correspondence but missing from the report, and perhaps not all the letters were discovered. The exchange included only one brief letter from Suradilaga, writing from Trincomalee, and what appear to be several follow-up responses from the exiles in Jaffna.

The note from Suradilaga was written, according to the Minutes, on an *ola* (T. *olai*), a palm leaf. This was a common writing practice at the time and may indicate that Suradilaga did not have access to paper as the addressees of his letter did. He sent his greetings and blessings (which were not detailed in the translation) and asked for some form of subsistence, writing that he had nothing at all (D. *ik in 't geheel niet en heb*) according to one translation, and that he was poor (D. *ik arm ben*) according to the other. There was no elaboration of his circumstances, and it is uncertain whether he was familiar with the Jaffna exiles or introducing himself as a fellow exile who had never met them in person.[3]

---

[3] The translation by Kyai Panji (spelled Kiaij Pantsje in the original) reads: "This letter is from Suradilaga" (in which case familiarity is possible, even likely), while Dian Grana's reads: "My name is Suradilaga," which may indicate a first introduction. However, subsequent letters imply that the exiles knew one another, as when those in Jaffna inquire about their friends in Java, suggesting that Suradilaga would know those friends' identities. Another perspective on Suradilaga's condition is found in a letter he wrote to his captors in which he requested return, complained about hardship, an inability to adjust and poverty. He claimed he had proven his loyalty by turning rebels in Java over

The remainder of the letters, three of them with two translations each, were sent from Jaffna. The first was sent by Pangéran Adipati, a title referring to the banished king of Mataram, Amangkurat III, exiled in 1708.[4] He acknowledged having received Suradilaga's letter and wrote that he wished to send him something but was afraid it would not reach him as planned. He requested another letter, perhaps as proof that the letters were not a trap set by the Dutch to test his obedience, or out of sheer curiosity and enthusiasm, and promised to then send as much as a poor person could afford. The deposed king then added: "I ask that you write a letter without fail, informing me of circumstances in Java before you came here. I am yearning for news, for as long as I have been in Ceylon I have received no news whatsoever from Java."[5]

The next letter was written by Pangéran Adipati along with his sons Pangéran Pakunagara and Pangéran Mangkunagara. It opened with greetings for Suradilaga, wishing that God and the Prophet Muhammad would grant him good health, a blessing that was especially appropriate considering the miserable conditions in which he lived. According to the translator Dian Grana, they wrote:

We have read the letter you sent, and our hearts are completely overcome, having heard of your misery. We ask why you were seized by the Dutch, where are your brothers and why are you kept separate from us? We inquire of you again how things are on Java and who was the emperor [D. *keiser*] when you departed? And how are our friends? Who is still living and who has died?

Again, the writers asked for an additional letter bearing news and expressed a desire to send Suradilaga provisions, but also communicated concern that these would not reach him. They ended with hope that God would grant him forgiveness and with good wishes and blessings. As is the case with all three letters, Kyai Panji's translation, although similar in content, seems to offer more subtle nuance that Dian Grana's: In his rendering the three writers greeted Suradilaga as brother (D. *broeder*); they addressed him in the third person which may have represented a

---

to the Dutch and that he had served more than his allotted time (Hague letters NL-HaNa, VOC, 1.04.02 inv. nr. 8942).

[4] The Dutch spelling appears as Pangerang Depatti. The details of Amangkurat III and his family's exile and return and their depiction in Javanese sources will be discussed in Chapter 4.

[5] *Verzoeke dat u voor al een brief schrijft sonder fout ... mij bekent maken hoe dat het op Java al staat sedert dat u van daar vertrocken bent. ik verlang na tijding, zo lange als ik op Ceilon geweest ben heb ik van Java geen tijding gekregen* (Political Council Minutes, June 13, 1727, SLNA 1/61B). The translation by Kyai Panji was similar in tone but stated that the letter was received by Pangéran Adipati's sons and that he had received no *goed beschied* (good, here implying reliable, news) since arriving in Ceylon.

rendering of Javanese terms of respect; they inquired if he was seized alone or along with his brothers; they expressed anxiety about sending goods but promised that if Suradilaga sent a messenger to collect the provisions they would help out, knowing of his miserable plight. Finally, they noted that when they were banished they had begged God's forgiveness – perhaps implying that he should do the same – and wished him luck and longevity.[6]

The final extant letter is but a short note, again written in Jaffna and sent to Suradilaga in Trincomalee. It was written on behalf of Prince Mangkunagara by his servant or servants. Dian Grana in his translation gave their names as Bannip and Siganding, while Kyai Panji mentioned a single, nameless servant but the Dutch caption to his translation referenced "a servant to Pangerang Mankoenogara named Bino of Jaffna."[7] The letter, at least as translated, opened hurriedly without any greetings and asked only one question: Who else from among the "great ones," indicating elders or people of high status, was currently in Trincomalee?[8] A reply, to be written on a small note, was requested.

Thus ends the exchange available in the archive. The Political Council Minutes go on to summarize the discussion following the arrival of the letters in Colombo and the two translations ordered in addition to the one already available from Jaffna. The Council's conclusion was that Dian Grana and Kyai Panji's translations did not differ significantly from the translation made in Jaffna (which was not recorded) and that what was most palpable about the letters was the "itching curiosity" (D. *jeukerige nieuwsgierigheid*) they exhibited to know of developments in Java at the time of Suradilaga's departure to Ceylon. To the Dutch, this inquisitiveness, and perhaps above all the desire expressed on the part of Javanese royals to obtain current political news, coupled with the threatening awareness that there was a "large number of Moors or Mohammedans to be found everywhere on this island," co-religionists

---

[6] One intriguing question arising from the translations, the originals of which are missing, is to whom the use of the title *keiser* in these texts referred. In the question about Java, did it refer to the contemporary Javanese ruler? To the Dutch governor-general (in 1727)? In the letter's closing lines, the uncertainty continues: In Dian Grana's translation, Suradilaga was encouraged to request goods from the *keiser* in his next letter, while Kyai Panji suggested making that same request to Pangéran Adipati. The former could imply a request from the Dutch authorities, who typically supplied royal exiles with allowances of cash and food, the latter that the exiled Javanese king would be the target of the request.

[7] *Een dienaar van den Pangerang Makoenogara genaamt Bino van Jaffanapatnam* (Political Council Minutes, June 13, 1727, SLNA 1/61B).

[8] In Dian Grana's translation the question refers specifically to "our friends": *wie dat er van de grote van onse vrunden op Trinconomale zijn* (ibid.).

who were clearly viewed as potential allies of the Javanese-Muslim exiles, signaled latent dangers looming in the shadows. The recommendation therefore was to warn the Jaffna exiles to refrain from ever again engaging in such illegal activity, on penalty of their current freedom (D. *tegenwoordige vrijheid*) being restricted or eliminated. The need for closer oversight of Suradilaga and others in Trincomalee was also emphasized.[9]

The letter exchange took place in 1727, nineteen long years after Amangkurat III was deceived by the Dutch in east Java in 1708 and sent along with his family and retinue to Ceylon. The urgency of the letters conceals the fact that a significant period, nearly a generation, had elapsed since the banishment: The king was growing old, his sons who had arrived as children had reached adulthood, the family had expanded considerably (as evident from requests made to increase cash and food allowances), yet the "itching curiosity" to have news from home remained undiminished. The letters offer small hints of the royal exiles' living condition, thoughts and aspirations.

The royal exiles offered Suradilaga sustenance in exchange for news. The desperation on both sides – for provisions or a report from Java – seems almost equal. The statement that Amangkurat and his sons had received no news at all, or no reliable news since their banishment, even if not entirely accurate, speaks to the gulf separating their past and present circumstances. How does one imagine the helplessness and frustration of falling from the apex of power in the Kartasura palace, through a state of war and fugitiveness yet still on home territory, to that of outcasts living under Dutch surveillance, lonely, distant and forbidden even to inquire for news of relatives and friends who could be dead or alive? The Jaffna exiles depicted themselves repeatedly as "poor," which was certainly also the image that arose from their periodic pleas for an allowance increase. They highlighted the misery that had befallen them, and Suradilaga as well, by recalling their appeal to God "when we were banished," evoking a shared fate of anguish and regret, and the Islamic framework within which this fate was experienced and interpreted.

The royal exiles' eagerness for contact with a man recently arrived from Java whose note asking for help may have come as a complete surprise feels almost overwhelming, despite the brevity of the notes and their distance across time and multiple translations. Conveying longing and anxiety, they asked for any news at all from Java but also probed more specifically into the social and political realms, perhaps entertaining a tenuous hope of eventual return and glory: old friends and relatives, the

---

[9] Ibid.

current ruler, who else was exiled and why, the reasons they were kept apart from others. All these questions must have haunted them over the years of imposed ignorance and marginality. The Dutch concern about the letters – despite their almost absolute control over the banished – is revealing as well. The illicit contact made with Tumenggung Suradilaga, the reminiscing it elicited in Jaffna and the questions raised in the exchange about individual fates, domestic politics, the ongoing practice of exile and contemporary divide-and-rule arrangements in Ceylon, along with the perceived threat of Muslim collaboration against the European rulers, all raised anxiety levels in the Political Council and posed memory itself as a dire threat: The letters provided explicit proof that the exiles remembered their land, longed for it and for their previous lives, their memories infused with emotion and urgency. The pan-island Islamic connection, whether conspiratorial or real, signaled a broader form of religious memory that relied on shared understandings of history, causality and divinity. Perhaps most revealing was the anxiety elicited among the Dutch authorities by yet another dimension of memory expressed through the letters: the ongoing use of the Javanese language. The Javanese writing, carrying nuances of meaning and tone that can no longer be recovered from the missing original documents, encoded yet another, complementary form of memory of pre-exile life whose potency and elusiveness even three independently commissioned translations of the notes were unable to dispel.

In considering writing produced in Ceylon and evoking memories of the Indonesian Archipelago and especially Java, archival fragments written in the Javanese language or translated from it provide important clues. In addition to glimpses of individuals' states of mind and recollections available in the set of translated covert letters, there are also textual sources carrying cultural and historical echoes of Java, its traditions, arts and remembered past that were transmitted to Ceylon to be preserved and made relevant in a new diasporic context. Among these, references to the nine walis and Java's Islamization are especially telling.

Coming from afar with a wealth of knowledge and insights and a capacity to introduce a new belief system couched in many of the old terms and practices, the walis, according to accounts preserved in Javanese texts and oral traditions, made the foreign familiar and the familiar novel by demonstrating how even the "most Javanese" of cultural traditions – like the shadow puppet theater (J. *wayang*) and gamelan instruments – could be infused with Islamic meaning. With their individual, often localized biographies, different walis gained prominence across various sites in Java, sometimes in opposition to one another, yet no less important was their collective persona that signaled a certain "unity in diversity" in the way Islamization was recounted and remembered. The nine walis' narratives are common throughout the Malay world, and fragments of this tradition are among the hints of Javanese occasionally and serendipitously found interspersed within Malay writing from colonial Ceylon. Three examples from Ceylon have come to light: the *Kidung Rumeksa ing Wengi*; a fragment of Sunan Bonang's biography; and the much more substantive *Hikayat Tuan Gusti*. These three Java-centered texts serve in considering how and why the walis, figures of momentous importance in the Javanese imagination and inseparably linked to the theme of conversion, figured in the Malay diasporic milieu in Ceylon.

The stories of the nine walis, although possessing certain Javanese particularities, are not unique. They form part of a broader and variegated corpus by which conversion to Islam was narrated in countless texts (as well as oral and performative traditions) in many South and Southeast Asian languages. Such accounts, despite their diversity, often shared a great deal. For example, many emphasized the powers and charisma of individuals who carried Islam to new regions, thus highlighting the tropes of travel and mobility; miracles such as feeding the hungry and curing the sick featured prominently; dreams, too, were often evoked, with rulers waking to find themselves circumcised, conversing in Arabic or still in awe having experienced a personal encounter with the Prophet.[10]

The 1897 *Hikayat Tuan Gusti* from Ceylon is one such account, and it testifies to the persistence of circulating conversion narratives across South and Southeast Asia. The *Hikayat* recounts the biography of one of the nine Javanese "saints," Sunan Giri, employing it to retell the story of Java's Islamization.[11] The genealogy of the *Hikayat* is unknown, nor is there certainty about when and how it arrived in Ceylon, where its only known copies are in the form of handwritten manuscripts, yet it is likely that it was transmitted early on. Some of its elements are very similar to those appearing in Javanese tellings of Sunan Giri's biography.[12] However, no such Javanese tellings have been found in Sri Lanka. Interestingly, its narrative is not traceable to any known Malay literary work from across Southeast Asia.[13] This is unusual, as the majority of

[10] See, for example, Russell Jones, "Ten Conversion Myths from Indonesia," in Nehemia Levtzion (ed.), *Conversion to Islam* (New York and London: Holmes and Meier, 1979), 129–158; Rinkes, *Nine Saints of Java*; Shaik Hasan Sahib S. A. Qadhiri, *The Divine Light of Nagore* (Nagore: Habeen & Fahira Publishers, 1998).
[11] According to tradition, Sunan Giri died in 1506 and is buried in Gresik.
[12] For a recent retelling in Indonesian, based on the eighteenth-century Javanese *Serat Centhini*, see Hariwijaya, *Kisah Para Wali* (Yogyakarta: Nirwana, 2003), 62–102.
[13] Hussainmiya, *Orang Rejimen*, 137.

Malay works written in Ceylon are also well known in the wider Malay world. Another rare Malay telling of Sunan Giri's biography was written in the form of an interlinear translation from Javanese, again suggesting the *Hikayat*'s very probable Javanese roots.[14] Whether the *Hikayat* manuscript exemplar is a copy or a translation of an older text, brought to Ceylon in the early eighteenth century by Javanese exiles, or whether it was introduced there in later years, its very existence as well as its content are suggestive of an ongoing consciousness of Javanese historical tradition, its relevance to contemporary circumstances in Ceylon and the amenability of its narratives to reinterpretation. The *Hikayat* may have been told initially in oral form and later put into writing, reimagining conversion on Java to suit local circumstances and indicating both a transregional connection to the archipelago and a relevance for the local community in Ceylon, offering a particular perspective on the wali stories, conversion and the process of creating and preserving memories of a distant ancestral land.

The manuscript on which the discussion is based was written by Subedar Mursit, self-identified as a retiree of the Ceylon Rifle Regiment, who completed it on Saturday, at two o'clock in the afternoon, on Shaʿabān 21 and January 22, 1897.[15] In closing he added the following comment, stressing the delight, and also the religious significance, of engaging with the text: "I instruct all those who find pleasure in reading this *Hikayat*: do not allow it [to leave, drift from] your heart so that you may be granted God's – may He be glorified and exalted – mercy in this world and the next."[16]

The *Hikayat* may well represent the furthest limits of the circulation in manuscript form of the wali tales. Sunan Giri (ascribed the honorific Javanese titles *radèn* and *gusti* as well as the Malay *tuan* throughout) is portrayed as the son of the Arabian sheikh Muḥīddīn. The sheikh, by virtue of his powers of intercession, averted a calamity about to befall the kingdom of Palembang (on the island of Sumatra) and in return was given the king's daughter in marriage. He later returned to his land, and the princess, who had converted to Islam, died in childbirth.

---

[14] Antoine Cabaton, "Raden Paku, Sunan de Giri (légende musulmane javanaise). Texte malais, traduction française et notes," *Revue de l'histoire des religions* 54 (1906): 374–400. This is a much abridged version.

[15] Mursit, *Hikayat Tuan Gusti*, 1897. Hussainmiya Collection, Department of National Archives, Sri Lanka, MF 182, 133 (pagination is internal to the manuscript). "Subedar" refers to the author's rank in the British colonial army.

[16] *Jua adapun aku pesan pada sekalian tuan yang suka membaca hikayat ini jangan saka qalbunya supaya dirahmatkan Allah subhan wa taʿala dari dunya sampai keakirat* (ibid.). I have added the punctuation to the translation.

Palembang's king feared his infant grandson, whose face glowed like the full moon, and, putting him in a basket on the river (in a motif familiar from the biblical story of Moses, the Javanese chronicles of the Prophet's uncle Ménak Amir Hamzah, and elsewhere), sent him away, only for him to be subsequently found and raised by a wealthy merchant woman. The boy grew into a man exhibiting many of the characteristics typical of the walis and other Muslim saints: traveling widely, interceding on behalf of the needy, performing miracles, marrying a local princess and propagating Islam.

The portrayal of Sunan Giri as the son of Sheikh Muḥīddīn is suggestive. The title Muḥīddīn (A. Muḥyī al-Dīn, "reviver of religion") is most often associated with the renowned philosopher and mystic Ibn al-ʿArabī (d. 1240) but is also widely identified with the great Muslim saint, ʿAbd al-Qādir al-Jīlānī (d. 1166). Although several of the walis are said to have had foreign, and most notably Arab, fathers or ancestors, the intimate connection in this telling between Sunan Giri and a figure of such magnitude in Muslim history and culture is striking. In addition, as a descendant of Sheikh Muḥīddīn, himself a great preacher of Islam, Sunan Giri's genealogy stretched back to the Prophet Muhammad. The appearance of this motif in a manuscript from Ceylon may reflect its Javanese source. Javanese biographies of the sheikh circulated in central Java and were especially popular in the western part of the island.[17] Portraying Sunan Giri as Sheikh Muḥīddīn's son may also be attributed to close contacts between the Malay and Tamil-Muslim communities in Ceylon, as the sheikh was a central focus of devotion among Tamil Muslims in south India and Ceylon and the subject of a wide array of Tamil literary works written across genres since at least the seventeenth century.[18] According to localized hagiographic traditions, Sheikh Muḥīddīn traveled to Tamil Nadu, Sri Lanka and Java during his many years of wandering and asceticism before returning to Baghdad at the age of forty, in which case he could have fathered Sunan Giri during his journeys. Whatever the source of this tradition, it extended the Malays' memories spatially and temporally: back to Java and, beyond that, through a sacred genealogy to Arabia and the Prophet.

Recounting conversion to Islam in the form of stories focused memory on a pivotal process of personal and communal transformation, while the

[17] See Julian Millie (trans.), *Celebration of the Desires through the Narration of the Deeds (Manaqib) of the Crown of Saints and the Convincing Beacon among Allah's Beloved Friends; Sheikh Abdul Qadir al-Jaelani* (Queenscliff: Joseph Helmi, 2003).
[18] Schomburg, "'Reviving Religion.'" On 240–299, Schomburg discusses no fewer than fourteen Tamil genres in which works on the saint were composed.

stories' particular details emphasized priorities of piety and affirmed their commemoration. As one such account, the *Hikayat Tuan Gusti* stressed several conversion elements repeatedly while neglecting to mention others. The erection of mosques, prayer (both communal and individual), the recital of the shahāda and the complete shunning of idolatry (M. *berhala*) are consistently upheld. The latter in particular was highlighted when the narrative opened with an idol worshipped by the Palembang king falling to the ground and shattering, signifying approaching doom for the nonbelievers. Throughout the *Hikayat*, different communities encountered by Sunan Giri and his representatives were reminded to refrain from resorting to idolatry. This may have reflected the author's concerns in late nineteenth-century Buddhist-majority Ceylon, projected on an earlier, imagined Java. The belief in, or devotion to, the Prophet was also emphasized, as was the adoption of a new name upon conversion. For example, when the Palembang princess Dewi Aranadani converted before marrying the sheikh, she was given the name Siti Jini.

War, violence and a threat toward those who refused to convert were also significant in this telling. This tendency distinguishes the *Hikayat* from many Javanese wali narratives which tend to stress accommodation and peaceful means in the conversion process. For instance, when the great infidel king of Kartasuru (Kartasura in central Java) sent a messenger to demand that Sunan Giri pay him tribute, the messenger was told to convert. He refused, only to be humiliated and sent home. The king was furious, gathered many allies and a large army and charged toward Giri. The Sunan called upon God for help and a great swarm of bees appeared, attacking the enemy. After the king was killed, Sunan Giri announced that any opponent captured would be bound, but not put to death unless they refused to accept Islam. The people of Kartasuru joyfully agreed to convert and returned to their land along with two hundred teachers, leaders and muezzins from Giri, who would teach them the Five Pillars of Islam, how to build mosques and recite the shahāda. The *Hikayat* contains several such episodes, all portraying an acceptance of Islam after military defeat and under circumstances of significant threat.

An anxiety about the possibility of a reversal of faith – of converts reverting to their old ways – is palpable in the *Hikayat*. In several instances, audiences of those who had converted under the influence (spiritual or military) of Sunan Giri were reminded, by him or by his confidante Sunan Panji, not to renege on their commitment. For instance, after the king of 'Alenggar was defeated by Sunan Giri, he embraced Islam. His subjects followed his path and he instructed them to limit or eliminate their idol worshipping, build a mosque, and recite the shahāda and daily prayers, after which they were pronounced to be "perfected in the faith" (M. *sempurna beriman*). Then,

One Friday all gathered at the mosque along with the gurus, leaders and king. They convened at the mosque and prayed and read the sermon. Then Sunan Panji spoke to those attending the Friday prayer, saying: "Listen all of you: old and young, leaders and king. I command you not to forget the five daily prayers and the Friday prayer. I will soon return to my land. After spending four years here I shall sail away tomorrow."

When all those present had heard Sunan Panji's words they replied: "Yes our lord, Sunan, none of us will forget to pray and recite the Qur'an and all that you have taught us we will never forsake. And if you meet Tuan Gusti please convey our respect and greetings so that he may not forget us."[19]

Following this episode Sunan Panji sought out the king and spoke to him in person, reinforcing his message that he must remember all that he had been taught:

"Do not rule as you previously did. Rule according to the Qur'anic prescriptions and maintain the words of the Qur'an as your highest priority."[20] The king replied: "Yes, I will never give precedence to anything above the words of the Qur'an and those of Sunan Giri."

Before Sunan Panji took his leave the following day the king asked him, as did his subjects before him, to convey the king's respect and greetings to Sunan Giri.

The concern that those newly converted would forget Islam – depicted in this scene and others – is countered, or mirrored by, the converts' eagerness to be remembered by Sunan Giri (referred to as Tuan Gusti), the man who first introduced them to Islam. A sense of doubt, loss and elusiveness inherent in the conversion process as perceived by both sides highlights its stakes. It is a process pervaded with ambiguity, with a sense of insecurity mixing with triumphant confidence, military imposition colliding with long-held beliefs, and charismatic personalities from afar encountering local kings, ministers, ascetics and gurus.

The sense of precariousness regarding the depth of conversion was perhaps related to the imposed acceptance of Islam as depicted in the *Hikayat* or, once again, a reflection of the Muslim community's sense of vulnerability living as a minority within Ceylon's society. There is an ambivalence emerging from the *Hikayat Tuan Gusti*, a narrative that

---

[19] Mursit, *Hikayat Tuan Gusti*, MF 182, 96–97. Here and below I have added punctuation, which does not appear in the Malay manuscript.
[20] Ibid., 97.

translated and transmitted the experience of Javanese conversion to Ceylon, in which new converts to Islam, perceived as still wavering among deeds, words, and new and old beliefs, were admonished to remain Muslim while concurrently depicted as eager to be recognized and remembered, to be accepted into the fold.

While the emphasis of the *Hikayat* on the erection of mosques, communal prayer, and the Friday sermon (A. and M. *khuṭba*) points to the significance accorded to Islamizing practices that would strengthen the emerging community, leading individuals who had only recently subscribed to it to fortify their faith, an anxiety about the strategy's success is evident in the brief exchanges between Sunan Panji, the king and those gathered in the mosque. These highlight not so much memory per se but a demand, and its acceptance, to refrain from forgetting (M. *melupakan*, *dilupakan*), discarding, discharging (M. *ditumangikkan*), leaving behind or slipping away (M. *diluputkan*) from the newly acquired religion. Before the king and his subjects could truly remember Islam, before it could pervade their lives, practices and ways of being in the world, they had to conquer unawareness.

Beyond his emphasis on normative worship, Sunan Giri also resorted to other means of obtaining and preserving his authority, and thus the power Islam would hold over his followers, to be passed down through his line of descent.[21] Toward the end of the *Hikayat* he is depicted as telling Sunan Panji to deliver iron to a blacksmith (M. *tukang besi*) so that the expert craftsman could produce a *keris*. The keris, a kind of dagger, was both a weapon and a highly charged spiritual object, a sacred heirloom passed down through the generations, particularly valued and guarded within the families of Java's ruling class. Sunan Panji immediately asked Sunan Giri to specify the quantity of iron required and the latter instructed him to give the blacksmith 40 *kati* so that the weight of the keris could amount to 20 kati.[22] Sunan Panji summoned an expert blacksmith by the name of Pandita Qadiman, who hurried to meet Sunan Giri, trembling with awe and repeatedly paying obeisance and conveying his respect to the Sunan. After receiving the iron and being informed of the desired weight of the keris, Pandita Qadiman took his leave and journeyed to a place called ʿAsiqin, where he meditated and performed austerities (*bertapa*), including refraining from food, for forty days

---

[21] Sunan Giri was the founder of a line of spiritual lords that lasted until 1680, while none of the other walis had successors to their authority. See Merle C. Ricklefs, *A History of Modern Indonesia since c. 1200* (Stanford: Stanford University Press, 2008), 41.

[22] A kati equals 625 grams, or 16 *tahil*. The tahil (Javanese *tail*, Chinese *tael*) was a widely used weight for gold, silver and opium. See Wilkinson, *Malay–English Dictionary*, 1149.

and nights. These ascetic practices were meant to generate the special powers needed to produce a keris, as the *Hikayat* stated explicitly that the heat for welding the keris should come not from a burning flame but from the inner fire created by the Pandita's practice (M. and A. *'amal*). Although the *Hikayat* does not dwell on the complex details of the art of keris making, the mention of the iron's weight and the blacksmith's retreat and austerities while producing it hint at the critical importance of precise measurements, particular materials and especially the spiritual powers of the keris-maker that were thought indispensable for producing a potent, supernaturally endowed keris in Javanese and Malay societies.[23]

Sunan Giri was pleased with the keris, described as exceedingly beautiful, and paid the artisan 40 dirham in gold, perhaps a gold coin payment for every kati of iron he initially received. Then Sunan Gusti endowed the keris with a name, Bintang Awan, a common practice that personalized the keris and was often related to its owner's character, deeds or wishes. Finally, Sunan Giri took the keris and stored it above the pulpit (A. *minbar*) at the mosque, in a niche in the wall (A. *miḥrāb*) that indicates the *kiblat*, the direction of Mecca and thus of Muslim prayer.[24]

In the context of considering collective memory and the ways in which the Islamization of Java was narrated in Ceylon to a Malay audience through the *Hikayat*, this brief scene is telling. Javanese histories link tales of great armorers with the appearance of the walis, the bearers of Islam, often depicted as the patrons of the armorers' art.[25] This connection between the walis' wisdom and blacksmiths' knowledge, especially in the literature of the Pasisir period (fifteenth to seventeenth centuries), likely points to a coinciding of the early arrival of Islam on the coasts of northeastern Java (including, especially, Giri and Surabaya) with the flourishing of trade and the arts at the time.[26] It may also have been an

---

[23] Blacksmiths and other master craftsmen (including poets) were often endowed with the title Empu or Mpu, one that carried magical or mystical associations. The *Hikayat* does not employ this title for the Pandita. Several Malay families in Sri Lanka still possess kerisses brought by their ancestors from Indonesia.

[24] Sunan Giri's keris can apparently still be viewed by privileged visitors to the mosque. In 2009, the then vice-presidential candidate Prabowo Subianto paid a visit to Sunan Giri's tomb in Gresik and was allowed to see and even touch the keris: "Pegang Keris Sunan Giri, Prabowo Bakal Jadi Wapres? [Will holding Sunan Giri's keris propel Prabowo to the vice presidency?]," *Kompas,* June 24, 2009; www.kompas.com (accessed August 12, 2010). The practice of placing a keris in the *miḥrāb*, perhaps combining or conflating the potency of Mecca with that of the keris, deserves further research, but appears to be unusual.

[25] The walis are also often depicted as patrons of other art forms, including music and the wayang shadow theater.

[26] Pigeaud, *Literature of Java,* I: 278. Pigeaud speculates on the possibility that increasing amounts of steel were traded along the coast during this period. According to Tome

attempt on the part of Javanese authors to reconcile pre-Islamic sites and objects of power with the newly emerging authority of Islam. The connection made between Sunan Giri, the art and practice of keris making, and the centrality of the mosque as the keeping place of the keris (where it is placed in the wall toward which all believers turn in prayer) suggest that the *Hikayat* was transmitted to Ceylon from the Pasisir region of Java, a region that can be said to be the "cradle of Javanese Islam." The region was also the seat of power of Sunan Giri's descendants, where they ruled during the sixteenth and seventeenth centuries, maintaining political and religious command.

In both these respects – as the site of early conversion and a center of expanding Islamic influence – the region possessed a powerful hold on the imagination when the Islamization of Java was recollected.[27] In addition, the keris scene in the *Hikayat* recalls the episode of the "missing pusakas" or royal heirlooms of the Kartasura court in central Java that were believed to have been taken to Ceylon by the exiled Amangkurat III in 1708. These highly charged objects, including kerisses, gongs, saddles and more, which were considered essential to a Javanese king's authority and legitimacy, first disappeared from the Kartasura court in 1705 when Amangkurat III fled rather than face the VOC-backed army of his rebelling uncle, Pangéran Puger. During the more than three decades that followed, until the original pusakas were said to have been brought back from Ceylon along with Amangkurat's surviving relatives and retinue, the fate of these heirlooms and impending questions regarding their authenticity caused much consternation in both Dutch and Javanese quarters. Although Amangkurat claimed he no longer had the desired objects in exile, three dozen kerisses and six pikes were taken from him on the assumption that he was being untruthful and were shipped back from Jaffna to Java, reaching Semarang in 1710.[28] Without knowing precisely how much of this history of the Pasisir, metallurgy and the pusakas was known to those reading the *Hikayat* or listening to its recitation in late nineteenth-century Ceylon, it may well be that it was the kind of story

Pires, the fifteenth-century Portuguese traveler, Gresik, the nearby trading center, was "the jewel of Java in trading ports" (cited in Ricklefs, *A History*, 41).

[27] The main reason for asserting that the *Hikayat* was of eastern Pasisir provenance is that Sunan Giri figures so prominently in it. The veneration of particular walis was often region-specific.

[28] The scene of the pusakas' return, as depicted in Javanese chronicles, is discussed in Chapter 4. The best account of the "missing pusakas," based on Dutch and Javanese sources, is Ricklefs, "The Missing *Pusakas*." The reference to the return of kerisses and pikes from Ceylon is on 611.

that was passed down through the generations, itself – like the keris – a kind of heirloom to cherish and revere.

The *Hikayat Tuan Gusti* has been discussed as introducing and reinforcing broad, collective memories of Java and its past. The second wali-related source from Ceylon, the *Kidung Rumeksa ing Wengi* ("A Song Guarding in the Night"), was mentioned in Chapter 2 as a rare instance of a Javanese song that hints at the transmission of generic and poetic elements from Java to Ceylon. Appearing in three different Sri Lankan Malay manuscripts, the *Kidung* expressed popular Javanese beliefs about a person's susceptibility to a host of unseen yet forceful beings populating the world which the song, when recited, had the power to keep at bay. In considering how Java was remembered in Ceylon, the *Kidung* can be understood as linking the personal and collective dimensions along the continuum of memory, and as occupying a liminal space that is connected to the very personal by seeking protection "for oneself," by guarding so that "no one shall dare approach me" (J. *tan wani ngarah mring mami*), while simultaneously evoking the collective history of Islamization on Java through its authorial attribution to Sunan Kalijaga, leader of the nine walis. In the more personal sense, the poem was a literary amulet capable of sheltering the reciter from the many dangers lurking in the night and, more generally, from all evil, harm and vulnerability, drawing on a sense of the miraculous associated with Sunan Kalijaga's deeds and personality. It is plausible that the preservation of this particular poem within the Malay community spoke to a desire to be guided and guarded through the "night" of exile in days past, using collective forms of knowledge and spiritual powers brought from faraway Java to overcome its hardships, and to the way in which the expression of that earlier sentiment continued to reverberate across the generations. Here is an example of how an individual's sung plea for protection overlapped with, and flowed into, the wider currents of memory reflected in the *Hikayat*, capturing as it did the more conventional, semi-mythic grand narrative of the Islamization of Java.

The third example of textual association with the walis from Ceylon is a mention of Sunan Bonang, whose biography seems to have formed a part of a compendium of various texts. Yet the manuscript, at present available only on microfilm, is missing many pages, including all but two that attest to familiarity with the Sunan's story.[29] Sunan Bonang, known also as Radèn Ibrahim Makdum, was the son of Sunan Ampel. He was born in the fifteenth century and is believed to have died at the age of 120.

---

[29] *Sunan Bonang Fragment*, Hussainmiya Collection, Department of National Archives, Sri Lanka, MF 178, 346–348.

After studying with a great sheikh in Pasai (the first Islamic kingdom in the archipelago, established by the late thirteenth century on Sumatra's northern tip), according to some traditions along with Sunan Giri, he was sent to spread the faith in Tuban, on Java's Pasisir northern coast. As a talented musician and poet, he is remembered for having taught Islam by way of music, especially by artfully playing the bonang, with its beautiful sounds captivating many hearts – including, following some accounts, those of robbers and murderers – and opening the way to religious instruction.[30]

In the textual fragment, within a manuscript owned by Mas Muham-mad Ghaise (M. M. G.) Weerabangsa and dated 1121/1709–1710, it is related that Pangeran Kediri, of Kediri in east Java, anticipated the coming of God's guidance (M. *hidayat*). Having had the title of *adipati*, crown prince, bestowed upon him, he one day received divine inspiration (M. *ilham*) to seek out profound secret knowledge, and off he went wandering in search of answers. Passing through Tuban on the north coast, he encountered Sunan Bonang, who inquired why the prince had left his wife and children behind. The prince told him about his revela-tion, the essence of which was the mystery of life and death or, as phrased in the fragment, the conundrum of "life without death and death without life" (M. *rahasia hamba apa hidup yang tiada mati dan apa mati yang tiada hidup*). Sunan Bonang, whom the prince greeted as his guru, then smiled, addressed him as *anak ratu* (royal child), and saying he did not know the answer, directed him toward a certain sage (M. *pandita*) medi-tating on a mountaintop. That sage's name was Sunan Gunungjati, another one of the walis, who possessed the proper knowledge to reply to the prince's query. Sunan Bonang and the prince then parted ways and the prince set out to find Sunan Gunungjati.[31] Whereas Sunan Bonang proselytized in Java's northeast, Sunan Gunungjati, son of an Egyptian noble and a descendant of the Pajajaran court on his mother's side, was credited with founding the sultanate of Cirebon in west Java and

[30] M. B. Rahimsyah, *Biografi dan Legenda Wali Sanga dan Para Ulama Penerus Perjuangannya* (Surabaya: Penerbit Indah, 1997), 115–136. Considering the relationship between music, memory and Islamic teachings, it is of note that the owner of the manuscript in which the Sunan Bonang fragment appears, the late Mr. Weerabangsa, was a talented musician who studied music in India and used to play several instruments and sing Malay songs for his children, often accompanied by recitations of hikayats and additional texts: personal communication, Mr. M. J. (Joe) Weerabangsa, January 2014; Mrs. Mas Naleera Rahim (née Weerabangsa,) February 2015.
[31] *Sunan*, MF 178, 348.

spreading Islam in that region.[32] However, the vast majority of the biographies of both these walis, Sunan Bonang and Sunan Gunungjati, is missing from the incomplete Ceylon manuscript, and with the prince's departure toward the mountain the relevant fragment comes to an end.

Despite the brevity of the surviving manuscript pages, several themes familiar from stories of the walis' lives and their efforts to spread Islam across Java emerge. The fragment suggests a "hagiographic geography" that maps Java from east to west, with the walis' famous locations figuring as nodes for the study and proselytization of Islam, while the prince, through his quest for knowledge, connects the dots as he travels from one guru to another.[33] Many of the walis' biographies, including those of Sunan Bonang and Sunan Gunungjati, emphasize their relationships with disciples and the ways in which they conducted one-on-one debates or other forms of encounter which were followed by their interlocutors embracing Islam. Such, for example, was the story of the learned Hindu *pandhita* who came to Java's shore in search of Sunan Bonang with whom he wished to debate Hinduism and Islam, but who lost all his religious books when his boat capsized on the way. When he finally reached shore and met Sunan Bonang, the latter struck the sand with his cane. Water came gushing out and with it all the books reappeared, convincing the pandhita to convert on the spot.[34]

The familial status of the crown prince of Kediri would have spoken to descendants of royalty in Ceylon and his interactions with the walis, to the web of connections between the diasporic community and religious and spiritual teachers who offered sustenance and guidance. The riddle pursued by the prince resonated deeply with similar questions that were at the heart of the walis' engagement with Javanese society and were later explored in depth in the Islamo-mystical genre of Javanese poetry, *suluk*: the Unity of Being, the relationship between God and all else in the world, especially mankind, questions often explored through metaphorical means, including the consideration of life in this world as death and the hereafter as life.[35] As they navigated Java's transition from earlier

---

[32] On Sunan Gunungjati's traditional biography, see Rahimsyah, *Biografi dan Legenda*, 199–210. For a historical assessment, see Martin van Bruinessen, "Gunungjati, Sunan," in *Encyclopaedia of Islam*, THREE, Part 2014-3, 148–150; dx.doi.org/10.1163/1573-3912_ei3_COM_27552 (accessed August 26, 2018).
[33] For an elaboration of this concept within a different religious tradition, the Hellenistic world of the third century CE, see John Elsner, "Hagiographic Geography: Travel and Allegory in the Life of Apollonius of Tyana," *Journal of Hellenic Studies* 117 (1997), 28.
[34] Rahimsyah, *Biografi dan Legenda*, 134–135.
[35] This idea was especially central to the teaching of the most controversial of the walis, Seh Siti Jenar. See P. J. Zoetmulder, *Pantheism and Monism in Javanese Suluk Literature*, trans. and ed. Merle C. Ricklefs (Leiden: KITLV, 1995 [1935]), 304–306.

forms of belief to an Islamic worldview in manners that did not discard the familiar, the walis found ways to accommodate long-held beliefs while framing them within the doctrines they promoted.[36] These fundamental questions and themes remained important within the Malay writing tradition in Ceylon.

The *Hikayat*, *Kidung* and Sunan Bonang's story were known within the Malay community in colonial Ceylon. The *Hikayat Tuan Gusti*, especially, was held in high esteem and retold repeatedly and enthusiastically into the twentieth century.[37] What did its reading convey about the importance of memories of Islamization, and of Javanese historical and cultural traditions, those of the walis in particular, within a diasporic community?

In the final lines of the *Hikayat*, Sunan Giri is preaching at the mosque on Friday and, once again, reminding his audience not to neglect the shahāda, to pray five times a day, recite the Qur'an and refrain from doing evil and from eating forbidden foods. The list goes on until, for the first time in the *Hikayat* and immediately before its closing lines, he speaks of the Day of Judgment, the threat of hell, and the promise of Paradise. This section is laced with untranslated Arabic terms (*ḥarām, mu'min, yaum al-qiyāma, 'amal, yatīm*) indicating the Muslim ethos pervading the story, one that nonetheless required repeated reinforcement. Although admonitions to remain Muslim appeared throughout the story, their detail and tone gradually intensified, reaching a climax in this final section. Here conversion and its stakes were projected onto long-ago Java, but the translated text's closing lines also resonated for contemporary listeners in Ceylon engaging with, and remembering, the story and its message. Sunan Giri's words – represented as direct speech in addressing his audience – resound beyond the inner realm of the text, figuratively reaching the ears of those gathered in Colombo and Kandy, instructing and guiding them in their own lives, collapsing the boundaries between past and present.

But reading the *Hikayat* in turn-of-the-twentieth-century British-ruled Ceylon was not solely about remembering conversion, and Java, per se. It was also, in part, about reaching back toward an earlier age, one in which Islamic civilization was spreading into new terrain – including Southeast Asia – incorporating additional peoples and cultures into its global fold. Although that earlier period did not witness the steamship or budding

---

[36] Thus, for example, Zoetmulder suggested that a negative view of God found in Javanese Islamo-mystical poetry "recalls what the various Hindu-Buddhist sects had as their final destination, whereby they hoped to be united in redemption; sunya, the Void, the Nothing": ibid., 174.

[37] In interviews with community members, Hussainmiya (*Lost Cousins*, 100–101) found that Tuan Gusti was a venerated figure among Malays in the late nineteenth and early twentieth centuries.

nationalism – as did the Malays reading the *Hikayat* – it too was represented in textual sources as characterized by powerful forms of mobility, connectedness and interdependence. At a time when the various religious and ethnic communities making up colonial Ceylon's social fabric were exploring new ways of identification and expression, including through emerging nationalist sentiments, the Malays – a minority even within the Muslim population of the island – could through the *Hikayat* recall a proud past and employ it to shape their distinct communal identity also in the present.[38] That identity – and its emerging political dimension – became increasingly important in the first decades of the twentieth century. In 1921, following a mass meeting in Colombo, a decision was made to establish the first Malay political association in Ceylon and to petition the British authorities to concede a Malay seat on the legislative council. In words that resonate with the tale of the Islamization of the Malays' forefathers narrated in the *Hikayat*, the memorandum sent to Governor William Manning urging a consideration of political rights for Malays stated that "[t]he Malays of the island form a distinct and separate community, still preserving the ancient habits, customs and their own language … They are members of the great Malay community, spread over the Far East and counting some fifty million souls."[39]

This statement underscored a sentiment of belonging to a wider Malay world, a world to the southeast from which many of the early ancestors of the petition writers were sent away by force. And, indeed, the exilic dimension of Sri Lankan Malay history was part of a larger picture of exile and diaspora across the Indian Ocean under colonialism, one which constituted an immediate lived reality for some or a distant, imagined memory for others. Although those living in the late nineteenth century were personally removed from the experience, its echoes continued to resound in their present, as clearly evident in the way the plea to the governor was phrased.

Another prism through which to consider the significance of the writings from Ceylon explored in this chapter and their relationship to the broader issues of memory, distance, the walis and a history of

---

[38] For the social and political activism of Sri Lankan Muslims during this period and a comparison with contemporary Sri Lankan Hindu and Buddhist movements, see Vijaya Samaraweera, "Aspects of the Muslim Revivalist Movement in Late Nineteenth Century Sri Lanka," in M. A. M. Shukri (ed.), *Muslims of Sri Lanka: Avenues to Antiquity* (Beruwala: Jamiah Naleemia Institute, 1986), 363–383.

[39] Cited in Hussainmiya, *Lost Cousins*, 14. Hussainmiya also discussed certain tensions between the Malay and Moor Muslim communities during this period and contended that in the process of strengthening differentiated identities, the Malays "endeavored to define their identity more clearly as the scions of an Eastern civilization rather than the inheritors of a Muslim civilization claimed by the Tamil-speaking Moors as the descendants of the Arabs, and the Indians."

Islamization is to view them as encapsulated by the word "travel." The early eighteenth-century letters exchanged between royal exiles in Jaffna and Trincomalee stand for travels in their concrete, corporeal sense. They are brief, translated yet haunting remnants of individuals who were taken by force from their land and sent on the grueling journey by sea to Ceylon. Long held in Jaffna, the exiled king and his sons were eager to hear news of Java from a traveler more recently arrived. The "wali writings," transmitted to Ceylon from across the seas, in turn convey metaphorical, yet no less real, travels undertaken across time and space by those engaging with them through a diasporic lens.

The *Hikayat Tuan Gusti* was, in a way, a form of early travel literature. Although it shares some of the features of later literature of this genre that emphasizes discovery and detailed descriptions, it possessed different goals and a different texture. It underscored movement and travel for the purpose of trade, acquiring knowledge and propagating Islam; it highlighted the journeys of Sheikh Muḥīddīn, Sunan Giri's father, from Arabia to Southeast Asia, and those of Sunan Giri himself throughout his career, as well as the travels of sailors, merchants and soldiers. Thinking about the *Hikayat* within paradigms of travel writing shows clearly the significance of mobility – of individuals, ideas and beliefs – both within the narrative and in its interpretive frameworks. And these forms of mobility, with the contacts, disseminations and contraction of distance – whether physical or symbolic – that they allowed, were prevalent long before the *Hikayat* was inscribed in the late nineteenth century.

The travel back in time presented in the *Hikayat* – toward the walis' period, Islamization and Java – is also worth considering when assessing a chronicle like the *Hikayat Tuan Gusti* as a source for thinking about history and its diverse representations. Although the histories of the walis have often been regarded as fantastic, mythical tales that are either entirely fictional or, at best, may contain a grain of barely recognizable truth, the biographies of these important figures – if placed in context both in Java and, much later, in Ceylon – can reveal how authors, in both places, revised the past transmitted to them by their predecessors in a way that brought it in line with contemporary needs. One seemingly minor difference between Sunan Giri's biography as told in Java and in Ceylon hints at this direction: In Javanese tellings, Sunan Giri eventually met his long-lost father. In the Malay *Hikayat*, Sheikh Muḥīddīn returned to Arabia after fathering Sunan Giri, planting a seed in faraway Java but never traveling back to meet his son. We may think of the diasporic Malays in Ceylon as never meeting, in a metaphorical sense, their "father" or "family," but being nonetheless a group that, like Sunan Giri, was able to create a new community of Muslims.

In his introduction to the anthology *Other Routes: 1500 Years of African and Asian Travel Writing*, Tabish Khair writes that "travel, then, is not just a matter of going away. It is also a matter of coming back, even when the return never takes place in person. It is this Janus-faced aspect of travel that makes it impossible to separate the 'imaginary' elements of travel from the 'real' elements."[40] For the Malays of Ceylon, the *Hikayat* was a way of returning, even if not in person, and only as a journey or a pilgrimage of the imagination: The travels it depicted foregrounded and represented their travels to their own shared past – a shared ancestry and places that used to be called home – a past that connected them to Java, to the nine walis as foundational Javanese religious and cultural heroes, and to the Muslim communities of Southeast Asia, as well as to the global Muslim community.

Conjuring the walis in the exilic, diasporic and colonial setting of Ceylon served to tap their protective powers in a foreign land and under difficult circumstances. It constituted one element in a repertoire of ways in which guidance and safeguards from danger were sought, drawing on the Javanese belief in the unseen as a force that pervaded the visible world and often determined its affairs.[41] The *Hikayat* sections written in direct speech allowed its audience to hear Sunan Giri speaking, instructing and explaining why one should choose to become and remain a Muslim. It also clarified how, by embracing Islam, new believers could join a community that was guided by figures like the Sunan, a performer of miracles covering many aspects of human life, be it the attainment of military victory, recovery from illness or the demolishing of competing gods. This source from Ceylon carried an echo of the walis' famed capacity for potent speech that effected change in the world.

The potency of particular forms of language and recitation to preserve from harm is evident also in the *Kidung*, a song "guarding in the night," its lyrics vocalizing a list of threats that were both concrete (water, fire, thieves) and more enigmatic (*jinn*, *sétan*, *paneluhan*) which the recitation, composed in Sunan Kalijaga's own words, would effectively keep at bay. Its recitation in Ceylon may have been viewed as incurring the added benefit of providing refuge from an exilic "darkness" permeated with its own ambiguous figures and dangers. The appeal to the walis' powers

[40] Tabish Khair, "African and Asian Travel Texts in the Light of Europe: An Introduction," in Tabish Khair, Martin Leer, Justin D. Edwards and H. Ziadeh (eds.), *Other Routes: 1500 Years of African and Asian Travel Writing* (Oxford: Signal Books, 2006), 2.
[41] On this belief and its implications in Java during the century that coincided with exile to Dutch Ceylon, see Ricklefs, *Seen and Unseen*, 1–16.

through poetry and prose should be understood as linked to the larger phenomenon of seeking protection from life's perils through magical means which encompassed, besides retellings of the walis' biographies and songs, sacred material objects such as Sunan Giri's keris and the heirlooms carried from Java into exile by Amangkurat III, supplications at the site of holy tombs, dreams, amulets and, most popularly, a wide range of prayers and incantations recited on multiple occasions to secure desired outcomes and freedom from threat and misery. These small texts, known as *doa*s or *wasilan*s, constituted an important and popular genre among the Malays, and they, too, carried memories of a Javanese past.

The word "doa" in Malay and Javanese – referring to a prayer for some definitive purpose – has two main meanings: a prayer to God (for example, *doa arwah*, prayers for the dead) or charms that serve goals such as keeping a rival suitor at bay, silencing a hostile witness or attaining invulnerability.[42] Both types were found in manuscripts from Ceylon; however, the latter is highlighted here: mantra-like doas or wasilans, talismanic texts, typically mentioned by title only and occasionally including the full recitation. These were passed down to the initiated by fathers, elders or gurus.[43]

Several of the doas/wasilans had Javanese titles as, for example, *Ratu Hewan* (J. animal queen) and *Sirep* (J. to calm; *nyirep*: to put someone under a magic spell), the latter said to assist in seeking angelic protection. The doas were sometimes prescribed along with fasting, walking in the forest and additional ascetic practices. The recitation of doas (not necessarily under this title) for personal gain, success and prosperity, as well as

---

[42] Wilkinson, *Malay–English Dictionary*, 283.

[43] The oft-used term for such texts, wasilan, deriving from Arabic *wasīla*, is used in Indonesia to refer to an intermediary or intercessor, a person or an object that can assist one in gaining access or a connection to God and His powers, and *tawassul* (from the same Arabic root w.s.l) is a ritual of naming Muslims considered to be in close proximity to God and making an offering for their benefit. On the importance of the "tawassul archive" in west Java and "the texture of supplication practices holding authority at specific locations in space and time," see Julian Millie, "Supplicating, Naming, Offering: *Tawassul* in West Java," *Journal of Southeast Asian Studies* 39.1 (2008), 118–122. In contemporary Sri Lanka those reminiscing about the wasilan they witnessed performed in their childhood did not typically mention practices of naming or offerings. Rather, they emphasized the powers required by the reciter, gained through specialized training, that guarantee the wasilan's efficacy. Talismanic texts, known as *ajimat* (from Arabic *'azimat*: amulet) and similar in content and purpose to those found in Sri Lanka, were very popular also among the "Cape Malays" in South Africa, another site of exile and forced migration from the Indonesian Archipelago during colonial times. See Saarah Jappie, "Jawi dari Jauh," *Indonesia and the Malay World* 40.117 (2012): 143–159. The reference to talismanic texts is on 148–149.

for the purposes of recovery from illness, overcoming danger in travel, childbirth and war, and seeking blessings for marriage and old age, was widespread in the Malay world and not unique to Java. However, their use, the practices accompanying them and the belief in the many unseen yet powerful beings inhabiting the world whose powers could be both harnessed and subdued by reciting doas were central to Javanese spiritual traditions and were likely exported to Ceylon.

A handwritten notebook bearing the title *Angkatan Menulis Ism* contains a collection of doas. In its opening pages its contents are defined explicitly as guidance or advice (M. *nasehat*) for the younger generations of the Weerabangsa family, passed down by Mas Murat ibn Mas Juri ibn Mas Anom Weerabangsa to his descendants. The notes were written or copied in 1942 and may comprise one of the most recently dated copies in a chain of transmission of this form of knowledge extant from colonial Ceylon. Examples of doa titles in the collection include *Doa Kesaktian Manusia*, *Doa Balikan Sumpa* and *Doa Lucut Badan*. A concrete connection to Javanese is found in linking these and other doas with the *Kidung Rumeksa ing Wengi*. That poem, as mentioned, possessed many of the attributes of a doa or wasilan in its perceived ability to fend off dangers and threats lurking in darkness, many of them – like jinn, thieves and fire – common to other charms. The link between the genres of *kidung* and doa, and the link between Malay and Javanese, was made explicit in the *Angkatan Menulis Ism* which contained a range of doas as well as the *Kidung* and fragments of additional kidung, side by side, claiming the same protective functions and thus suggesting that the two genres may have been viewed as interchangeable.[44]

These sources from Ceylon – the *Hikayat*, *Kidung* and wasilan – resonate with the conviction that words, often in the form of charms and uttered by the right person under particular circumstances, affect reality, a form of power closely associated with the walis and with memories of their accomplishments. A famous example of this attribution is found in the Javanese story of the meeting of Prince Darmakusuma, i.e. the eldest of the Pandawa brothers, Yudhishtira from the Mahabharata, with Sunan Kalijaga.[45] Following the Great War and the ensuing destruction and death, the prince wished to die but to no avail. Told that only one known as Sunan Kalijaga could assist him, he wandered across Java until he found the Sunan, who inquired whether he possessed an amulet of immortality. The prince replied that there was only the

---

[44] *Angkatan Menulis Ism*, BL, EAP609/17/3. The *Kidung* is on 198.
[45] For a telling of this story, see "Matinya Raden Darmakusuma," in A. M. Noertjahajo, *Cerita Rakyat Sekitar Wali Sanga* (Jakarta: Pradnya Paramita, 1974), 32–35.

Ngamarta amulet hidden in his hair which was tied up in a bun, as was the custom, but that he was doubtful it could ever be released. All the walis then meditated (from Sanskrit, *semedi*) and asked God to allow the amulet to emerge. Their pleas were accepted, and the amulet emerged in the form of a bit of torn paper inscribed with the Arabic words "kalimah syahadat." As it turned out, Prince Darmakusuma would only attain death once he could read those words himself, and so the walis taught him the Arabic script and, reading or proclaiming the words of the charm, he finally passed away. The story ended by citing the amulet's content which was no other than the Muslim profession of faith, which in Javanese tradition was given the name Kalimasada. Thus, the charm of a previous era, now bygone, turned out to be the shahāda, the hero of the great Indian epic thereby unknowingly protected by Islam's sacred words and language. Furthermore, like Sunan Giri's speech in the *Hikayat*, the *Kidung*'s verbal refuge, and the wasilan's potent words, the Kalimasada amulet in the story about Sunan Kalijaga, entangled as it was in Darma- kusuma's hair, represented the entwining of local forms of faith and protection with Islamic tradition, recalling the walis' access to, and manipulation of, powerful forms of language, as well as their ability to accommodate pre-Islamic cultures, as narrated in Java and tapped anew in Ceylon.

The trope of the pusaka, referring in high Javanese to "inheritance" and typically connoting royal regalia or heirlooms that were crucial to a Javanese ruler's ability to govern, has been expanded here to consider a cultural, spiritual inheritance carried into exile, along with its protective capacities. The *Kidung*, *Hikayat* and wasilan can be understood as "poetic pusakas." The walis, those core agents of Javanese memorializa- tion of the transition from a pre-Islamic to an Islamic past, figured in all these genres as transmitted to Ceylon, with their words and deeds offering guidance and shelter from life's challenges and also protection from the forgetting of a particular past. These poetic pusakas formed part of a larger category that included the sacred material objects carried into exile by the deposed king of Mataram, Amangkurat III. The protracted dealings with, and anxieties about, these pusakas in both Java and Ceylon at the time make their significance clear. The pusakas, as well as the keris depicted in the *Hikayat*, highlight in addition to their spiritual dimen- sions also a material aspect of Javanese culture and an embodied link to its past and potential future. Here too a significant wali connection was evident: One of the pusakas that returned from Ceylon in 1737 along with the deceased Amangkurat's body and surviving family members was a garment (J. *rasukan*), believed to be the famous pusaka Kyai Gundhil, a garment bestowed miraculously on Sunan Kalijaga by the Prophet

Muhammad.[46] That such an important pusaka was brought to Ceylon, or was believed to have been brought there, greatly strengthened the walis' diasporic presence and significance.

Memories of Java's Islamization, as recalled through foundational episodes in the walis' biographies inscribed in Javanese sources later transmitted to Ceylon, traveled and expanded the space throughout which that crucial process, with its diverse ramifications, reverberated. The extended space was geographical, as when those same wali tales were recounted anew in the Ceylon diaspora, and it was also a literary space constituted by the shared Javanese language of the *Kidung*,[47] the shared memories and echoes of an earlier conversion narrative, generic, orthographic and prosodic commonalities, modes of translation and transmission. The process of Islamization in Java and other regions of the archipelago whence came the "Malays" gave rise to cultural products that reached Ceylon much later and encompassed it within a single realm of memory, shared associations and poetic echoes, contracting distance and blurring boundaries.

Perceived boundaries between categories of memory – those of living individuals thinking of home and of later generations, more constructed and conventional – blurred as well. The letters exchanged and the *Hikayat Tuan Gusti* contained biographical and genealogical fragments that were personal and public concurrently; both possessed a political dimension, the letters written by a deposed ruler who was contemplating return, the *Hikayat* narrating a major religious and political shift in Javanese history; both connected authors or audiences to Java, to travel, to the experiences of mobility, displacement, novel places and new "homes," whether private or communal. The languages employed in writing, Javanese and Malay, were those brought from the archipelago and maintained through the generations in unlikely circumstances, forming a living, creative link with the past. The next chapter continues to explore links and memories, but shifts the perspective to Java's shores.

---

[46] On the link between Kyai Gundhil and the *rasukan* mentioned in the scene depicting the return of the pusakas to Java in 1737 in the *Babad Tanah Jawi*, see Ricklefs, "The Missing *Pusaka*s," 620. The garment Kyai Gundhil is taken out and ritually cleaned annually on 10 Dhū al-Ḥijja, drawing large crowds to Sunan Kalijaga's grave at Kadilangu where the ceremony takes place; see H. Imron Abu Amar, *Sunan Kalijaga Kadilangu Demak* (Kudus: Menara Kudus, 1992), 22.

[47] As was the case with the *Hikayat*, the familiarity with the *Kidung* in Ceylon likely represents the farthest limits of its dissemination at the time. According to Arps, the *Kidung* was known in many parts of the archipelago, including Java, Bali, Lombok and South Kalimantan: see Bernard Arps, "The Song Guarding at Night: Grounds for Cogency in a Javanese Incantation," in Stephen C. Headley (ed.), *Towards an Anthropology of Prayer: Javanese Ethnolinguistic Studies/Vers une anthropologie de la prière: études ethnolinguistiques javanaises* (Aix-en-Provence: Publications de l'Université de Provence, 1996), 47–113. However, there is no known evidence of a more expanded circulation.

4   "Ceyloned": The View from the Other Shore

Beginning with the Javanese verb *disélongaké* – "to be Ceyloned," i.e. exiled – this chapter and the next investigate a set of questions related to Javanese documentation and memorialization of exile to Ceylon. Drawing on eighteenth- and nineteenth-century Javanese manuscripts of the historical babad genre, the chapters suggest that, although depictions of exile to Ceylon are relatively few and far between, mining local chronicles for references yields a body of insights on how life in exile was imagined and understood in Java, how exile affected those left behind as well as those returning home from Ceylon, and what meanings, tensions and creative possibilities infused narratives of exile.[1]

The story of the Javanese exiles to Ceylon can be read, in part, as a familial one, stretching from Amangkurat III, the first Javanese king ever to be exiled by the Dutch in the early eighteenth century, through many exiles and returns during that century, a very tumultuous one in Java's history. Descendants of the House of Mataram exiled to Ceylon in the eighteenth century included, besides Amangkurat III, his children and wives, and Pangéran Arya Mangkunagara and his family; Sunan Kuning; Radèn Tumenggung Sasradiningrat and Radèn Tumenggung Ranadiningrat, sons of Cakraningrat IV of Madura, whose wife Radèn Ayu Maduretna was the sister of Pakubuwana II; Pangéran Purbaya; several of Pangéran Mangkubumi's brothers; and others. Also relevant to this analysis are the various exiled court officials who were often related by marriage to the royal family.[2]

Thinking about exile in the House of Mataram locates the experience of banishment as one guiding thread in its genealogical biography. It allows a contemplation of exile across generations, experiences and places, and explores the intertwining of ancestry, historical developments

---

[1] The question of whether and how Javanese authors wrote about exile to Ceylon has been rarely pursued to date, despite the large number of exiles from Java and their frequent social and political prominence.

[2] Although this chapter focuses on Javanese, and especially central Javanese, cases of exile, there is documentation of the experiences of exiles from other regions, including those of the sultan of Bacan, Siti Hapipa of Makassar, the sultan of Banten, and others.

76

of war, ascensions to the throne and colonial expansion, and the workings of cultural memory. In considering how writing in the Javanese language reflected and engaged with such processes, there is perhaps no better place to begin than with the Javanese verb forms *disélongaké*, *dipunsélongaken* and *kasélongan* – "to be Ceyloned" – which came to signify exile. This verb – part of a larger pool of words used in the eighteenth and nineteenth centuries for "banishment," "exile" and "expulsion" – was also used in Malay, taking the form *disailankan*. The significance of Ceylon as an exile site – in lived and imagined experience – must have been very great for it to transform from a noun into a verb.[3] This verb, which initially meant exclusively "to be banished to Ceylon," came to encompass, through its wide usage, banishment more broadly, including to additional specific, faraway sites. Thus, we find the phrase *disailankan ke negeri Kap* ("He was 'Ceyloned' to the Cape of Good Hope"), although the Javanese verb *ngekap* ("to go to the Cape," "to be sent to the Cape") was also employed. The newspaper *Kajawèn*, published twice-weekly by Bale Pustaka in Batavia, explained in a 1931 article that "in the past Ceylon was a site of exile for Javanese nobility and even to this day high officials who were banished from the kingdom are referred to as having been 'Ceyloned' because at first they were indeed placed in Ceylon, but then the term came to mean 'banished,' therefore a question can be posed: 'Ceyloned' to where?"[4]

In order to better understand the phenomenon of exile as discerned from Javanese viewpoints, this chapter and the next examine evidence from eighteenth- and nineteenth-century Javanese manuscripts relating experiences of exile and return of members of royal families, court officials and their accompanying retinues from Java to Ceylon (and back again) in the eighteenth century. These typically very brief depictions have the potential to offer information and a perspective, however fragmentary, on what remains a vague but dramatic and significant chapter in the larger history of exile in colonial Asia, as well as on specifically Indonesian and Sri Lankan understandings of the past.[5]

---

[3] Other Javanese terms for "to exile" were *mbuwang, nyingkiraken, ngéndhangaken, mbucal*. For definitions of the verb, see Poerwadarminta, *Kamus Bausastra Jawa*, 357.

[4] *Sélon punika ing kinanipun dados papan pangendhanganing bangsa luhur Jawi, malah katelahipun sapriki, prayagung luhur ingkang kakendhangaken saking praja punika, tiyang mastani dipunsélong (Sélon), kajengipun sakawit, dipunprenahaken wonten ing Sélon, nanging lajeng dados teges dipunsingkiraken, mila lajeng wonten pitakenan: dipunsélong dhateng pundi.* (*Kajawèn* no. 59–60, 9 Mulud Je 1862, July 25, 1931, 917).

[5] For case studies of exile across colonial Asia and a comparative discussion of the exile phenomenon, see Ricci (ed.), *Exile in Colonial Asia*.

In her book *Networks of Empire: Forced Migration in the Dutch East India Company*, Kerry Ward examined the Dutch East India Company's networks of forced migration as one of several types of networks that constituted the Company's empire (1602–1799). She noted how the High Government's diplomatic relations with indigenous polities, formalized in the signing of contracts, were underpinned by the systematic use of exile: "Batavia created a network of exile sites throughout its empire that enabled it to choose specific places of banishment according to the High Government's perceptions of the dangers of particular prisoners." Moreover, "Batavia used the nature of its far-flung domain to help consolidate its interest within particular archipelagic polities, and, most especially, at the center of the Company empire in Java."[6] These twin aspects of exile – the distance of particular exile sites, in this case Ceylon, and the complex politics of decisions made about exiles and returns – are manifested in the Javanese sources discussed below.

Java (and especially central Java) in the eighteenth century was home to many of the most prominent among those exiled to Ceylon. In part due to their elevated status, such persons were not sent into exile alone but rather were accompanied by wives, children, additional relatives and retinues of servants, thus expanding the numbers of those departing Java's shores. Studying exile from Java during this period sheds light on its very complex internal-familial politics (as exile was often a solution to rivalries among brothers or cousins competing for the throne), as well as on the evolving dynamics of Javanese–European entanglements (with the Dutch intervening on behalf of one contender whose loyalty was then secured, along with economic and political concessions that gradually limited indigenous power). At a more practical level, Java's rich and long-standing literary tradition going back at least to the ninth century and Javanese scribes' tendency to produce long historical chronicles enhance the possibility of finding written testimonies of events related to exile that may not be as likely in a less literate society. Furthermore, Java is still remembered today as the land of origin of several prominent Malay families in Sri Lanka; thus a better understanding of its role in the history of exile could prove significant in both personal and collective ways.

Drawing on Javanese sources, the exilic episodes discussed present glimpses of a complex picture that contains specific events and relationships while also revealing some of the broad themes that relate to exile in Ceylon and its aftermath as viewed from the "other shore" of Java.

---

[6] Ward, *Networks of Empire*, 186.

In 1703 the reigning king of Kartasura in central Java passed away; his son was crowned and had the title Amangkurat III bestowed upon him. Not long after this event the new monarch's uncle, Pangéran Puger, brother of the deceased king, rebelled against his nephew and claimed to be rightful heir to the throne. Amangkurat III fled the palace in 1705. For the next three years this king, known also as Sunan Mas and later as Sunan Kendhang ("the Exiled King"), lived and fought in the mountains of east Java, allying himself with various parties, most famous among them the Balinese rebel, fugitive and legendary leader Surapati.[7] In this struggle, known as the First Javanese War of Succession (1704–1708), the Dutch supported Pangéran Puger who, under their protection and at the price of great territorial and political concessions, ascended to the throne in 1704 with the title Pakubuwana I.[8]

When Amangkurat III concluded that his struggle was hopeless, he decided to contact the Dutch commander of Surabaya. His sense of desperation was especially keen after his troops were said to have been smitten by a terrible disease which left those ill in the afternoon dead by morning.[9] He sent an emissary to Commander Govert Cnoll, outlining his conditions for surrender, and was promised that they would be honored. Reality, however, was different, and Amangkurat III was betrayed by his captors, imprisoned and sent to Batavia and later to Ceylon.[10] In Ceylon, as discussed in Chapter 3, he was held in Jaffna, at the far northern end of the island.

The *Babad Kartasura*, a history of Java during the early to mid eighteenth century, narrates these events:

> Great was the king's happiness
> Upon hearing the Company's message,
> Along with all his officials,
> Not realizing they were victims of deceit.

The next few lines depict an exchange between Amangkurat III and Pangéran Blitar, then:

---

[7] On the life and historical afterlives of Surapati, see Ann Kumar, *Surapati: Man and Legend* (Leiden: E. J. Brill, 1976). Several of Surapati's descendants were exiled to Ceylon.

[8] On the war, see Merle C. Ricklefs, *War, Culture and Economy in Java, 1677–1726: Asian and European Imperialism in the Early Kartasura Period* (Sydney: Asian Studies Association of Australia, 1993), 129–151.

[9] *Babad Sangkala* canto III: 64–65; see Ricklefs, *Modern Javanese Historical Tradition*, 119.

[10] Amangkurat III was not alone in experiencing such trauma. For another exile verdict depicted as brief and sudden, see the case of Sasranegara, bupati of Surabaya, who supported Pangéran Mangkubumi with troops and money, was spied upon, caught and immediately put on a ship to Ceylon (Yasadipura I, *Babad Giyanti* [BP], 5: 61–63). For a famous example of Dutch betrayal and the banishment that followed, see the detailed depiction of Dipanagara's capture in Carey, *Power of Prophecy*, 677–698.

> Other matters will now be discussed.
> Susunan Mas was quickly carried
> Aboard the ship,
> Many of his subjects followed
> And all his family members,
> And all the pusakas were carried too
> Aboard the ship.[11]

The Javanese source did not elaborate on the identity or number of those who accompanied the king into exile. *The Makassar Annals*, a genre of Makassarese historical writing that contain specific and dated information about a range of topics, noted that on October 20, 1708, Amangkurat III was taken to Jakarta and that on December 4 of that year he was exiled to Ceylon with Daeng Massepe.[12]

The scene, even in the context of portrayals of exile which are often fleeting, is especially concise and laconic. Since Amangkurat III was the first Javanese king to be exiled by the VOC, the fact that the text devoted so few words to the event merits some consideration. Also noteworthy is the mention of the royal heirlooms, the pusakas, made in the final lines cited above. In Java such objects, which included particular spears, gongs, daggers, garments and saddles belonging to the royal house, were considered vital to a king's authority and ability to rule and to overcome the many obstacles he might face such as war, rebellion, famine and powerful supernatural forces and beings inhabiting the world. Hence, the loss of the Kartasura pusakas with Amangkurat III's flight and later exile caused great consternation in the court, driving several attempts to regain them both in the years before and following his banishment, all of which were unsuccessful. Despite the brevity of the exile scene as depicted in the *Babad*, mention of the pusakas is not omitted, foreshadowing the relatively plentiful allusions to them yet to come.

---

[11] *Langkung trusthanira Sri Bupati/amiarsa kumpeni turira/tuwin sagung punggawané/tan wruh yèn kenèng apus…*
Gantya ingkang winuwus/Susunan Mas binekta aglis/minggah dhateng ing kapal/kang wadya kèh tumut/lan sagung ingkang santana/tuwin sagung pusaka binekta sami/minggah dhateng ing kapal (*Babad Kartasura*, Surakarta: Reksa Pustaka Library, Kadipatèn Mangkunagaran, MS MN 199, inscribed 1869, transliterated as B21d by Mulyo Hutomo, 102–103). The manuscript was commissioned by, and belonged to, Bendara Radèn Ayu Purbasumarsa; see Nancy K. Florida, *Javanese Literature in Surakarta Manuscripts: Manuscripts of the Mangkunagaran Palace*, vol. II (Ithaca: Cornell University Press, 2000), 126. The verses are in Dhandhanggula. This scene is also depicted in the *Babad Tanah Jawi* (BP), 18: 23–25, sastra.org/kisah-cerita-dan-kronikal/69-babad-tanah-jawi/1027-babad-tanah-jawi-balai-pustaka-1938-41-1024-jilid-18.
[12] "Daeng" was an honorific title in the Gowa kingdom. See William Cummings (trans. and ed.), *The Makassar Annals* (Leiden: KITLV, 2011), 192.

The next instance of a Javanese source relating exile to Ceylon depicts an unlikely meeting at sea. In 1728 Pangéran Arya Mangkunagara, older brother of the ruling king of Kartasura Pakubuwana II (both were grandsons of the aforementioned Pakubuwana I), was exiled on charges of having an affair with one of the king's women. The *Babad ing Mangkunagaran* dates his departure from Kartasura to Jumadilakir 1, *Éhé* 1652 Windu Kunthara (1727).[13] Left behind was his third child, the two-year-old Radèn Mas Said, and five younger children, two of whom would later join Sunan Kuning's forces. Pangéran Arya, who was grieving the loss of two of his wives, was accused of giving a precious cloth (*sinjang lurik*) owned previously by the queen to a woman favored by Pakubuwana. The latter, reports the *Babad Tanah Jawi*, was furious when he saw her wearing it at the royal audience, confirming what his spies had reported.[14] The truth behind the accusation was an intractable matter but one the Dutch apparently did not believe.[15] What is quite clear, however, is that the king's powerful chief counsel (J. *patih*) Danureja was deeply implicated in the move to rid the court of Pangéran Arya Mangkunagara. He was arrested by the Dutch and sent to Batavia, where he remained for several years.[16] Despite Pakubuwana II's recurring requests that he be exiled further, this did not transpire until 1733, when he boarded a ship to Ceylon.

Meanwhile, also in 1733, Patih Danureja himself fell out of favor with the king. The *Babad Tanah Jawi* depicts Danureja's anger when he discovered that Pakubuwana II had appointed a bupati without consulting with him. Following this episode, Pakubuwana instructed his advisor Tirtawiguna (on whom more below) to write a letter to the Dutch governor proclaiming that the king entertained no more sympathy for the patih and wished him shipped across the ocean.[17] The king's mother

---

[13] This babad, which briefly narrates the lives of the Mangkunagara rulers and is a compilation based on earlier sources, erroneously names the Cape (*tanah Kaap*) as Pangéran Arya's site of exile, but notes correctly that he died in Ceylon: Citrasantana, *Babad ing Mangkunagaran*, Surakarta: Reksa Pustaka Library, Kadipatèn Mangkunagaran, MS MN 208B, inscribed 1918, 2. *Éhé* is the name of the Javanese year, a windu is an eight-year cycle (in which *Éhé* is the second year) in the Javanese calendrical system.

[14] *Babad Tanah Jawi* (BP), 21: 31–35, in Mijil.

[15] Although they did not trust the rumors, the Dutch feared that Arya Mangkunagara would rebel and be followed by many dignitaries and therefore felt compelled to exile him: Ricklefs, *A History*, 108.

[16] The *Babad Kartasura* mentions that Pangéran Arya fathered another son, or sons, while in Batavia: *Babad Kartasura*, Surakarta: Reksa Pustaka Library, Kadipatèn Mangkunagaran, inscribed 1844, transliterated as B21c by Mulyo Hutomo, 26, in Dhandhanggula.

[17] *Si uwa Danureja│wus ilang ing tresna mami… sun titipaken Kumpeni │ dèn prenahna pulo sabrang* (ibid., 22, in Sinom).

tried to intervene on behalf of the patih but to no avail.[18] Danureja was turned over to the Dutch authorities, to be exiled as well. In a somewhat different description of events, but culminating in the same result, the *Babad Kartasura* claimed that after the death of his wife, Queen Ratu Kencana, the king opened a letter she had once received from her brother Urawan, later to be known as Purbaya. The letter, which revealed to him the truth about the gifted cloth and the *"kain lurik Bugis* affair," infuriated him and caused him to condemn Danureja to a life in exile.[19]

Pangéran Arya Mangkunagara was traveling by ship when, after a month had passed, he was surprised when the ship anchored unexpectedly in mid sea. Not long afterwards a smaller boat slammed into the ship, its hull cracking open. Its mast was in pieces and the frightened passengers were crying out for help. Pangéran Arya along with the captain rushed on board to see what had happened:

> Deeply startled by what he saw,
> Pangéran Arya Mangkunagara,
> Astonished, he patted his chest:
> "Uncle Danureja,
> How did you come to this,
> Experiencing misery
> Akin to my own hardship?"
> Boarding the ship
> He was startled to meet Pangéran Arya
> On that boat.[20]

> The Patih ran to him in haste
> And bowed deeply at the feet of Pangéran Arya.[21]
> Loud was his weeping.
> Pangéran Arya spoke softly:
> "Why did you follow me here
> O, Patih, what happened,
> What did you do?"

---

[18] *Babad Tanah Jawi* (BP), 21: 59–60. A very similar depiction appears in *Babad Kartasura*, B21c.

[19] Ronggawarsita, *Babad Itih IV: Kartasura*, Surakarta: Reksa Pustaka Library, Kadipatèn Mangkunagaran, composed mid nineteenth century, inscribed mid to late nineteenth century, transliterated as MN 88 TT by Djajeng Susarno, 167. According to this manuscript, the patih was exiled to Karimun island, not Ceylon.

[20] *Langkung kagèt dènira ningali/Pangéran Arya Mangkunagara/ngungun amijet jajané/siwa Danurejèku/déné kongsi mangkéné iki/nemu papa kaliwat/kaya susah ingsun/duk prapta minggah ing kapal/kagyat Pangran Arya kang pinanggih/wonten palatar palwa* (*Babad Kartasura*, B21c, 27, in Dhandhanggula). *Amijet jajané* means "to pinch, squeeze or massage the chest," here a gesture of great surprise or consternation.

[21] *Anyungkemi* refers to touching the feet of another with one's head as a sign of respect and deference.

He replied, gasping:
"O, son, I now sweeten
The treason committed against you.
I beg your forgiveness truly."[22]

Patih Danureja asked forgiveness within earshot of the shocked ship's captain, who was astounded to witness the meeting of a fallen court official and the prince he had betrayed, now both on a ship bound for Ceylon, sharing the same fate.[23] Pangéran Arya Mangkunagara's anger at Danureja had subsided over the years, and the two spent time together, perhaps conversing of home on the long journey. In the final section depicting the two, Patih Danureja, as he had promised, "sweetened" the prince's bitter fate that resulted from Danureja's act of treason by offering Pangéran Arya Mangkunagara a vision of the future based on prophecies he had heard from the astrologers (*alul nujum*) back in Java:

> Your son, Radèn Mas Said,
> Shall be a king-maker,
> Shouldering great battles,
> His excellence famed far and wide.
> Should he be destroyed, Radèn Mas Said,
> The sustenance of Java
> Destroyed will be rice and paddy
> That sustenance entirely gone.
> For among the people of Java not one will have food.
> As for the other[24]
>
> Who is included in the story,
> Your younger brother Mas Sujana,
> In the future shall be called powerful,
> Considered a noble king
> Bearing the burden of fierce battle.

---

[22] *Kiya Patih gupuh malayoni/anungkemi mring Pangéran Arya/pan sarya asru tangisé/Pangran Arya lingnya rum/yapagéné nusulirèki/wah Patih kenèng apa/mangkana tingkahmu/saurira megap-megap/adhuh angger pun uwa mangké manisi/duraka ing panduka/mangkya nuwun apunten sayekti* (*Babad Kartasura*, B21c, 27, in Dhandhanggula). An almost identical rendering appears in Mas Ngabèhi Rongga Panambangan III, *Babad Kartasura*, Surakarta: Reksa Pustaka Library, Kadipatèn Mangkunagaran, 1852, transliterated as MN 185 TT by Hatmo Wasito, 27–28. The subtitle describing the content of the manuscript opens with *wiwit panyélongipun Pangéran Mangkunagara* ("beginning with the 'Ceyloning' [*panyélong*] of Pangéran Arya Mangkunagara," i.e. his exile to Ceylon).

[23] In Ronggawarsita, *Babad Itih* (MN 88 TT), according to which Danureja was exiled to Karimun rather than Ceylon, a similar conversation and request for forgiveness took place in Batavia, where the two met (178–180).

[24] *Putra paduka Radèn Mas Said/tembé kuwawi adamel raja/ing prang awrat sasanggané/urageng jagat panjul/yèn sirnaha Radèn Mas Said/rejeki Tanah Jawa/sirna beras pantun/ rejeki nabrang sadara/pan wong Jawa tan ana kang bisa bukti/déné ta kang satunggal* (*Babad Kartasura*, B21c, 28, in Dhandhanggula).

Should he be destroyed
In Java then,
Not one shall be clothed.
Yes, those are the two noblemen to be cherished
As garments and food.[25]

After the recitation of this prophecy, Patih Danureja and Pangéran Arya Mangkunagara are said to have smiled, grasping in their hearts that which had been spoken, just as the boat was about to dock at the shores of Ceylon. At this moment, when the destination of their long journey and the exilic life they would lead there became a reality, the disgraced official offered the betrayed prince a sense of comfort and hope. Patih Danureja's words implied that, although Pangéran Arya Mangkunagara himself was doomed to a life far away from his land and people, the future held great things in store for his son and younger brother, both of whom would indeed become rulers of newly established Javanese courts.[26] Exile in this case did not signal the end of his line: His close kin were, claimed the prophecy, the very livelihood of Java, concretely depicted as its nourishment and clothing, and more figuratively as its sustenance and protection.[27]

Such a story can be taken at face value, as describing an unlikely yet not impossible coincidence. Dutch sources, which could have corroborated or negated its occurrence, are not entirely clear on whether Pangéran Arya Mangkunagara and Patih Danureja were on a single ship bound for Ceylon. They seem to suggest the two arrived on the same day yet on board different ships.[28] But regardless of its factual validity, the story can be read as striving to put to rest some of the tensions tearing

---

[25] *Kang kalebet ing wirayat nenggih/rayi paduka Mas Sujana/tembé ampuh paparabé/aran satriya ratu/kang ananggga wawraté jurit/yèn punika sirnaha/Tanah Jawa bésuk/tan ana kang bisa nyandhang/gih satriya kakalih kang dènpanuti/ing sandhang lawan pangan* (*Babad Kartasura*, ibid.). The word *satriya* (from S. *kṣatriya*, traditionally the military or ruling class in Hindu society) is translated here as "nobleman" but can also mean "warrior prince," especially in the context of the wayang theatrical tradition.

[26] The son, Radèn Mas Said (upon whom was later bestowed the title Mangkunagara I), was to become the first ruler of Surakarta's minor court, the Kadipatèn Mangkunagaran (r. 1757–1796). For his life and achievements, see Merle C. Ricklefs, *Soul Catcher: Java's Fiery Prince Mangkunagara I, 1726–1795* (Honolulu: University of Hawai'i ASAA Southeast Asia Publications Series, 2018). The brother Mas Sujana (Pangéran Mangkubumi), was to reign as the founding sultan of the newly established Karaton Yogyakarta, Sultan Hamengkubuwana I (r. 1749–1792). For a study of his life, see Merle C. Ricklefs, *Jogjakarta under Sultan Mangkubumi 1749–1792: A History of the Division of Java* (London: Oxford University Press, 1974).

[27] In other sources, the prophecy about Radèn Mas Said's future abilities as warrior and leader were attributed to Purbaya, to whom the child was entrusted by Pangéran Arya before he was exiled; see below.

[28] SLNA 1/69, Political Council Minutes, November 14, 1733. From this document it appears that Pangéran Mangkunagara was on the ship *Wesendijxhoorn* and Patih Danureja on *de Jonge Willem*.

away at the fabric of the Kartasura court in the 1720s and which continued to reverberate for many years to come; it may signal an attempt to absolve Pangéran Arya Mangkunagara through Patih Danureja's admitting his treachery or to vindicate the Patih by portraying his anguish and remorse. The narrative could also constitute a retroactive endeavor to explain the rise of two of Pangéran Arya Mangkunagara's family members to powerful positions of authority despite his exile, or even with his exile as the particular background against which their success would unfold. In the case of these speculative scenarios, the story could be a later addition that was inserted to provide context and reason for events either past or future and, as such, raises questions about how exile was recounted and remembered.

Pangéran Arya Mangkunagara and Danureja never returned home. Many others lived out their lives in Ceylon or spent time periods there that ranged from the relatively brief to the extended. What do the Javanese sources reveal about contacts among the exiles in Ceylon, about information circulating, about ties of friendship and family that were or were not allowed to persist?

At the very end of the section of the *Babad Kartasura* depicting the meeting at sea of Danureja and Pangéran Arya Mangkunagara, the two arrive at the coast of Ceylon, depicted as lined with gardens and large houses.[29] Although the *Babad* does not offer details, the men may have been looking across the Colombo shore at Wolvendahl, to the northeast of the fort, where land was given by the Dutch authorities to a group of Javanese who had served them well in their anti-Portuguese campaigns several decades earlier. The Dutch superintendent at the time had wished to secure "a fertile spot, in order to settle them there with their families, and to found there a village, according to the limits and ordinances that shall be appointed for them," where they would grow rice and fruit trees.[30] But that populated area was not to be Pangéran Arya Mangkunagara's place of residence, as the text states he would live separately and without access to his "older brother" (*raka*) the Patih, likely under the watchful eye of the Dutch as other high-ranking exiles did.[31]

---

[29] *Kuneng lampahnya palwa prapta/nagri Sélong pasisiré/ing inggahaken sampun serayaté pinernah sami/jinajar kebonira/wisma gedhong agung* (*Babad Kartasura*, B21c, 28, in Dhandhanggula).

[30] Political Council Minutes, September 8, 1660, cited in *Jubilee Book*, 158.

[31] *Nging sanes panggenaira/pan pinisah Pangran Harya Nagaréki/lan enggené kang raka* (*Babad Kartasura*, B21c, 28, in Dhandhanggula). This information is corroborated in a Dutch source that states that Pangéran Arya Mangkunagara would be kept at the Colombo Fort while Patih Danureja would be housed outside the town (SLNA 1/69, Political Council Minutes of November 14, 1733).

The *Babad* also clarifies that Pangéran Arya Mangkunagara was unable to visit Pangéran Mangkunagari, son of the exiled king Amangkurat Mas (Amangkurat III), who lived with his relatives at a great distance (*tebih panggenanipun*) from him.[32] Although contemporary Dutch sources reveal that this distant site was Jaffna, whereas the *Babad* reference offers only an ambiguous hint on location, the latter provides telling and rare evidence as far as Javanese sources are concerned about Amangkurat's son's presence in Ceylon at the time Arya Mangkunagara arrived and the fact that these two members of the Mataram lineage were kept apart and prevented from meeting. In fact, the *Babad* suggests that due to the distance (which was both geographical and imposed by a ban on communication) the prince in Jaffna was unaware (J. *datan ana udani*) of Pangéran Arya's arrival.[33] With much of what was happening in Ceylon seemingly unknown in detail to Javanese authors depicting histories of exile, mention of this particular case – recalling kinship relations and the frustration of alienation in a foreign land – shows that news of the most high-status exiles did filter back to Java, however partially, and that despite the exiles' often pitiful circumstances – as emerges from their letters and petitions – the authorities were nonetheless concerned about potential unrest that might draw on their power and prestige in a previous life.[34]

It is instructive to consider not only ongoing and severed relationships during exile but also the ways in which knowledge of Ceylon and the exilic experience and, even more pertinently, imaginings of the place and life there, and of individuals banished, often permeated the life of those left behind. For example, the *Syair Hemop* (also known as *Syair Kompeni Welanda Berperang dengan Tjina,* "The Dutch Company Goes to War with the Chinese"), a Malay chronicle written in Batavia and recounting Dutch policies in Ceylon in the early eighteenth century and events leading up to the Chinese Massacre of 1740, depicts how when Gustaaf Willem van Imhoff (known in Malay as Hemop) had reached a truce with the king of Kandy he asked Adriaan Valckenier, the governor-general of the Dutch East Indies, to send poor unemployed Chinese from Batavia

---

[32] *Babad Kartasura*, B21c, 28. Pangéran Mangkunagari was Pakubuwana I's grand-nephew whereas Pangéran Arya Mangkunagara was his grandson.

[33] *Nenggih Pangéran Mangkunagari/putranira Pangéran Mangkurat Mas/anèng Sélong sakadangan tebih panggenanipun/dadya datan ana udani* (ibid.)

[34] Testimony to this anxiety appears in the Dutch Political Council Minutes from Colombo in 1794 which note that "State exiles though guilty of crime are not to be punished here without further orders from Batavia" (SLNA 1/225, January 9, 1794; cited in Anthonisz, *Digest,* 249). The *Digest* was prepared by R. G. Anthonisz (1852–1930), the first Government Archivist (1902–1921), in manuscript form. It was published, with an introduction by K. D. Paranavitana, in 2012.

to trade in Ceylon. Valckenier instead deviously called a meeting with the leaders of Batavia's Chinese community and informed them that an order had come from the Netherlands stating that all Batavia Chinese would be sent to Ceylon within several days. The headmen were shocked and, weeping, they begged and appealed, proposing a large per capita bribe to avert the calamity, an offer the governor-general accepted.[35]

Although the *Syair* does not reveal to what extent specific knowledge of Ceylon was available to those threatened with exile, it was the image of Ceylon as a site of banishment that caused the Chinese to collect a huge sum of money to avoid this fate. The *Syair* does, however, include a harrowing description of travel by sea, the journey between Java and Ceylon portrayed as a near-death experience, the ship bobbing up and down like a small boat on the stormy sea, its waves high as mountains, an image that could certainly have been evoked when the prospect of "being Ceyloned" was raised.[36]

In some cases, imaginings and anxieties related to exile preceded an actual banishment which certain individuals would later experience. For example, two of Pangéran Arya Mangkunagara's sons were left behind with relatives on Java, and both guardians were later exiled themselves. The *Babad Kartasura*, where the prophecy about Radèn Mas Said's future abilities as warrior and leader was attributed not to Danureja but to Pangéran Purbaya (brother of Pakubuwana II's queen), recounts that the child was entrusted to Purbaya's care when his father Pangéran Arya was banished and that Purbaya spoiled him, perhaps trying to compensate for the missing father. One day Purbaya was sitting on the pavilion of his house when Radèn Mas Said came and sat nearby. Watching the child intently, Purbaya felt his heart throb and asked the boy to come closer, noticing his tongue twitch (*rinogoh*) as he approached, signaling to Purbaya that Radèn Mas Said and his descendants were destined to be outstanding soldiers. He then instructed the boy to practice asceticism (J. *tapa*) so that the prediction would eventually be realized.[37]

---

[35] J. Rusconi, "Sja'ir Kompeni Welanda Berperang dengan Tjina" (academic dissertation; Utrecht: Wageningen Veenman, 1935), lines 530–552, p. 33. This transliterated and printed version is based primarily on MS Farquhar 3, Royal Asiatic Society, London (text dated 1750s, manuscript 1817), synthesized occasionally with MS Cod. Or 2095, Leiden University Library (dated after 1869). Reference is to the numbered couplets/lines of the printed edition. For a study of the *Syair*, see W. Kern, "Aantekeningen op de Sja'ir Hémop (Sja'ir Kompeni Welanda berperang dengan Tjina)," *Tijdschrift voor Indische Taal-, Land- en Volkenkunde* 82.2 (1948): 211–257.

[36] This depiction is in Rusconi, "Sja'ir," lines 1390–1400, pp. 54–55.

[37] In Ronggawarsita, *Babad Itih*, MN 88 TT, 145. Purbaya is not addressing the prince directly (or not just him) but various officials. The language used is in some phrases

After pronouncing the prediction, Purbaya felt stiff (J. *keju*) and stunned with grief (J. *jetung*) when his heart recalled Radèn Mas Said's father, Pangéran Arya Mangkunagara, who was in Ceylon. Here Pangéran Purbaya is described as remembering Pangéran Arya, languishing across the sea and unable to see his son, who was destined for glory. These thoughts and memories of relatives and friends formed part of the web of associations and connections to exilic life in Ceylon although they are clearly, by their very nature, unrecoverable in all but a very few cases when they were recorded in writing. Purbaya himself (as will be discussed in the next chapter) would be exiled to Ceylon in 1738 after his sister and patron at court, Queen Ratu Kencana, passed away, and so his connection to Ceylon would cease to be imaginative and become real. As for Radèn Mas Said, who lost both his father and adoptive father to exile in Ceylon, that island of banishment must have loomed large in his imagination and his life, without his ever having set foot there.

Another, much less famous son of Pangéran Arya Mangkunagara, Radèn Sambiya, was also left in Java and raised by Pangéran Ngabèhi, an uncle of the boy and brother of Pangéran Mangkubumi, first sultan of Yogyakarta. On the occasion of Pakubuwana III's ascension to the throne in 1749 he banished several of Pangéran Mangkubumi's brothers, Ngabèhi among them. Again, the guardian of a prince whose father was exiled was later exiled himself, highlighting how banishment to Ceylon was part of these royals' lives in the most personal of ways.[38] An additional and very significant aspect of the exile experience was the question of return: hoped-for but unrealized returns, returns in life and in death.

King Amangkurat III, whose capture and exile in 1708 were discussed above, lived out the rest of his life in Ceylon. His plea to the Dutch authorities to allow him to return to Java in his old age was rejected, and this unlucky monarch passed away in wretched circumstances, after an illness. When word of his death reached Batavia in 1734, Pakubuwana II received a letter from the governor-general informing him that the deposed king had passed away in exile, that his body had not yet been

---

identical to what Danureja later told Pangéran Arya Mangkunagara about his son when they met at sea.

[38] Another example of contemplating Ceylon and the consequences of exile before experiencing it personally is found in Patih Natakusuma's participation in the embassy to Batavia (September 1734–April 1735), charged among other matters with sorting out the question of the "missing pusakas" after Amangkurat III's death in Ceylon (Ricklefs, *Seen and Unseen*, 180–183). Natakusuma was exiled to Ceylon in 1742.

Figure 4.1 Detail from a dynastic tree-diagram of Java's rulers, compiled in 1814, presenting Amangkurat III as "Mangkurat Selong" (leaf 53B).
© The British Library Board Or 15932, f. 72

buried and that the Dutch were awaiting Pakubuwana II's preference regarding Amangkurat III's posthumous repatriation.[39]

The *Babad Kartasura* recounts how Pakubuwana II, upon reading the letter brought by a messenger, was astounded. The Javanese word *ngungun* (astonished, dumbfounded, amazed) is repeated three times in this short passage, as the king assembled his close advisors and relatives to ask for their thoughts on the matter. Despite his repeated attempts to elicit an opinion about what he should do, all those present avoided voicing one and deferred to him, perhaps because of the issue's great sensitivity, Pakubuwana II's grandfather having usurped the throne from the legitimate line of his brother and nephew whose return, even posthumously, could give rise to competing claims to authority. It seemed the Dutch were also not eager to weigh in and so the decision was left squarely in Pakubuwana's hands. Increasingly bewildered of heart (J. *èmenginirèng galih*), the king lost himself in thought for a long time, finally emerging to announce that he wished Amangkurat III to be buried in the royal cemetery in Imogiri; that he would allow his surviving sons and families to return; and, importantly, that he asked that all the missing regalia that had disappeared with Amangkurat III's flight in 1705 be returned to the

---

[39] Although the text claims the body had not yet been buried (*kang layon samangké dèrèng pinetak*), it must have been interred temporarily in Ceylon but had not yet received the official burial due to a Javanese king. A similar example is found in the case of Cakraningrat IV (r. 1718–1746), who died in exile at the Cape in South Africa and was later reburied in Madura.

court.[40] It seems the desire to reclaim those sacred objects played a major role in his decision.[41]

How did Javanese chronicles depict the return of the group of exiles which included, besides the deceased king's body, approximately two hundred of his relatives and members of his retinue, some of whom were surely born in Ceylon during the years of banishment?[42] Upon receiving Pakubuwana II's decision, the governor-general sent a message to two of Amangkurat III's sons in Ceylon, Pangéran Mangkunagara[43] and Pangéran Pakuningrat, to prepare to accompany their father's body back to Java and for their own return along with their wives, children and retinues. The departure from Ceylon and the journey home were not recounted in the *Babad*, but it did narrate how the princes arrived in Batavia with their families and the heirlooms in tow, were greeted with eleven military cannon salutes and boarded a boat to travel by sea, along Java's north coast, to Semarang:

Then they all came ashore. The Commander got word that Sunan Mangkurat Mas' sons had arrived at the mouth of the river, accompanying their late father's body. Displaying respect, the Commander came forth to receive them along with all of Kartasura's court officials.

When they arrived at the mouth of the river they bowed to those two princes. When the two princes saw Radèn Pringgalaya and Radèn Natakusuma their hearts were filled with emotion and they wept, [and] both Radèn Pringgalaya and Radèn Natakusuma wept along with them.

[40] This scene is described in Ronggawarsita, *Babad Itih*, MN 88 TT, 92–93.
[41] For a comparative perspective on Ceylon-related royal regalia in exile, the last king of Kandy's regalia taken to London and later returned, see Robert Aldrich, "The Return of the Throne: The Repatriation of the Kandyan Regalia to Ceylon," in Robert Aldrich and Cindy McCreery (eds.), *Crowns and Colonies: European Monarchies and Overseas Empires* (Manchester: Manchester University Press, 2016), 139–162. The circumstances in the two cases differed markedly: The Javanese pusakas were brought by a king to Ceylon, not taken from a king by a colonial power as in the case of Kandy; the royal Kandy regalia gained new significance for Ceylonese nationalists, and the case of the heirlooms' return constituted an early example of repatriation of booty by colonial powers as resolution to an international relations issue between former colonizer and colonized states, dimensions the Javanese instance lacked. The common thread, however, was the significance of these potent objects to rule, to memory, to the imagination.
[42] Details of expanding and contracting households, especially those of royal exiles, were noted regularly in Dutch documents from Ceylon. For example, SLNA 1/3956 lists Dutch state exiles residing in Ceylon in 1788, noting those who had recently been added to an earlier list (through birth or arrival in Ceylon) or subtracted from it (through death or repatriation).
[43] This prince had the same name, but was not the same person, as the above-mentioned Pangéran Arya Mangkunagara.

They then embraced each other in turns for some time, then emerged from the river mouth and headed toward the Commander's house for the night, and left Semarang in the morning honored with eleven cannon salutes.[44]

A section from another *Babad Kartasura* volume highlights additional aspects of this particular return: In it Amangkurat III's four sons are mentioned, thus in addition to Pangéran Mangkunagara and Pangéran Mangkuningrat, Pangéran Jayakusuma and the youngest son Pangéran Emas also appear. Collectively all four are referred to in the text as the "Ceylon Princes" (*Pangéran Sélong*) while their father is referred to as Sunan Kéndhang, the Exiled King.[45]

Immediately after this mention of the returning family, the heirlooms make an appearance:

> It was the king's intent
> That the heirlooms of the land of Java
> Would all return home to Java:
> Spears, kerisses and garments,
> The small gong Kyai Bicak,
> Carried to Ceylon in the past,
> By Sunan Mangkurat Mas.
>
> In the year Alip,
> The month of Rabingulakir,
> On the eighth day of the month they left,
> On a Monday.
> As for those who accompanied them
> Formerly going along
> They were all returned home.[46]

A triumphant, proud and relieved tone can be detected in this passage as the return of the pusakas was probably a major goal of allowing

---

[44] *Nulya sami mentas ing baita. Ingriku kumendur wus amiyarsa lamun putrané Sunan Mangkurat Mas sampun prapta muara, sarta angiringaken layoné kang rama. Nulya komendur ngormati methuk lan sagung punggawèng Kartasura sami methuk sedaya.*

Yata sak praptané muwuru sampun tundhuk lawan Pangéran kalih mau, Pangéran kekalih duk aningali Radèn Pringgalaya lawan Radèn Natakusuma, kathah ingkang taraosèng galih dadya sami karuna. Kalihipun Radèn Pringgalaya lawan Radèn Natakusuma sami tumut karuna.

Nunten sami rangkul rinangkul gantya, wau sareng sampun antawis dangu, lajeng budhal saking muara, anjujug wismané kumendur, among rerep sadalu, énjing gya budhal saking Semawis sarta kinurmatan mariyem saking sawelas (Ronggawarsita, *Babad Itih*, MN 88 TT, 94).

[45] "Sunan" was a title applied to the ruler of Kartasura and later Surakarta. It was also applied to the wali sanga.

[46] *Pamrihira sri bupati/pusaka ing Tanah Jawa/mantuka mring Jawa kabèh/waos dhuwung lan rasukan/bendhé Kiyai Bicak/binektèng Sélong rumuhun/mring Sunan Mangkurat Mas//Anuju ing taun Alip/Rabingulakir kang wulan/tanggal ping wolu angkaté/marengi ing dina Soma/déné ta kanthènira/kang samya tumut rumuhun/winangsulaken sadaya* (*Babad Kartasura*, B21c, 28, in Asmaradana).

Amangkurat's descendants to return to Java despite a certain anxiety that they might try to reclaim their earlier, pre-exile status. Another depiction of the same return draws attention to the human dimension of repatriation, after many years during which there was little hope of return:

> All reached Betawi,
> The members of the House of Mangkurat
> Who had lived in Ceylon:
> Pangéran Mangkunagara,
> Pangéran Mangkuningrat,
> Radèn Jayakusuma
> And the youngest, Pangéran Emas.

> Along with their households, men and women
> Great and small, yes everyone,
> Two hundred in total,
> Were met by the Patih.
> Like those dead coming to life
> Great was their happiness.
> No more will be said.[47]

The return of the Ceylon princes is narrated also in the *Babad Jawi Kartasura,* where the description of events is similar, though less joyful sentiments also emerge: Those awaiting the princes in Kartasura are said to be weighed down with sorrow as they watch the Ceylon princes arrive;[48] when the princes came before King Pakubuawan II they felt heartbroken;[49] in this source, as in the others cited, new names were bestowed on the princes upon their return to Java and they were given tracts of land by the king.[50]

Considering these references together, a discrepancy emerges between the level of detail in passages relating the return of Amangkurat III's sons, depicted in several chronicles and presenting different emphases, and the brevity of description related to their father's exile, about which the texts had little to say. The *Babad Kartasura*'s depiction of the arrival of the

---

[47] *Sadaya prapta Betawi/Santana kamangkuratan/kang sami wonten ing Sélong/Pangéran Mangkunagara/Pangéran Mangkuningrat/Radèn Jayakusumèku/wuragil Pangéran Emas// Sarayaté jalu èstri/geng alit nenggih sadaya/wong kalihatus cacahé/wus panggih lan Kiyai Patya/lir pejah manggih gesang/samya langsung sukanipun/mangkana sah ing bicara (Babad Kartasura,* B21c, 29, in Asmaradana).

[48] *Jibeg kang samya ningali/rawuhira pangéran kang saking Sélan (Babad Jawi Kartasura),* transliterated by Sri Soehartini (Jakarta: Departemen Pendidikan dan Kebudayaan Proyek Penerbitan Buku Sastra Indonesia dan Daerah, 1987), 4: 82, in Sinom.

[49] *Samya sumedhot tyasira* (ibid., 83).

[50] Ibid., 84. The practice of receiving a new name often accompanied certain life transitions including promotion or attaining a new position within the court, recovery from illness, ascension to the throne and various other moments that signaled a new beginning.

princes' retinues in Betawi, for example, continues as they travel onward toward Kartasura and the palace. Their journey home, which had begun when they departed the shores of distant Ceylon, took them across the sea to Java, first landing in Betawi, then traveling by boat to Semarang and continuing to Kartasura. Once there they were taken first to the hall of the king's chief counsellor (*kepatihan*), then to the palace (*pura*), and finally to the royal audience hall (*panangkilan*). This and other examples of attentiveness to detail suggest that this exilic return marked an event considered highly significant, and one that these texts, often passing over emotions in near silence, could not refrain from depicting with affective words.

Another instance of posthumous return from exile in Ceylon narrated in Javanese sources is that of Pangéran Arya Mangkunagara, whose travel by sea and conversation with Patih Danureja marked his one-way journey into exile. Like his older kinsman Amangkurat III, he too requested to return to Java but the ruling king, his brother Pakubuwana II, consistently refused.[51] In 1738, only several years after his arrival in Ceylon, Pangéran Arya passed away and was buried in Colombo. According to Burah, Prince "Amangku Nagoora" was buried at Peer Sahib Makam in the Pettah area east of the Colombo Fort.[52] The tomb, known as the resting place of Tuan Pangéran, is today still visited by devotees, and regular prayers and rituals are conducted there. Various stories about past events surrounding the tomb circulate among local Malay families but their core motifs are shared: There was long ago a Javanese prince who was exiled to Ceylon, where he died. Several years after his burial one of his relatives in faraway Java dreamed that the dead prince wished to come home and be buried properly in the soil of his forefathers. The Dutch authorities were petitioned to this effect and they agreed to exhume the body, but on one condition: Upon opening the grave the body must still be complete, as if just buried, a condition the Dutch officials inserted into the agreement only because they were convinced it could not possibly materialize. However, when the grave was opened the body within it was not just in perfect shape but it was said to be warm, and when pricked with a pin drops of blood appeared, all proving that the prince, in all likelihood Pangéran Arya Mangkunagara, possessed special powers that allowed him to reach out to his distant relative through a dream and to remain intact in the grave despite time passing, thus defying not only the strict demands of the Dutch but also acceptable paradigms of life and death. The officials present were so amazed, the

---

[51] Ricklefs, *Seen and Unseen*, 194n.
[52] Burah, *Saga of the Exiled Royal Javanese Unearthed*, 55.

story continues, that they immediately saluted the prince with their cannons, took his body to the nearby port and sent it back to Java.

Relevant Javanese sources describe how, a decade and a half after Pangéran Arya Mangkunagara's death, and as part of complex negotiations in Java and the increasing estrangement of Pangéran Arya's son Radèn Mas Said from Pangéran Mangkubumi, the Dutch authorities consented to the request to return his body to Java for proper burial at Imogiri.[53] The miraculous state of his body when exhumed and the respect accorded it by the colonial officials were not mentioned in the Javanese text, whose account begins with Radèn Mas Said approaching the Company via an exchange of letters with *delèr Semarang*[54] and ultimately receiving word that the body would be returned, which transpired in 1753. The Javanese source recounting the event is the *Serat Babad Pakunegaran*, an autobiography of Radèn Mas Said, the son who according to the prophecies – which were now gradually coming to fruition – would become a great warrior and leader.[55] The *Babad* offers a brief description when reporting on the execution of the Company's decision, noting that the body of Pangéran Arya, who had died in Ceylon in the past (J. *kang séda Sélong rumiyin*) would be met by emissaries upon arrival.[56]

The son did not himself go to Semarang to reclaim the body, and the *Babad* names the officials sent to do so.[57] Pangéran Arya's body, placed in a coffin (J. *tabela*), was carried by a group of *santri*, those adhering strictly to the rules of Islam. As Radèn Mas Said awaited the arrival of his father's body and the coffin in which it lay approached, nature signaled the gravity of the event, with its tumult (J. *gara-gara*) felt all around:

[53] The son's wish to bring his father's body back is discussed in Yasadipura I, *Babad Giyanti* (BP), 13: 78–79. Another source is van Hohendorff's secret letter to Batavia, dated May 24, 1753, in which he discusses Mangkunagara's request for his father's body and his own support of it (VOC 2825, Overgek. Brieven & Papieren 1754). Even earlier, in 1751, Pakubuwana III had asked for the bodies of "Ariaas Mancoe Nagara and Poerbaija" to be returned for burial in Java, accompanied by their surviving family members (see VOC 2787, Overgek. Brieven & Papieren 1752). It appears his letter received no response at the time (Merle C. Ricklefs, personal communication, May 26, 2016).

[54] *Delèr* was a title for a member of the Council of the Indies, from D. *edeler* (nobles).

[55] Mangkunagara I, *Serat Babad Pakunegaran*, Surakarta, composed c. 1757, inscribed 1779, British Library Add. MS 12318. For an in-depth study of this chronicle, see Ricklefs, *Soul Catcher*.

[56] Mangkunagara I, *Serat Babad Pakunegaran*, BL, Add. MS 12318, 303, in Dhandhanggula.

[57] The head of another member of the Mataram royal house, Pangéran Adiwijaya, was returned on the same occasion (ibid.). Rather than sending Pangéran Purbaya's body, too, as requested, the Company officers in Colombo mistakenly sent back the body of Mangkunagara's brother Tirtakusuma (Pancuran); see Ricklefs, *Soul Catcher*, 132–133.

Lightning (*obar-abir*) flashed, an ominous red glow (J. *téja*) appeared in the sky and a strong west wind blew.

As the terrifying omens appeared and the world around him quaked and rumbled, the prince found calm and resignation as he sat in meditation, his arms folded, drawing inward and surrendering himself to the favor of the Creator of the Earth, before heading toward Mataram to perform the burial.[58] Foreboding signs and the active participation of nature in events of often seminal importance to human life, and to kingship in particular, are common in babad literature, creating emphasis, suggesting the likelihood or inevitability of events yet to come, and underscoring powers that are beyond human reach. Here the burial of Pangéran Arya Mangkunagara, despite his years in exile and his death far from Java, was portrayed as a significant homecoming in which all of nature partook.

Following the burial, Radèn Mas Said paid his respects to his deceased father by distributing alms (J. *sidhekah*), food and drink. He felt intuitively in his heart the benefits bestowed upon him by his father, and the intensity of his feeling was accentuated by the *Babad*'s repetition (J. *osik ing tyas/raos ing galih*). He sensed that his father was still alive and present upon return, despite the years that had passed since he had died in exile. This forceful insight reveals Radèn Mas Said's spiritual dimension, evident in his meditative practice. It also echoes with other textual depictions that evoke images of life and death when narrating returns from Ceylon: living returnees seeming as though they have come back from the dead, the dream-like quality of unexpected reunions that creates uncertainty for those coming together, the liminal nature of returning bodies which retained a powerful presence and sometimes miraculous abilities, the latter casting doubt upon the rigid boundaries between the dead and the living.

Mas Said's insights connect especially well, and are in dialogue, with the oral traditions circulating about the Javanese prince Tuan Pangéran in Colombo. Despite the distance, the different languages and writing traditions, and the time that has elapsed since the events took place, and although many of the elements appearing in Tuan Pangéran's story are typical of holy men's biographies (the dream, communicating from the grave, the body exhumed untouched by the passage of time), there are significant indications that the Sri Lankan Malay tradition and the Javanese one offer two similar perspectives of events and their interpretation. In both accounts Pangéran Arya Mangkunagara, who was powerless to

---

[58] Mangkunagara I, *Serat Babad Pakunegaran*, BL, Add. MS 12318, 305–306, in Dhandhanggula.

avoid his own exile and never able to return in life, emerged as a man whose powers were superior to those of the men who had banished him and wished him ill. His impeccable physical condition upon the opening of his tomb, putting Dutch assumptions to shame, links with his son's visceral feeling that he had returned alive; the dream of the relative, in which Pangéran Arya communicated his wish to be returned, recalls Radèn Mas Said's deep meditation and concentration through which he knew his father's proximity and God's oversight; and the respectful farewell and cannon salutes offered by the Dutch to the departing prince mirror their "mistake" of sending the wrong body back, a bureaucratic error to some but proof of Pangéran Arya's ability to outsmart his captors, even in death, to others. Both tellings highlight the importance of the miraculous, of that which goes beyond mundane perception, and which offers power to the displaced and comfort to the disempowered.

Conducting the rituals, and above all the interment of Pangéran Arya in the dynastic cemetery along with his ancestors and where future generations would lie, was of great significance to his son, who had last seen his father when he was only a young child, but whose commitment to conducting the cultural and religious rites of Javanese royalty remained intact despite the lifelong separation imposed on them both. The reburial of his father at Imogiri must have been important not only for personal reasons but also to legitimate Radèn Mas Said, himself in the process of asserting his power and founding his own court (J. *kadipatèn*), and to show that his direct ancestor rested in the proper place, a member of the Mataram lineage. Thus, in this case, as seen in the prophecy predicting Mas Said's future glory and in the burial rites, exile failed to undermine the future for which Pangéran Arya's son was destined nor did it remove the exiled prince from his rightful position within the Javanese social and dynastic order. Meanwhile in Colombo, the old and now empty tomb continued to draw those craving the blessings of a Javanese prince, whose life was indeed disrupted by exile, but only to a degree, as he has continued to exert his power via his descendants in the land of his birth as well as in the land of his banishment long after both he, and the regime that banished him, had passed away.

5   Exilic Journeys in Time, Place and Writing

Chapter 4 explored a range of dimensions of exile from Java to Ceylon as portrayed in Javanese sources: royal exile, movement toward Ceylon and away from it in ship voyages and dreams, communication challenges faced by the banished even with those who shared their fate, ways in which Ceylon and exilic life were imagined by relatives and others in Java and the recurring process by which that imagined life suddenly turned real, and the category of "posthumous" returns from exile sometimes afforded to a select few. The current chapter continues dwelling on the theme of exilic life as depicted and remembered in Javanese texts, emphasizing the challenges and emotional turmoil experienced by long-term exiles returning to Java, and a gendered perspective on exile and return. The anxieties of return are explored primarily through the textual testimonies narrating the homecoming of Pangéran Juru, previously known as Natakusuma, who was the chief counsel to King Pakubuwana II until being accused of leading a pro-Chinese court faction and exiled to Ceylon in 1742. In 1755, as one of his first acts upon making peace with the VOC, Sultan Hamengkubuwana I of Yogyakarta (brother of the late Pakubuwana II) petitioned the Dutch, requesting that Pangéran Natakusuma be returned to Java. The request was granted, Natakusuma was renamed Pangéran Juru, and was appointed advisor to the sultan, becoming an honored senior figure at the Yogyakarta court.[1] Depictions of his return after more than a decade in exile provide evidence of the transformative effects of the experience and the struggle to reintegrate into court life.

As for gender, although women's voices recounting exile and depictions of their exilic journeys are even rarer than men's, delving into the female dimension of banishment shows that it is women who tend to be depicted as delivering the more detailed, emotional and thus revealing accounts. This comes through clearly in a scene in which a Javanese

---

[1] For Natakusuma's return, see *Babad Giyanti* (BP), 21: 69–76. On the broader episode, see Ricklefs, *Seen and Unseen*, 266–267.

woman recently returned from Ceylon recalls some experiences and events she witnessed there, offering memories of exilic life that combine the ordinary and the fantastic. It is also women's exilic lives whose traces tend to come to us through narrations of marriage, love relationships, motherhood, widowhood and divorce, bringing out more fully the human dimension of living through exile and return. The biography of Putri Sélong (the "Ceylon Princess"), as reconstructed from several sources, serves as testimony: Born in Ceylon to an exiled prince, she returned to Java with her husband, later followed a brother into exile and a third husband back to Java where she was again widowed, then remarried for the fourth time.

After considering these memories – of women and men – which speak to geographical and social mobility, adjustments and reintegration, sacrifices and survival, the chapter concludes by considering the shared themes of, and connections between, the exile-centric depictions discussed in Chapters 2 (Ceylon) and 3 and 4 (Java).

Pangéran Juru was no doubt among the fortunate exiles, allowed not only to return in life to Java but also receiving much recognition by and respect from the sultan of Yogyakarta and an appointment to high office at court. His status upon return was reflected in the grand welcome afforded him, with troops marching and music playing and Juru himself dressed in finery.[2] This event may have reminded him of the time, years earlier in 1734, when he had gone to Batavia on Pakubuwana II's orders to negotiate with the Dutch authorities the return of Amangkurat III's body and his surviving relatives from Ceylon.[3] Or perhaps he recalled the ceremonies marking their arrival, along with the lost pusakas, in 1737. Pangéran Juru was a man who had been involved in others' return from exile, exiled himself, and allowed to return; thus his perspective on the matter was a complex and personal one. Moreover, in the attempt to reconstruct exilic experiences Pangéran Juru's case is unusual, not only due to his nuanced view on exile and return but also because he was important enough to be included in the chronicles and to have his voice represented in narrating his experiences and encounters in exile and his challenges upon return. These depictions show the ambiguous nature of

---

[2] S. Hatmowasito, *Babad Giyanti dumugi Prayut: Gancaran.* Inscribed Surakarta, 1977, Reksa Pustaka Library, Kadipatèn Mangkunagaran, Surakarta, MN 693 (c), 102. This is a prose rendition of Yasadipura I, *Babad Giyanti dumugi Prayut*, Surakarta, composed late eighteenth century, inscribed 1976, MS MN 692. The latter in turn appears to be a handwritten transliteration into Latin script of the Radya Pustaka Library MS RP 40; see Florida, *Javanese Literature*, vol. II, 445. The handwritten MN 693 was typed in three volumes (a–c). The letter appended to each citation is a reference to the typed volume.

[3] On the embassy to Batavia in 1734–1735, see Ricklefs, *Seen and Unseen*, 183.

his return, with high rank, land grants, joy and relief offset by uncertainty and traumatic memories that could not be easily discarded.

The *Babad Giyanti* portrays the initial confusion and emotional turmoil that accompanied Pangéran Juru's return to Java. Not long after his arrival, while in the Yogyakarta palace, he noticed much movement and noise outside, where he could see many troops assembling and hear the sounds of the tambourine, flute and *serunai* that filled the air. Pangéran Juru was startled as he observed the great number of soldiers arranging themselves on the *alun-alun* in a show of force. Looking in all directions, he felt exceedingly sorrowful for his ignorance yet was too embarrassed to inquire about what was unfolding in front of his eyes, his mind bewildered, clueless about the event, asking himself what this could possibly all mean (*iya iki ana apa*, his internal conversation transpiring in informal Javanese). The longer he watched, the less he considered his shame at revealing his simplicity, wishing to know so that his mind could find relief. He then approached the official Martalaya and spoke apologetically: "I am the son of a *tumenggung* turned hick [*wong désa*], having spent two *windu* in Ceylon. What is going on? The palace troops all arranged in rows, and the *dandanan jro* are out on the field, going northward carrying the great parasol on a golden platter?"[4] Laughing, Martalaya told Pangéran Juru that a letter-bearing messenger had arrived from Surakarta, sent by "your grandson, the king,"[5] and that the ceremonial welcome he was witnessing was the Yogyakarta court's way of showing respect on the occasion of the letter's receipt.

Pangéran Juru continued to voice his wonder at what he saw in Yogyakarta on this occasion: the discipline of the troops, the beauty, order, skill and charm of the kingdom as reflected in the unfolding event, a kingdom that did not yet exist when he was exiled and which he felt exceeded what he knew in the past in Kartasura. The music played on melodiously while the military drills were repeatedly performed and the court officials, as well as the Dutch Major Dungkur and the messenger from Surakarta, assembled in the Srimanganti pavilion. The messenger paid his respects to the king and then conveyed his letter. Once again Pangéran Juru's astonishment is noted, as he listened and watched with his mouth agape at the messenger's manner, his conduct as he engaged with the king, the way he spoke and carried himself.[6]

---

[4] *Babad Giyanti* (BP), 21: 77, in Dhandhanggula.
[5] Ibid. *Wayah paduka sang nata*, ibid. The use of familial titles is very common in babad literature with younger men often referred to as "child," or "grandson," and older men as "uncle," "father," or "grandfather," regardless of actual biological ties. Here the reference is to Pakubuwana III.
[6] Ibid., 21: 78–79.

After staring intently, Pangéran Juru whispered to the nearby Adipati Danureja that the man they were watching was just a small child in the old days, one who could not yet even speak, whereas now he was an adult conversing with the king,[7] his sentences correct and respectful, and he was watchful of his words and alert. Danureja smiled at Pangéran Juru's admiration and reminded him of where to place that long-gone child: He was the son of the palace official (*gandhèk*) Gandhingan, a follower of the late Pangéran Purbaya. Filled with wonder, Pangéran Juru heard his words and once more, as if unable to release himself from disbelief, exclaimed: "Yes, that child could not yet speak, way back in the old days!"[8]

The vocabulary in this brief passage emphasizes Pangéran Juru's state of shock and amazement with words that express his range of overlapping yet nuanced emotions and reactions: *ngungun* (amazed), *dongong* (stare with mouth open), *gawok* (astonished), *kagèt-kagèt* (startled). In addition to conveying Pangéran Juru's wonder and awe, the passage highlights his sense of insecurity and instability as he faces the changes that took place during his years away from Java: the chasm between himself and court life in terms of practices, rituals and formalities, generational shifts, language use, and etiquette. The full significance of this gap is best represented by the indirectly narrated transformation of a small child who could not yet speak when Juru was sent away but who during the two windu of his absence had grown into a man refined and knowledgeable enough to approach the king of Yogyakarta, whereas Pangéran Juru, a former patih at court, had seemingly moved in the other direction and morphed into a simple, childlike being, whom exile had robbed of the ability to speak correctly, in a culturally and politically appropriate manner. Responding to this state of affairs, Pangéran Juru retreated into partial silence, as he first watched events eager to know their meaning yet being too timid to ask, stared with his mouth agape, and resorted to whispering. His thrice repeated *duk ing alam kula rumiyin* can be translated as "back in the old days," or "way back when," but more literally as "in my old world," even "in my previous life," indicating the very real boundary he experienced between his pre- and post-exile periods.

In another episode, haunting memories of the period leading up to, and culminating in, Pangéran Juru's exile come to the fore. On a visit to Surakarta, conversing with court officials about various people he recalled from before his banishment, Pangéran Juru noticed a person of unusually small dimensions in the room, one who was like a child, and

[7] Ibid., 21: 79.   [8] Ibid., 79.

asked who he might be.[9] The grandson of Tumenggung Tirtawiguna was the reply. At this Pangéran Juru was shocked, his heart beating with fright (*atrataban*). Upon seeing the grandson Juru felt that he was again standing face to face with the grandfather, his head throbbing (*kumepyur*). It was as if he was caught by a snake, his tongue quaking, sticking out repeatedly as if hissing and spraying venom. He felt apprehensive, as if Tirtawiguna himself was there, and fear overcame him lest there was someone wishing ill upon him again, just when he had finally returned to Java from a foreign land. A moment later, as if awoken from a bad dream, Pangéran Juru uttered the *astafirlah* ("may God forgive me"), realizing he was saved from potential harm, as Tirtawiguna was dead.[10]

Pangéran Juru's traumatic reaction to the grandson reflected the depth of his anxiety when recalling the role Tumenggung Tirtawiguna played in his own demotion and exile.[11] Tirtawiguna was a powerful, shrewd courtier in Pakubuwana II's court during the years when Danureja and later Natakusuma (as Juru was previously known) had served in the position of patih. Tirtawiguna, a man of literary and linguistic skills who served as head scribe and translator in Pakubuwana II's court, opposed Danureja and was more influential than Natakusuma, despite the latter's elevated rank.[12] In 1729 Tirtawiguna was appointed as regent (*tumenggung*). During the major crisis of 1740–1741, when the court was near collapse and a debate of vital importance was taking place regarding whom to side with, the VOC or the Chinese forces, Tirtawiguna failed in his responsibility to provide guidance and leadership. While Natakusuma, who thought the VOC could be expelled from the region by the court joining the Chinese, expressed his opinion, Tirtawiguna did not utter a word but only glowered at the participants, a threatening, unpredictable presence likened in the *Babad Tanah Jawi* to a small cannonball waiting to explode.[13] Although he kept silent, the *Babad Kraton*, complied in Yogyakarta in 1777, suggests that Tirtawiguna favored maintaining the VOC alliance and thus he and Natakusuma stood on opposing sides of the war policy; that Tirtawiguna was the one who informed Pakubuwana II that Natakusuma was behind the installation of Sunan

[9] *Pangran Juru tanya/sinten punika ta adhi/cilik temen punika pan kadi bocah//* (Yasadipura I, *Babad Prayut*, Surakarta: Reksa Pustaka Library, Kadipatèn Mangkunagaran, composed late eighteenth century, inscribed 1857, MS MN 211, transcribed as MN 211 TT by Mulyo Hartono and M. Husodo, 3, in Pucung.

[10] *Serat Babad Prayut*, MN 211 TT, 3–4, in Pucung.

[11] The following is based on Ricklefs, *Seen and Unseen*, 171–173, 249.

[12] On Tirtawiguna's literary and linguistic abilities, see ibid., 172.

[13] Perhaps there is a reference here to Tirtawiguna's physical size, which would explain in part why the small features of the grandson reminded Pangéran Juru of the elder Tirtawiguna (*Babad Tanah Jawi* [BP], 23: 4, in Dhandhanggula]).

Kuning; and that he was likely present in Semarang when Natakusuma was arrested in 1742.[14] After Natakusuma's exile to Ceylon and Pakubuwana II's reconciliation with the VOC, Tirtawiguna was appointed as patih with Dutch support in 1743 and was renamed Radèn Adipati Sindureja.[15] He died in 1751, several years before his old rival Natakusuma returned from exile, was welcomed by the sultan of Yogyakarta, and encountered Tirtawiguna's grandson.

Although it seems at first that Pangéran Juru felt relieved when recalling that Tirtawiguna had passed away and could therefore no longer pose a threat to the returning exile, his mind was gripped by memories and new worry, and he quickly returned to the subject. He cast sidelong glances at the grandson, his features – a curved backside and bulging eyes – reminiscent of the elder Tirtawiguna, and raised the topic with Adipati Mangkupraja. Finally, Pangéran Juru is described as sitting in the *pendhapa* with a group of court nobles, some of whom he had known in his pre-exile days, and they converse and reminisce.[16] He then shares with them his reaction upon seeing Tirtawiguna's grandson. Again, as in the earlier passage, both physical and emotional aspects of the experience are noted: Pangéran Juru turned suddenly pale with surprise (*biyas*), he felt faint like one who had labored for an entire year (*alumipun kadi wong berah setahun*) recalling the tragedy of old. With no prior warning, emerging from an intuition of the heart, his emotional state shifted when he saw the grandson, and he felt as if he was still living in that distant moment, fearful that it would repeat itself and that he would again be the target of ill wishes. Upon hearing his account, all present laughed out loud (*gumuyu, gumer*), as Tirtawiguna was long gone and Pangéran Juru had no reason to fear. The *Babad* makes it clear, by its threefold depiction of Juru's apprehension, how significant a moment this was. Although for all others at court Tirtawiguna and his manipulations of power were a thing of the past, for the recently returned Juru time had in some ways stood still while he was banished, and he felt as if it was resuming from the point when it had left off. The trauma of Tirtawiguna's impact on his fate felt entirely fresh and the memories ignited caused him deeply visceral terror of disastrous repetition, showing how vulnerable he remained, how deeply wounded he was by the memory of pre-exile politics and power struggles and their impact on his life.

In addition to revealing his own memories as related to exile and return, Pangéran Juru also depicted the lives of other Javanese exiles in

---

[14] On Sunan Kuning, a grandson of the exiled Amangkurat III, see below.
[15] Ricklefs, *Seen and Unseen*, 306–307.
[16] This section is based on Yasadipura I, *Serat Babad Prayut*, MN 211 TT, 3–5, in Pucung.

Ceylon. Beyond the "Tirtawiguna scene," the *Babad Prayut* recounts a conversation of the returned Pangéran Juru with officials and courtiers in the Yogyakarta court which turned to several princes who had been exiled to Ceylon.[17] The princes – Danupaya, Adinagara, Ngabèhi and Arya Mataram – were brothers of Mangkubumi, later Sultan Hameng-kubuwana I, in whose palace Juru was now discussing their plight.[18] They were turned over to the Dutch to be exiled to Ceylon by their nephew Pakubuwana III on the occasion of his ascension to the throne in 1749.[19] According to the *Babad Giyanti*, one reason for their exile was the transfer of land they owned into Dutch hands.[20] Contemporary Dutch records mention six princes who were arrested and exiled at the time, the only princes who remained in Pakubuwana's palace after his succession rather than joining the followers of his rebelling brother Mangkubumi.[21]

In Ceylon, the *Babad Sultan Mangkubumi* reports, the princes mixed with the commoners (*awor lan kawula alit*), an erasure of class boundar-ies that crushed their hearts with grief. Upon arriving in Ceylon their faces were wan and pinched-looking, as if after a long illness, and they felt remorse for having been captured, thinking of how, had they followed Mangkubumi, they would not be facing death in a foreign land.[22] Once in Ceylon their lives were miserable. The *Babad* narrates further how they were constantly ridiculed throughout their time there, listing several reasons. For one, they were not dressed properly and did not carry a keris (*bedhugul*), as would be expected of men of their status; they went bald, looking like Buddhists or slaves (*wong buda*), incapable of doing anything.[23] Again their outer appearance is noted (*baligung*, shirtless), as are their illiteracy (*nora weruh alip bengkung*) and the way they were made

---

[17] Ibid., 2, in Pucung. A very similar scene, at times at the word level, appears in Yasadipura I, *Babad Prayut*, Surakarta: Reksapustaka Library, Kadipatèn Mangkunagaran, composed late eighteenth century, inscribed 1854, MS MN 212, transcribed as MN 212 TT by Suroso, 1980. Because of missing and unclear words in the two texts, I draw on both accounts to make sense of the events described. One source of confusion is the inconsistency regarding the princes' names.

[18] In the *Babad Prayut*, MN 212 TT, only three princes are mentioned, and their names are Danupaya, Adiwijaya and Adisurya (Yasadipura I, *Babad Prayut*, MN 211 TT, 2, in Pucung).

[19] Ricklefs, *Jogjakarta under Sultan Mangkubumi*, 102.

[20] *Babad Giyanti* (BU), 4: 3–15, in Dhandhanggula.

[21] The Dutch documents are discussed in Ricklefs, *Jogjakarta under Sultan Mangkubumi*, 56–57.

[22] Yasadipura I, *Babad Prayut*, MN 211 TT, 2, in Pucung.

[23] In terms of dress, Javanese batik textiles were likely important in this context: The colors, patterns and modes of tying the cloth revealed genealogy and rank. Without their batiks, one of the princes' major status indicators was missing.

the laughing stock of many who asked incredulously if these were the sons of a Balinese king, perhaps, rather than the Muslim sons of the king of Mataram. Lacking respect, ridiculed and deeply grieving for the length of their time in exile, the three princes passed away in Ceylon.[24]

This depiction, although brief, invites the *Babad*'s audience to imagine certain aspects of the princes' life in Ceylon vividly while neglecting to mention others. Nothing is said of their journey by sea (although their pale faces upon arrival may tell that story), of their whereabouts or deeds while in exile, nor of their families and the "little people" they encountered. What does come through with force is the humiliation of lives which recall those of fish out of water: sons of the Mataram dynasty who have no proper batik garments nor kerisses and who, whether because of living conditions, lack of guidance or the unavailability of elders and teachers, have not reached or maintained the level of etiquette and cultural and religious literacy expected of them, so much so that they were constantly ridiculed by others. This latter aspect of their lives hints also at the ways in which exile upended the known social order and created unexpected interactions across classes.

The picture emerging from portrayals of exilic life so far emphasizes moments of difficulty, awkwardness and a lost or diminished sense of self. Juru's depiction of his challenging attempts at reintegration into court life, taken together with the account of the Javanese princes' misery in Ceylon, due in part to their loss of status and the absence of the social structures that upheld their rank, including the accepted boundaries between court members and commoners in terms of dress, etiquette, language and access to particular forms of knowledge and ritual, shed light on the grave difficulties faced by high-status exiles and returnees.

A different perspective emerges from a section of the *Babad Giyanti* that stresses the exiles' longing and desire for the often-elusive familiar yet contains a portrayal that is, on the whole, positive: It recalls networks of study and prayer, close relationships among Muslims from diverse backgrounds, and the comfort found in gatherings and food. It is none other than Pangéran Juru's wife whose recollections give the impression that, although exile posed challenges, those living in Ceylon were able to

---

[24] A form of the verb *ngguyu* (to laugh, ridicule, joke) appears in each of the three verses preceding the report of the princes' death. The names of the three princes only partly match the names given at the beginning of the account. The three said to have died in exile were Pangéran Danupaya, Pangéran Adinagara, and Pangéran Arya Mantaram (Yasadipura I, *Babad Prayut*, MN 211 TT, 2, in Pucung). Since more than three Javanese princes were exiled to Ceylon during this period, there may be some confusion in the source or, in describing the princes' plight, it may be speaking more broadly than about any particular three.

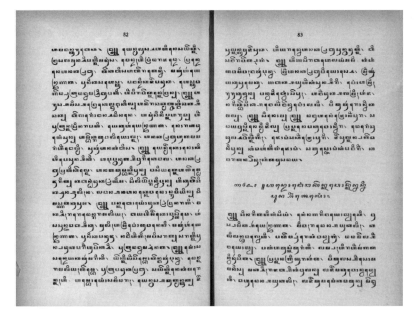

Figure 5.1 *Babad Giyanti* (Bale Pustaka, 1937), 83. The heading reads "Narrating circumstances in Ceylon"

counter them with solidarity, faith and special blessings, and that these in turn may have even prepared a man like Pangéran Juru for his new role as esteemed court official. These recollections also shine a light on gendered aspects of exilic narratives (see Figure 5.1).

In an atypical, detailed and insightful account, the *Babad Giyanti* recalls the exiles' lives in Ceylon by way of a female voice. The speaker is the wife of Pangéran Juru, Radèn Ayu Juru, while on a visit to Pakubuwana III, ruler of Surakarta, whose late mother Ratu Kencana was Radèn Ayu Juru's sister, and whose father Pakubuwana II had sent her and her husband Pangéran Juru into exile. She is accompanied by another aunt of the king, Radèn Ayu Kulon, whose husband Pangéran Purbaya (formerly Urawan) was also a sibling of Ratu Kencana and Radèn Ayu Juru, exiled in 1738 following a demand by the VOC. Stated differently, Pakubuwana II had exiled his wife's brother and sister, as well as his brother-in-law and sister-in-law, to Ceylon and now the two returned women were visiting their nephew, Pakubuwana III, who had succeeded his father.[25] The familial terms *bibi* (aunt) and *éyang* (grandmother) are employed throughout for the women. The female voice

[25] This section is based on Yasadipura I, *Babad Giyanti* (BP), 21: 83–87, in Sinom.

speaking is personal, emphasizing small moments of sadness and resilience, relationships, and the powers of the unseen. As the long-parted relatives met,

> With open arms they embraced, weeping,
> They never imagined they would reunite.
> It felt like they were dreaming,
> Long they all wept.[26]

The body language and sounds of the moment come through, as does the silencing of words at this emotional and unexpected reunion. The women then enter the palace, and the king greets them in an overly deferential way, an act that elicits their protest, insisting that a king should show such respect only to one of equal status – i.e. another ruler – and therefore only his queen, Ratu Kencana, paid her respects (*ngabekti*). This brief mention of etiquette transgressed shows both the king's emotional state at seeing his two long-lost aunts and their own awareness of the rules, quite different from Pangéran Juru's confused state at court, despite a lengthy absence from Java. Following the greetings, food is brought in and they dine together. Sitting comfortably after the meal, with snacks served, the stage is set for recollections and stories to be shared with relatives for whom Ceylon was a distant and unknown reality.

Radèn Ayu Juru portrays the Ceylon experiences of the two couples: Pangéran Purbaya (referred to as *kakèk*, grandfather) and his wife, referred to as *éyang* (grandmother) Kulon, Pangéran Juru (referred to as *paman*, uncle) and herself (referred to as "bibi," aunt). She includes no "objective" indications illuminating where on the island the exiles lived, what conditions they endured, what their surroundings were like. The emphasis of the passage is on the emergence of a group of disciples convening around the charismatic Islamic teacher, Sayid Musa Ngidrus, whom they encountered, by God's grace, three months after arriving in Ceylon. He is depicted as a true holy man, able to work wonders (*karamat sayekti*), a true descendant of the Prophet (*satuhu sayid*) and a man close to God (*auliya*), whose powers were such that anything at all he wished for materialized. Entering his circle of disciples, the exiles' pain and sadness were dispelled. After some time Purbaya and Juru became the guru's most senior disciples, a position that must have accorded them respect and a sense of fulfillment. As Sayid Musa refused to receive the many gifts brought to him by his followers, the two

---

[26] *Ngebyaki ngrangkul karuna/tan andipé yèn papanggih/kadya ciptané supena/adangu karuna sami* (ibid., 84).

Javanese exiles handled his affairs and accepted the gifts and other tokens of respect on his behalf, becoming known to many.

The *Babad Giyanti*'s depiction offers a glimpse of the religiously inspired contacts and relationships that must have been significant to the exiles in their attempts to overcome the many challenges they faced. In part, this was achieved by joining particular circles of disciples and thus also building and maintaining ties to larger devotional and intellectual networks in Ceylon and beyond.[27] Sayid Musa is depicted as attracting a very large and diverse crowd of disciples, numbering in the thousands, including ship's captains from Surat and Selangor, Bengal and Hyderabad. The recurring mention of captains and seafarers highlights Ceylon's location as a crossroads within the Indian Ocean and the reliance of travelers on religious networks and the blessings of teachers along the routes of their long and often risky journeys.

The passage offers a depiction of gatherings in which the exiles took part: Every Friday night the disciples (*murid*) would convene to recite the Qur'an. The crowd was so large that no fewer than fifteen goats had to be slaughtered to accommodate all those present, a task undertaken by Bibi Juru and likely some of the other women. The gathering took place every week and, with God's compassion, food was plentiful, surpassing what the exiles used to have in Surakarta.

Besides dwelling on the community's religious functions, the text emphasizes the difficult emotional state of exilic life and how men of special powers and vision ably assisted those afflicted with homesickness and longing. Having noticed one day that Purbaya seemed deeply dejected, Ibrahim Asmara, another guru of clear insight and a fellow Javanese who was related to the exiles, turned to him and asked about his favorite food while still back home in Java.[28] The question itself brought a smile to Purbaya's lips, and he replied immediately:

> Fish, tempé – that's what I miss,
> Yes, and the fruits:
> Salak, durian and pundhung,
> Jackfruit, malinjo, potatoes
> Every Friday appeared
> Emerging from the [guru's] jubbah.[29]

---

[27] The emergence of such religious networks was often an unintended result of banishment as far as the Dutch were concerned. On the case of exiles from Indonesia contributing to Islam's spread at the Cape of Good Hope, see Ward, *Networks of Empire*, 20.

[28] *Dinangu kadoyanira/kala wonten Tanah Jawi* (Yasadipura I, *Babad Giyanti* [BP], 85, in Sinom).

[29] *Ulam tempé dèn kangeni/lawan woh wohan nenggih/salak durèn lawan pundhung/nongka malinjo kenthang/ing saben Jumuwah prapti/wedalipun saking ing rasukan jubbah* (ibid.).

From that day onward fruit and other Javanese delicacies, including freshly produced tempeh, arrived in Ceylon from Surakarta every Friday, healing the disciple's heart, thanks to the guru's special powers, expressed through his ability to transport the foods, his keen understanding of his disciples' psychological needs, and his compassion. The desire for certain flavors, smells, textures and sensations depicted in Radèn Ayu Juru's narrative of Purbaya's encounter with Ibrahim Asmara combines a concrete form of longing for the familiar – the basic, everyday fruits and dishes that were unavailable in a foreign land – and a broader longing for all those known objects, people, places, traditions and habits that became inaccessible in exile and that one could not trust would one day be attainable again.[30]

Meanwhile in Surakarta, the tempeh seller, whose livelihood depended on his profits, found that every Friday night six bundles of fresh tempeh which he left outside his door would disappear without explanation, creating an illusion of loss and disadvantage. However, the text claims, appearances are often deceiving: The man found money hidden under his mat every week, compensating for the missing tempeh, and he told his prying neighbors that in the past he had supplied Purbaya with tempeh daily and that he was certain those whisking the tempeh away were spirits (*jim*), commissioned by this client, the now exiled Purbaya in faraway Ceylon.

Upon hearing the recollections of these events, as related to him years later, the Sunan of Surakarta was filled with awe. His brief words, uttered as if lost in thought, on how astonishing was the "walis' *keramat*," referred to the gurus in distant Ceylon but encompassed them within the Javanese wali tradition with its resounding cultural echoes. As was shown in Chapter 3, fragments of the wali sanga tradition found their way to Ceylon and circulated there, while in this instance a ruler in Java projected his knowledge of local tradition on the exilic community, both

---

Ulam is ambiguous as it can refer to meat, fish or side dishes eaten with rice. However, since in a previous section in the story the Friday meal of goat meat enjoyed by the disciples is mentioned, I am assuming that it is a longing for fish which is expressed here. This particular scene does not appear in several additional *Babad Giyanti* versions consulted.

[30] As recent studies have shown, exploring material belongings opens a window to understanding their owners' forms of belonging. For an example that centers on inventories of possessions of deceased Indonesian slaves in the eighteenth century, see Jean Gelman Taylor, "Belongings and Belonging: Indonesian Histories in Inventories from the Cape of Good Hope," in Ricci (ed.), *Exile in Colonial Asia*, 165–192. Another example of longing for familiar scents and flavors is found in a letter written on December 31, 1725, by Pangéran Purbaya in Ceylon to his wife Ratu Purbaya in Batavia, asking her to send him various kinds of oils as well as *ketjap* (soy sauce) and Javanese tamarind: NL-Ha.Na, VOC, 1.04.02 inv. nr. 8942, 1227.

cases highlighting the interconnectedness of Ceylon and Java as nodes in a "hagiographic geography."[31] This ability of the "Ceylon walis" to perform wonders, concluded the Sunan, constituted God's retribution on behalf of Pangéran Purbaya and Pangéran Juru, suggesting a divine justice at work and the extension of the walis' protective powers beyond the physical limits of Java.[32]

These emotional aspects of exilic life, both personal and collective, depicted in a brief passage of a Javanese historical chronicle, provide a glimpse of the human face of exile and return: disbelief and joy at reuniting with relatives; the longing for the familiar and its power to comfort and heal; the importance of Qur'anic recitations, Friday gatherings and devotion to teachers blessed with special powers to sustain those living in exile and unsure of their prospects of returning home. Mention of Sayid Musa's knowledge of curing pain and sadness (J. *mulihken lara prihatin*) weaves together these thematic threads of an individual's challenges and the solace found in leadership and community. The passage also evokes the intertwined experiences and histories of the exiles, the many other Muslim individuals who crossed their paths in Ceylon, and the relatives who remained on Java but listened to the tales, perhaps drawing lessons from them and trying to imagine what life was like on that island which lay across the sea from their own.

In recounting their lives in exile, the women conjure images of mundane yet deeply significant moments. Their tone is personal, even intimate. Retelling one's life story is always shaped by particular circumstances past and present, agendas, selected memories, yearnings and regrets. The way the *Babad*'s author conveyed these particular accounts emphasized how the women framed their biographies in terms of their, and their husbands', attempts to find meaning in their exilic lives through a sense of community, an attachment to particular individuals endowed with magical powers and possessing a capacity to control events within a context that was far beyond the command of the now-powerless exiles, and a devotion to a religious tradition that connected them to many others passing through Ceylon or residing there. The accounts accentuate relationships: each woman as part of a couple, experiencing exilic life and its tribulations with a partner; their familial and close relationship to each other as sisters-in-law facing challenges in a foreign land; encountering Ibrahim Asmara who turned out to be of shared ancestry; the ties

---

[31] Elsner, "Hagiographic Geography," 28.

[32] *Lamun karamat ing wali/walaltullah ing kaki miwah ing paman* (Yasadipura I, *Babad Giyanti* [BP], 21: 86, in Sinom). There appears to be an error in the phrase *walaltullah*. I take its initial part to mean *walat* (J. heaven-sent retribution).

to the admired guru, the involvement in the group of disciples, conveying the impression that these bonds were crucially important to their ability to face adversity, remain hopeful and perhaps even survive. The emphasis on the ample quantities of food, so much so that it was "as plentiful as rubbish," and on the gifts and donations piling up in honor of Sayid Musa, stands in stark contrast to the reports typical of the Dutch colonial archive from Ceylon, in which petitions and pleas for sustenance sent by exiles are abundant. This trope points to a path of overcoming difficult economic circumstances and a dependence on the Europeans who exiled them by maintaining strength and self-respect through the devotional and the miraculous, a theme that is common to the portrayal and imaginings of subaltern exilic existence.

The women's participation in communal events comes through in the depiction of their responsibility for the large feasts that followed the Friday Qur'anic recitations. Someone had to cook and prepare those copious amounts of food served to the thousands who gathered to recite, pray and receive blessings, and the women rose to the challenge. Thus, they were active members of the community with a particular role that was central to the religious circle's thriving. The comments on the tempeh seller back in Surakarta, and the insistence on providing an explanation showing that justice prevailed and that the exiles' joy at receiving the Javanese food they craved did not occur at the expense of a man among whose clients they used to count themselves, highlight their awareness of others and prevent the story they told from seeming biased, unjust or arbitrary.

And it was women, whose recorded voices on exile are even scarcer than men's, who emphasized these webs of friendship and family, the personal, the details of yearning, anguish, compassion and piety. They located food in its various forms – cooked, served, distributed, longed for, conjured, missing, in abundance, replaced, freshly made, emerging from the guru's sleeve as if almost one with his body – as a central trope that connected home and exile, familiar and foreign, bridging the two places and states of mind. These particular emphases emerge especially clearly when read side by side with the depicted conversation between Patih Danureja and Pangéran Arya Mangkunagara on the ship taking them into exile: In that exchange between two men, who like Bibi Juru and Éyang Kulon were members of the Kartasura court, it was martial courage and dynastic politics that took center stage. The two scenes portraying Javanese exiles – men sailing toward Ceylon, women who left it behind – are however also linked, both providing images of fundamental sustenance: The women's images are of food as offering physical, spiritual and psychological comfort, as well as a link and bond with the past, loved ones, and one's identity. Food was a sign of the guru's, and of God's, benevolence and powers, His perpetual care for the believers. Danureja's prophecy was expressed in more narrow political terms as it posited Pangéran Arya's brother and son as future rulers, yet he equated the two to food – a basic necessity and means to survival and prosperity – and to shelter. His proposed image was not of wali or learned guru as leader but of political rulers who in their ability to serve as their people's sustenance and refuge revealed a spiritual dimension also considered essential to Javanese kingship.

Another revealing example of a woman's exilic journeys and the way they were recounted and remembered in Javanese chronicles highlights once more, as seen in Chapter 4, the theme of how contesting and competing claims to the throne of Mataram continued to play out in biographies of exile and return. The return of Amangkurat III's body along with the pusakas and the late king's sons and extended family in 1737, depicted in the *Babad Kartasura*, did not signal their final appearance in the pages of Javanese history, and the history of exile in particular. It appears that ongoing claims to the throne by Amangkurat's descendants, whose pretensions to royal legitimacy seem to have survived Pakubuwana I's usurpation of the throne in 1705 and the many years of exile in Ceylon, or at least anxieties regarding such claims or hopes, continued to haunt the Kartasura court.[33] A glimpse of these tensions becomes evident by following the trajectory of Tepasana (previously known as Pakuningrat), one of the returned *Pangéran Sélong* ("Ceylon Princes"), sons of Amangkurat III, and his family. And, to continue the gendered exploration, especially the life of his daughter, best known by her title *Putri Sélong* ("Ceylon Princess").

Tepasana, son of the banished king Amangkurat III, had five children, likely all born in Ceylon, who traveled to Java with their family when their grandfather's body was sent back for burial in Imogiri.[34] The eldest son, Radèn Wiratmeja, had a *selir* (minor wife of royalty) in Ceylon and married Pakubuwana's daughter Ratu Alit. After his own father was murdered by his father-in-law Pakubuwana III, Radèn Wiratmeja found refuge with the Chinese but was soon turned over to the Javanese troops and killed.[35] The second child was a daughter, Radèn Ajeng Banowati, on whom more below. Another daughter, the third child, Radèn Ayu

---

[33] The *Surakarta Major Babad* narrates forewarnings of such claims upon the throne at the time; see Ricklefs, *Seen and Unseen*, 237–238.
[34] This section is based on an untitled *Babad*, inscribed Semarang, 1834, John Rylands Collection, University of Manchester Library, MS Javanese 18.
[35] Ricklefs, *Seen and Unseen*, 251–252.

Sumilah, was married to the king in 1738 and later divorced. The fourth, another girl, married Pangéran Buminata. The youngest child, Radèn Mas Garendi, was kept alive by the Chinese and crowned as their king in a short-lived attempt to rule over Kartasura, receiving the title Sunan Kuning, the "Yellow Sunan." It was he, as well as his sister Radèn Ajeng Banowati, who continued to feature in the ongoing story of eighteenth-century exiles and returns between Java and Ceylon.

The *Babad Tanah Jawi* also discusses the five offspring of the family and offers expanded detail: The eldest son Wiratmeja was handsome and wanted by the king for his daughter, Ratu Alit, likely in order to cement the loyalty of Amangkurat III's descendants to the ruler of Kartasura.[36] Ratu Alit was still very young while Wiratmeja was older, and so he waited for her. His sister Radèn Ajeng Banowati had married earlier in Ceylon. According to the *Babad* she was given to the son of one Wirakabluk, a close acquaintance of her grandfather, the "Banished Sunan" (Sunan Kendhang, Amangkurat III). The son Anggakusuma was very ugly, perhaps even deformed, and the couple was mismatched in looks, yet Radèn Ajeng Banowati dutifully followed him. However, when back in Java she met the handsome Puspadirja, younger brother of the deposed Tumenggung Puspanagara of Batang, and Tepasana permitted their marriage, which resulted in two sons and a daughter.[37] Heartbroken and unable to eat or sleep, the grieving Anggakusuma wished misfortune upon his former wife and her new husband.

Whether in response to his prayers or for other reasons, disaster soon struck. Radèn Ajeng Banowati, known in the Javanese sources as Putri Sélong, lost her husband and father within the span of four days. Puspadirja and his brothers Puspanagara and Jayakusuma were publicly executed on July 6, 1741, their heads displayed in the market and their bodies tossed into the river. Dutch officials believed they were murdered for passing court secrets to the VOC as Tepasana's emissaries. Tepasana and his brother Jayakusuma (formerly known as Radèn Mas Kasdu) swore innocence to Patih Natakusuma, but Pakubuwana II ordered them to the palace to swear accordingly in his presence. Suspected of treason, they were murdered that night, July 10.[38] The *Babad Kraton* claims Tepasana hoped to capture the throne for himself and revealed court secrets to Kartasura's Dutch commander Johannes van Velsen, using his son-in-law Puspadirja and his brothers as messengers. The *Babad* also asserts that Pakubuwana II's decision to go to war with the Company in

---

[36] *Babad Tanah Jawi* (BP), 21:75, in Mijil.   [37] Ibid., 76–77.

[38] The Dutch sources documenting these events are meticulously covered in Ricklefs, *Seen and Unseen*, 250.

July 1741 arose from fear of an alliance between Amangkurat III's descendants and the Chinese if he failed to join the anti-VOC cause.[39]

Such an alliance, although very short-lived, did in fact transpire. Upon learning of the murders of Tepasana and Jayakusuma, their brother Wiramenggala (formerly Pangéran Mangkunagara) fled with other members of Amangkurat III's family, including Tepasana's two sons, and took refuge with Chinese forces near Semarang. The latter soon turned Wiramenggala and Tepasana's older son over to the Javanese troops to be killed but protected the younger son, Radèn Mas Garendi, who was only twelve at the time (so a small child when he left Ceylon), and in early 1742 proclaimed him the new Susuhunan with the name Amangkurat.[40] He was even given the title Mangkurat Mas, by which his grandfather Amangkurat III was posthumously known. The young king was popularly known as Sunan Kuning, the "Yellow Sunan,"[41] and Sunan Alit, the "Little King." On June 30, 1742, Pakubuwana II abandoned his palace to the Chinese, and Sunan Kuning occupied the crown prince's residence and led the plundering of the court for three days. These events and their narration and interpretation in the babads and Dutch contemporary sources indicate that almost three decades spent in Ceylon had not eradicated the Amangkurat line's sense of entitlement to power over central Java.

Tepasana's daughter Putri Sélong would soon follow her brother Sunan Kuning back to Ceylon when he was exiled in 1743 due to his involvement in the Chinese War. There she met with a son of the late Pangéran Arya Mangkunagara and brother of Mas Said (Mangkunagara I), Pangéran Pancuran (also known as Pangéran Kartakusuma or Tirtakusuma).[42] This marriage between a granddaughter of an exiled king and son of an exiled prince (a great-great-grandnephew of that same king), both from the Mataram dynasty, signaled the potential for continuity of the deposed line, and offers evidence of the ongoing importance of royal marital politics in exile.[43]

---

[39] For a detailed study of this war, see Willem G. J. Remmelink, *The Chinese War and the Collapse of the Javanese State 1725–1743* (Leiden: KITLV, 1994).

[40] Ricklefs, *Seen and Unseen*, 265.

[41] This title may hint at his connection to the Chinese or indicate "light," "fair," as referring to skin.

[42] Hatmowasito, *Babad Giyanti dumugi Prayut*, MN 693 (c), 388.

[43] As Peter Carey and Vincent Houben show, despite Javanese court women's vital importance to ceremonial, military and financial affairs in the pre-Java War period, their main functions were domestic and procreative; see Carey and Houben, "Spirited Srikandhis and Sly Sumbadras: The Social, Political and Economic Role of Women at the Central Javanese Courts in the Eighteenth and Early Nineteenth Centuries," in Elsbeth Locher-Scholten and Anke Borkent-Niehof (eds.), *Indonesian Women in Focus:*

Putri Sélong's biography and its depiction within Javanese chronicles did not end at that. Her third husband Pangéran Pancuran also passed away and his body was sent back from Ceylon to Semarang in 1753, in what appears to have been a bureaucratic error on the part of the Dutch authorities in Colombo, who were asked to return Pangéran Purbaya's body but instead sent Pancuran's along with that of his late father Pangéran Arya Mangkunagara.[44] Now back yet again in Java, the sources depict Putri Sélong's fourth marriage, the circumstances of which were dramatic even within a turbulent biography such as her own.

The man she would marry, Raja Darab, is depicted as a former criminal from Banyumas who escaped to the village of Botobabad where a local kyai took pity on him and taught him the science of *padhukunan* (healing, indigenous medicine, black magic). He attained special powers (*sakti*) and was able to cure any sickness, but soon used the skills gained for less benevolent aims as well. The *Babad* depicts the sultan of Yogyakarta warning the Dutch in Semarang against an impending attack by "the man of sakti" Raja Darab Maulana Maghribi and indeed, when he entered battle, it was by way of the miraculous (*mujijat*), bringing about a storm with heavy rains upon the Company troops whose weapons attempted retaliation with a rain of bullets. In the competition between the two "downpours," the one caused by Raja Darab steadily increased, bringing about the death of the Company's captain and many of the soldiers.[45]

One day, after losing her husband Pangéran Pancuran, Putri Sélong entered the Ketangi River region with her son by Puspadirja, Radèn Bagus Bening, where they were apprehended by an "enemy," Panembahan Kowok, who was none other than Raja Darab. Not wishing to put herself in harm's way, Putri did not resist.[46] Her son, too, followed the

---

Past and Present Notions (Leiden: KITLV, 1987), 25. As much as circumstances permitted, this dynastic emphasis seems to have been maintained in exile. The *Babad Prayut* (MN 212 TT, 148, in Dhandhanggula) notes explicitly that following their marriage no son was born to Putri Sélong and Pangéran Pancuran despite a long time passing. This may indicate the hope for a son who would be descended from Mataram on both his paternal and maternal sides. Another example of marital politics among the Ceylon exiles was the marriage of the crown prince of Banten, who was exiled in 1747 due to internal conflict at court under the rule of his uncle Sultan Mustapa, returned by the Dutch in 1752 and crowned in 1753. While in Ceylon he married Den Ajeng Tambur, daughter of Adipati Natakusuma (later Pangéran Juru); see Yasadipura I, *Babad Giyanti* (BP), 9: 42, in Gambuh.

[44] For the administrative mix-up, see Ricklefs, *Soul Catcher*, 133.
[45] Hatmowasito, *Babad Giyanti dumugi Prayut*, MN 693 (a), 11–12.
[46] This section is based on Hatmowasito, *Babad Giyanti dumugi Prayut*, MN 693 (c), 388–396, complemented by Hatmowasito, *Babad Giyanti dumugi Prayut*, MN 693 (a) 11–13.

Panembahan, was adopted as his son and was given the name Radèn Arya Jayapuspita. Panembahan Kowok was strongly attracted to Purti Sélong, whose beauty and grace are depicted in detail: The myrtle green pattern of her batik, her sash with its delicate flowers and her matching earrings all made her a joy to behold, and "when compared with the young maidens of Java, this woman still captivated the heart."[47] The Panembahan desired Putri but was for a while reluctant to approach her, perhaps because of her status or well-known past. He ultimately dispatched a pair of messengers who went to speak with her daily, until in time she agreed and the two were married. The celebrations lasted for a week, with 26 cows, 50 goats, and 400 ducks and chickens slaughtered for the occasion and gamelan music playing throughout. Then the couple entered their chambers and did not emerge for four days and nights.

On the fifth day, Radèn Bagus Bening was called in. After praising her new husband's sexual prowess, Putri told her son to view Raja Darab not as an adopted father but as his genuine one. She spoke of genealogy and kingship, telling her son that he was a scion (a great-grandson) of Sunan Amangkurat through her own bloodline but also of noble descent on his new father's side, since the latter was heir to the legendary Ciyung Wanara.[48] Therefore, she claimed, Radèn Bagus Bening possessed the right to rule Java as king, adding that he should seek instruction from Raja Darab as his guru, emphasizing the sexual nature of the teachings which were inseparably linked with the ability to gain power, maintain legitimacy and guarantee continuity of the lineage as a Javanese ruler. Although the lessons would be taught by watching his mother and her husband practicing acts of love, she chided the son for seeming reluctant, or shy, emphasizing the centrality of this form of knowledge while Raja Darab chimed in: "In the future, son, when you rule as king and boast a hundred wives, you must still be a lover [to them all]. That is what kingship is about."[49]

Not long after, Radèn Bening, "as if possessed by Setan," revealed to his mother that he wished to be instructed directly by her.[50] Attempting at first to refuse, saying he was her own son and she his guru's wife, with Raja Darab's support she eventually relented and the three practiced forms of love making together. Then Raja Darab appeared before a large gathering and announced he was anointing himself ruler of Kartasura,

[47] Hatmowasito, *Babad Giyanti dumugi Prayut*, MN 693 (c), 389.
[48] Ciyung Wanara was one of two competing brothers who ruled Java according to a Sundanese legend that explains the origin of the relationship between the Javanese and Sundanese.
[49] Hatmowasito, *Babad Giyanti dumugi Prayut*, MN 693 (c), 392.   [50] Ibid., 393.

taking the title of the founder of the Mataram dynasty in the sixteenth century, Senopati ing Alaga. He also declared his adopted son crown prince (*Adipati Anom*), and all those present paid their respects. Meanwhile the ongoing threat stemming from Raja Darab's powers, coupled with word of his actions, moved the local Penghulu, Lepen Katangi, and Pangéran Kadilangu to conspire against his ability to cast spells which assured his victory in battle. The Penghulu prepared some food into which he mixed a certain ingredient supplied by Pangéran Wijil, a descendant of Sunan Kalijaga, and the food was consumed by Darab. The ensuing battle unfolded in a downpour, coming full circle to the earlier attack when Raja Darab's *sakti* had brought deluge and defeat. This time, the *Serat* claims, it was the pusaka of Demak whose potency caused the rain and paved the way to Raja Darab's utter failure, death and decapitation. Soon after, Radèn Bening and Putri Sélong were discovered in their bed, and were tied up and taken to Semarang where the son, too, was decapitated and his head displayed beside that of his adopted father. The mother's fate was not recorded.

The details of Putri Sélong's biography salvaged from the babads are enlightening for several reasons. Her 1737 arrival in Java did not constitute the same type of return as experienced by many of her older relatives and family retinue members. As she had been born in Ceylon, raised there during her early years, and married there, hers was not a personal homecoming but more of a symbolic one, as a granddaughter of a deposed king. Consequently, following her brother Sunan Kuning to Ceylon several years later signaled a return to the land of her birth, complicating the notion of exile and blurring the lines between banishment, return and perceptions of "home" and belonging. Her story and even more so that of her brother, the young Sunan, attest to the ongoing tensions regarding the loyalty or lack thereof of the Amangkurat line toward the reigning king in Kartasura and the deepening involvement of the Dutch in local and familial Javanese politics. It shows that Ceylon remained an important site in which this and other power struggles were resolved, overcome, or at least pushed out of sight. No less important, this brief, fragmented biography offers a rare perspective on a female figure whose life was entangled in a history of exiles and returns.

Radèn Ajeng Banowati (who during her marriages was known as Radèn Ayu Puspadirja and later as Radèn Ayu Pancuran), alias Putri Sélong, appears in the chronicles more often without her given name than with it.[51]

---

[51] For example, the *Babad Tanah Jawi* notes both, while *Babad Prayut* refers to her only as Putri Sélong (MN 212 TT), as does Hatmowasito, *Babad Giyanti dumugi Prayut*, MN 693 (c).

The repeated references to Putri Sélong may demonstrate that she was well known and no further indication of her identity was needed; that she spent significant portions of her life in Ceylon and was associated with that country; and that there was no doubt regarding her status as princess, daughter of a "Ceylon Prince," and the high rank into which she was born and which was retained despite the family's history of banishment, humiliation and loss. Her own voice does not for the most part come through in the chronicles; rather, her life is told by way of her relationships to the men around her: First, she was a granddaughter of Java's banished king who gave her in marriage to his trusted advisor's son; then she was the daughter of a prince who may have sought to regain the throne, and who was murdered in cold blood in the dead of night at the court once ruled by his father; she was the obedient wife of a man who must have been a clear mismatch for her, whom she later left for another with her father's consent; she was a woman whose father allegedly sent her husband into harm's way, resulting in his death; she remarried a third man whose father, a prominent prince, was exiled from the Kartasura court by the devious Danureja; she was a mother of three children; she was wife to an ex-criminal who gained miraculous and destructive powers, and who encouraged her to form a sexual bond with her son; and she was a sister who accompanied her brother in exile.

In many of these roles, Putri Sélong paid a distinctly painful price. And even if all that remains are tantalizing hints of the person she was, or more precisely of the way she was represented, these hints suggest a woman whose turbulent life she endured with fortitude. Having left her homeland at a young age, crossed the Indian Ocean three times by ship – from Ceylon to Java, back to Ceylon, and again to Java – she remained beautiful, graceful and resourceful. This was not an obvious depiction considering all she had been through – exile, travels, deaths, murders and heartache. What is clear is that her biography exemplified the ongoing tensions and aspirations related to legitimate kingship in central Java despite recurring exiles: granddaughter of a king, daughter of a prince, sister of a boy anointed as competitor to the ruler, wife of Pangéran Arya Mangkunagara's son, mother of two potential male heirs to the throne. In all these roles, she embodied the threat to the usurping line of the Kartasura and later Surakarta courts. It is most likely that when claiming power for himself, and anointing Putri's son Radèn Bening as heir to the throne, her husband Raja Darab was drawing on her lineage, creating anxiety among the ruling family, their allies and the Dutch. The decapitation of Putri Sélong's husband and son symbolized the wish to dissociate this competing lineage, this "alternative head," from the body of Javanese royal genealogy and terminate its threat once and for all.

The textual sources explored in this chapter and the preceding ones, written in Javanese and Malay (at times translated into Dutch), reveal diverse perspectives and voices related to exile to Ceylon as viewed from both shores. They display fragments of the available archive but in no way exhaust it. To the examples presented could be added many more, among them Amangkurat III's letter regarding his illness and imminent death in exile, images of Ceylon as an exilic land in the Malay *Syair Hemop* and sections of exiles' letters expressing their wishes for return. Viewing these sources' depictions of exile in a comparative light underscores some commonalities across genres, authors and languages. It appears, for example, that the great distance between the islands of Ceylon and Java, the voids of uncertainty, doubt and anxiety of exile, were countered in textual depictions by the (part concrete, part imaginary) materiality of familiar food, sacred heirlooms, corpses and stories traveling between the two sites. Similarly, states of helplessness and hopelessness brought about by banishment were offset by prophecies of future glory and power, by (sometimes posthumous) homecoming scenes, and depictions of the ongoing potency of a deposed royal line viewed as a threat to a reigning king despite formidable temporal and geographical barriers.

Status – lost, diminished, compromised, altered, gained – comes across as an important theme for members of court elites, whether banished or returned. Pangéran Juru's disorientation at court upon return and his feeling that despite his pedigree he had become a simple hick show a keen awareness of how time in exile chipped away at familiar codes of civility. Éyang Kulon's reply to Pakubuwana III when he invited her to remain in Surakarta, that she would be ridiculed as an old senseless woman, ungrateful to the sultan of Yogyakarta who had arranged for her return, demonstrates how for some the rules of engagement remained clear. Especially striking was the example of the princes mocked in Ceylon for their lost signs of rank, whether related to outward appearance or their behavior and upbringing, a question being raised by some whether they could possibly have been true sons of Mataram.

How royal exiles were treated in Ceylon was, however, a complicated and often ambiguous matter on which the available sources offer only a very partial picture. The letters exchanged between exiles in Jaffna and Trincomalee made clear that Amangkurat and his sons were facing challenges and hardship. Yet reports from Jaffna depict how those same princes and their father were treated with respect by Dutch officials with whom they maintained bonds of familiarity and even closeness. Such a relationship is noted in the travel diary of Isaac Augustine Rumpf, Governor of Ceylon (1716–1723). On December 28, 1719, Rumpf arrived in Kolombogam, not far from Jaffna, where "the Reverend Prendicants, other qualified officers and Pangarang Adipattij, along with his three sons, welcomed His Excellency."[52] The governor listed the military ranks of twenty-four men who were serving the Pangarang, i.e. Amangkurat III, indicating that although he was held captive he was honored with his own guard.[53] During Rumpf's visit, he met with Amangkurat and the princes several times. At the first meeting, on January 2, 1720, they were "welcomed warmly by His Excellency, and after some discussions they left [for] the lodge, satisfied"; at the second meeting, on January 25, Amangkurat III told the governor he needed an allowance increase to care for his growing family. He also expressed remorse for "the crimes he [had] committed against the Honorable Company and asked to be allowed to return to Batavia." This could not be allowed, replied the governor, and yet he suggested that Amangkurat and family might move to Colombo "if he did not like it here." Finally, on the 31st, the former ruler of central Java and his three sons accompanied the governor to his ship to bid him farewell.[54] These interactions recall, among others, the social dynamics between the British governor of Ceylon and the former king of Gowa in the early nineteenth century, when the latter was regularly invited to dine at the governor's residence, and show the different, sometimes contradictory dimensions of the status question as it related to royals in exile and in return.[55]

The instability of status was also evident when relationships between the exiles and European rulers were depicted, at times indirectly, as filled with potential misunderstandings. As mentioned in Chapter 3, citing the Council Minutes from 1727, Dutch anxiety levels regarding Ceylon's Muslim population, perceived as a threat, were high. Also cited was the sense of urgency regarding attaining a precise translation of Javanese letters sent secretly between exiles, the Javanese language itself

---

[52] Isaac Augustus Rumpf, *Travel Diary of Isaac Augustus Rumpf, the Dutch Governor of Ceylon (1716–1723)*, trans. and ed. K. D. Paranavitana (Colombo: Department of National Archives, Sri Lanka, 2015), 65.

[53] These included one ensign, two sergeants, three corporals, seventeen ordinary soldiers and one drummer (ibid., 68).

[54] Ibid., 72, 91 and 139 respectively. Of course, these passages record the Dutch perspective of their captive's "satisfaction." The suggestion that Amangkurat III move to Colombo did not materialize. At the other end of his journey, upon return to Colombo, Governor Rumpf was welcomed by another royal exile, Pangarang Arij Pourbaija, rebel brother of Amangkurat IV exiled in 1723 (ibid., 142).

[55] On the case of the king of Gowa, see Suryadi, "Sepucuk Surat." For similar relationships between Dutch officials and Javanese exiles at the Cape, see Ward, *Networks of Empire*, 225–227.

constituting a secret code that could not be entirely broken. The gurus and gatherings appearing in the *Babad Giyanti*, with their Islamic content, readings of the Arabic Qur'an and Javanese spiritual dimensions, suggest that, in addition to the challenges posed by the Javanese and Malay languages, these events and personalities "spoke" in a language that was incomprehensible to the Dutch authorities and that created ongoing apprehension and uncertainty about being fully in control.

The unseen pervades many of the texts, providing a framework within which exile was depicted and comprehended, comprising an element within a worldview that privileged the invisible: a set of forces that could generate success and calamity. This perception was central to Javanese court culture in the early eighteenth century, where an adherence to Java's pre-Islamic traditions along with Islamic ones emphasized "ideas of supernatural powers, of mysterious forces and magical potencies, through which unseen energies could be brought to penetrate into and shape the phenomenal world."[56] The tendency was evident in the narration of Tuan Pangéran's emergence from his Ceylon grave unscathed, fresh tempeh arriving weekly from Java, the wasilan incantations and charms, fragments of the walis' words and deeds, and the recurring mention of potent heirlooms. Yet another example was found in the final chapter of Putri Sélong's biography to be included in the chronicles, the Raja Darab episode, in which most events were formulated in magical terms: As a former criminal, Raja Darab was pitied by a kyai and taught the science of curing all illness; he used his powers to bring about supernatural rain, causing destruction and death; the scenes of his love making with Putri and Radèn Bening, his sexual prowess and claims to kingship were tied to his acquired talismanic skills; a potent ingredient added to his food caused him to lose his concentrated focus; and after he left for battle, mother and son, engrossed in their sexual practice, were unable to detach their bodies from each other until taken to an expert healer (*dhukun*), kyai Nologuna, who treated them with a special, likely supernatural, remedy. Whereas in many of the instances depicted in the exile-related texts, unseen forces were credited with offering comfort, wisdom and justice, this latter episode highlighted the dangers and risks of the magical arts, the potential consequences of their abuse in the wrong hands and the shifting fortunes of those daring to employ them.

Another framework for considering the exile of Javanese royalty to Ceylon is genealogical. The thread from Amangkurat III, the first Javanese king exiled to Ceylon, wove its way to a letter written in the early

---

[56] Ricklefs, *Seen and Unseen*, xxiv.

nineteenth century and addressed to the governor-general in Batavia by a descendant of the same royal family who still claimed special status and a connection to Java. Writing from Colombo in 1806, almost a century to the day after Amangkurat III was exiled, one of his offspring via Pangéran Arya Mangkunagara's son Mas Kreti beseeched the Dutch authorities in Batavia for protection from Ceylon's British rulers. The writer, grandson (*cucunda*) of Radèn Tumenggung Wirakushuma ibn Mas Kreti, explained at length how his grandfather (or an ancestor more generally) had fought on the side of the VOC with the rank of captain against the British attack, was sent to Madras after the Dutch defeat, then returned to Ceylon after three long years. He asked that his family's loyalty and sacrifice for the Company be remembered and that he be sent home to Java from Ceylon, which he twice referred to grimly using the Arabic phrase *dār al-ḍalālāt*, a realm of errors, aberrances or obscurity. This letter, composed in Malay rather than Javanese, can be viewed as an early sign marking the gradual transition of identity from Javanese royals to Sri Lankan Malays, but also reveals an ongoing sense of belonging to a lineage and a desire for its recognition (see Figure 5.2).[57]

Returns, when granted, were no less significant than banishments in this dynastic biography of the Mataram dynasty. Both formed elements in a temporal and spatial continuum that produced many variations on a common theme. At the continuum's edge lay returns to the grave: bodies sent back to Java from Ceylon for whom the rites performed served as rituals for the dead and the living alike, emphasizing narratives of ancestry and continuity in which those who died in exile were sometimes, but not always, included. Returning the bodies of family members and giving them a proper burial in Islamic and dynastic terms turned the dead into a pusaka of sorts which in the case of particularly powerful figures could provide keramat – a form of potency and sanctity – for surviving relatives and those who might rule in the future. The incident of Mas Said

---

[57] Letter from Cucunda Radèn Tumenggung Wira Kushuma ibn Mas Kreti to the governor-general and Council of the Indies, Colombo, 1806, Leiden University Library, MS LOr 2241-I(24). Another relevant example is found in the letter from Pangéran Mas Adipati Mangkurat, also written in Colombo in 1806 and addressed to the governor-general in Batavia, detailing the writer's family circumstances. He was married to Siti Awang, daughter of the sultan of Gowa, with five children, and had a brother and two sisters who were also married with children. All of them, in addition to their relative (M. *sanak saudara*), Baginda Susunan Kuning Mangkurat, shared an insufficient living allowance and had suffered much in Ceylon to the point they could bear it no longer (M. *tiada tertahan lagi*), and therefore requested emotionally to be returned to Batavia. As is clear from this example the names of the Amangkurat line, including Mangkurat and Susunan Kuning, were bestowed across generations in the family; see MS LOr 2241-I (23).

122   Banishment and Belonging

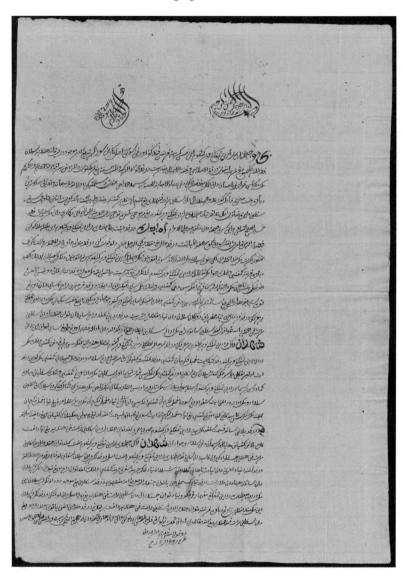

Figure 5.2 Letter from Cucunda Radèn Tumenggung Wira Kushuma ibn Mas
Kreti to the governor-general and Council of the Indies, Colombo 1806, MS LOr
2241-I(24).
Courtesy Leiden University Library

accompanying the body of his late father Pangéran Arya Mangkunagara to Imogiri is a case in point.

Others who were buried in Ceylon and were never sent home nonetheless continued to exert their power within Javanese historical memory and imagination. Here the life of Sunan Kuning may serve as illustration: A grandson of Amangkurat III (and brother of Putri Sélong), who was born in Ceylon, returned in 1737 to Java as an eight-year-old child with his family, his grandfather's remains and the missing pusakas, was then crowned as Sunan Kuning, only to rule briefly and be exiled back to Ceylon where he lived out his life. A tomb in the Malay mosque in the town of Chilaw, north of Colombo along Sri Lanka's west coast, is honored as his final resting place. Known locally as Raja Kooning, he continues, more than two and a half centuries after his death in exile, to wield his influence, blessing those who pray at his tomb.[58]

Going on pilgrimage to the tomb of a Javanese royal in Ceylon was not performed only on a local scale. On November 18, 1936, the *Ceylon Observer*, priding itself on being "the oldest newspaper in Ceylon," featured a front-page article titled "Javanese Prince Visits Ancestor's Tomb in Colombo."[59] Accompanied by a photo bearing the caption "H.H. The Sultan of Solo and his wife who were in Colombo today," the article reported how Mangkunagara VII, ruler of "one of the four native principalities of Java," joined by his queen and fifteen-year-old daughter, stopped in Ceylon en route to Princess Juliana's wedding in the Netherlands to pay his respects at the tomb of his ancestor (see Figure 5.3). The Sultan and his family visited the Peer Saib Mosque in the Pettah area, where the "father of the founder of the Sultan's dynasty is buried." The dynasty's founder was Radèn Mas Said, later known as Mangkunagara I, and his father was the exiled prince, Pangéran Arya Mangkunagara. The tomb visited was the site where, according to popular belief, a Javanese prince known as Tuan Pangéran was once interred, before he informed a relative in a dream of his wish to return to Java. The events that followed, most pertinently his emergence from the grave unscathed despite the time that had elapsed and the respectful cannon salutes offered by Dutch officials, were narrated in Chapter 3. Yet despite his posthumous return and interment at Imogiri, as known from local oral traditions and from the Javanese babads, the site visited by Mangkunagara VII was still considered potent and one possessing great significance from the lineage's point of view. This approach toward the tomb shows how the power of royals, just as that of holy men like the walis and

---

[58] Personal communication, Mr. Sadar (b. 1925), Colombo, December 2015.
[59] *Ceylon Observer*, November 18, 1936. The *Ceylon Observer* was first published in 1834.

Figure 5.3 The *Ceylon Observer* headline of November 18, 1936, announcing Mangkunagara VII's visit to Colombo.
Courtesy Department of National Archives, Sri Lanka

others – the line between prince and powerful "saint" often blurred – played an important role in the exilic culture that developed in Ceylon which drew on, and retained, elements of Javanese belief and practice. It also shows that ancestors exiled, even for many years, were not forgotten and their lives were woven into the Javanese dynasty's history which came to encompass Sélong. Tuan Pangéran's tomb, simultaneously vacant and full, and its importance as a pilgrimage site where rituals are performed and offerings made to this day, recalls at once the ephemeral and concrete, yet also symbolic and miraculous, dimensions of exilic journeys.

6 Nabi Adam: The Paradigmatic Exile

This chapter and the next are about fragments, about echoes, about the imagination – and also about prior text and its workings: how stories, words, and characters circulate and transform depending on site, religion and historical context, carrying with them their particular pasts. Within this broader phenomenon, exile provides an especially poignant arena for exploring such processes and imaginative recreations and expressions, because of its dimensions of human struggle and endurance and its often-unanticipated outcomes. Taking the foundational Muslim tradition of Adam's banishment from Paradise and his fall in Sarandib as a starting point, a tradition known from early Arab sources and widespread in Muslim Southeast Asia, this chapter explores the relevance of Adam's fall to Sarandib to colonial exile to Ceylon. How might this ancient tradition of banishment have informed experiences and memories of more recent exile?

Rather than approach this question, as well as the story and its transmission, in a linear, chronological manner, the chapter weaves its way through different periods, places and languages – early Islamic works written by Arab and Persian scholars in the tenth–twelfth centuries, a twentieth-century Malay poem from Ceylon, a fourteenth-century travelogue, a series of tales from eighteenth-century Java – invoking the movement of Adam's story and its manifestation in different genres and contexts.

The story of Adam's fall constitutes a religious and textual tradition in which Sarandib – the Arabic name for Ceylon and Lanka – is the site of exile of the most fundamental kind: banishment from the realm of the divine to human life and suffering. This primordial exile was God's punishment for Adam and Eve's disregard of the command never to approach the tree. Tricked and tempted by Iblīs (Satan, who was assisted by the *naga* snake and the peacock), the two tasted the forbidden fruit, resulting in their expulsion from Paradise, an event that would have profound implications for all of humanity. As the Persian scholar, historian and exegete al-Ṭabarī wrote in his interpretation of Qurʾan 20: 115–126, verses depicting Adam's disobedience to God, "Adam, to

125

whom God had given the high rank of honor above the angels and to whom he allowed the enjoyment of Paradise, lost his place and was given the miserable life of the inhabitants of the earth: tilling, hoeing, and planting the soil."[1]

The tradition that Adam, the first man and first prophet in Islam, fell to Sarandib gained traction and fame within Arabic and wider Islamic literature.[2] Although the specifics of Adam's fall are not recounted in the Qur'an, the story appears already in the writing of early geographers and historians.[3] Al-Ṭabarī (d. 923), who wrote a universal history from Creation to the year 915, mentioned it in his *Ta'rīkh al-rusul wa 'l-mulūk* ("History of Prophets and Kings"). Following a discussion of Friday as the day on which Adam was created, brought into Paradise, and driven out of it, al-Ṭabarī included a section titled "The place on earth to which Adam and Eve came when they were cast down." Most traditions collected by al-Ṭabarī state that Adam fell in al-Hind, the Arabic designation for the Indian subcontinent, and two among them depict Adam as landing on a mountaintop. Toward the end of this section al-Ṭabarī cites a different view, writing that "Others said: rather, Adam was cast down in Sarandib upon a mountain called Nūdh."[4]

The Arab historian and geographer al-Mas'ūdī (d. 956), himself widely traveled, reported in his tenth-century world history, *Murūj al-dhahab wa ma'ādin al-jawāhir* ("The Meadows of Gold and Mines of Gems"), that God caused Adam to land (*ahbaṭa*) in Sarandib, Ḥawwā'/Eve in Jiddah, Iblīs in Baisan and the snake in Isfahan. He then added that, along with several leaves from the trees of Paradise, "Adam landed [*habaṭa*] in India, on the island of Sarandib on Mount al-Rahūn." The account

---

[1] Cited in Brannon M. Wheeler, *Prophets in the Quran: An Introduction to the Quran and Muslim Exegesis* (London and New York: Continuum, 2002), 23.

[2] According to Sir J. Emerson Tennent the earliest recorded mention of the sacred footprint of Adam is in a fourth-century manuscript that contains the Coptic version of the discourse on Faithful Wisdom. Gnostics likely communicated to the Arabs this mystical veneration for Adam (cited in William Skeen, *Adam's Peak: Legendary Traditional and Historic Notices of the Samanala and Sri Pada with a Descriptive Account of the Pilgrims' Route from Colombo to the Sacred Foot Print* [Colombo: W. L. H. Skeen & Co., 1870], 279).

[3] Adam's story is scattered throughout the Qur'an. There are references to it in, for example, suras 2, 4, 5, 7, 15, 20, 21 and 38.

[4] Franz Rosenthal (trans. and annot.), *The History of al-Ṭabarī. Vol. I: General Introduction and From the Creation to the Flood* (Albany: State University of New York Press, 1989), 290–292. There are traditions that locate the site of Adam's fall in Mecca or its vicinity. Ibn 'Abbās, for example, wrote that "Adam was made to fall to earth, to a place called Dahna, between Mecca and Ta'if" (Wheeler, *Prophets*, 26). However, these traditions seem far less popular than those locating the fall in Sarandib/al-Hind. A name closely resembling Nūdh appears in Genesis 4: 16, where Cain is said to have gone to the land of Nod, "east of Eden."

points to a conflation of India and Sarandib in this and similar reports, where al-Hind refers to the Indian Ocean or conveys a sense of "greater India" that encompasses the subcontinent and nearby islands within a single domain.[5]

Al-Bīrūnī (d. 1048), one of medieval Islam's greatest scholars and scientists, tells the story of Adam's fall in Sarandib in his *Ṣifat al-ma'mūra 'alā al-Bīrūnī* ("Al-Bīrūnī's Picture of the World") where the mountain, Jabal al-Rahūn, is designated as *mahbaṭ Ādam 'alaihi al-salām*, Adam's place of descent.[6]

Al-Idrīsī (d. 1165), the Arab geographer, cartographer and advisor to Roger II, Norman king of Sicily, incorporated in his writings knowledge of Africa, the Indian Ocean and the Far East gathered by Muslim merchants and explorers and recorded on maps, along with information brought by the Norman voyagers. In his twelfth-century *Kitāb nuzhat al-mushtāq fī 'khtirāq al-āfāq* ("The Book of Pleasant Journeys into Faraway Lands"), al-Idrīsī mentioned Sarandib as a "large and widely known island," the site of "the mountain upon which Adam descended." He then went on to describe the mountain and its environs in detail: The mountain has a lofty summit and a high peak that rises into the sky and can be seen by sailors from their boats when they are at a distance of several days' journey; the mountain is known as al-Rahūn, and the Brahmins believe that Adam's footmark is imprinted in the stone on its summit, and that a light permanently shines over the footprint like lightning. On and around the mountain, rubies and other types of precious stones are found, as are perfume-producing flora such as aloe-wood. Rice, coconuts and sugar cane grow there, while diamonds and crystals abound in nearby rivers.[7] Thus the site of Adam's fall dominates the landscape: Lofty and lit, it stands like a pillar beckoning from afar.

---

[5] *Habaṭa Ādam bi-l-Hind 'alā jazīrat Sarandīb 'alā jabal al-Rahūn* ('Alī b. al-Ḥusayn al-Mas'ūdī, *Murūj al-dhahab wa-ma'ādin al-jawāhir: les prairies d'or*, ed. and trans. C. Barbier de Meynard and Pavet de Courteille [Paris: L'Imprimerie Impériale, 1861], 60).

[6] A. Zeki Validi Togan (ed.), *Memoirs of the Archeological Survey of India No. 53: Biruni's Picture of the World* (Delhi: Latifl Press, 1937), 60. Togan intended to translate al-Bīrūnī's text into English, but the project did not materialize and his volume, despite its English title, includes the original Arabic only. Al-Bīrūnī's *Ta'rīkh al-Hind* contains an entire chapter on Lanka (chapter 30) but does not mention Sarandib; see Edward C. Sachau (ed.), *Alberuni's India. An account of the religion, philosophy, literature, geography, chronology, astronomy, customs, laws and astrology of India about AD 1030* (London: Kegan Paul, Trench, Trubner and Co., 1910). For further discussion, see Chapter 7.

[7] S. Maqbul Ahmad (ed. and trans.), *India and the Neighbouring Territories in the Kitāb nuzhat al-mushtāq fī 'khtirāq al-āfāq of al-Sharīf al-Idrīsī: A Translation, with Commentary, of the Passages Relating to India, Pakistan, Ceylon, Parts of Afghanistan, and the Andaman, Nicobar, and Maldive Islands, etc.* (Leiden: Brill, 1960), 27–28. Possible etymologies for al-Ruhūn include Sanskrit *rohaṇa* (ascent): ibid., 108.

Figure 6.1 Paradise scene prior to Adam's banishment to Sarandib, as depicted in Java. The archangel Jibrail is speaking from the cloud, Iblis crouches beneath him, while the naga and peacock appear in the front right-hand corner. *Tapel Adam*. Inscribed c. 1800. John Rylands Collection, University of Manchester Library, Javanese MS 6, 10.
Copyright of The University of Manchester

Its slopes are abundant with beauty, sweet aromas, precious stones and nourishing food, reminiscent of the paradise left behind.

The core features of Adam's story relate to his descent to Sarandib, on a mountaintop. There are variations to this story, especially regarding where on earth, precisely, Adam's companions in his fall found themselves. Most commonly, Eve is said to have landed in Jeddah, the snake in Isfahan and Iblīs in south India, but Adam, or *nabī* Adam (the prophet Adam) as he is known in Islamic sources, consistently found himself in Sarandib, sometimes encompassed within al-Hind, banished from the riches and pleasures of Paradise to a life of toil and pain for him and all his descendants thereafter.

This story circulated far and wide and can be found in multiple textual sources in the Islamic world, including in South and Southeast Asia (see Figure 6.1).[8] For example, in the earliest extant Javanese telling of the

---

[8] For India, see Carl W. Ernst, *Refractions of Islam in India: Situating Sufism and Yoga* (New Delhi: Sage, 2016), 31–34, 110–112.

Serat Samud (c. late seventeenth century), the Jewish protagonist Samud Ibnu Salam questions the Prophet about a range of topics when he arrives at the subject of the Garden of Eden. He wishes to know how large was the forbidden *kuldi* tree, how many fruits it bore and what their size was. Muhammad gives those details and adds that one of the forbidden fruits was eaten by Adam, another by Eve, and a third was brought down to earth along with them and planted here, becoming the source for all of the world's trees. Another question followed:

How many accompanied Adam on his descent from Paradise, when God's wrath was upon him? And that prophet Adam, which land did he fall in? Please tell me where each one of them fell.

And the Prophet replied: Along with Adam, who descended with the kuldi fruit and fell in Sarandil, Eve fell in Jiddah. Iblis, who was tied up, fell in Keling. The naga guarding the gate fell in Nisfahid, while the peacock who guarded Heaven fell in the land of Egypt. Samud said: True, and I have a further question:

What did Adam and his wife do when sent away from Paradise?

God's Messenger spoke: They were sorrowful always, and by God's wrath Adam was assailed by the wind, his clothes blown away, he was naked. Eve was also exposed. Adam then took three of the kuldi leaves and made a *kampuh* with one, a *dhesthar* from another, and from a third, a blanket. Eve made a kampuh from her hair which was thick and exceedingly long, growing down to her heels.[9]

In another telling of the same story, written at least two hundred years later in Java at the Pakualam court in Yogyakarta, a very similar depiction of events is found. There is a greater emphasis on Adam's remorse and his praying for a long while, asking forgiveness from God and wishing to reunite with Eve, which eventually transpired. Here a small but important detail was added: Adam is said to have fallen "in Sélan, indeed on

---

[9] *Pinten sarenging Adam/duk tumedhak saking swargi/daweg ira binedon dening Ywang Suksma// Lan nabi Adam punika/tiba anèng bumi pundi/lah tuwan ucapakena/ing sanunggal nunggal nèki/dan saurira nabi/kang sareng Adam tumurun/lan wohing kuldi ika/tiba ing bumi Sarandil/ Awa tiba ing bumi Judah punika//*
Ibelis kang ambandana/tiba anèng bumi Keling/naga kang atunggu lawang/tiba ing bumi Nisfahid/merak kang tunggu swargi/tiba ing Mesir puniku/Samud lingira ngucap/bener ing wuwus puniki/lan malih amba atakèn maring tuwan//
Kados punapa kang tingkah/nabi Adam lan kang rayi/daweg késah saking swarga/angandika sang dutadi/tansah duka priyatin/yatah nabi Adam iku/kasilir ing maruta/saking bebendu ning Widi/kang busana ilang kari awuwuda//
Awa pan wus awuwuda/yatah nyandhak ron ing kuldi/nabyadam angsal titiga/kinarya kampuh sawiji/kang salembaré malih/kinarya dhastar puniku/salembaré punika/kinarya salimut singgih/Awa kang kinarya kampuh rémanira// Mapan kalintanga kathah/panjang tekèng tungkak neki/ (*Samud*, inscribed late seventeenth–early eighteenth centuries, Leiden University Library, MS LOr 4001, n.p., canto 3.3–8 [Sinom]). A kampuh is a batik garment; a dhesthar is a head cloth.

Mount Serandil,"[10] drawing an explicit connection between two of the island's names – Ceylon and Sarandib.

Such brief depictions offer a surprising number of details that bring this tale of ancient banishment to life: the geographical dispersal of the fallen – each completely alone with his or her fate – but within the geographical boundaries of present-day "South Asia" and the "Middle East"; the worldly forces of nature, the scramble to cover the naked body, the new shame attached to nudity; the first creation of clothing with its cultural specificity, here Javanese textiles and style. The passage evokes the implications of exile: the loss of freedom and innocence, a sense of longing, separation, sorrow, loneliness and a changed relationship with God, with other living species and between fellow humans, women and men.

Meanwhile in Sarandib, or Ceylon, the core story of Adam's fall was also known, cited by Tayka Shuʿayb ʿĀlim as a major reason for the Arabs' early attraction to the island.[11] Compilations of qiṣaṣ al-anbiyāʾ (stories of the prophets) written in Arabic and Arabu-Tamil retold the episode. Imāmul Arūs, the great poet, Sufi scholar and "saint" of Kila-karai, and a prolific author, described Sarandib's landscape in detail in his Minḥatu Sarandīb fī madḥil ḥabīb ("A Gift for Sarandib in Praise of the Prophet"), beginning with Sarandib's importance as the site of Adam's descent, and employed the exact same words as al-Bīrūnī.[12]

In the Malay Compendium the story of Adam's creation, attributed to Ibn ʿAbbās, is told at length as part of a sequence depicting the prophets' lives.[13] The well-known story of God sending the archangels to collect a handful of earth and bring it back so that He can create a king for the earth (raja bumi) is recounted, as each returns empty-handed after the earth resists. Finally, Adam is created from earth gathered from several places (all in the Arab lands except for one in India) and is infused with life. In Paradise he is warned of Iblis, his eternal enemy, but is not too worried, believing Iblis to reside on earth. Iblis manages to enter Paradise by trickery and tempts Eve, and she in turn Adam, with the fruit of the forbidden tree. They are banished, with Adam falling in Sarandib, Eve (Hawa) in Jiddah, the peacock in Hindustan, the snake in Isfahan and

[10] Adam neng Sélan/iya ing Srandil arga. The complete passage appears in Serat Samud, Yogyakarta, inscribed 1884, Pura Pakualaman Library, Yogyakarta, MS PP St. 80, 79–84, in Sinom.
[11] ʿĀlim, Arabic, Arwi and Persian, 15.
[12] Imāmul Arūs depicted the island as jazīrat Sarandīb mahbaṭ Ādam ʿalaihi al-salām ("the island of Sarandib, site of Adam's – peace be upon him – descent"), cited in ʿĀlim, Arabic, Arwi and Persian, 660–661.
[13] Malay Compendium, BL, EAP450/1/2; see Chapter 2.

Iblis in Mazan.[14] Many years and generations later, Ibrahim (Abraham) was commanded by God to build the Ka'ba at the spot where, put to the test by God, he almost sacrificed his son Isma'il (Ishmael). Ibrahim asked where he should get the stones to erect the site and God sent Jibrail (Gabriel) to bring them from five different mountains, including Mt. Sarandib.[15]

In this account, Islam's holiest site, the Ka'ba, is partly constituted from the rock of the mountain where Adam fell to earth. The account is in dialogue with the story of Adam's creation from earth collected in several places, used to make the first human who would, ultimately, return to the earth (first via banishment, then upon death), while Adam's descendant Ibrahim would resituate the site of primordial exile at the heart of the Muslim world. The names of the four other mountains whence stones were brought (Juda, Abu Qabas, Tursina and Kharah) suggest they were located within the boundaries of the Middle East, thus Mt. Sarandib was a distant, displaced mountain in relation to the others, just as that same mountain was "in exile" from all other sacred pilgrimage sites located within Islam's heartlands.

The stones which are said to have been brought to Mecca to be used in the creation of the Ka'ba suggest a material link between Islam's most sacred of sites and Sarandib. This connection is reminiscent of the Javanese tradition that a handful of Mecca's earth was transported every Friday to Java by the seventeenth-century king of Mataram, Sultan Agung (r. 1613–1645), eventually piling up to form the sacred hill at Imogiri where Java's royalty have since been buried. In both cases concrete, earthly bonds were forged between the Islamic "core" and distant "peripheries" that located themselves within a universal sacred geography whose boundaries have been contested and expanded.[16] Although we have no reflection by the nineteenth-century author or scribe on the appearance of Sarandib and Mt. Sarandib in his Malay manuscript produced in Ceylon, nonetheless a connection is made for writer and audience between the sacred sites of Adam's fall and the Ka'ba, between Mecca and Sarandib, exiles of the distant and not-so-distant pasts.

The site where Adam first touched the earth is known in English as Adam's Peak, the summit of a towering mountain that is visible from a great distance and whose peak casts a remarkable shadow at sunrise.

---

[14] Ibid., 58.   [15] *Bukit Sarandib*; ibid., 260.

[16] Another well-known Javanese tradition echoed here is that of Sunan Kalijaga orienting the mosques at Demak on Java's north coast and Mecca toward one another. All these stories speak to relationships based on forms of mutuality between Arabia and Java or Ceylon.

The peak is not associated with a single religion but is sacred to several, pointing to the interconnectedness of beliefs, stories and commemorative acts among religious communities living in close proximity. To the Buddhists it is known as Sri Pada, marking the site of the Buddha's footprint left on one of his three visits to the island (recorded as early as the Mahawansa); the Hindus believe that it was Shiva or Vishnu who left the sacred trace; and there is also a Christian tradition that the footprint was left by St. Thomas. Followers of all these religions have made the mountain into an important pilgrimage site, one that in the past was accessible only with great difficulty as its elevated terrain was surrounded by dense forests. Even today the 5,000-plus steps leading up to its summit require patience and determination. But although there is much that is shared among the faithful as they approach the mountaintop and it is sacred to them all, it is only the Muslims who view it as a site of exile, where a pivotal event for all humanity transpired. This significance has been translated into an expansion of the core elements of Adam's story and its increasingly deep implantation into the Islamic imagination across genres and languages.

The importance of this site is palpable, for example, in the account by Ibn Baṭṭūṭa, the great Muslim traveler who in the fourteenth century journeyed from his native Tangiers all the way to China. In 1341, Ibn Baṭṭūṭa was on his way from India to China when he stopped in Ceylon. He recounted how while still nine days away from shore he saw the famous mountain towering in the distance. After arriving at the site of present-day Puttalam and finding favor with the king, he was asked to make a wish and replied: "my only desire in coming to this island was, to visit the blessed foot of our forefather Adam, whom these people call Baba."[17] The wish was granted and Ibn Baṭṭūṭa, accompanied by several yogis and Brahmins, set off for the mountain. The journey was difficult and also fascinating, and he met pearl divers and saw large rubies. Although he encountered the dangers of rough roads, rivers and forests and many wild elephants along the way, he remained unharmed. It was, noted Ibn Baṭṭūṭa, thanks to the blessings of a great sheikh, the first to have opened up the path to pilgrims, that none of the elephants disturbed those traversing it.[18]

---

[17] Rev. Samuel Lee (trans.), *Travels of Ibn Batuta; Translated from the Abridged Arabic Manuscript Copies, preserved in the Public Library of Cambridge* (London: Oriental Translation Committee, 1829), 183–192. The quote is on 185 (Nabu Public Domain Reprints).

[18] Ibid., 186.

Ibn Baṭṭūṭa described a ridge with a cave and well at the entrance to the mountain, and continued: "this mountain of Sarandib is one of the largest in the world … when we ascended it, we saw the clouds passing between us and its foot. On it is a great number of trees, the leaves of which never fall. There are also flowers of various colours, with the red rose about the size of the palm of the hand, upon the leaves of which they think they can read the name of God and his Prophet." He went on to depict a series of chains fastened to iron pins along the arduous path, which those ascending could hold on to. Interestingly, the final chain was known as "the chain of witness," because, Ibn Baṭṭūṭa explained, when one reached it and looked down one was seized by the frightful notion that one would fall.[19] Perhaps this last stage of the ascent and the view from above offered a reenactment of Adam's experience as he glanced down before his fall into this world – an ominous moment indeed. According to custom, pilgrims at the time spent three days in the cave, visiting the footprint depressed in the rock two miles above them morning and night. There, they stood face to face with the concrete spot on earth where man first set foot, bewildered, afraid and remorseful, having left behind the pleasures and certainties of heaven. Just before the final, steep ascent, the cave and well of Khiḍr are located, thus tying one important prophet to another, one sacred biography to the next.[20]

The theme of banishment, so central to Adam's fall and thus deeply ingrained in the Islamic imagination, appears especially poignant when thinking of those contemplating this tradition in colonial Ceylon, exiles or their descendants. The question is pertinent: Did they link their own plight with Adam's paradigmatic human and Muslim banishment?

Yusuf al-Makassari was among the most prominent exiles sent from the Indonesian Archipelago to Ceylon and certainly the one most commonly remembered and celebrated into the twenty-first century. Exiled by the Dutch in 1684, he spent a decade in Ceylon before being sent aboard the *Voetboeg* to the Cape Settlement. While in Ceylon, Sheikh Yusuf, who had spent many years living in Mecca and had been initiated into several Sufi orders, is known to have composed religious treatises and to have taught disciples both local and foreign. Despite his centrality

---

[19] Ibid., 189.

[20] Some traditions claim that Khiḍr was Adam's son and that he recovered Adam's body after the flood; see the fourteenth-century collection by Ibn Kathīr, *Stories of the Prophets*, trans. Mohammed Hilmi al-Ahmed (Beirut: DKI, 2013), 457. There is an important shrine to Khiḍr in Kataragama, less than 200 km from Adam's Peak. Like the Peak, Kataragama is a site sacred to more than one religion and, in addition to Khiḍr's shrine, it boasts a temple complex dedicated to the Buddhist guardian deity Kataragama deviyo and a temple of the Hindu deity Murugan.

to the Muslim community at the time and his current status as a national hero in modern Indonesia and South Africa, little is known of the years he spent in Ceylon. Clearly, however, he was active enough – despite his advanced age and years of exile – to warrant Dutch anxiety about his ongoing, long-distance influence back in Java and the need to banish him even further afield.[21]

One of the treatises composed by Sheikh Yusuf, in Arabic, is titled *al-Nafḥat al-Sailāniyyah fi manḥat al-raḥmāniyyah*: "The Whiff/Fragrance of Ceylon Concerning the Setting Out of Mystical Topics." Interestingly, he chose to insert Sailān into the title to designate the place of writing. In the initial section of the text Sheikh Yusuf recounted its circumstances of writing, offering more detail: "the reason for this writing was our presence in the land of Ceylon [*arḍ Sailān*], known as the island of Sarandib [*jazīrat Sarandīb*], place of banishment [*marmiya*] for the disobeyers [*al-maʿāṣī*] and site of destiny [*māwiya*] for the alienated [*al-gharīb*], [a presence] brought about by God's decrees that have no beginning and His acts which have no end. As an act of wisdom from Him who is glorious and exalted."[22] The key words in this brief but revealing passage are *marmiya*, place of banishment, the site one is hurled to; *al-maʿāṣī*, the disobeyers, rebels, referring to those who did not obey the Dutch or revolted against them, as Yusuf had done; *māwiya*, a place of destiny for those who are remote; and *al-gharīb*, the foreign, strange, alien, remote or uncommon, all adjectives touching upon the condition of Yusuf and his disciplines in Ceylon.

Yusuf did not elaborate on his choice of title. Although the use of *nafḥat* in Arabic titles is not unheard of, other authors have employed it in the plural.[23] In Yusuf's case, the title may well be evoking the story of Adam's banishment. Many of the Arabic traditions of Adam's fall, already noted, claim that as he was sent away from Paradise leaves of the beautiful, fragrant trees that grew there fell down with him: covering his head in a wreath, sewn around his newly discovered naked body which he was suddenly ashamed to expose, or just descending beside him. Al-Ṭabarī wrote that "it is said that when Adam fell to earth he had a

---

[21] For a comprehensive study of Sheikh Yusuf's life and writing, see Abu Hamid, *Syekh Yusuf Makassar. Seorang Ulama, Sufi, dan Penjuang* (Jakarta: Yayasan Obor Indonesia, 1994). However, even this book dedicates a mere five pages (106–111) to Yusuf's decade in Ceylon and notes the dearth of studies on this period (110, n. 41).

[22] Yusuf al-Makassari, *al-Nafḥat al-Sailāniyyah fi manḥat al-Raḥmāniyyah* in ʿIlm at-Taṣawwuf, n.d., Perpustakaan Nasional Republik Indonesia, Jakarta, MS PNRI A 101, 1.

[23] Most famous among such works may be Jāmi's (d. 1492) *Nafaḥāt al-uns*, a compilation of biographies of Sufi saints.

wreath on his head from the trees of paradise and when he reached the earth the wreath dried up, its leaves scattered, and from them grew types of perfume. Others say: This was from the clothes that Adam and Eve sewed together from the leaves of paradise ... Adam fell to India. It is the land with the sweetest smell on earth because when Adam was cast down there some of the smell of paradise clung to the trees."[24] The earliest traditions that relate Adam's fall thus mention the perfumed leaves of Paradise that descended along with him, whose marvelous scent filled the land and clung to it, creating a fragrant sphere with no rivals on earth.

Al-Mas'ūdī, who recounted similar developments as related to the perfumed leaves, elaborated also on the thirty types of fruit that Adam brought down with him. These were divided into three categories (with shells/skins; with pits; with neither shells nor pits). Furthermore, he noted that the mountain where Adam fell was glittering with rubies and diamonds, and the surrounding sea and its deep cavities were rich in pearls.[25] As discussed in the section on the qiṣaṣ al-anbiyā' below, tradition positions Mt. Sarandib in close proximity to Paradise. The depictions of multiple fruit and fragrant trees conjure a Sarandib that is not only close to the heavens but constitutes a paradise on earth. Mention of pearls and gems is in tandem with the island's fame since the first centuries of the Common Era as a pearling hub and an abundant source of emeralds, rubies and sapphires, their highest concentration indeed found in the vicinity of Adam's Peak.[26]

Sheikh Yusuf's decision to title his work "A Whiff of Ceylon" or "Ceylonese Fragrance" suggests a dialogue with these ancient traditions: recalling the heavenly scents filling the land of wretched exile, he could remind his disciples that, despite their experiences of remoteness, alienation and life in a strange land, they were gathering in a site marked by a foundational event of Muslim history which was blessed by an eternal heavenly perfume. This inspirational dimension of his text went hand in hand with its content, as the *Nafḥat* stresses the crucial importance of finding and following a teacher, of practice and of community, and of the comfort and confidence offered by adhering to the right path which is understood as an inner one, no matter the external circumstances. Taken together, the text and its title reaffirmed a connection to Ceylon/Sarandib – the significance of the site in the "big picture" and *longue durée* of Islam's history – even while the contemporary episode of exile was difficult and strange. Adam's displacement from Paradise, traumatic as

---

[24] *The History of al-Ṭabarī*, 296.   [25] Mas'ūdī, *Murūj*, 61–62.
[26] Adam's Peak is in the Ratnapura district of modern Sri Lanka, with the city of Ratnapura the center of its gem industry and trade.

it was, had constructive outcomes, symbolized by the uplifting, sensual and lasting scents he brought along, such perfumes an element in a sphere of beauty, prosperity, nourishment and sweetness that Adam was able to carry along as he entered earthly life, forming memories, traces or whiffs of a paradise that was lost, but not in its entirety. Such allusions suggested empowerment for those banished, also, and reading the text with Sheikh Yusuf (in body or spirit) afforded a way for those around him to see beyond present realities into other temporal and spiritual realms.

There are additional instances in which Malay writing in Ceylon established a connection – explicitly or subtly – between Adam's banishment from Paradise and a history of exile. In a Malay manuscript containing more than 1,300 pages and filled with the popular tales of the prophets, Adam's biography takes up several dozen pages, seventeen of which focus explicitly on his relationship to Sarandib by occasionally mentioning it and tying Adam's actions to it.[27] As in many other Malay manuscripts inscribed in nineteenth-century Ceylon, including those discussed in Chapter 2, this text is interspersed with Qur'anic quotations relevant to the story which are then explained – usually with some elaboration upon the original – in Malay. Serving as nodes of religious authority within the largely Malay text but written in the same script, such Arabic quotes stand out due to their vocalization and are linked back into the Malay flow of the narrative by the single word "artinya": "meaning," "can be explained as." The lengthy section dedicated to Adam begins with the same depiction already noted from many sources, of Adam falling in Sarandib, Eve in Jiddah, the peacock in Hindustan, the snake in Isfahan and Iblis in Mazan. The tears that flowed from Adam's eyes over the next three hundred years eventually created several rivers. Adam was then commanded to go on pilgrimage. While on his way, every place he passed turned into a flourishing settlement. Finally, after passing through Mt. ʿArafat he reached Mt. Rahman and reunited with Eve. Stories follow, all of which have their roots in older traditions: the angels complimenting Adam on his circumambulation (ṭawāf) of the Kaʿba, Musa (Moses) questioning Adam's decision to listen to Iblis while in Paradise, the order of standing – of Muslims and infidels – in

---

[27] *Tales of the Prophets and miscellaneous*, BL, EAP450/2/1. The manuscript is anonymous and contains no dates. A similar sequence of the prophets' tales appears in an *Arabu-Tamil Compendium* that was written by Tuan Muhammed Maas Misbahu Cuttilan, a member of a prominent Malay family in Ceylon that traces its ancestry to Mas Kerti, an eighteenth-century royal Javanese exile. The *Compendium*, the writing of which was completed on Ramadan 30, 1324 (1906), was inherited by Maas Syrni Sookoor from her mother Radèn Jawi Cuttilan; see BL, EAP609/10/1.

relation to Adam on the Day of Judgment. Eventually Adam was com-manded by God: *Hai Adam pergilah engkau ke Sarandib dengan Hawa di sana tempatmu diam. Maka penuhilah dunia ini dengan anaq cucumu* ("O Adam, go to Sarandib with Eve and live there. Fill the world with your descendants"). Adam then follows the command with the text using the expression *ke bawa angin*, "to [a land] below the winds" to refer to Sarandib's location.[28]

In this instance Adam was sent back to Sarandib, designating it not only as his site of banishment but also a place of return and settlement. God's decree depicts it as a place of plenty, of fertility and growth, where the process of filling the world with humans will commence. Additional events unfold, presumably in Sarandib, where Adam and Hawa were living: Adam asks God for fire, Jibrail teaches him the blacksmith's craft, which in the Malay world was a profession that combined technical expertise with spiritual powers, especially in the context of keris produc-tion. Further, the tradition of *Ayyām al-Bīḍ* ("White Nights," the fast on the thirteenth–fifteenth days of every month during the full moon) is revealed to Adam. Then, although the repetition is unnecessary for the storyline, the text states again: "God's prophet Adam, peace be upon him, settled in Sarandib, making a place for his children and grandchil-dren."[29] The offspring were born in pairs, always a boy and a girl, and eventually each married a spouse from a different pair of twins at a time when, according to the text, pregnancy and childbirth were painless, thus disregarding the more common tradition of Eve's punishment for dis-obeying God taking the form of giving birth in misery. It was also a time when death was unknown, and next appeared the story of Qabil and Habil (Cain and Abel) and the first murder, death and burial. As it turns out, Adam was away on the hajj when his beloved son Habil was killed by his envious brother and so again the movement to and from Sarandib is explicit, as Adam's return and search for Habil are described. Finally, after weeping for three hundred years for their dead son (the same number of years Adam wept after parting with Hawa), the father and mother of humanity are said to have left Damascus where they had been grieving and returned one final time to Sarandib.[30]

This undated Malay manuscript offers a clear extension of Sarandib's presence within the traditional Islamic depiction of Adam's life: Sarandib first appears, conventionally, as the site of banishment from Paradise, but is then reinserted into the narrative repeatedly as a reminder of Adam and Eve's earthly home, the place where they bore children and watched

---

[28] Ibid., 59. "Above" and "below the winds" referred to the monsoon.   [29] Ibid., 64.
[30] Ibid., 74.

future generations come into being, where they knew prosperity and growth but also the pain of loss and the original, traumatic human encounter with death. Encapsulated in their Sarandib biographies is the full cycle of human life, from conception to birth, life and death, thus consolidating Sarandib's foundational role as a site in whose particular history all that would accompany humanity from Adam and Eve's time onward, for all generations, first transpired and was first framed in Islamic terms.

Mountains appear repeatedly throughout the section on Adam's life, including as sites of significant events like Qabil and Habil's sacrifice competition and the spot where Adam's son Shish (Seth; A. Shīth) prayed for a fruit of Paradise for his ailing father.[31] Although the mountains are not named, their appearance as sites of critical developments in the narrative and their location in Sarandib suggest that the references allude to *the* mountain on which Adam first fell in that same land. In the case of Shish's prayer, particularly, Paradise seems very close to the mountaintop on which he is standing, recalling the hadith that of all the mountains in the world the one Adam fell to in Sarandib was the closest one to Paradise. Al-Ṭabarī wrote that the distance was so small that when Adam was cast down upon the mountain his feet were upon it while his head was in heaven and he could still hear the angels giving praise to God.[32] The physical proximity is compounded by a heavenly *bidadari* sent down to marry Shish, thus the story almost joins, although not fully, the realms of the earthly and heavenly in which Adam resided during his lifetime.

By occasionally noting that Adam visited other sites, the text confirms Sarandib's role as a site of return, the place that Adam came back to time and again: to his family and the human continuity they represented, to sorrow and finally to his own death. The latter event, the ultimate return, is again linked to the mountain. Al-Ṭabarī, citing the authority of Ibn ʿAbbas, claimed that Adam died in the same place where he was cast down. As it turned out this would not immediately become Adam's final resting place: During the Flood, nabi Nuh (the prophet Noah) disinterred the body, placed it in a coffin and carried it around in the ark until the waters receded, when it was returned.[33]

The depictions and allusions in the Malay volume of tales of the prophets as they relate to Adam suggest their relevance to their particular

---

[31] Ibid., 66 and 75, respectively.   [32] Rosenthal (trans.), *The History of al-Ṭabarī*, 292.

[33] Ibid., 334, where al-Ṭabarī also notes the tradition that Noah reburied Adam in Jerusalem. The episode of carrying Adam's body in the ark appears also in the *Malay Compendium*.

audience in colonial Ceylon. The broader-than-usual emphasis on Adam and Eve's life and death in Sarandib, their bringing forth future generations there and the emergence of envy, anger, deceit, grief, longing and fratricide as attributes of human life, cemented Sarandib's importance far beyond even the constitutive event of divine banishment. Sarandib, later to be known as Ceylon, was unrivaled in this regard, and the stories were a reminder that nabi Adam's history was firmly planted there, as was that of humanity. In this way, the Malays engaging with the text could find in it both a local and a universal history that was relevant to their past and present. The proximity, yet ultimate separation, between Sarandib – and especially the mountaintop upon which Adam fell – and Paradise, could be felt, symbolically, to echo with the spheres of "home" and "away" of exilic lives.

Finally, an additional source that suggests a connection between different exilic eras and ordeals is the *Syair Faiḍ al-Abād* ("Bounty of the Ages"), written in 1905 by the prominent Malay community leader, publisher and literary figure Baba Ounus Saldin, whose life and works will be discussed further in Chapter 9. This small volume was written, as Saldin states explicitly in his introduction, in order to convey to a young Malay generation an understanding of the community's past. It primarily includes depictions of battles in which Malays took part in the service of Empire, as well as a section on mystical teachings and some brief stories of the prophets, but opens, after salutation to the Prophet and a context for its writing, with what might be termed a "telegraphic history" of the island prior to the arrival of the British. Its initial lines are below (several more lines sum up 300 years of consecutive Portuguese and Dutch rule, while the next 18 pages are dedicated to the British period):

> *Bahwa pulau ini pada permulaan/pulau Sarandib nama dikatakan*
> *Allah Ta'ala akan Adam/diturunkan di atas bukit di tengah hutan*
> *Ama Hawwa turunkan di Jeddah/beberapa lama kemudian berjumpah*
> *Kedua laki istri bersuka cita/diperanaq akan beberapa juta*
> *Kemudian dikata Seylong namanya/buminya amat banyaq kekayaannya*
> *Sangat meliputnya bandaharanya/mutiara dan permata beberapa jenisnya*

This island in the beginning was known by the name Sarandib.
God sent Adam down to a mountaintop deep in the forest;
Eve was sent down in Jeddah; a while later they met.
Man and wife were delighted; they begat millions of children.
Later it was known as Ceylon by name, its earth abundant with riches
Completely inundated its ports with pearls and gems of many kinds.[34]

---

[34] Baba Ounus Saldin, *Syair Faiḍ al-Abād* (Colombo: Alamat Langkapuri, 1905), 3. See also BL, EAP609/5/6.

The island's history, according to the *Syair*, thus begins with Adam, first man and prophet, who was banished by God to the island, at the time known by its first, or original name, Sarandib, and later to be called Ceylon. These opening lines are clearly based on Arab traditions that were transmitted across the Islamic world. The reference to Adam's fall from Paradise onto a mountaintop in Sarandib, recounted in early Arabic sources as well as in Ibn Baṭṭūṭa's travelogue and in many local retellings in South and Southeast Asia, highlights in the *Syair*'s opening section Sarandib's status as the oldest, original home on earth for the Malays, for all Muslims and for humanity, via the sacred biography of Adam. It frames the *Syair* and gives the history it tells a temporal depth that extends far prior to, and also beyond, the history of colonialism, the latter being, although recounted in much greater detail, but a fleeting – and therefore less consequential than often perceived – moment within a much grander narrative. Adam's fall on this particular mountaintop, an important pilgrimage site for centuries, locates Ceylon at the forefront of humanity's worldly existence: not just a place of exile where forsaken royals languish or a coveted possession for profit-hungry colonial administrations, as some may have perceived it, but the unique site where Man first touched this earth and to which all humans ultimately trace their ancestry. As in the earlier sources, in the *Syair* too Ceylon's riches, pearls and gems echo those of Paradise, which was left behind but remained, both physically and metaphorically, nearby. As the *Hikayat Tuan Gusti* extended its audiences' collective memories both spatially and temporally by linking its protagonist Tuan Gusti and Java's emerging Muslim community with Sheikh Muhideen, a descendant of the Prophet, the *Syair* suggested that the Malay past in Sarandib stretched all the way back to Adam, these textual claims both harboring the potential to alter the temporal lens and the balance of power and status between colonizer and colonized.

Saldin's framing of the *Syair* was directed at his audience, the Malays in colonial Ceylon eager to know more of their community's past. Recalling Adam's fall in Sarandib positioned the Malays' history in Ceylon as extending all the way to the dawn of humanity and yet also encompassing more recent episodes of mobility and displacement between their ancestral and current homelands. Saldin's inclusion of Adam's fall at the start of his historical account also located his work within overlapping literary and historiographic traditions, including those of Arab and Persian historians, geographers and travelers writing in different locales and centuries, and formed a thematic and generic link with the wider networks of history writing in the Islamic world.

Saldin wrote of Ceylon's past, both distant and more familiar to him personally from his own life and that of his elders. What of the other

Figure 6.2 Title page of Baba Ounus Saldin's *Syair Faiḍ al-Abād*, BL, EAP609/5/6.
Courtesy Thalip and Jayarine Iyne

shore? How did those who were not displaced but remained in Java conceive of, and imagine, that island of banishment whence rulers, relatives or friends were sent away aboard Dutch ships, often never to return, and which coincided with the site of Adam's fall to earth?

This question will be addressed by reading another work by R. Ng. Yasadipura I (1729–1803), whose *Babad Giyanti* was discussed in Chapter 5 in the context of returning exiles depicting their lives in Ceylon. In that case, Yasadipura's *Babad* offered a glimpse of what may have been known of the site of exile, the lived conditions and experiences of those banished, and their representation in Javanese writing. The scene he depicted, of study and prayer with a popular Muslim guru, recounted how feelings of longing were soothed by the miraculous arrival of familiar Javanese food on Fridays. Yasadipura's *Serat Ménak Serandhil* offers an additional eighteenth-century perspective on Ceylon, one that suggests how the island was understood and imagined from afar, in part through the familiar lens of Islamic and Javanese religious and literary models, including those related to Adam's biography.[35]

The tales of Ménak Amir Ambyah, one of the Prophet Muhammad's uncles and a great warrior, traveler and lover, became widely popular across the archipelago from at least the sixteenth century. Adapted from Persian, they were known in Malay as the *Hikayat Amir Hamzah* and were among the Malay texts circulating in Ceylon in manuscript form.[36] The *Hikayat Amir Hamzah* was often a very lengthy text and could exceed a thousand pages, but it was not usually divided into separate volumes, each with its own title, as would be the case after the tales were adapted into Javanese in the seventeenth century. The story told in *Serat Ménak Serandhil* is set, as the title implies, in Serandhil, the Javanized form of Sarandib. As in the *Syair*, Sélan and Serandil are used interchangeably in this text.

Here is found not an eyewitness account of the island, as in the case of Ibn Baṭṭūṭa, nor an allusion to exile in Ceylon as a personal or familial experience. Set in the era of Islam's early expansion, the volume opens with the king of Sélan, Sahalsyah, being unseated by a powerful rival, Lamdahur. The deposed king turns to his allies in Medayin and asks for help and, after some deliberation, they decide that Ménak is the right

---

[35] Yasadipura I, *Ménak Serandhil* (Betawi Sentrum: Bale Pustaka, 1933).

[36] On the history of the Malay *Hikayat Amir Hamzah*, including its Persian origins, see Ph. S. van Ronkel, *De Roman van Amir Hamza* (Leiden: E. J. Brill, 1895), 91–180. For a manuscript from Ceylon, see *Hikayat Amir Hamzah*, inscribed by Muhammad Yusuf Jailani Jurangpati in Kampung Katukele, Kandy, Perpustakaan Negara Malaysia, Kuala Lumpur, MS PMN 1056. The manuscript is undated but based on the scribe's biography probably dates to the 1870s or 1880s.

person to assist. In this early section, Sélan is depicted as led by an
extremely powerful king and possessing a huge army. The journey to
Sélan was arduous and Ménak and his army faced many dangers, including encounters with various types of invisible beings. As they sailed closer
to Sélan's shoreline, they saw a large mountain in the distance and
Ménak asked Ki Buyut Wirigaluh, a local man who had loyally helped
them, about it. Ki Buyut replied that this was Mt. Serandhil, and he
pointed out to Ménak a very large rock on the summit where Adam's
footprint could be found. He added that many ship's captains and kings
visited the site and performed acts of devotion there.[37] Ambyah asked to
do the same and he, along with all accompanying kings and officials,
climbed to the top.

Then all descended but his general Umarmaya, who remained by the
big rock, fell asleep and had a dream in which four holy men came down
from the sky. One of them was nabi Adam, from whom Umarmaya
requested a pusaka, a sacred, powerful object. Adam promised Umarmaya a pouch out of which anything he desired would emerge.

Umarmaya then spoke to the second man, who revealed himself to be
the prophet Ibrahim. Telling him he was a follower of his religion, Islam,
Umarmaya requested "supernatural powers" – kesaktian – and Ibrahim
promised him great speed as a runner, knowledge of half the world's
languages (260 out of 520), and the opportunity to travel and see many
places and peoples. The third celestial man was nabi Iskak (Isaac) from
whom Umarmaya also asked for kesaktian. In this case he was promised
the ability to take any human form (including that of bulé, a foreigner), as
well as that of fish and animals. Finally, the fourth prophet, Sulaiman
(Solomon), promised Umarmaya gold and precious stones.[38] Umarmaya
indeed received these boons and used them to his and Ambyah's benefit
later in the story. The relevant point is that, as in the other texts examined, Ménak Serandhil shows knowledge of Adam's fall to Sarandib, also
known as Sélan. Moreover, beyond this accepted truth, the author Yasadipura was familiar with tales of the specific mountaintop and its fame as
a pilgrimage site and a place to ask for blessings and miracles, where
direct access to the prophets of Islam was possible. Whereas Ibn Baṭṭūṭa's
account offered a firsthand testimony of the site, Yasadipura's depiction
recalled many of the same details but relied on his imagination and
received imagery to tell its story. Both accounts, of the Arab traveler

---

[37] *Nggih punika sang inggiling wukir/séla geng kinaot/inggih tapak Adam kamulané/pra nakoda
kang langkung ing ngriki/miwah para aji/pan sami angujung* (Yasadipura I, *Ménak
Serandhil*, 35, in Mijil).
[38] Ibid., 36–38.

and the Javanese poet, writing in their respective genres, expanded the core tradition of Adam and kept it alive through practices of pilgrimage and documentation.

Depictions of Ceylon in the *Babad Giyanti*, a historical chronicle, can be linked with those in *Ménak Serandhil*, part of a longer series of tales documenting the life of one of early Islam's greatest warriors. Taken together, the two works show that Sélan was on the poet Yasadipura's mind, that he made attempts to imagine and depict it, living as he did through a century of contemporary, lived exile to Dutch Ceylon, including that of high-ranking members of the Surakarta palace where he served as court poet. Possessing at least some awareness of Ceylon's geography and sites facilitated the imagining of exiles in particular places, or in proximity to sacred sites such as Adam's Peak. The descriptions found in *Ménak Serandhil*, of ship's captains coming from far and wide to express their devotion at the site of Adam's fall, is echoed closely in the *Babad Giyanti*, in which ship's captains from many a land encircle with reverence not the sacred footprint, but the Islamic guru Ibrahim Asmara. The boons received by Umarmaya after four prophets descended from the sky (including Adam's second descent to that spot, constituting a return) and fulfilled his wishes in a dream, are reminiscent of the Javanese delicacies arriving every Friday to console the exiles' hearts, highlighting the miraculous in both texts.[39] Umarmaya's desire for a pusaka – a sacred, powerful object – while in Ceylon resonates with the complex historical episode of the banished Javanese king Amangkurat III who managed to carry off royal heirlooms to Ceylon in 1708.

The question of nomenclature is conspicuous in these texts. In *Ménak Serandhil* and the *Syair*, Sarandib and Ceylon are both used as designations. Employing both suggests that when writing *Ménak* Yasadipura's literary imagination was informed by traditional Islamic tales, as well as his view from Java on contemporary exile. Whereas he used Sarandib and Sélan interchangeably, Baba Ounus Saldin in his *Syair* put forth a more "developmental" model: Sarandib, it claimed, was the original name for the island, its only images those of mountain and jungle, while later (*kemudian*) it came to be known as Ceylon, its land fertile and abundant with riches. And yet toward the end of the *Syair*, in the brief section narrating the prophets' lives, Sarandib, and Adam, reappear: Saldin mentions again that Adam fell to "the island called Sarandib, in this world" (*pulau nama Sarandib di dunia ini*) and that he and Eve wept, indicating that landing in this world, and in Sarandib, was an experience

---

[39] For a discussion of this scene, see above, Chapter 5.

filled with sorrow. And so, even if forested, desolate Sarandib became over time gem-filled Ceylon – a place where Malay history unfolded through battles, travel and personal lives – in closing the *Syair* returns to the older name: It is, in Gerard Genette's terms, a paratext, a brief but crucial insertion which frames the poem on both ends, encasing it with the figures of Adam and Eve as parents, vulnerable humans, exiles in a new land.

The appellation "Sarandib" maintained its power and its hold on the imagination in colonial Ceylon, like an ancient pusaka summoned to caution and protect. And that power, or at least its remnants, can still be felt in Sarandib's manifestation in the English language, in the form of the word "serendipity," coined in 1754. Its inventor, Horace Walpole (1717–1792), who had read the Persian tale "Three Princes of Serendip," wrote to a friend that those princes "were always making discoveries, by accidents and sagacity, of things they were not in quest of."[40] He called that ability they possessed "serendipity," and the word has since come to designate an aptitude for making desirable discoveries by accident, as well as good fortune or luck more broadly. Its core meaning remains tied to finding the unexpected, to a search, a quest, an adventure, to faint echoes of Persian tales and princes as imagined in eighteenth-century England. Although these associations are largely positive, they also resonate with the exilic experiences of Adam, as well as the Malays' forefathers, finding themselves in unexpected, unintended circumstances.

By framing itself with Adam's fall, the *Syair* suggests that exile can also constitute a return. Adam's banishment from Paradise signals the end of that heavenly existence for all humans, known typically in Malay as *anak cucu Adam* (literally "children and grandchildren of Adam," his descendants). This seminal event forms a paradigm for all future exiles, including that of the Malays' ancestors, many of whom were banished from across the Indonesian Archipelago. With Adam's story in mind, and with its appearance in the *Syair*'s opening and closing sections, readers were reminded that the colonial power that exiled their community's forefathers had transported the Malays to the quintessential exilic site. The recognition that exile to Ceylon was not solely an expulsion but also, via Adam's sacred biography, a return, was potent and comforting: It held the potential to encourage attempts at connecting, searching for roots in a foreign land, looking for ties to the site and justifications for being

---

[40] The letter, dated January 28, 1754, was addressed to Horace Mann. See Douglas Harper, *Online Etymology Dictionary*, www.etymonline.com/search?q=serendipity (accessed September 3, 2018).

there, affirming a sense of "at-homeness" that was incongruent with the early exiles' experiences but nonetheless, as evidenced in repeated references, offered sustenance and gradually, for subsequent generations, transformed into a lived reality. This later sentiment is clear as the *Syair*, throughout its pages, portrays mobility of many kinds, via travel, enlistment and transmission, but makes palpable a sense of community, an attachment to place, the telling of a history that has connected Malays to their "new" home, a history that converges on Ceylon – but also highlights Ceylon or Sarandib's status as the old, original home on this earth for the Malays and all humans as descendants of Adam.

Thus far, this chapter has explored sources from various places, periods and genres that engage with Adam's fall in Sarandib and the way this tradition offered a framework for considering and experiencing exile to Ceylon in the colonial period, most pertinently under Dutch rule in the seventeenth and eighteenth centuries. The next, and final, source is the most heartrending, and it also draws the clearest, most direct connection between the two episodes of banishment. On July 11, 1724, a letter was received in Batavia from Tumenggung Surapati, a Javanese exile in Colombo who wrote to his wife, children and mother, who had remained in Java. The letter was written in pégon, Javanese written in a modified form of the Arabic script, and translated into Dutch. The final section of the letter, addressed to Surapati's mother, reads:

Oh dear mother, wheresoever you may be and with whomsoever you may be, among our women and children, be careful and take care and be sure to please and satisfy whomsoever you serve and that your grandchildren are also like that and trust in God with patience thinking of me as I am now not by your side.

I live here in the town named Colombo, at the beach of the mountain Sarandib, the mountain where Adam fled when he had angered God, and stayed there separated from our mother Eve for some time, but was again through the mercy of Exalted God, after acknowledging his sins and praying for forgiveness, restored to his wife's side and accepted in mercy, which we must all take as an example and hope that after ardent prayer we may again be brought together in eternity, which we will all beg of God and hope to be heard.[41]

In this brief passage Surapati located himself in relation to Adam and his exilic fate: He described Colombo as a town on the shore, whereas inland from that coast stood Mt. Sarandib, the only point in the

---

[41] Translation of a Javanese letter in Arabic letters written by the sender Tommengong Soerapattij from Ceylon to his mother, wives and children, received in Batavia on July 11, 1724, in NL-HaNA, VOC, 1.04.02, inv. nr. 8939, 471. I have added to the scant punctuation in the original. The writer addresses his mother in the honorific (D. *uwe Edele*), which he likely would have done in the Javanese.

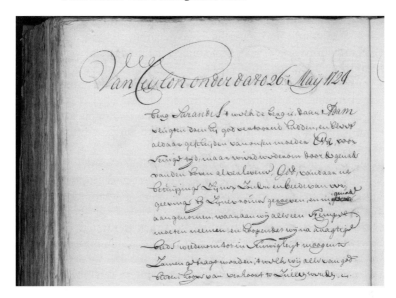

Figure 6.3 Detail from the exiled Surapati's 1724 letter to his family in Java, in Dutch translation. The top line mentions Mt. Sarandib (*berg Sarandib*) as the site of Adam's banishment. NL-HaNA, VOC, 1.04.02, inv. nr. 8939, 471.
Courtesy Department of National Archives, Sri Lanka

landscape of the island that he took care to mention. He depicted the mountain as the place where Adam fled after angering God and, separated from Eve, alone, declared his sins and prayed for forgiveness, which God ultimately granted. Surapati took Adam's plight explicitly as a model for his own: He was like Adam, having angered God and thus received the punishment of exile from his native land, separated painfully from the distant family he wrote to with such longing. He referred to Eve as "mother," i.e. the mother of humanity, while writing to his own, particular and beloved mother, thus conflating the two; and he called on her to pray ardently, as he would do too, and beg before God, with the hope of reuniting one day. Surapati did not dare expect a reunion that would soon transpire, a return home and a meeting with his own "Eve": All he felt he could aspire to was an eventual meeting in the afterlife.

Surapati's letter, despite its brevity and its inaccessibility in the original, conveys the loneliness and pain of exile but also the hope and resilience that Adam's example provided. It offered comfort and inspiration, and insight into an experience which, due to Adam's plight, is deeply instilled in humanity. The ancient story of Adam's banishment from Paradise to earth, a paradigm for all future banishments – from original home to a strange land; from divine realm to human suffering – was deployed to frame and partially give meaning to exile to Ceylon, fostering connections and echoes that shaped the way Ceylon was experienced. For one, recalling Adam's fall shifted the temporal frame of political exile under colonial domination, and located contemporary, worldly events within a divinely determined chronology. It offered an alternative approach to time and causality, putting colonialism's structures of authority and its durability in perspective within a much larger, even cosmic, framework.

Referencing Adam put Ceylon on the map, adding a spatial dimension to those of meaning and time: It was no longer just a godforsaken place of exile but home to the important Islamic sacred site of Adam's Peak, itself somewhat "exilic" in its location far from the Middle East, yet according to some traditions its rocks contributing to the structure of the Ka'ba. The important site, and the possibility that their arrival in Ceylon was not only banishment but also a return, introduced some measure of familiarity to a foreign land in which, over time, the Malays established a new home. In considering Adam and Sarandib the link to place was further strengthened by the Hebrew etymology of Adam's name and its relationship to the word for earth, *adama*, the feminine form of *adam*, i.e. human, man, highlighting not only the trope of paradigmatic exile but also that of an acquired attachment to place, be it the post-Paradise human world or, specifically, Ceylon.

As Chapter 6 explored the links between the story of Adam's banishment to Sarandib and exile to colonial Ceylon, this chapter asks whether the Ramayana – with its central theme of banishment to Lanka – played a role in the Malay exilic imagination. Contemplating Lanka and banishment, one cannot but think of the Ramayana, a pivotal religious, cultural and literary force across South and Southeast Asia for many centuries. Did exiles and their descendants implicitly or explicitly connect Lanka with Ceylon and Sarandib, and the story of Rama and Sita's exile to the forest, and especially Sita's banishment to Lanka, with their own collective biography? These questions are considered within the context of the Ramayana's importance in the Indonesian–Malay world whence it was brought to Ceylon in its Malay telling as part of the Malays' literary and cultural repository and where, moreover, its significance may have been maintained and even enhanced through its principal theme of exile.

In exploring these themes, while building on the discussion of Adam's fall, the chapter considers nomenclature histories, delving further into the ways in which different names that converge on the "same" site can shape profoundly divergent imaginaries and perspectives. Additionally, the chapter offers a close reading of relevant sections of the Malay *Hikayat Seri Rama*, a Ramayana telling that was known and copied in colonial Ceylon, and in which nabi Adam – the protagonist of Chapter 6 – made several appearances. Recalling Massey's reconceptualization of space as "a simultaneity of stories-so-far,"[1] the concrete place with its shifting names is taken as a starting point to examine how these two seminal episodes of exile – those of Adam and Rama/Sita – focus their imaginings on the very same island, and how their stories intertwined with one another and with that of the Malays.[2] The theme of mobility,

---

[1] Massey, *For Space*, 9.
[2] The question of whether the island forms a shared site of exilic traditions due to coincidence or to a history of interreligious contact and appropriation is not of central importance here. Clearly the footprint on the mountain was a site sacred to Muslims,

in multiple directions, is again palpable: in the transmission of stories across the centuries and religious traditions, in the horizontal image of the bridge that connects Lanka and southeast India, known both as Rama's Bridge (*Rama Sethu*), on which the monkey army crossed in search of Sita, and as Adam's Bridge, on which Adam crossed while searching for Eve, and in the vertical climb of pilgrims, inspired by competing and intertwining stories, to the mountaintop where a sacred footprint awaits.

As A. K. Ramanujan wrote in his seminal essay "Three Hundred Ramayanas: Five Examples and Three Thoughts on Translation," "in India and in Southeast Asia no one ever reads the Ramayana or the Mahabharata for the first time. The stories are there, 'always already.'"[3] The Ramayana – the story of Rama, an incarnation of the god Vishnu, a great king and, in some tellings, a fallible human – has circulated for many centuries and has been expressed through poetry, prose, sculpture, dance, music and theater; it has permeated the languages of India in the form of idioms, quotes, riddles and songs. Told and retold in many languages and genres, the Ramayana – from the seventh century onward if not earlier – commenced its "epic voyages" to Java, Bali, Thailand, Burma, Cambodia and further afield, transforming in its wake the cultural traditions of these societies.[4]

No justice can be done here to the hundreds of tellings of the Ramayana, the many voices and perspectives, events and relationships emphasized by particular authors and reciters. Therefore, only some of the broadest and most common themes are mentioned, chief among them the story of exile that lies at the Ramayana's core. After his father King Dasharatha must fulfill an old promise to one of his wives who wished her son to be king, Rama is banished to the forest for fourteen years along with his wife Sita and younger brother Laksmana. During this period of exile from Ayodhya occurred the event that would propel the rest of the narrative forward: Sita was kidnapped by the ten-headed

---

Buddhists, Hindus and Christians. Thus, Adam's landing on that spot could be tied to Hindu sacred space, i.e. not to the Ramayana directly but still within a cultural sphere in which both Rama and the Buddha were often viewed as incarnations of the god Vishnu.

[3] A. K. Ramanujan, "Three Hundred Ramayanas: Five Examples and Three Thoughts on Translation," in Paula Richman (ed.), *Many Ramayanas: The Diversity of a Narrative Tradition in South Asia* (Berkeley: University of California Press, 1991), 46.

[4] On evidence that the Ramayana was known in Champa as early as the seventh century, see Jan Fontein, "The Abduction of Sita: Notes on a Stone Relief from Eastern Java," *Boston Museum Bulletin*, 71 (1973), 21; Laurie J. Sears, "Epic Voyages: The Transmission of the Epics from India to Java," in Stephanie Morgan and Laurie J. Sears (eds.), *Aesthetic Tradition and Cultural Transmission in Java and Bali* (Madison: University of Wisconsin Press, 1984), 1–30.

demon king of Lanka, Ravana, and taken to his palace, to be held in captivity across the sea until Rama came to rescue her. Depictions of the island of Lanka vary, but in many Ravana was a great king who ruled a powerful land of riches. For Sita and those searching for her, Lanka was an island of exile and captivity and, within it, the site that encapsulated the loneliness, longing and pain of the exilic condition was a grove of Ashoka trees near the palace where Sita was held and watched over by her demoness guardians, withering away as she refused Ravana's advances and prayed for Rama's arrival.

In Ramayana scholarship, as well as within the tradition, the exile *par excellence* of the Ramayana is understood to be that experienced by Rama during his years in the forest, when he sacrificed power, palace and prestige to respect his father's wish. Sita's plight has been commonly viewed as abduction and imprisonment, her great suffering a "byproduct" of conflicts or destinies in which she was entangled, but which were not her own. Moreover, in Ramayana studies and in popular devotion, the physical island known as Sri Lanka does not command much importance, as can be evinced from the dearth of Ramayana-associated sites across the landscape, most of which are of relatively recent commemoration.[5] There is no agreement as to whether contemporary Sri Lanka coincides with the island and kingdom depicted in the Ramayana.[6] Sri Lanka itself, quite strikingly, as Ananda Guruge stated, "is unique among the countries of Southeast and South Asia in that the Ramayana neither has been nor is a part of the living cultural tradition."[7] No dance or theatrical adaptations have entered its folk culture, neither sculptors nor painters created in Sri Lanka any artwork even remotely reminiscent of the Ramayana representations in Prambanan or Angkor Wat, and no national version of the Ramayana was produced (as happened in Thailand, Laos and Cambodia). The only relevant

[5] The main Ramayana sites in Sri Lanka are the small Seetha Amman temple at the location where Sita is believed to have been held captive, and the nearby Hakgala Botanical Gardens where Hanuman is said to have found the medicinal herb needed for Laksmana's revival. Rawana is associated with the Koneśwaram Temple built on a cliff overlooking the Indian Ocean near Trincomalee, where he is believed to have worshipped Shiva and to which he contributed one of the original *linga* he brought from Mt. Kailaśa in Tibet. Some say the ruins of his own palace lie in the sea below.

[6] For an archeological perspective on the Ramayana, see H. D. Sankalia, *Ramayana: Myth or Reality?* (New Delhi: People's Publishing House, 1973). For a discussion of the link, or lack thereof, between the name "Lanka" and the island, see C. E. Godakumbura, "Ramayana in Sri Lanka and Lanka in the Ramayana," in K. Krishnamoorthy and Jithendra Nath (eds.), *A Critical Inventory of Ramayana Studies in the World: Foreign Languages* (New Delhi: Sahitya Akademi, 1993), 99–100, 114–115.

[7] Ananda W. P. Guruge, "Sri Lankan Attitude to the Ramayana: A Historical Analysis," *Indologica Taurinensia*, 19–20 (1993–1994), 131.

literary works in Sinhala are recent adaptations of Kamban's twelfth-century Tamil Ramayana found in several manuscripts, this absence most likely due to a Buddhist rejection of the Ramayana (and Mahabharata) as "futile talk," which prevented their entry into the main-stream of literature.[8]

The traditional priority given to Rama's exile and the lack of popularity of the Ramayana within Sri Lanka's cultural history aside, in this chapter it is Sita's, rather than Rama's, banishment that explicitly takes center stage, and echoes with other banishments – metaphorical and historical – whose destination was Lanka. The point is not that the Lanka of the Ramayana and the physical island were taken to be one and the same within a broader Sri Lankan or even South Asian cultural context, or that the Malays' forefathers arrived in a place where the Ramayana tradition and its connection to exile were paramount, but that Lanka was famed and significant in the culture whence the royal exiles came, and could have therefore resonated in their thoughts and imagination when they were sent to its shores.

The Ramayana was known in Java from at least the ninth century, to which century the earliest written version extant, the *Kakawin Ramayana*, is dated. This is a poetic work considered among the most intricate and beautiful to have been produced in Javanese and attributed traditionally to the poet Yogiswara. The Ramayana's long-standing popularity is clear from the inspiration it gave to a range of literary genres, its widespread incorporation within performative traditions of shadow puppetry and dance, and the carving of its heroes and episodes in stone on temple walls across Java, including Prambanan (c. tenth century) and Panataran (c. fourteenth century).[9] With Java's gradual Islamization, the Ramayana's popularity did not diminish. Rather, the meanings ascribed to it shifted. In the early eighteenth century, as Ricklefs has shown, pre-Islamic works were read as expressing a

---

[8] Guruge, "Sri Lankan Attitude," 145. Interestingly, however, both Rawana and Vibhisana are mentioned in folklore, as well as in Sanskrit Buddhist literature, as disciples of the Buddha (ibid., 142–144), and Vibhisana, Rawana's estranged brother who crossed over to become a devotee of Rama, was deified and worshipped at Kelaniya (ibid., 139). Godakumbura discusses a Sinhala folk tradition related to the Ramayana in which several of its main characters appear and the connection of this story to a local occult ceremony, but notes that it is known only to traditional performers and students of folklore. See Godakumbura, "Ramayana in Sri Lanka," xcv.

[9] For a theory based on epigraphical evidence from ninth-century Java combined with textual evidence from the *Kakawin Ramayana* that the temple site now named Prambanan was originally known as Langkapura, see Arlo Griffiths, "Imagine Laṅkāpura at Prambanan," in Andrea Acri, Helen Creese and Arlo Griffiths (eds.), *From Laṅkā Eastwards: The Rāmāyaṇa in the Literature and Visual Arts of Indonesia* (Leiden: KITLV, 2011), 133–148.

thoroughly Sufi worldview: In the *Serat Cabolek*, where the relationship between Java's rich pre-Islamic heritage and devout Sufi Islam was addressed, Ketib Anom of Kudus claimed that even if his opponent Mutamakim were to ship all the books of Arabia to Java it would be in vain, for in the hands of the knowledgeable interpreter Old Javanese books such as the Ramayana, *Bima Suci* and *Arjunawiwaha* were works of Islamic mysticism which contained all the necessary teachings. Pre-Islamic literature was thus incorporated into Javanese Islamic civilization, and the Ramayana clearly retained a place in its revised canon.[10] With the Ramayana receiving such interpretations, its ongoing visibility in Javanese architecture and arts, and its availability in central Java's court libraries whence came many of the eighteenth-century exiles to Ceylon, it can be safely assumed that it was familiar to at least some of them, and later to their descendants.[11]

An allusion to this familiarity is found in the Javanese *Babad Tanah Jawi*, a multiversion corpus that dates to the eighteenth century and chronicles Java's history from Adam to the Mataram dynasty. The *Babad* relates briefly that Pakubuwana II, who was anointed in 1726 after the death of his father Amangkurat Jawi (r. 1719–1726), refused to sit on the throne in Kartasura for an entire year, insisting on sitting on a mat and pillow whenever he held audience (J. *tinangkil*) in his palace.[12] The chief minister Danureja could not convince him to do otherwise and eventually turned to the king's older brother, Pangéran Arya Mangkunagara, asking him for assistance in convincing the young monarch that his conduct was improper. As was discussed in Chapter 4, Pangéran Arya was the expected heir to the throne of Kartasura but was deprived of rule at the

---

[10] Merle C. Ricklefs, *Mystic Synthesis in Java: A History of Islamization from the Fourteenth to the Early Nineteenth Centuries* (Norwalk, CT: EastBridge, 2006), 116–117.

[11] Old Javanese/Kawi pre-Islamic works including the Ramayana were still well known and understood, discussed and interpreted in central Java in the 1730s, yet this tendency may have been severely challenged, or even largely eliminated, after the fall of Kartasura in 1742, the sacking of the court's treasures and death of many of those knowledgeable about the tradition; see Ricklefs, *Seen and Unseen*, 336. I am unaware of any Old Javanese works that were transmitted to Ceylon but in theory such texts that were no longer widely read in Java could have been preserved there. Interestingly in the context of the Sri Lankan Malays, some of whom trace their genealogies to Sumenep on the island of Madura, the Madurese king Cakraningrat IV ordered many of the Javanese manuscripts of Kartasura looted and brought to his palace, and evidently for some time his descendants could still preserve and patronize a classical literature that after 1742 became marginal to court culture in central Java. On the looting of manuscripts, see Ricklefs, *Seen and Unseen*, 337. On a letter from 1843 in which the ruler of Sumenep was described as an authority on Kawi, see Pigeaud, *Literature of Java*, II: 91.

[12] *Sampun jangkep sataun/yèn kalané miyos tinangkil/tan arsa munggèng dhampar/nèng pangrawitipun/mung lanté lawan kasuran* (*Babad Tanah Jawi* [BP], 21: 19, in Dhandhanggula). The complete episode is narrated on pp. 19–21.

last minute, based on an agreement between his dying father and the Dutch. The episode recalls the scene in the Ramayana in which Bharata learned that his elder brother Rama was deprived of ruling the kingdom and refused to sit on the throne in his place. Bharata rushed after Rama and, when unable to persuade him to return, placed Rama's sandals on the throne, sat on the floor beside it, and announced that he would not ascend it himself until the true king – Rama – returned from exile. The circumstances narrated in the *Babad* are different, yet there too a younger brother who had kingship bestowed upon him refuses to sit physically on the throne in place of the elder sibling until he returns or, in the case of Pakubuwana II, until a meeting took place between the brothers, after which the king began sitting in state as expected. This depiction suggests that the two members of the court who were soon to be exiled to Ceylon, Pangéran Arya Mangkunagara and Patih Danureja, were well, even intimately, acquainted with the Ramayana, in ways that influenced their conduct and their ideas about kingship, hierarchy and family.

And yet the question remains, did exiles and the generations that followed make a connection between the Lanka of the well-loved Ramayana and the island to which they were banished? What might it have been like to read, or listen to, tales of earlier exiles to the same island once they had arrived at their destination? Writing of Hindu communities, Kenny Kevin in his work on diaspora mentions the Ramayana as a text that was read across great distances, becoming "the central text of the Indian diaspora." He further elaborates how "migrant workers from Trinidad to Fiji, South Africa to Suriname, and Guyana to Malaysia recited verses from Tulsidas' Hindi Ramayana in public performances, just as wealthier migrants to Britain and America host readings of the text today."[13] For example, for indentured laborers sent from north India to Fiji from 1879 to 1920, the Ramayana's narrative of Rama's fourteen-year exile to the forest carried a special resonance as they recognized their own experiences of dislocation in the epic. The descendants of such laborers, migrating away from Fiji in the past several decades as a result of Fijian ethnonationalism and economic factors, have been called the "twice banished", a term that "collapses the contemporary migrant's experience with both the indentured labourer's 'exile' of a century before and Ram's 'banishment' to the forest during antiquity."[14]

---

[13] Kenny Kevin, *Diaspora: A Very Short Introduction* (New York: Oxford University Press, 2014), 44.

[14] Kevin C. Miller, "Beyond Exile: The Ramayana as a Living Narrative among Indo-Fijians in Fiji and New Zealand," in Farzana Gounder (ed.), *Narrative and Identity Construction in the Pacific Islands* (Amsterdam: John Benjamins, 2015), 236.

For those far from their places of origin, whether due to political exile, the demands of forced labor, or servitude, the connection with Lanka as a site of exile could be concrete or symbolic. Anand Yang writes of survivors of the south Indian Poligar Wars of the late eighteenth century, who were exiled by the British to Penang in 1801. In a series of moving petitions, consistently rejected, they asked to be allowed to return home after years of separation and misery. In a petition from 1815 the prisoners noted specifically that a banishment of fourteen years could not be considered "a light punishment even for atrocious crimes," very likely alluding to Rama's fourteen years in the forest. As Yang explains, it is not surprising that the prisoners drew on the storehouse of the Ramayana, part of popular religious imagination, with stories of exile and of Lanka, the island capital of the evil demon Ravana, appealing especially to prisoners and convicts transported to different islands across the Indian Ocean. Moreover, convicts, regardless of where they were transported, often "considered their penal settlements to be their Lanka."[15] For example, the archive contains the testimony of an escaped prisoner who was heard by a police informant telling his audience that he had returned from Lanka, even though he had been in Penang.[16]

If the story has been so important to South Asian diasporas around the world, and certainly to political exiles and defeated warriors who resisted British rule, as it resonated deeply with their tribulations and sense of longing and loss, all the more so for the Malays in Ceylon who found themselves – physically and not just metaphorically – in the same site of banishment as Sita. Through an identification with her experiences in that very place, they forged a concrete link with her ordeal and her yearning to reunite with Rama, which corresponded to their own desires for familiar places and loved ones. It is not at all obvious that such an identification would emerge in the Malay imagination and in literary references. Whereas the Ramayana's place within a Hindu cultural sphere was pivotal, and it served as a warehouse for ideas, ideals and images of kingship, divinity, love, social hierarchy and gender relations, this was not the case, for the most part, for Muslims. Although familiar to many living in South Asia, the Ramayana did not typically constitute a repository to draw on for inspiration or analogy.[17] For example, Tamil Muslims in Ceylon, where they often lived in close physical and cultural

---

[15] Anand Yang, "Bandits and Kings: Moral Authority and Resistance in Early Modern India," *Journal of Asian Studies,* 66.4 (2007), 891.

[16] Anand Yang, personal communication, November 5, 2012.

[17] In an example to the contrary, devotees of the regional deity Kullayappa in Andhra Pradesh, south India, view him as Rama incarnated in a Muslim *pīr*. Within this tradition Fatima, the Prophet's daughter, assumes characteristics similar to those of Sita. See

proximity with Malays, did not possess a tradition of reading the Ramayana or performing it as did their co-religionists coming from the Indonesian–Malay world. It appears that the Ramayana's importance among Malays remained intact even at a great distance from the archipelago, even when other Muslim communities in Ceylon did not engage with it in any way or form, even when, as discussed, the broader society in the midst of which they lived did not possess a substantial Ramayana tradition.[18]

Thinking about Rama and Sita, and about Sita's plight, in the Malay world meant imagining the kingdom of Langka, Langkapuri or (in Javanese) Alengka, Lengka or Ngalengka. This was a fabulously wealthy kingdom ruled by the ten-headed demon king Rawana who, despite all his power and riches, was doomed to failure because of actions contradicting morality and his own dharma as warrior and king. Portrayed in texts, oral tellings and the wayang shadow puppet theater, "Lengka" was a name that conjured awe, beauty and power, Sita's pain and longing, epic battles and death and, ultimately, Rawana's destruction. As the names Sarandib and Ceylon were employed for framing the same island in particular yet different ways, tied to specific understandings of history and genealogy, so "Lengka" was firmly rooted in the intimately familiar world of the Ramayana. To consider if and how these nomenclatures were linked is to ask whether these were parallel, synonymous or perhaps competing nomenclatures for a single place or, possibly, names that were employed for what their users believed to be distinct sites rather than a shared location. Far from constituting a technicality or a marginal scholarly quibble, this is a query that can help assess whether the different exile narratives of Adam, Sita and the eighteenth-century banished were, or could have been, linked in people's imagination and lived experience. As discussed in Chapter 6, Ceylon and Sarandib did appear together, as synonyms, in at least some Javanese sources, including the late nineteenth-century *Samud* and the eighteenth-century *Ménak Serandil*. Less obvious, however, at least explicitly, is if and how Lanka was associated with Sarandib and, even more pertinently if lived exile is considered, whether Lanka was associated with colonial Ceylon.

Finding self-reflexive eighteenth-century accounts that describe life in exile in Ceylon, including its cultural, religious and literary aspects, is

Afsar Mohammad, *The Festival of Pīrs: Popular Islam and Shared Devotion in South India* (New York: Oxford University Press, 2013), 16, 76.

[18] Another example of a Southeast Asian-Muslim Ramayana tradition is found among the Maranao Muslims of the southern Philippines, whose Ramayana is titled *Maharadia Lawana*. See Juan R. Francisco, "The Ramayana in the Philippines," in Krishnamoorthy and Nath (eds.), *A Critical Inventory of Ramayana Studies*, 119–145.

rare. In order to address the nomenclature conundrum as well as the broader implications of connecting exilic stories and memories, the *Hikayat Seri Rama*, a Malay telling of the Ramayana which was known and narrated on the island in the nineteenth century, will be explored. The *Hikayat Seri Rama* weaves together the different traditions discussed thus far, the lived experience of exile in Ceylon, and an association between the disparate yet related names of the island and the echoes they carried.

The *Hikayat Seri Rama* was popular in the Malay-speaking world from at least the early seventeenth century as the oldest extant copy (MS Laud Or. 291), now at Oxford, was purchased by a merchant and taken back to England in 1633. This manuscript is not only the oldest Malay Ramayana extant but among the oldest of any surviving Malay manuscripts. Its content, a Hindu devotional text written in jawi and incorporating Islamic terminology and references, constitutes a monument to the kinds of connections and syntheses that were forming during the transition from pre-Islamic to Islamic culture in the Malay world. As is common in Malay writing, this is a literary tradition with considerable internal variability, and the manuscripts tend to be lengthy, ranging from three hundred to eight hundred pages. Several prominent scholars of Malay have devoted efforts toward studying this Malay Ramayana and analyzing its structure and components, with an emphasis on mapping the different sources that influenced its writing.[19]

As might be expected of such philological comparisons, the first point of call tended to be Valmiki's Sanskrit Ramayana, long considered the gold standard, especially before the internal diversity of the vernacular Ramayana tradition across South and Southeast Asia was fully recognized by scholars. As early as 1843, Philippus P. Roorda van Eysinga published what he called a "Malay translation" of the Indian epic, and others followed.[20] More fruitfully, scholars have searched broadly for

---

[19] See for example R. O. Windstedt, "An Undescribed Malay Version of the Ramayana," *JRAS* 76. 1–2 (April 1944): 62–73; Russell Jones, "One of the Oldest Malay Manuscripts Extant: The Laud Or. 291 Manuscript of the *Hikayat Seri Rama*," *Indonesia Circle*, November 1986 (41): 49–53; H. Overbeck, "*Hikayat Maharaja Rawana*," *JRAS* Malayan Branch 11.2 (1933): 111–132.

[20] P. P. Roorda van Eysinga, *Geschidenis van Sri Rama, beroemd Indisch Heroisch Dichtstuk, oorspronkelijk van Valmic en naar eene Maleische vertaling daarvan uitgegeven* (Amsterdam: L. van Bakkenes, 1843). See W. G. Shellabear, "Hikayat Sri Rama: Introduction to the MS in the Bodleian Library at Oxford," *Journal of the Straits Branch of the Royal Asiatic Society* 70 (1917): 181–207, for a summary of Valmiki with notes on the main differences with the Malay *Hikayat*. For a detailed study comparing Malay versions with Valmiki, see Alexander Zieseniss, *The Rama Saga in Malaysia: Its Origin and Development*, trans. P. W. Burch with an introduction by C. Hooykaas (Singapore: Malaysian Sociological Research Institute, 1963).

connections and echoes rather than precise lines of transmission. They have found hints of Jaina Ramayanas, possible Javanese sources, and have repeatedly pointed to evidence of south Indian, most likely Tamil, elements adopted into the *Hikayat*.[21] The Dutch philologists H. H. Juynboll and Philippus Samuel van Ronkel both made suggestions to this effect in the early twentieth century, based primarily on name forms that they considered to be south Indian.[22] In an illuminating article comparing Ramayana tellings in Sanskrit, Tamil, Thai and Malay, Sachithanantham Singaravelu pointed to the great diversity of the Ramayana tradition but also called attention to clear connections between south Indian, Malay and Thai tellings.[23] For example, he cited similarities between the Thai and Malay texts in their emphasis on descriptions of the birth and early life of Ravana and Hanuman over those of Rama's birth and early achievements. As for the south Indian element, Singaravelu noted events within the Malay narrative such as Sita's birth as Ravana's daughter and her dropping of a ring into Jatayu's beak, both known from Tamil, as proof. Moreover, and like his predecessors referring to nomenclature as hinting at routes of textual transmission, he showed that the name Patala Maryam (a character in the *Hikayat* and a son of Hanuman in Javanese shadow theater tellings) comes from the Tamil form Patāla Maharāyan, with *maharāyan* a variety of *mahārājā* or *mahārājān*, "great king" in Tamil. R. O. Windstedt in his study also highlighted Dravidian name forms such as names ending in "ammā," and Hans Overbeck in a discussion of a telling titled *Hikayat Maharaja Rawana* found in it hints of south Indian sources.[24] The title of a Javanese adaptation of the *Hikayat*, *Serat Rama Keling*, points in the

[21] For a hypothesis concerning Javanese, see L. F. Brakel, "Two Indian Epics in Malay," *Archipel* 20 (1980): 143–160.
[22] H. H. Juynboll, "Eene Episode uit het Oudindische Ramayana Vergeleken met de Javaansche en Maleische Bewerkingen," *BKI* 50.1 (1899): 59–66; H. H. Juynboll, "Eene Episode uit het Oudindische Ramayana Vergeleken met de Javaansche en Maleische Bewerkingen," *BKI* 54.1 (1902): 501–565; Ph. S. van Ronkel, "Aanteekeningen op een Ouden Maleischen Ramajana-Tekst," *BKI* 75.1 (1919): 379–383.
[23] S. Singaravelu, "A Comparative Study of the Sanskrit, Tamil, Thai and Malay Versions of the Story of Rama, with Special Reference to the Process of Acculturation in the Southeast Asian Versions," *Journal of the Siam Society* 56.2 (1968): 137–185. As an example of the crosscultural reach of the Ramayana and its characters and the different claims and significance attached to them, Singaravelu shows that the Laṅkāvatāra Sūtra of the second to third centuries CE mentions Ravana as a person of unmatched learning who had a discourse with the Buddha (ibid., 151).
[24] Windstedt, "An Undescribed Malay Version of the Ramayana," 66; Overbeck, "*Hikayat Maharaja Rawana*."

same direction, as "Keling" (from Kalinga) refers to south India, especially its Tamil region, or to people originating there.[25]

Such comparisons, and the highlighting of similar narrative and linguistic elements across languages and traditions, can be valuable although, as argued by Achadiati Ikram, author of the most extensive study of the *Hikayat* to date, the *Hikayat* may be best studied as a work in its own right – and as an expression of the cultural, linguistic and religious perspectives of those who composed it – rather than a collection of influences and borrowings pieced together.[26] When links are nonetheless drawn, they are at their most relevant when a broader point is pursued beyond the tracing of "influence," one that sheds light on, for instance, histories of contact and exchange. In the case of the Malays in colonial Ceylon, that more comprehensive point has to do with the question of return. Ancient Sarandib, later also called Ceylon, was discussed as an abode of banishment and exile but also one of return: Adam, according to several Malay texts from Ceylon, was commanded to return to Sarandib in order to settle and procreate; Malays sent away to Ceylon from the archipelago were also returning to the site of Adam's paradigmatic exile; individuals were sometimes exiled, sent home, then banished again. In the case of the *Hikayat Seri Rama* the discussion can be expanded also to stories and texts that circulated, taking unexpected routes of travel and return: The Ramayana that the Malays were reading in eighteenth- and nineteenth-century Ceylon initially drew on Indian models – whether "classical," vernacular, written, oral or all of these – in all likelihood, at least partly modeled on nearby south India's significant Tamil literary tradition. Theirs was a Rama story which had traveled to the archipelago and its vicinity several centuries earlier, had been adapted and recast, and now returned to Ceylon in its Malay incarnation.[27]

---

[25] In many of the Southeast Asian accounts of Adam's fall, Iblis lands in Keling; see Chapter 6. In the *Hikayat Seri Rama* from Ceylon (on which see below), Rama is said to be the ruler of Keling (*dalam Benua Keling ada seorang raja terlalu besar kerajaannya*); see M. M. G. Weerabangsa, *Hikayat Seri Rama*, Trincomalee, n.d., Hussainmiya Collection, Department of National Archives, Sri Lanka, MF 176, 1.

[26] Achadiati Ikram, *Hikayat Sri Rama: suntingan naskah disertai telaah amanat dan struktur* (Jakarta: Universitas Indonesia, 1980).

[27] Concurrently, hints of Tamil in a mid-nineteenth-century Sri Lankan Malay manuscript of the *Hikayat* could also be contemporary, recent additions by a scribe or reciter who was considering an audience whose language had been inflected by that spoken by many fellow Muslims, and others, in Ceylon at the time. Thus, in the scene when Hanuman visits Cintadewi (Sita's Malay name) in Lankapuri where she is held captive, she offers him some fruit. The depiction reads: *Maka diambilnya oleh Cintadewi mam palam artinya mangga dua buah yang sentapan itu* – "And then Cintadewi took *mam palam*, meaning mango, [and gave him] two ripe fruits" (*Hikayat Seri Rama*, 1865, Perpustakaan Negara Malaysia, Kuala Lumpur, MS PNM 1056, 473). Using a construct very typical of

Despite a sense of relevance and familiarity, it is difficult to assess the precise place of the *Hikayat Seri Rama*, and the Ramayana tradition more broadly, within Malay cultural life in Ceylon and, even more so, to point to the ways in which it inhabited people's imaginations. It is certainly challenging to assess how widely it was read, on what occasions, and what its ambit of associations consisted of. To date, two manuscripts of the *Hikayat* have been found in Sri Lanka, both dating from the second half of the nineteenth century and both incomplete. The first manuscript, inscribed by M. M. G. Weerabangsa of Kandy Road in Trincomalee, ends abruptly after approximately two hundred pages in the midst of the scene depicting Rama and Laksmana's meeting with the bird Jatayu who had tried to prevent Sita's kidnapping and was fatally injured by Rawana. Just before he breathed his last, Jatayu was able to tell Rama the direction in which Sita was taken, and to give him Sita's ring as proof of the encounter. This episode precedes those depicting Sita's plight of banishment in Lanka, and much of the narrative remains untold.[28] The second manuscript, inscribed by Encik Hakim ibnu Guru Salim in Trincomalee, on the other hand, includes all the later episodes, but its opening pages and sections of its two final pages are missing.[29] Despite the challenges presented by such fragmentary sources, the compelling centrality of Lanka and of banishment, both to the Ramayana and to Malay history in Ceylon, merit consideration and comparison. This is the case, moreover, because the *Hikayat Seri Rama* presents a remarkable intertwining of Ceylon's exilic traditions and their place in the literary and religious imagination.[30]

The *Hikayat Sri Rama* opens with the following scene: At the age of twelve Rawana was so strong that when he smacked his playmates they would fall dead. His grandfather Bermaraja therefore decided to send him into exile (*membuang*). The young Rawana was placed in a boat and taken to Mt. Sarandib. He wandered about but could not find any food. For twelve years he performed austerities by hanging upside down from a

translation between Arabic and Malay in the Malay writing tradition, i.e. a word or phrase appearing in Arabic followed by "artinya" – "the meaning of which is," "this is to say" – and then a Malay translation, the *Hikayat* casually translates the Tamil word for mango, *mām paḷam*, into Malay *mangga*. Whether a remnant of an old translation effort or a contemporary addition, such instances strengthen the impression of the *Hikayat*'s relevance to its particular audience in Ceylon and to its South Asian links.

[28] M. M. G. Weerabangsa, *Hikayat Seri Rama*, Hussainmiya Collection, MF 176.
[29] Encik Hakim ibnu Guru Salim, *Hikayat Seri Rama*, Trincomalee, 1859, Perpustakaan Negara Malaysia, Kuala Lumpur, MS PNM 1055.
[30] Due to the incomplete state of the two Sri Lankan Malay exemplars of the *Hikayat* and because they appear to be very similar in content, wording and style to the telling edited by Ikram, several examples from her edition have been included in the discussion.

tree. At that same time, Allah sent down nabi Adam from Paradise (*sorga*) and one morning, as he was walking the earth, he came across Rawana.[31] Curious, he asked: "Why are you in this state and for how long have you been hanging down like this?" "Twelve years," was the reply. Adam asked if Rawana wished to ask Allah for anything and expressed hope that he would be able to make the request on Rawana's behalf. Rawana then disclosed his wish to possess four kingdoms: this world (*dunia*), the earth (*bumi*), the sea (*laut*) and the heavens (*keinderaan*).

Adam (whose name is followed by the blessing 'alaihi al-salām, "peace be upon him") told Rawana that if he promised to abide by his word then he – Adam – would petition God on his behalf, and Rawana committed to doing so. Adam then put forth the conditions for possessing the four kingdoms: Rawana must not defame his parents or subjects and must rule justly and never disobey Allah. And he must accept that if he ever committed a wrong, or his people did and he did not punish them, God would destroy him. Adam then repeats his claim that if Rawana promises to fulfill these conditions he will pass on his wish to God and reminds him that whatever kingdoms and powers he may possess they are all ultimately "*pinjaman saja*": borrowed, only his temporarily, implying that God alone owns everything. Finally, Adam cautions Rawana: "Don't be like me – sent away from Paradise because I didn't follow God's command." To show he concurs, Rawana states that if he ever commits any of the wrongs mentioned he shall be cursed a thousand times by Allah. Then Adam turns to God and Rawana is granted the four kingdoms he desires. In several instances throughout the story Rawana is reminded of, or challenged by, his promise to nabi Adam, always claiming he is committed to his words.[32] Thus begins the Ramayana, with Rawana, and with Adam, both exiled, at the same time, to the same place: Sarandib Mountain. The two cross paths, as do their stories.[33]

In another, much later episode, Hanuman speaks to Sita, whom he secretly visits in the Asoka grove, and tells her how he crossed over to

---

[31] This opening scene of the *Hikayat* resonates with Ramayana tellings in which Shiva, rather than Adam, meets Rawana as he meditates and offers him the boons.

[32] Ikram, *Hikayat Sri Rama*, 136, 167. When after his son Indrajit's death Rawana asks Sita if she wishes to return to Rama, she reminds him of the rewards (*pahala*) he was promised when he met with Adam while meditating (M. *bertapa*, from Sanskrit *tapas*): *yang dipertuan beroleh pahala tatkala yang dipertuan bertapa bertemu dengan nabi Adam 'alaihi as-salam* (Encik Hakim, *Hikayat Seri Rama*, MS PNM 1055, 553). Rawana, enraged, refuses to listen.

[33] Intriguingly, one of the names for the mountain where Adam fell in Arabic sources is al-Rahūn, which may be associated through sound with Rawana.

Lanka, unhurt by any of the mountains, rocks and trees along the way.[34]
Sita advises him that prior to his return he should go to the top of
Mt. Serandib (M. *Bukit Sarandib*), where he will find a black stone with
a footprint marking the site where nabi Adam descended from Paradise
(*di sanalah ada sebuah batu hitam bekas tapaqnya nabi Adam 'alaihi
al-salam tatkala turun dari dalam sorga itulah tempatnya turun demikian*).
The verb *turun*, "to descend," is repeated twice, emphasizing that the
stone is precisely the spot where Adam came down.[35] Hanuman should
hug and kiss the stone, then leap back across the ocean to Rama. After
hearing this, Hanuman climbs to the summit of the mountain and finds
the black stone. He pays his respects to it, shrinks his body to make
leaping through the air easier, steps on the stone and takes off from there,
quickly reaching Rama. The black stone evokes the perfectly square,
black rock of the Ka'ba, the heart of the Muslim world, circled by
pilgrims as they pray, ask for blessings and repentance. Sita's words to
Hanuman suggest that the smaller black stone on the mountain – modeled on the Ka'ba and perhaps more specifically on the *batu hajar
al-aswad*, the eastern cornerstone of the Ka'ba which according to tradition goes back to the time of Adam and Eve when it fell from Paradise to
show them where to build an altar – has the keramat (holiness, ability
to work wonders) power of sacred sites and individuals that will give
Hanuman the ability to fly through the air and reach Rama quickly.[36]
Adam's distant history is known to Sita. Banished to Lanka herself, she is
aware of Adam's biography and descent to earth in that very place:
One story of exile is enveloped within another.

When the battle between Rama and Rawana finally transpires, their
two armies face one another on the plain. Rawana asks his generals
about the man he sees in the distance, the one who stands tall like a
lontar palm, whose body glows like a green emerald and who resembles
the prophet Adam.[37] In this instance Adam is evoked as a model of

---

[34] Encik Hakim, *Hikayat Seri Rama*, MS PNM 1055, 481–482; Ikram, *Hikayat Sri
Rama*, 321.

[35] Encik Hakim, *Hikayat Seri Rama*, MS PNM 1055, 481. The same verb appears again
when Hanuman is on the mountaintop: *maka bertemu dia dengan batu itu tempat bekas
nabi Adam turun ke dunia itu* ("and so he came across that stone, site of the trace of the
prophet Adam's descent into the world.")

[36] The Prophet is credited with setting the stone in its current place after which he hugged
and kissed it. His actions will be emulated by all pilgrims who perform the hajj on the
Day of Judgment. The history of the stone is narrated in an anonymous Malay
manuscript from Ceylon, *Tales of the Prophets and miscellaneous*, BL, EAP450/2/1, 50.

[37] Ikram, *Hikayat Sri Rama*, 227. Adam is likened to a palm tree also in Qur'anic exegesis.
For example, Ubayy b. Ka'b cited the Prophet Muhammad as saying that "God created
Adam to be a tall man with a lot of hair on his head like the top of a palm tree." See
Wheeler, *Prophets*, 25. In its comparisons, whether explicit or subtle, the *Hikayat*

gendered beauty and Rama – who is depicted also in conventional Indian terms as green-blue in color, like the emerald or the dark raincloud – is compared to Adam as he stands upright in a show of courageous manliness. A bit later in the story, Laksmana is hurt by Indrajit's arrow and Bibusanam, Rawana's brother who had joined Rama's forces, tells Anila Anggada to go quickly to the top of Mt. Nabi Adam (peace be upon him), find a certain tree and bring back its root, bark and leaves so that the injured Laksmana may be treated. In a variation on the classical episode in which Hanuman is sent to the Himalayas to fetch a particular medicinal plant, here the cure is found nearby, again on that same sacred spot of the mountaintop, and Laksmana awakens.[38]

These examples of Adam's presence will conclude with just one more episode, though it is an especially significant one. As recounted, the *Hikayat* opens with the scene of Rawana meditating on Mt. Sarandib, meeting Adam and promising to do good in exchange for power and domination. Toward the end of the *Hikayat*, after Rawana's utter defeat, Rama is ruling Lanka. His two siblings Citradana and Bermadana tell him they wish to see Rawana who – so they have heard – is still alive and residing at the foot of Mt. Sarandib. Rama goes with them and with Laksmana, and they find Rawana leaning on a rock at the foot of the mountain. His body is covered in cuts, the flow of his blood and pus accumulating into a small river. They have a brief, laconic exchange with him and return to the palace.[39]

What is the significance of Rawana, wounded, sitting at the foot of the mountain? The scene reads as a closing of a circle, a return to the place where he first met nabi Adam and was promised great power and riches if he behaved justly and, now that he has not, he has returned to the same spot, injured and powerless, in an exile of sorts from his own nearby kingdom. As the story opened with the seed of Rawana's ruin sown in the Islamic terms of obeying Allah and remaining on His true path, so it narrates his downfall and decay (of power and body) by locating him at that same site and highlighting his failure to abide by those particular religious terms. His downfall moved him from mountaintop to -bottom, from commitment to its abuse, from a meeting with the first human and prophet to defeat by one of Adam's descendants. The story started with his exile to the mountain by his grandfather, continued with him

questions the validity of the analogies it evokes and asks about the specificity of the exilic condition vs. its openness to generalization: At different points in the story Adam, or his condition, evokes that of Sita, Rawana, and Rama.

[38] Ikram, *Hikayat Sri Rama*, 255.

[39] Encik Hakim, *Hikayat Seri Rama*, MS PNM 1055, 576–577, where the mountain is described as "*bukit tempat nabi Adam*"; Ikram, *Hikayat Sri Rama*, 295.

banishing Sita from her husband and land, only to find himself in
renewed exile from his kingdoms, riches and dominance — in the spot
where it all began. Adam's cautioning words – "do not disobey God as
I did" – were left unheeded, with both figures possessing great opportunity and potential but doomed to fail because of passions, ignorance
and the inability to find clarity of vision, their stories passed down
through the generations as cautionary lessons.

These "Adam references" within the Malay Ramayana are neither
extensive nor frequent if the length of the text and its multiple details
are considered, yet they are telling. Clearly, they weave together disparate
religious and cultural elements and make a connection among them
through depictions of, and ideas about, geography, sacred space, ideals
of kingship, courage and beauty, prophecy, memory, and exile. The
theme of exile, so central to the Ramayana and also to Adam's fall, and
tied together in the Malay *Hikayat*, provides an important lens through
which to view those listening to its recital in colonial Ceylon, exiles or
their descendants. What, if any, kinds of connections did those audiences
make, explicitly or in their minds, between the long, winding and often
enchanting story recited and their own condition? What might they have
made of the mention of Adam and the site of his fall?

A connection between the banishments of Adam and Sita does not end
with a detailed comparison of their stories nor with the explicit mention
of Adam within the Malay Ramayana. In order to contemplate both
narratives, as well as their links to experiences, understandings and
memories of exile in Ceylon – including on the "other shore" in Java –
the wider realm of literary imagination merits consideration, and especially the ways in which the Ramayana permeated writing traditions far
beyond the limits of its own narrative.

Depictions of Ceylon in Yasadipura's *Ménak Serandhil* (discussed in
Chapter 6) and in the Ramayana invite comparison. The appearance of
the king of Serandhil/Sélan, Raja Lamdahur, is described in detail,
including his tusks, huge hairy body and mighty club (*gada*), and he is
compared explicitly to a giant demon, a *danawa*. In other words, he
seems very Rawana-like.[40] In a scene in which Umarmaya brings a letter
from Ménak to King Lamdahur and tricks him into thinking there was a
problem with a gem on his crown, then quickly jumps up and escapes
with the precious crown, running at lightning speed with chaos ensuing,

---

[40] The king is said to possess black troops from Bengal and Surat, and white ones from
Selangor, the Maldives, Spain and France, yet all local troops are depicted as red, a
possible reference – thinking in "Ramayana terms" – to the always-red countenance of
the demons (*raksasa*) in Javanese shadow puppet theater.

echoes of Hanuman's escape from his audience with Rawana are heard; when King Lamdahur challenges Ménak, giving him his special club while being certain he will not be able to move it, Ménak easily lifts it and brings it crashing down, like Rama raising Shiva's bow at Sita's *swayamvara*; as Ménak celebrates his victory in battle, his heart fills with longing for the princess and his mind wanders, and he asks a rival for a remedy to be brought from Medayin for his heartache, the scene reminiscent of Rawana's obsession with Sita and the vulnerability it brought upon him. Found here are a range of motifs similar to those in the Ramayana (what Ramanujan called a "signifiers' pool"), yet their logic or attribution to particular characters varies. And so, although Lanka is not mentioned by name in Ménak's story, these elements that connect with and recall the Ramayana tradition in the *Ménak Serandhil* testify to Lanka's very real presence in, or affiliation with, the world it depicted, if only by association.[41]

In thinking further of the wider literary sphere in which the stories were couched, nomenclature again assists in drawing connections. Beyond the intertextual web of associations and instances of documented exilic experiences and longings, the *Hikayat Seri Rama* from colonial Ceylon offers the most concrete, suggestive example of the intertwining not just of religious and literary traditions related to banishment to the island but also of its different nomenclatures. The question was raised of whether Lanka and Ceylon were ever associated in the texts, whether they appeared side by side as did the names Sarandib and Ceylon, and Sarandib and Lanka. In the manuscript's penultimate page, Rama establishes a new kingdom in Ayudyapuranagara, moves into his palace accompanied by Laksmana and Hanuman, and lives happily with his wife Cintadewi in the kingdom that will be passed down to their descendants. The following and final section of the page, which is unfortunately torn and therefore only partially legible, reads (see Figure 7.1):

[41] One can speak of a certain "Islamization" of the Ramayana in its Malay tellings, although how "deep" or "superficial" this process was has been debated and remains to be studied further. But no less interesting is the question of a "Ramayanization" of Islamic tales: Might this process (in the sense of incorporating themes, scenes and language, and the notion that the Ramayana is about the anesthetization of grief, longing, pain) be a broad phenomenon but one that is especially salient when Sri Lanka is considered as a site within and outside the stories? The particular context of eighteenth-century exile (and nineteenth-century descendants of exiles) in Ceylon provides a suggestive setting in which to consider this matter.

Figure 7.1 Penultimate page of the *Hikayat Seri Rama* MS PNM 1055, 567.
Courtesy National Library of Malaysia

Demikian diceriterakan oleh dhalang yang empunya cerita daripada maharaja Seri Rama dan Laksmana yang termashur namanya di tanah benua Kaling benua Sha..ng dan ke benua Turki datang ke benua Walanda...[42]

Thus [the *Hikayat*] was told by a dhalang who "owns" the story of King Rama and Laksmana whose names are famous in the land of Keling, in Sha..ng and Turkey, all the way to the Netherlands...

The remainder of the page is gone, but the word missing a letter or two in the above quote looks very much like Shalong, i.e. Ceylon, and this is all the more likely because of the mention of neighboring Keling, or south India. Two important hints appear in the brief sentence. First, the person "owning" the story (M. *empunya cerita*, with *empu* meaning also "master craftsman" and linked to ideas of creativity and powerful magic, including those of the keris maker) is depicted as a *dhalang*, master of the shadow puppet theater (J. *wayang kulit*) who, singlehandedly, leads the nightlong performances in which he impersonates all the different characters with his movements and voice, while giving cues to the gamelan

---

[42] Encik Hakim, *Hikayat Seri Rama*, MS PNM 1055, 567. The exchange of the letters *sīn* and *shīn* (as in Shelong for Selong) is common in Malay writing from Ceylon.

orchestra and telling a complex story of intrigue, love, war, politics and destiny. The vast majority of wayang kulit performances have been based on episodes from the Mahabharata and the Ramayana, and this small insertion suggests the possibility that such manuscripts may have also been used for performative purposes in colonial Ceylon or, at the very least, that such a performative tradition could have been known to the Ramayana's audience there. The second hint in this truncated sentence invokes the question of naming and offers a rare example in which the name "Ceylon" appears in close proximity to the name "Lankapuri," whose depiction filled many of the previous pages and whose fame – through the heroic story of Rama and Laksmana – was now said to have spread throughout Ceylon.

The closing lines of the *Hikayat* on the following page offer additional clues to the context in which the Ramayana was retold among the Malays in Ceylon:

Bahwa ya ini Hikayat Maharaja Seri Rama yang menulish hambah Allah enchi Hakim ibnu guru Shalim peranakan Selong serta telah hadia akan pada kakandaku sarjen Abdulrasap namanya pas kampeni Selon Rifel Rejimen Tringkomali 17 dari bulan March hijrat tahun welanda 1856 juadanya

This is the *Hikayat Maharaja Seri Rama* written by God's servant Mr. Hakim son of Guru Shalim *peranakan* Selong and gifted to my elder brother sergeant Abdulrasap of the Ceylon Rifle Regiment Company. Trincomalee, March 17, the Dutch year of 1856.[43]

Here, at the very end of the 594-page manuscript, appears this telling paratext, framing the locally produced Ramayana. Whereas the previous page proclaimed the fame of the text and its protagonists, including in the region of southeastern India and Ceylon where it had now been inscribed, this final sentence reveals brief but important information about the author or scribe. Beyond the scribe's name, his father's name and occupation, the fact that he had a brother serving in the Ceylon Rifle Regiment and the date of completing the manuscript is found the term *"peranakan Selong."* "Peranakan," the Malay term designating "locally born foreigners," and referring to people of mixed parentage in the Malay world or those descended from a foreign ancestor, however

---

[43] *Hikayat Seri Rama*, MS PNM 1056, 594. Pages are misnumbered, hence p. 594 follows p. 567. *Hikayat Maharaja Seri Rama* could be a title of the *Hikayat* or refer to "the story of king Rama." The verb *menulis*, "to write" (here spelled *menulish* in the common exchange of the letters *sīn* and *shīn*, as noted) could also mean "inscribe," referring to the act of inscribing the *Hikayat* but not necessarily to authorship. The word *pas* may refer to a soldier's pass number, but no number is noted.

distantly in the past, here indicates a locally born Malay.[44] Whether this man's mother was Malay or not is impossible to detect from the passage but it does provide, importantly, evidence of the category of peranakan in Ceylon and the associations of a diasporic community it conveys. Thus, a locally born descendant of Malay origins had created a locally produced Ramayana, highlighting the ongoing relevance of this narrative to a diasporic community with exilic roots that was maintaining its cultural and linguistic traditions over time in the place that was now home, linked as it was to this home's dimensions as Sarandib, Ceylon and Lanka.

The name Langkapuri surfaced in a novel, forward-looking context in 1869 when Baba Ounus Saldin, a Malay community leader and a pioneer in the field of printing in Ceylon, founded the world's first Malay newspaper in Colombo and gave it the title *Alamat Langkapuri*, with *alamat* meaning "sign," "signal," "indication of things to come" and, most pertinently, "news." The newspaper appeared fortnightly and was written in Malay using the gundul script, making it accessible – at least theoretically – to a broad readership beyond Ceylon's borders in British Malaya and the Dutch East Indies.[45] Disseminating international as well as local news, promoting Malay poetry, experimenting with advertising techniques and inviting its readership to connect with each other and the broader communities by way of letters and an early version of editorial opinions, the *Alamat Langkapuri* possessed transformative potential. Yet despite the keen interest in the Malay community's religious affairs expressed throughout its pages, as well as the consistent reporting on matters having to do with British rule of the island, neither the name Sarandib – echoing with Islamic tradition and identity – nor the name Ceylon with its contemporary relevance was selected for the newspaper's title.[46] Rather, it was Langkapuri: That choice, and the excerpt of a letter published in the newspaper, testify to the ongoing relevance of Ramayana imagery among the Malays.

The author opened his letter of July 6, 1869, by recounting how he had come across several letters of praise for the newspaper in previous issues and, inspired by the model (*teladan*) they presented, decided to write his

---

[44] In contemporary Indonesia the term is most often applied to Indonesians of Chinese descent. In colonial Malaya and Singapore, *Jawi Peranakan* often referred to Tamil-speaking Muslims born in Malaya, to a Malay mother, as well as to people of mixed Chinese–Malay parentage.

[45] *Alamat Langkapuri* 1869–1870, Department of National Archives, Sri Lanka.

[46] This choice is suggestive in light of Saldin's later decision, in his 1905 *Syair Faiḍ al-Abād*, to mention the names Sarandib and Ceylon, but not Lanka, in his brief retelling of the island's history. See Chapter 6.

own applauding piece.[47] He inserted the conventional apology for his dearth of knowledge and expressed his hope that his ignorance would be forgiven by his readers. Such apologies appeared regularly in Malay manuscript literature and were incorporated into additional forms of writing, including the newspaper. The author then presented his composition, defined as *"pantun seloka,"* combining in this title two forms of poetry. The first, pantun, was a popular Malay genre of four-lined poems with internal assonance, often improvised and sung, and *seloka*, from Sanskrit *śloka*, quatrains of four rhyming lines:[48]

Pulau ini pulau Langkapuri

ku pohonkan bagi juru Alamat Langkapuri[49]

Oleh pemerintaan raja Rawana

Supaya mashurkan dengan sempurna

oleh pemerintaan raja Rawana

supaya dapat mashurkan dengan sempurna

dilanggarlah oleh Seri Rama

yaitu dapat akan diterima

This is Langkapuri island

I ask the editors of *Alamat Langkapuri*

Ruled by King Rawana

To spread its fame far and wide [to perfection]

ruled over by King Rawana

that they spread its fame far and wide

attacked by Seri Rama

so that it is [well] received

The author named the island where he was writing as neither Sarandib, nor Ceylon but as Langkapuri, and defined it as the land that was ruled by Rawana, then attacked by Rama, whose name was prefaced by the honorific Seri, just like in the *Hikayat*'s title. The rhyme of the first halves of the first two lines – Langkapuri – joined the island and the Malay newspaper as one, drawing a link between the kingdom depicted in the Ramayana and the newspaper, between a Malay man writing for a strictly Malay audience and Raja Rawana and Seri Rama, heroes of the Ramayana. The repetition of *supaya mashurkan dengan sempurna* ("so that its fame spreads far and wide") most likely referred in this context to the

---

[47] *Alamat Langkapuri* issue 3, July 11, 1869, Rabiʿ al-Akhir 1286. This was only the third issue published and the excitement at the availability of a Malay newspaper is palpable; see below.

[48] Intriguingly, the orthography of *seloka*, spelled s.l.w.k in this instance, and suluk (songs sung by the dhalang during wayang performances, often in Old Javanese; also Javano-Islamic mystical poetry) could be one and the same. The first, as noted, derives from a Sanskrit word, the second from Arabic, and they represent two different literary and religious traditions, often intertwined in Malay writing.

[49] The word *juru* refers to "expert," typically followed by a word that defines the type of expertise, i.e. *juru tulis* ("expert in writing," clerk), *juru bahasa* ("expert in language," interpreter). The phrase *juru Alamat Langkapuri* most likely refers to the newspaper's editors or staff, and presents an example of how *juru* was employed in introducing new professions of the modern age.

newspaper but could also imply proclaiming the fame of Rama's victory over Rawana and that of the island, especially in light of what followed.[50]

The next part of the letter recounts very briefly the transfer of the island (without referring to it by name, only as *pulau ini*) from Dutch to British rule in 1795 under the last Dutch governor-general Johan Gerard van Angelbeek. The writer noted that approximately seventy-four years had since passed (1795–1869), and only recently have "we" (employing the exclusive first-person plural pronoun *kami*), here referring to the Malay community in British Ceylon, encountered that which was like a rising sun whose rays were brilliantly shining: the *Alamat Langkapuri*.[51] Like the sun that rises, stands high in the sky and follows its path day by day, the newspaper arose among the Malays and was appearing regularly, providing them with details of local events and fascinating news stories. And all this was taking place, the author added, as if incredulous, in the Malay language (*Itu dengan bahasa Malayu adanya*). No explicit connection was made between the poem and the depiction of recent history and contemporary developments, yet the reference to the transition of power from Dutch to British rule, and the unambiguous emphasis on the positive change – in the form of the newly established newspaper, spreading information and enhancing community via the Malay language – that occurred only after the Dutch departed and the British had arrived, rings out like an echo of the juxtaposition of Rawana and Rama in the poem and the former's rule as having been upended by the latter. Even though the letter-writer did not insert any details depicting Rawana and Rama as rulers, military leaders or moral beings in his brief four lines of poetry, their names alone stood for a vast repository of cultural and political knowledge which could easily be tapped by a Malay man writing for a local Malay audience, whose understanding of the code words "Rama" and "Rawana" he could rely on. This kind of hint, or brief yet unelaborated signifier, is very common in pantun literature which tends to be ambiguous, elusive and associative by definition.

---

[50] Such repetitions are common as part of the pantuns' interlinked (M. *berkait*) form, repeating one hemistich in the next verse throughout the poem. In the case discussed here, it appears that the designation "pantun" was used more broadly than was typical in Malay writing. The rhyme scheme of ABAB was not followed, and the pantuns have more narrative coherence than most, which tend to include the kernel of their message (often implicitly) in lines 3 and 4 while the first two lines may be related in assonance, in allusion or not at all. The author in colonial Ceylon seems to be using "pantun" in a generalized sense of "poem." On pantun literature, see Fang, *A History of Classical Malay Literature*, 442–447.

[51] *Maka baharulah ini kami dapat bertemu/yaitu seupama matahari berterbitkan diri.*
Maka sinarnya pun cemerlanglah berbangkit2 sedemikian itu maka Alamat Langkapuri pun telah bangun lalu berdiri antara pihaq kami maka sekarang ia memulai berjalan sambil mencitrakan peri tiap2 kejadian dan habar2 yang 'ajaib (Alamat Langkapuri issue 3).

Having likened the *Alamat Langkapuri* to a brightly shining sun, the author then expressed his joy at its publication and his gratitude to the newspaper's staff for their efforts and accomplishments and the good they had wrought for all those friends and relatives who were avid readers of the newspaper. He stated that it would forever be an example for adults and children – the next generation of readers – and concluded by noting his pleasure (*maka hiburlah hatiku*) when he read some of the interesting, even wondrous ('*ajaib*) items reported, so much so that he decided to compose another pantun:[52]

kota ini kota perawan	*belumlah lagi dilanggar orang*
Alamat Langkapuri perbuatannya yang setiawan	*wajib sekali dipujikan orang*
Belum lagi dilanggar orang	*bijaq sekalilah Laksmana*
Wajib sekali dipujikan orang	*sebab terbuat dengan sempurna*

Seorang yang berusahakan Alamat Langkapuri ini dari jajahannya

This city is a maiden	not yet attacked by a man
Alamat Langkapuri its deeds are loyal	must be praised by all
Not yet attacked	the very wise Laksmana
Must be praised by all	made to perfection

One who strives for *Alamat Langkapuri* from his district.

This second and final poem praised the newspaper and those working to produce it, but was also in dialogue with the earlier pantun. Taken together, the two offer a comparison between the past, when Langka was ruled by Rawana then attacked by Rama (representing Dutch and, later, British rule of the island), with the present times, when the city, or fort (*kota*), alluding more specifically to Colombo where the newspaper was published and where the author lived rather than to an island-wide territory, was safe, with no attack or intrusion on the horizon. The Ramayana was here evoked somewhat less explicitly than before but it still hovered over the poem: The word *perawan* ("maiden," "virgin") is close to Rawana in sound but calls forth the antithetical image of Sita, awaiting Rama like an innocent maiden, unviolated by a desiring and greedy Rawana and resisting his attacks on her purity; her loyalty, like

---

[52] Here and above, the pantun is prefaced by the phrase *demikian bunyinya* (literally "such is its sound," less literally "it goes like this"), precisely the phrase that is used in Malay hikayat literature in which prose is often interspersed with pantuns and syairs. For a Malay example from Ceylon, see *Hikayat Indera Quraishi*, Colombo, 1881, Perpustakaan Negara Malaysia, Kuala Lumpur, MS PNM 431, 90–168. The shared use of the phrase and the easy transition between prose, poetry and back again provide examples of the overlap between Malay manuscript and print cultures in the nineteenth century.

that of the *Alamat Langkapuri*'s staff dedicated to high standards of journalism and production, and to providing Malay language reporting, should be praised by all; and the mention of Laksmana recalled Rama's wise and courageous younger brother, and invoked his role as Sita's defender in the forest when Rama was away. It also strengthened the theme of loyalty within the pantun as Laksmana had left everything behind in order to follow Rama and Sita into exile. His name, which in its common Malay usage has come to mean "admiral," may have here also hinted at the newspaper's leadership navigating it like a ship across the waters.[53] As with the repeated reference regarding the need to spread *Alamat Langkapuri*'s fame far and wide, but also Rama's, the praise-worthy evoked by this second poem are again the newspaper and its staff, striving as they did on behalf of the Malays, but also Sita, Laksmana and the British rulers who deserved the Malay community's loyalty as their era of rule was filled with brilliant sunlight representing knowledge, information and new forms of connectivity that allowed the Malays to open up to the world as never before. In their brief and ambiguous lines, then, the pantuns alluded to questions of politics and history, to the Malays' position under two colonial regimes, to evolving forms of new media of the day and to linguistic and cultural identity, all couched in Ramayana imagery and employing it as a shorthand accessible to a readership for whom the succinct allusions were sufficiently evocative.

Laksmana, Rama's younger and exceedingly loyal brother, appears elsewhere in Sri Lankan Malay culture, in the category of texts known collectively as wasilan. This Malay term covers a range of charms and incantations that were to be recited on various occasions including childbirth, illness, wishing good fortune or disaster upon an individual and, importantly, in averting danger of many kinds, from snakes to storms to the perils of the battlefield, the latter hardly surprising for a community that affiliated itself overwhelmingly with the military in the first half of the nineteenth century.[54] It was thus in the context of war that

---

[53] Hang Tuah, the famed Malay hero of the *Sejarah Melayu*, compared himself to Laksmana in fifteenth-century Melacca; see R. O. Windstedt, *An Unabridged Malay–English Dictionary* (Kuala Lumpur and Singapore: Marican and Sons, 1967), 197.

[54] Ramayana imagery was also evoked in military contexts in Java during the same period. During the Java War (1825–1830) the Dutch supreme commander, Lieutenant-General Hendrik Merkus de Kock, was compared by the Javanese to Dasamuka (the "Ten-Headed One," i.e. Rawana). See Carey, *Power of Prophecy*, 247, n. 172. The Javanese commander of the war, Pangéran Dipanagara, who would be exiled by the Dutch to Ambon and later Makassar, identified with Arjuna, a hero of the Mahabharata and the wayang plays deriving from it, another epic narrative that explores the theme of exile, but not to Lanka. See ibid., 153–154, 156, 404, 572.

Figure 7.2 Ramayana-themed pantun. *Alamat Langkapuri* issue 3, July 11, 1869.
Courtesy Department of National Archives, Sri Lanka

Laksmana's name was evoked: A recitation titled *garisan Laksamana* was used against an approaching enemy and, if the adversary attempted to advance after it was uttered, he was expected to drop dead.[55] The *garisan Laksamana* – "the Laksamana Line" – conjures a Ramayana episode: While Rama went in search of the golden deer coveted by Sita, Laksmana remained with her in the forest hermitage. After some time passed, the two of them heard Rama's voice calling out in pain in the distance. Even though Laksmana assured Sita that this was not in fact Rama (rather it was the demon Marica, disguised as the deer and imitating Rama's voice, dying as he was pierced by Rama's arrow), Sita was worried and begged him to go find Rama, in some tellings even accusing him of coveting her so as to force him to go. Laksmana, who feared leaving her alone, finally relented but before going drew a circular line on the ground around her, promising her she would remain safe as long as she did not cross that line. When Rawana came along dressed as an old Brahmin, Sita put caution aside in order to assist him, disregarded Laksmana's line and was kidnapped. The wasilan recalled Laksmana's protective, powerful boundary which would have saved Sita from the demon king had she been less careless, and promised that same safeguard to Malay soldiers should they recite it at the right moment.

Thinking about Adam's and Sita's exilic episodes in Lanka together can be taken further, with links and echoes resonating with the exilic condition on Ceylon. The theme of Lanka's natural richness was common to both. In Indian Ramayana traditions Lanka was often portrayed as a "heaven on earth," with Rawana bringing many types of trees, including the wish-fulfilling ones, and other beautiful things, from Indra's world to plant in his realm. The *Kakawin Ramayana* offered similar portrayals, the following depicting Lanka as it returned to its former self after the battles and destruction of the Great War, under its new king, Wibhisana:

> Now when that excellent nectar fell down and penetrated in the city of Lenka-pura,
> Its excellence increased and everything wrought by his elder brother flared up again;

---

[55] This information was recounted to me by Mr. Iqbal Weerabangsa of Badulla. He received this wasilan as well as many others from his father M. M. G. Weerabangsa (personal communication, January 1, 2014). Most wasilans were not actually recited out loud, by Mr. Weerabangsa and others I spoke to, in awareness of their power and potential effects.

Mount Mahendra was restored, and overcome by rain it now
   returned to former loveliness,
Everything destroyed was now rained on by god Indra and took its
   former shape.[56]

Such depictions appeared also in the eighteenth-century Javanese *Serat
Rama*, when Hanuman, who had leapt across the ocean in search of Sita,
first saw Alengka's beauty, the city as if shrouded in gold, filled with
beautiful structures, its gardens overflowing with flowers, gems and
pearls at every turn.[57]

As discussed in Chapter 6, Sarandib was also viewed as fantastically
rich and fertile in Arabic sources, thanks to the heavenly seeds, fruit and
leaves that fell from Paradise along with Adam. Again, the two traditions
of the island's beauty and wealth are linked in the *Hikayat Seri Rama*
when, after Rama won the war and entered Langkapuri with his followers, they went to a beach where they found many pearls from the sea
(from T. *mutu*), some the size of a chicken's egg while others were as
large as goose eggs. Rama then took Berdana and Citradana to the foot of
the prophet Adam's mountain (M. *kaki bukit tempat nabi Adam*) where
they encountered gems, opals (from S. *permata* and *baiduri*), emeralds
(A. *zamrud*), sapphires (T. *nīlām*), alabaster (T. *pualam*) and jewels of all
kinds.[58] This is reminiscent of the description of the mountain's environs
in Ibn Baṭūṭa's *Travels* as well as in many other representations of
Ceylon in general and of the gem-producing region in particular. As
Sharae Deckard wrote in her "Exploited Edens: Paradise Discourse in
Colonial and Postcolonial Literature," European travelers, who had
inherited Paradise myths of Ceylon, longed to penetrate to its heart "with
the hope of accessing unimaginable riches." Eventually, "Ceylon's
mythic significance as both a material and a spiritual paradise helped
spur the development of British colonial desire and the British East India
Company."[59] As far as considering the Malays' attitudes toward the
island, long-held images of plenty such as those appearing in Adam's
stories and the Ramayana connect with Baba Ounus Saldin's opening
lines in his *Syair Faiḍ al-Abād*, in which he claimed its earth to be
abundant with riches and its ports completely inundated with pearls

---

[56] The nectar falling on Lanka is the rain sent down by Indra. The "older brother" who
wrought destruction refers to Rawana. See C. Hooykaas, "The Paradise on Earth in
Lenka (Old-Javanese Ramayana XXIV. 87–126)," *BKI* 114.3 (1958), 269.

[57] Yasadipura I, *Serat Rama* (Weltevreden: Bale Pustaka, 1925), 142–143, in
Dhandhanggula.

[58] Ikram, *Hikayat Seri Rama*, 295.

[59] Sharae Grace Deckard, "Exploited Edens: Paradise Discourse in Colonial and
Postcolonial Literature," unpublished Ph.D. diss., University of Warwick (2007), 208.

and gems of many kinds.[60] Although this promising view was likely not shared by many of the first-generation exiles to Ceylon, subsequent generations of their descendants may well have seen it in that light, the shifting of perspective over time represented with brevity but force in Saldin's transition in his *Syair* from the name Sarandib to Ceylon. As Adam was forced from the "real" heaven to this "heaven on earth" and the Ramayana protagonists recreated the golden kingdom after it was devastated, the banished had ultimately to build new lives in Ceylon, a process that had often serendipitous outcomes despite being rooted in penal circumstances and hardship.

The two banished protagonists in the traditions explored – Sita and Adam – have names that are associated with the earth, and both were drawn toward it: Adam, etymologically connected with the Hebrew word for "earth" or "land" (*adama*), was created from earth (Q 2:30), was sent down to live on and toil the earth, and eventually, according to the biblical account, returned to it at death (Gen. 3:19). Sita, according to Valmiki and also in many other Ramayana tellings, was born from a furrow (the meaning of *sītā* in Sanskrit) where she was found by her father King Janaka and where, years later, she called upon her mother Earth to take her back into her depths. Her life, which even after her return from captivity in Rawana's Lankapuri continued as a form of exile in the forest hermitage due to Rama's distrust, suggests that there is no possibility of a true, complete, unblemished return.[61] Her plight, as well as the documents and texts that testify to, or creatively imagine, exile's multiple forms in Ceylon, Lanka and Sarandib, and sometimes also consider returns from exile, however late or partial, show that both exile and return are fraught conditions, lying on a continuum rather than being distinctly separate, attesting to the complexity, ambiguity and humanity of the exilic experience.

In thinking about the Javanese shore of eighteenth-century exile to Ceylon, and the literary and historical representations produced there, the exilic experience was nowhere better explored and captured in its multiple dimensions than in the writings of Kartasura court poet Yasadipura I. Having written *Serat Ménak Serandhil*, *Serat Rama* and

---

[60] Saldin, *Syair*, 1.

[61] The inclusion of the second banishment, and its details, are telling-specific. In the *Hikayat Seri Rama* from Ceylon, Sita is sent away to the forest when Rama suspects her of longing for Rawana after he sees an image of the demon king she had sketched reluctantly for a persistent relative who demanded to know his looks. Although in this telling Rama and Sita ultimately reunited and lived happily ever after, the reunion took place only after twelve years of further separation. The episode is related in Encik Hakim, *Hikayat Seri Rama*, MS PNM 1055, 583–587; the reunion is depicted on 590.

the *Babad Giyanti*, he engaged in his writings with Serandhil, Alengka and Sélong, respectively: In *Ménak Serandhil*, the narrative of which unfolds partly in Serandhil (i.e. Sarandib), he employed the Arabic name for the island and included the scene of pilgrimage to the mountaintop where Adam first descended to the world. In his depiction, it is a site of reconnecting with Islam's prophets via Adam's biography, dreams and boons; in *Serat Rama* Yasadipura recounted the Ramayana in modern Javanese, basing himself on the ancient *kawi* work and continuing the tradition of depicting Alengka's great beauty and power, as well as Sita's desolation and longing after her banishment;[62] finally, in the *Babad Giyanti*, the memories of exiles who were sent to Sélong and allowed to return to Java after many years were documented.

Yasadipura's role as a poet who engaged with all three nomenclatures of the island was unique. This focus of his literary production suggests the importance of the island, and the exilic imagination it inspired, in eighteenth-century Java. With knowledge of the Ramayana, Islamic tales and contemporary exile informing his writing, Yasadipura for the most part kept the sites designated by the three names separate in his writing, except in the case of the *Ménak Serandhil*, in which Sélan and Serandhil were used interchangeably. Still, a closer look at his writing suggests that common threads wove through the island's depictions and the images it inspired: All three accounts tied the site of exile to powerful forces, from Adam's footprint inspiring the dreams that would result in Umarmaya's meeting with the prophets, to Hanuman burning down Alengka in rage after finding the captive Sita, to the miraculous appearance of Javanese food after the weekly Friday prayers that would console the homesick exiles' hearts. All three sites were associated with dreams, or dreamlike states, with forms of divine invincibility, with bewilderment, yearning and hope. As such, and despite Yasadipura's silence on explicit links and overlaps among Ceylon, Lanka and Sarandib, his diverse tellings offer an integrated view of the three places making up an island to which the prophet Adam, Sita and people of his own era were banished. This view was by definition comparative, looking across genres and periods from hadith-based accounts, translations and adaptations of Arabic, Sanskrit and Persian texts, to Javanese *serat* and babad literatures, and encompassing eras from soon after Creation in Islamic cosmology, to Rama and Sita's epoch, to what for Yasadipura constituted the recent past and present. Yasadipura's evocative use of themes and scenes relating to

---

[62] On the process of rewriting, or translating, Old Javanese works into modern Javanese, see Barbara McDonald, "Kawi and Kawi Miring: Old Javanese Literature in Eighteenth-Century Java," unpublished Ph.D. diss., Australian National University (1983).

the island places his works in conversation with each other and positions him as a connector, through his writing and his living in the "Ceylon exile century," conveying something of its geography, sacred sites, religious significance, history and lived experiences – along with its mythic dimensions – to Javanese audiences.

Meanwhile, in Ceylon itself the tradition of Adam's fall in Sarandib was well known, as attested by the popularity of Adam's Peak as a pilgrimage site and from Malay writings. Letters written by exiles or their descendants in the eighteenth and early nineteenth centuries testify to the hardships of living in Sélong and express a desire for repatriation. And the appearance of Adam in the local telling of the Malay Ramayana and his depicted relationship with Rawana, king of Lankapuri, show that, albeit inexplicitly, Sarandib, Ceylon and Lanka were all conspicuous places, imaginatively intertwined, with the exilic elements of all three documented and represented in local writing, constituting a subtle but powerful theme of Sri Lankan Malay literary history.

Episodes of exile and return raise questions of space and directionality. Al-Bīrūnī, one of medieval Islam's most important scholars, dedicated a chapter to Lanka in his book on India and discussed its location as the "copula of the earth" or the place that lay "between the two ends of the inhabitable world and without latitude." Viewed as a land of demons, it gave rise to an idea of the south as the direction of foreboding evil and death.[63] In the traditions of Adam and Sita, both vertical and horizontal axes play a part: Adam and Sita descended to the island from above, Adam when banished from the heavens, while Sita is said to have arrived in Rawana's flying chariot, the Pushpaka. Crossing over to the island, or from it, is central to both stories. Rama and his armies, coming to rescue Sita, built and crossed a bridge over the ocean from southeastern India to Lanka,[64] while Adam, according to Islamic sources, wept bitterly and asked for God's forgiveness when he found himself alone and went

---

[63] Sachau, *Alberuni's India*, 306–307.

[64] Al-Bīrūnī gave a detailed description of the bridge and its importance to the Ramayana story. He reported, for example, the local villagers' habit of cooking rice and offering it to the monkey king and his hosts, in recognition that the monkeys are believed to be "a race of men changed into monkeys on account of the help which they had afforded to Rama when making war against the demons" (ibid., 209). Al-Bīrūnī offered a Muslim's view of the Ramayana tradition and its connection to Lanka, presented in a matter-of-fact tone that was unusual for his time. Interestingly, the chapter on Lanka mentioned Sarandib only very briefly, as a concrete place south of India (ibid., 209, 211), with no note of Adam's story, while in his *Picture of the World* he wrote of the pilgrimage to the mountain in Sarandib where Adam touched the earth, without mentioning Lanka, providing an example of addressing the two names and places, each with its own tradition, without linking them (Togan, *Picture of the World*, 1).

searching for Eve, walking across Sarandib until he reached the land bridge connecting it to south India, which he crossed with the hope of finding his wife. Exiles from the archipelago did not land from above or cross a bridge to reach Ceylon but rather had to bear long and often terrifying journeys by sea. And all three narratives – those of Adam, the Ramayana and the Malays in Ceylon – emphasize the nature of the site of banishment as an island (*jazīra*, *dwīpa* and *pulau*), an image that in this context suggests separation, enclosure and confinement.

The Ramayana and nabi Adam traditions thus make clear that the island of Lanka/Sarandib constituted an important site of exile, construed in religious, historical and literary terms. The two traditions, and their associated references in ever-widening circles of cultural associations from the battlefield to print media, lived on concurrently in Ceylon and Java, combining literary and religious elements from India, Arabia, and the archipelago and producing tellings that resonated with local lives. The two can evoke the common dichotomies of Hindu and Muslim, Ravana and Adam, human and divine. But more meaningfully, as construed within a Malay community with a significant exilic past, such stories constituted a weaving together of different religious and cultural traditions and dimensions of exile or distance from home: exile from a proximity to God or a husband, from kingdom, status, family, land, language, and an assumed future; and also exile to, or toward, certain conditions: the toiling of the land which was to become Man's fate after Adam's fall, an ever-present distance from the divine which Man would constantly and mostly futilely try to recover; a husband who would later be overtaken by envy and suspicion, leading to a second banishment; and, for Javanese and other Indonesian royalty, to a life of want, of petitioning for more food and allowances and a return often denied. Like the "bridge" of islets in the ocean known both as Rama's Bridge and Adam's Bridge, the connections and overlaps between the stories of Adam and Sita point to interreligious appropriations of stories, episodes and relationships to place, as well as to the ways in which competing and alternative narratives coexist. And Lanka, so prominent in the Hindu imagination, was adopted and adapted by Muslims in the archipelago and later connected to their story of ancient exile into the world as well as more recent exile and return to that same place.

The question of how significant reading the Ramayana in Ceylon was for exiles and their descendants cannot be answered in full. But it is likely that, like the religious gatherings and Javanese tempeh arriving from afar depicted in the *Babad Giyanti*, the Ramayana provided solace and a sense of community. As the final, fragmented lines of the *Hikayat Seri Rama* completed in Trincomalee in 1856, coming after the official closing lines of the text, testify:

Dan lagi barangsiapa sahabatku yang maminjam henda perbaca ceritra ini sehingga enam hari kemudian segerah yang mesti dibalik pada yang punya ...[65]

Furthermore, anyone amongst my friends who wishes to borrow and read this story may do so for six days after which it must be quickly returned to the owner...

These lines, added almost as an afterthought, suggest that the manuscript was in demand and often put to use. When joined with the words on a previous page depicting the story's "owner" as a puppeteer (dhalang), they are even more powerful. Reading and listening to, and possibly performing, the Ramayana's familiar stories offered perspective and inspiration. And it resonated with the Malays' attachment to the island which, as Sarandib, Lanka and Ceylon, had merged into their history and lived experience.

---

[65] Encik Hakim, *Hikayat Seri Rama*, MS PNM 1055, 594. The page is torn off after this word.

8   Ceylon Malays: Military and Literary Paths

Although not all Malays in early nineteenth-century Ceylon were associated with the military and some worked as cultivators, store keepers and fishermen and in additional occupations, as many as 75 percent of Malays served as soldiers in the British colonial army under Governor North.[1] And while this figure was reduced later in the century, the ethos of, and attachment to, military culture remained central to Malay life for at least several decades after the Malay Regiment was disbanded in 1873. Taking this phenomenon as its starting point, this chapter focuses on Malay military affiliation and its links and overlaps with the Malays' literary culture, including modes of writing as evident in letters, family diaries and manuscript colophons, practices of copying, inscribing and professing humility, and the role of soldiers in the production and preservation of texts. In addition, the chapter considers perceptions of the Malays as formulated and reflected in writings of the period in Dutch, English, Malay and Sinhala, representing diverse perspectives on Malay life and martial experiences in Ceylon. Finally, the chapter asks how exploring pivotal episodes in Ceylon's military history – colonialism, the Kandy Wars, the transition between empires – from a Malay vantage point affects the ways this history can be understood. Highlighting details and nuance in Malay sources achieves a certain change in resolution, anticipating the argument made in the next and final chapter about the importance of "bringing the Malays back" into Sri Lanka's history.

---

[1] Hussainmiya, *Orang Rejimen*, 73. North's term as governor (1798–1805) was marked by his successful initiative to establish a Malay Regiment as well as by a disastrous war with Kandy in 1803–1805, on which more below. Percival (*An Account,* 120) documented some of the Malays' nonmilitary occupations at the turn of the nineteenth century: "The Dutch, to avoid the expense of keeping coast servants, introduced the practice of rearing slaves of the African casts, and employing Malays who made excellent cooks and gardeners, and indeed good servants in every respect, although they were kept for a trifle in comparison of the others."

Men from across the Indonesian–Malay Archipelago served in the VOC army in the seventeenth and eighteenth centuries, a period that constituted a precursor to the one highlighted in this chapter, and it is important to understanding the various continuities and changes that transpired across the two colonial regimes.[2] The Dutch, who had observed the fighting skills of these men when wresting the island away from the Portuguese in the seventeenth century, appreciated them for their perceived courage and loyalty.[3] They wished to employ them in their own service after the takeover and indeed, in many cases, the men were sent to fight in the cause of Empire.[4] It was also not uncommon for slaves to be released in order to become soldiers, as a case from June 19, 1778, testifies: eighteen "eastern slaves," listed by name and place of origin, were declared to be employed from then onward as "soldiers under the Eastern Company." The list highlights a diversity that, although in no way exhausting the range of exiles' and soldiers' home regions or ethnicities, stands in stark contrast to the later British all-encompassing designation of "Malay," including as it does Sumbawa, Madura, Bugis, Bali, Batak and Makassar.[5]

The traits of bravery and dedication noted by the Dutch during the conquest of Ceylon were important not only in battle but also for the daily, more mundane tasks of policing colonial possessions in Ceylon and India. For example, the Political Council Minutes of October 5, 1757, mention two companies of Buginese, 157 men strong, that were sent to Galle to quell riots in the area.[6] In 1786, the Resident at Ponnekail specifically requested "Malays" to be deployed to south India for the protection of the merchants and washermen against disturbances by the Land Regent of Tinnelwelli.[7]

While many served loyally, such men also posed occasional challenges to their European superiors. At a Council meeting on August 24, 1745, the governor reported that a company of Buginese soldiers stationed in Coromandel had laid down their weapons and refused to continue serving the Company after their salaries had been reduced to an amount that could no longer sustain them. The Buginese were, however, willing

---

[2] For an account and analysis of the transition from Dutch to British rule framed by theories of regime change, see Alicia Schrikker, *Dutch and British Colonial Intervention in Sri Lanka, 1780–1815: Expansion and Reform* (Leiden: Brill, 2007). The book (especially chapter 3) importantly draws lines of comparison between Ceylon and Java.

[3] *Jubilee Book*, 158.

[4] SLNA 1/218, Political Council Minutes, May 19, 1792, mention the "Madurese and Sumanappers" who had been employed as soldiers since the recent English war.

[5] SLNA 1/176, June 19, 1778.

[6] SLNA 1/122, Political Council Minutes, October 5, 1757.

[7] SLNA 1/181, 1780, cited in Anthonisz, *Digest*, 205.

to serve in cheaper Ceylon, and so it was agreed that they would be exchanged for a company made up of Europeans and "*Toepassers*" on the condition that the Buginese should declare, in a document written in Malay, that having come to Ceylon they should be confined to the salary of three rix dollars per month.[8] There were also more explicit criminal cases in which such soldiers were involved. In 1791, Linban and Tangin, two Madurese men serving under Captain Joerang Patie in the Malay Company, were tried for theft of a bundle of clothes in Galle. During the trial, mention was made of a document routinely read to the soldiers as a reminder lest they cause any harm to members of the local population and their property. Although the bundle was found and the men confessed, the prosecutor recommended flogging them until they bled, after which they would be put in chains and confined to labor in the public works for three years with no salary, and compelling them to pay the costs of justice. The sentence was later changed to the offenders having to run the gauntlet among a battalion of "forty-four heads of Eastern militiamen," thus charging Linban and Tangin's fellow countrymen with carrying out their sentence.[9]

A noteworthy aspect of Malay military life emerging from archival documents, going back to the Dutch period and maintained under the British, was the centrality of family to the soldiers' lives and the related entanglements and considerations of the colonial governments in this sphere. The Political Council Minutes of May 22, 1745, recorded the case of Roda Crocot and Kadie Krokot, captain and ensign of the Balinese troops, respectively; Adjie Daga, lieutenant of the Malays; and Siti Leta, lieutenant of the Buginese, who each wrote a letter to the governor before setting sail from Galle to Batavia, making special requests to transport their wives and families at their own cost with the Company's boats to Batavia.[10] In another case, twenty-five women, wives of Eastern militiamen dispatched to Batavia and the Cape of Good

---

[8] *Toepassers* were people of mixed Portuguese–Asian descent. The document in Malay may have been requested as proof of the declaration's authenticity and as a measure to prevent later claims of misunderstanding. Perhaps a Bugis document was not suggested because the Dutch officials could read Malay but not Bugis. See SLNA 1/95, Political Council Minutes, August 24, 1745.

[9] SLNA 1/4722. The document stated that only if there were not enough Eastern militiamen to form the battalion carrying out the sentence should it be supplied with Moors and *sepoys* (May 23, 1791). "Sepoy" was a broad term used to refer to native soldiers from India serving European powers.

[10] SLNA 1/95. The requests were refused due to a shortage of water-carrying utensils on the ship, with the exception of Captain Roda Crocot's case, which was approved in consideration of his many years of good service and bravery shown on different occasions.

Hope, sent a petition to Ceylon's Governor van Angelbeek, written in their own name and that of many others. In it they detailed how approximately two hundred of their men had been stationed on Dutch ships since 1794 to protect them against attacks at sea and, having expected to return to Ceylon quickly, had not requested to take their families along, which would have been their undoubted inclination had they known the length of deployment. Meanwhile, the women's allowance (paid by consent from their husbands' own salaries) was cut by half and at the time of writing had not been paid for two months, reducing many of them and their children to poverty. The women reminded the governor and Council that their husbands had always served loyally and left the shores of Ceylon willing to risk their lives for the Company; therefore they humbly requested a reinstatement of their maintenance or the opportunity to reunite their families. In the deliberations that followed, aside from recognizing the women's hardship and the injustice of withholding the payments which were legally theirs, Council members explicitly noted that the Company's interests required that the wives and children of the Eastern militiamen not be allowed to walk the streets begging at a time when troops "from that nation" constituted the largest part of the military, and the Company must possess the utmost confidence in their loyalty.[11]

Desertions could and did occur during military campaigns. The ongoing tensions and competition over loyalty come through in the case of the former Eastern soldier Lanang, who in 1772 was whipped, branded and sent in chains to Galle over a theft but escaped shortly thereafter to Kandy. After some time there, he returned to Dutch territory and willingly took upon himself to try and enter Kandy unnoticed in order to bring back additional Malays living there and serving the king. Lanang was caught by the Kandyans on two different occasions and suffered great misery in their prison and so, in return for his sacrifice, the Council decided he had earned some relief from his punishment and would be sent away from Ceylon to Malabar.[12] As Kandy provided an alternative to living under Dutch rule, various sources depict the shifting loyalties of Malay individuals and families moving between the two. In 1745, the Council decided to ignore the escape of the exile Surapati and his family from Trincomalee to the king's territories in Kandy as the escapees would be "well protected there." It was added, perhaps in self-persuasion, that their absence would also save funds as their allowances would not be paid, but it seemed the runaway exiles were not worth the

---

[11] SLNA 1/232, Political Council Minutes, November 24, 1795.
[12] SLNA 1/173, Political Council Minutes, December 5, 1776.

risk of conflict with the powerful kingdom.[13] The question of Malay loyalty, especially that of troops and guards, was one that would continue to haunt the colonial administration until the very final days of Kandy's independence in the early nineteenth century.

After the British took control of Ceylon from the Dutch in 1796, and throughout the nineteenth century, many of the Malays joined the military regiments established by the British, serving the new colonial power.[14] This incorporation into the British army was due in no small measure to the bravery the Malays had exhibited in opposing the British, and subsequent British admiration for their military abilities, as well as a constant need on the part of the British to police the island and to occasionally send reinforcements to additional sites within their empire, especially neighboring south India. The main proponent of the Malays within the administration at the time was Governor North, who advocated, successfully, for the creation of a Malay Regiment in 1801.[15]

As time went by, ongoing attempts were made by the British to recruit additional soldiers in the archipelago and Malay Peninsula and bring them to Ceylon, but these were on the whole unsuccessful.[16]

---

[13] SLNA 1/95, Political Council Minutes of May 5, 1745. When they returned five years later, they claimed they had originally fled mistreatment in Trincomalee and begged forgiveness. No reason was given for why they decided to return (SLNA 1/109, Political Council Minutes, April 28, 1750). On Malay slaves who "on account of ill treatment made their escape to the Candian territories," see Anthonisz, *Digest*, 6. On Malays and other foreign troops in the service of Kandy, see Channa Wickremesekere, *Kandy at War: Indigenous Military Resistance to European Expansion in Sri Lanka 1594–1818* (Colombo: Vijitha Yapa, 2004), 60–63.

[14] B. A. Hussainmiya's *Orang Rejimen* is to date the most detailed and insightful study of the Malays' roles and experiences within the British colonial forces in Ceylon. The majority of the background and analysis it provides on these themes will not be reiterated here. Not all those serving the Dutch continued service under the British. Alicia Schrikker cites a case of old Malay military men who "had chosen not to enter English service but to support themselves with a small vegetable garden that produced too little to feed everyone," and who received a modest pension from Batavia in lieu of returning there; see Alicia Schrikker, "Caught between Empires: VOC Families in Sri Lanka after the British Takeover, 1806–1808," *Annales de Démographie Historique* 2 (2011), 141.

[15] For details on Malay attacks on the invading British, see Hussainmiya, *Orang Rejimen*, 57–58. On the question of the Malays' fate upon the Dutch capitulation and the decision to send the troops and their families to Madras as prisoners of war, to be returned to Ceylon once British rule was established, see ibid., 58–60. For Governor North's role in the creation of the Regiment and subsequent developments, see especially ibid., chapter 4, 57–77. On the departure of some of the descendants of royal exiles back to Java under Governor Thomas Maitland, who wished to avoid funding their subsistence, see ibid., 79–80. On the latter episode, see also Schrikker, "Caught between Empires," especially 135–137.

[16] The last time recruits came directly from the archipelago was in 1816. See Hussainmiya, *Orang Rejimen*, 83; *Jubilee Book*, 171.

Such attempts were made by sending recruiters to the region and by publicly promoting the possibility of enlistment. On June 16, 1813, for example, a notice appeared in both English and Dutch in the *Java Government Gazette* published in Batavia. Signed by C. Assey, Secretary to Government, it announced that Captain de Bussche of His Majesty's 4th Ceylon Regiment had arrived in Java to recruit volunteers to the Malay Regiment in Ceylon. Just a few lines above this notice was another, declaring the establishment of a close trade relationship between the colonies of Java and Ceylon (both under British rule at the time), for which Captain de Bussche was also responsible. The volunteers, the ad indicated, would surely be able to benefit from these close contacts.[17] Captain de Bussche was moderately successful, returning from his mission with 412 "fine young men" as recruits "from the Malay settlement in the island of Java and its neighbourhood" for the 1st Ceylon Regiment. Combined with a company of Malays from the 4th Regiment stationed in Trincomalee where their ship had arrived, they were now 1,013 strong.[18]

In 1830 Thomas Skinner, a major in the British army and prominent road builder in Ceylon, was tasked with accompanying Javanese soldiers who wished to return from Ceylon to Java. These were men recruited by the British and taken to Ceylon during the British interregnum on Java (1811–1816). Skinner was concurrently charged with recruiting additional men for military service in Ceylon.[19] In his memoirs, he described how after eight days at sea he could see the shores of Aceh. He visited Penang, Malacca and Singapore (where a local sultan's son offered to enlist with a group of Buginese soldiers) before reaching Batavia, where he requested permission to disembark some "time-expired" Javanese men whom he had brought on the ship.[20] Despite all of Skinner's attempts, the Dutch authorities refused to take the soldiers back, because they had been in the service of another power. More specifically, he was told that the recent Java War (1825–1830) had been much prolonged by the presence of soldiers who had acquired military experience while serving the British in Java, then discharged in 1816 and joined the anti-Dutch struggle.[21] Although Skinner reported that he was greeted with

---

[17] *Java Government Gazette* 2.69 (June 19, 1813), 1.

[18] SLNA 5/7, Brownrigg to Bathurst, August 17, 1814.

[19] This section is based on Thomas Skinner, *Fifty Years in Ceylon: An Autobiography*, ed. Annie Skinner (London: W. H. Allen & Co. 1891). The events discussed are described in chapters 5 and 6, pp. 96–156.

[20] Ibid., 119–122. Skinner depicted the Javanese on shore as excited to see the British uniforms of those on the ship, having as they did a saying to the effect of "when the rain comes, the goats run away; when the English come, the Dutch run away" (ibid., 123).

[21] Ibid., 128.

impressive hospitality and greatly enjoyed his exposure to Java's riches and beauty, the Dutch were firm in their decision and he did not accomplish his mission.[22]

While it lasted, military service constituted a critical link between the Malays and the British in colonial Ceylon and was, by its nature, ambiguous: Enlistment provided a profession, a livelihood for individuals and families, participation in a system governed by Europeans and opportunities for advancement within the colonial state; it entailed adopting new attire, new mannerisms and new allegiances; and it required putting one's health and sometimes life at risk for the sake of Empire.[23] In a somewhat more unexpected manner, service offered opportunities for participation in a vibrant literary culture.

A noteworthy aspect of Malay military service in the nineteenth century was the remarkable relationship between life in the Malay Regiment and Malay literary culture, which took several forms. Members of the Regiment copied classical Malay works that are known from other Malay-speaking regions, including present-day Malaysia and Indonesia. Among many others these included the *Hikayat Ahmad Muhammad*, *Hikayat Amir Hamzah*, *Hikayat Isma Yatim* and *Sirat al-Mustaqim*. In addition to reproducing the "old classics," Regiment soldiers also wrote their own stories and poems, some of which addressed particular events that unfolded in Ceylon and within the context of military life. These were often composed in the poetic genre of the syair. Malay literature's principal promoters and audiences were often related to the Regiment, which, as an institution, played an important organizing role in the Malay community's life. At schools established by the British in the military cantonments where Malays served, members of the Regiment and their children received a compulsory education that included instruction in Malay written in the Arabic script.[24] An ongoing familiarity with the script (especially as romanized Malay became gradually more prominent in the late nineteenth century) ensured that the literature remained intelligible to younger generations. Regiment soldiers who traveled to British Malaya and Singapore on assignment served as a bridge between the community in Ceylon and the large Malay centers to the east by guaranteeing a two-way

---

[22] It was suggested to him by his hosts, however, that he should go to Bali, an island not ruled by the Dutch, where he would have an opportunity to purchase men from the local ruler (ibid., 134).

[23] Commenting on the new attire, Skinner lamented the Malays' dressing in boots and being given habits and equipment of the European soldier that "utterly destroyed" them (ibid., 13).

[24] The schools' curriculum included also English and arithmetic. See Hussainmiya, *Lost Cousins*, 93.

movement of ideas, religious texts and people between them. For example, a manuscript of the *Hikayat Indera Putra* copied first in Kampung Gelam, Singapore, in 1844, and then copied anew (*disalin buat baru*) in Kampung Kertel in Colombo in 1866, declares both writing sites, in Ceylon and Singapore, to be the *barisan Melayu*, the Malay barracks (see Figure 8.1). The man inscribing the tale, at both times and in both places, was one Salimudeen, who in the closing lines of the 1866 telling described himself as a retiree, holding the rank of captain, of the Ceylon Regiment.[25] And indeed this multifaceted investment in Malay literary culture by members of the Regiment – as scribes, readers, teachers and promoters – is apparent in many of the manuscripts collected to date having been found in the possession of soldiers' descendants.

Salimudeen's brief lines attest to the transmission of Malay manuscripts produced in Singapore to Ceylon and to their recopying there after many years, likely due to the wear and tear of frequent reading or a demand for additional copies. In his case, more than two decades had passed since the writing of the *Hikayat* concluded in the Malay barracks in Singapore to its reproduction, also in Malay barracks, in Colombo. In both cases the barracks were located in *kampung*s – Gelam and Kertel – Malay settlements central in the respective communities' histories. The earlier colophon had already made it clear that Salimudeen was a Malay military man stationed in, or passing through, Singapore on his way to Ceylon, while by the time the second colophon was written, Salimudeen had reached the rank of captain and retired from the Regiment. In addition to the *Hikayat Indera Putra*, the same Salimudeen was responsible also for the production of the *Hikayat Qobad Shah* and the *Hikayat Isma Yatim*, both copied at the Malay barracks of Kertel in Colombo, and all three belonging to the classical Malay "canon." In his colophons Salimudeen, who again noted his status as Regiment retiree, included the phrase "*biladi jawi hindi*" as an element describing the writing circumstances. The phrase, which can be translated as "the jawi hindi land" seems to evoke a spatial designation which is both "jawi" – i.e. Malay or Southeast Asian – and "hindi," the term for British India, here apparently encompassing Ceylon. "Jawi hindi" could therefore connote "British Southeast Asia" or the British sphere within the jawi lands, and more specifically Singapore and Malaya, where texts were purchased or copied.[26] Aside from serving as signposts in one man's life,

---

[25] Salimudeen, *Hikayat Indera Putra*, Kuala Lumpur: Perpustakaan Negara Malaysia, MS PNM 1063, 360. The manuscript is a compendium 1,378 pages long.

[26] The copying (M. *bersalin*) of *Hikayat Qobad Shah* was concluded at the Malay barracks of Kampung Kertel on September 27, 1865. The copying anew (M. *disalin buat baru*) of *Hikayat Isma Yatim* was finished in those same barracks on December 10, 1871: MS PNM 1063, 828.

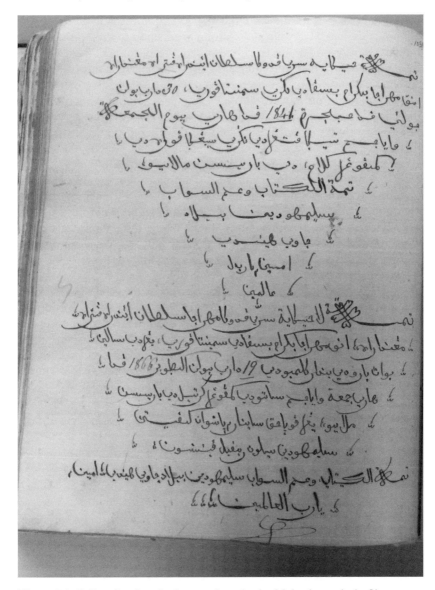

Figure 8.1 Salimudeen's colophons written in the Malay barracks in Singapore and Colombo. *Hikayat Indera Putra*, MS PNM 1063, 360.
Courtesy National Library of Malaysia

the colophons in Salimudeen's manuscripts more broadly attest to the ongoing ties with Malay life and cultural production to the southeast that military service under the British afforded Malay soldiers from Ceylon, keeping them informed and connected to a wider Malay sphere of language and literary culture.[27]

Salimudeen in no way constituted a singular example. Military service provided a framework within which men with an army affiliation invested in a textual tradition that linked them to their heritage and also allowed them a depiction of current events, aspirations and beliefs. The manuscript colophon, as shown above, was a paratextual site where servicemen's commitment to literature was manifested: Composed of several brief lines typically found on the final page, it offered succinct information about the scribe and place and date of completion. Although usually insufficient to trace a manuscript's source or the history of its arrival in Ceylon, there are many instances in which the link between Malay literary culture and army service – whether present or past – is clear.

The *Hikayat Qobad Shah* contains two colophons at its end. The first gives the date of completion and the location as the Malay barracks in Kampung Kertel, Colombo. On the next page is found an additional, more elaborate colophon written in the form of a syair. Although the exact date of completion is repeated, as is Colombo as the writing site, these lines offer additional details of the manuscript production process. By doing so, they reveal a glimpse of the cultural context in which Regiment scribes and audiences were operating, their challenges and goals:

> I spent months copying [this book]/the process lasted six months.
> Asking for determination [I] sat and endured/[until] with care the
>   source was [re]created.
> The benefits are not just a matter/of knowing a particular language.
> There is poetic language within it/if one is adamant it can be attained.[28]

---

[27] Instances of Malay books brought back from Singapore to Ceylon are known also from a somewhat later period. For example, the late Mrs. Fathin Basiron Abbas of Gampolla (1929–2018) recounted how her grandfather Mr. Mammath Hannan used to travel to Singapore to visit his brother and bring books back upon his return, some of which were still in her possession, including several hikayats and a booklet her mother used to teach her jawi during childhood (personal communication, February 14, 2012). For examples of books printed in Singapore and brought to Ceylon in the early twentieth century, see the Gnei Fathin Preena Basiron Abbas and Jayarine and Thalip Iyne collections, BL, EAP609/2 and EAP609/5 respectively.

[28] *Hamba bersalin berbulan bulan/ada qadarnya enam bulan*
Pinta pe[ng]gang duduq bertahan/kalah matah khalak pengawasan
Faedanya ini bukan suatu/sahaja mengetahui bahasa yang tentu
Ada kawi bahasa di situ/jika menuntut dapatlah itu (Salimudeen, *Hikayat Qobad Shah*, Colombo, 1865, Perpustakaan Negara Malaysia, Kuala Lumpur, MS PNM 1063, 150).

Employing the verb *bersalin*, used for one borrowing books in order to have them copied, Salimudeen described a lengthy process, stretching over six months, possibly because of other commitments but seemingly also because of the difficulty inherent in reading and making sense of the manuscript, a process that required endurance and determination and finally resulted in a carefully created new copy. The reward for this effort was not just gaining better knowledge of the Malay language but of gaining access to the *kawi bahasa*, the poetic language that emerged when texts such as the *Hikayat Qobad Shah* and others occasionally switched from the hikayat prose to sections written in the syair and pantun meters. The colophon itself exemplifies the scribe's success in the endeavor as he was able to add his own, however brief, rhymed poem, as proof of what he had learned.

Another dimension of the link between regimental life and Malay literary culture, also revealed in several brief colophons, was the practice of borrowing. Manuscripts were produced and funded by relatively few people, but their aspiring audience was much larger. And so, in some cases, they were lent out on a temporary basis so that others could gain from their reading or recital. This form of circulation enhanced the manuscripts' reach and positioned Regiment members and retirees as the core textual community within wider circles of Malay life. The *Hikayat Nabi Musa Munajat* contains a note asking that any borrower of "this tale of Musa" shall return it without delay to its owner; Dulhamit Fakir Gigul, owner of the *Hikayat Nabi Berperang dengan Raja Kaibar*, added a note to the manuscript in 1869 asking that anyone borrowing it should return it quickly, rather than store it for personal use; the *Hikayat Ahmad Muhammad*, copied in 1896, concluded with the following passage:

This is the *Hikayat Ahmad Muhammad* written in Colombo at Kampung Wekande. Owned by God's servant Tuan Subedar Mursit, retiree of the Ceylon Rifle Regiment. Whomsoever borrows [this book] wishing to read it may not keep it for more than ten days. Those who request it must return it clean: Do not stain it [or] I will not accept it back. Also, do not be offended by the many requests of [your] friend the scribe. The End.

Mursit retired Subedar

Light Ceylon Rifles[29]

---

[29] These borrowing references appear, respectively, in Tuan Jury ibn Husain Weerabangsa, *Hikayat Nabi Musa Munajat*, Kandy, 1892, Perpustakaan Negara Malaysia, Kuala Lumpur, in MS PNM 430, though much of the text is illegible; Saliman ibn Sarjan Asmara, *Hikayat Nabi Berperang dengan Raja Kaibar*, 1861, Perpustakaan Negara Malaysia, Kuala Lumpur, MS PNM 1061, 212. The quote is from Subedar Mursit, *Hikayat Ahmad Muhammad*, Kampung Wekande, 1890, Perpustakaan Negara Malaysia, Kuala Lumpur, MS PNM 1058, 204: *Yaini hikayatnya Ahmad Muhamad yang menulis*

The relative abundance of manuscripts that mention soldiers is a testimony to their role as guardians and transmitters of Malay writing in Ceylon. The same Subedar Mursit copied the *Syair Sultan Abdul Muluk* in Colombo. Another *Hikayat Ahmad Muhammad* was transmitted (M. *menurunkan*) in 1867, written by Samshudeen ibn al-Taif in Malapingi. The owner, who may have been the writer's son, was Encik Prawira Mahmud Samsudeen, of the Ceylon Rifle Regiment. On the next and final page, written in a different hand, Tuan 'Abdalhanan Kecilan noted that he had received the manuscript from the wife of Sergeant Samsudeen in 1871 and that he was now the proper owner. The *Hikayat Muhammad Hanafiyah* was copied by Captain Morset in 1894, in Kampung Kertel. The writing of the *Hikayat Shah Qobad* was completed on September 7, 1892, at 2:30 in the afternoon. It was written by Tuan ibn Cenci, serving as a police sergeant in Agrapatni. A compendium now listed as *Pelbagai Catatan* was signed on its inner flap by Mas Anom, Police Constable no. 417, Galgadara.[30] The dates and the positions held by these latter scribes in the police, rather than the army, represented the post-disbandment period in the Regiment's history when many Malays turned to other security-oriented organizations, including the police and fire brigades, for employment and a continuing sense of purpose, livelihood and pride. In these capacities their literary activities continued.

In addition to reproducing the "old classics," Regiment soldiers also wrote their own stories and poems, some of which addressed particular events that unfolded in Ceylon and within the context of military life. These were often composed in the poetic genre of syair. The *Syair Kisahnya Kabar Wolenter Benggali* ("Report on the Bengali Volunteers") is the earliest-known example of local Malay expression of its kind in Ceylon, testifying to an ability of local authors to employ the language's

---

dinegeri Kalambo di kampung Wekande yang ampunya haq sebenar2nya hamba Allah tuan subedar Mursit pension Selon Rifel Rejimet yaitulah barangsiapa pinjam hendaq baca tiada boleh lewat dari sepulu hari tetapi yang mintanya dibaliqkan dengan bersi supaya jangan kuturkan aku tiada nanti terima jua jangan guser terlalu pintanya henda menulis juadanya. An additional borrowing reference was given from the *Hikayat Seri Rama*; see Chapter 7.

[30] Subedar Mursit, *Syair Sultan Abdul Muluk* Colombo, n.d., Perpustakaan Negara Malaysia, Kuala Lumpur MS PNM 450; Samsudeen ibn al-Taif, *Hikayat Ahmad Muhammad*, inscribed Malapingi, 1867, Perpustakaan Negara Malaysia, Kuala Lumpur, MS PNM 1063; *Hikayat Muhammad Hanafiyah*, inscribed Colombo, 1894, Perpustakaan Negara Malaysia, Kuala Lumpur, MS PNM 453; Tuan ibn Cenci, *Hikayat Shah Qobad*, inscribed Agrapatni, 1892, Perpustakaan Negara Malaysia, Kuala Lumpur, MS PNM 446; Mas Anom Weerabangsa, *Pelbagai Catatan*, n.d., Perpustakaan Negara Malaysia, Kuala Lumpur, MS PNM 1062. This list constitutes only a sample of the many Malay manuscripts produced by Regiment soldiers and retirees.

contemporary literary conventions (rather than just reproduce texts brought from Southeast Asia) and to the desire to record and commemorate events of Regiment life through poetic means. The *Syair* offers an onlooker's perspective on a street fight between members of the Malay Regiment and those of the 20th Bengal Native Infantry, sent to Ceylon from Fort William in Calcutta to help quell the Uva rebellion in 1818.[31] Composed by Burhan Lye in 1819, shortly after the events depicted, it purports to depict the events truthfully, without bias or exaggeration. Beginning with the news of the rebellion in the Hill Country, the *Syair* describes the Malay soldiers sent to Kandy, the intense fighting and the many casualties as the war dragged on for months. The Bengali soldiers dispatched from India to fight the Sinhalese rebels arrived in Colombo toward the end of the war and were settled there in close proximity to the Malay barracks of Kampung Kertel. The clash erupted on January 1, 1819, initially between two groups of Malays – those of the 1st Ceylon Volunteers and those of the Regiment – with soldiers from both groups shouting abuse at each other and firing their guns. When the Bengali soldiers heard the clash, they hurried to the scene, intending to attack. New fighting broke out, men were injured, and eventually the British authorities arrived and restored calm.[32] After a search and the arrest of several men, the Malays were brought to trial before a military court. According to the author, the Malays presented their claims truthfully and humbly while the Bengalis were deceitful. The portrayal of the case ended with the Malays' acquittal.[33]

---

[31] The *Syair* has been romanized, edited and partially translated by Hussainmiya, who appended contemporary British sources engaging with the event depicted. See B. A. Hussainmiya, "Syair Kisahnya Kabar Orang Wolenter Benggali: A Sri Lankan Malay Syair, Introduction and Text," in *Lost Cousins*, 106–152. The information about the Bengali unit is on p. 107. While the discussion draws on Hussainmiya's edition, it is based mainly on the original manuscript, contained in *Pelbagai Catatan*, MS PNM 1062. The only known extant copy of the *Syair*, inscribed in the late nineteenth century and now housed in the National Library of Malaysia, it seems to contain errors and may not represent an original now lost. For speculation on these errors, see Hussainmiya, *Lost Cousins*, 114–115. In essence the *Syair* seems to come to a close at verse 62 but then returns to further depict the same events. The manuscript *Pelbagai Catatan* ("Various Notes") contains several additional texts and serves as an example of how a nondescript catalogue title may mask a fascinating and rare writing exemplar. The colophon states that the owner, and likely copyist, was Mas Anom Weerabangsa, son of Tuan Captain Husain, nephew of Captain Sawal, and grandson of Captain Weerabangsa, on whom see more below.

[32] Such violent occurrences among native troops of different origins were not rare. For a report of a clash between Malay and gun laskar troops in Trincomalee, in which at least forty-seven men, of both groups, were wounded and killed, see SLNA 5/78, Maitland to Windham, February 28, 1807.

[33] Burhan Lye, *Syair Kisahnya*, MS PNM 1061, verses 1–62.

What does the *Syair* reveal, beyond the sequence of events on that fateful day? Constituting the earliest extant original composition in Malay from Ceylon, the *Syair* divulges much about the particular use of the Malay language at the time in terms of vocabulary, orthography and the ability to manipulate the syair poetic form, all topics well covered by Hussainmiya which shall not be reiterated. In addition, the *Syair* offers an insider's view on the Malay character as presented by the author: Providing an explanation as to the initial cause of the event, Burhan Lye stated that the Malays "were a violent people who will quarrel when offered the slightest opportunity."[34] His writing exposed an internal rivalry between Malay troops as well as, no less importantly, a divide between those Malays who served in the army, depicted as trigger-happy and brash, and those like the author who self-identified as a "free man" (*preman*, a civilian), frightened by the aggressive outbreak and preferring to disappear from the scene.[35] This statement was followed by graphic descriptions of the violence (still between two groups of Malays), conveying the fear in the air and people scrambling to shut themselves in their homes while the soldiers, as if possessed by Satan, destroyed the shops (*kedai*) lining the streets. A description of running amok (M. *mengamok*) followed, the men likened to ghosts or evil spirits leaping in the air, rushing about, shooting, hurling stones, waving swords while wounded, as fainting and unconscious men lay in blood-filled streets.[36] When the Bengali troops joined in, similar descriptions were repeated, bringing into sharp relief the proximity of chaos beneath the veil of military discipline and order in this enclave of Malay life in Colombo where men who had just returned from months of brutal warfare lived in close proximity to others who belonged to the same military establishment yet differed from them in language, land of origin and religion.[37]

Cultural and religious dimensions of the struggle were mentioned briefly in the *Syair*. The Malays were depicted as humbly presenting their case before the court, asking forgiveness and evoking empathy in their superiors while the Bengalis were said to have lied outright. More importantly from the viewpoint of Burhan Lye, the Malays won the upper hand in the skirmish, despite their numerical disadvantage, on

---

[34] *Apala lagi hendaq bicara/di dalam nagari ampunya cedera*
Sebab Melayu orang angkarah/sedikit terboleh menjadi cederah (ibid., verse 17).

[35] *Karena hamba bukan orang Kompeni/henda berperang menunjuk berani*
sebabnya aku orang premani/makanya itu hendaq sembunyi (ibid., verse 23).

[36] Ibid., verses 26–33. Mengamok was a common trope, to be discussed below.

[37] Kampung Kertel was not only a barrack but the place of residence of many Malay regimental families: Hussainmiya, *Lost Cousins*, 107.

account of their Muslim faith, having received God's assistance and the blessing of the Prophet Muhammad in the land of Ceylon.[38] In later verses this message was further elaborated as the *Syair* juxtaposed the Bengalis and Malays. The Bengali volunteers were depicted as tall and eminent; however,

> What is the use of being great,
> lacking intention, losing their heads,
> Thoughts driven by anger,
> Short on intelligence later filled with regret,
>
> Acting as though ready to extinguish the world,
> Noble God in none of their thoughts,
> His grace is nothing to them.
> Thus they dare to act in this way,
>
> What is the use of being great,
> Lacking intention, as they follow their minds,
> Resembling Setan who does not attack,
> Disappearing with no permanent trace.[39]

The Bengalis were depicted as eminent (M. *orang utama*) whereas the Malays were portrayed as "little people" (M. *orang kecil*), yet the significant differentiation between the groups was not about physical power or rank but in intention and piety. In these passages the poet seems to be both making a statement regarding the Malays' standing and putting forth a plea that they live up to the religious standards he had delineated:

> The Malays are a useless people.
> Allah keeps them far from all danger,
> Blessed by Muhammad, the faithful Prophet.
> Protected are all His slaves, those useless ones.[40]
>
> We are Allah's slaves,
> Kept far from any affliction.
> If willing [to] commit no wrong
> The path shall be flawless.

---

[38] *Ditolongnya Tuhan seru sekalian alam/sekalian Melayu orang Islam*
    daripada berkat nabi akhir alam/di tanah Selong empunya dalam (Burhan Lye, *Syair Kisahnya*, MS PNM 1061, verse 55).
[39] Ibid., verses 65–67.
[40] The line reads *dipiarkan segala hamba dan siya*, literally "slaves *and* useless [ones]," but since it seems to be in dialogue with the first line of the stanza in which the Malays are depicted as useless (*tersiya*) I have omitted the connective in translation. The final word could also be read as *saya* ("I") however the author never uses it to speak of himself but rather consistently employs the self-deprecating *hamba*.

> Let us be filled with reverence
> Toward God, the Sublime Lord.
> Praise those believers
> Who rule over all Muslims.[41]

Burhan Lye offered a few autobiographical details as well as the conventional apology for his lack of poetic talent, stating that he wrote the *Syair* to console troubled hearts. He identified himself as the son of Tuan Kapitan Layu, a *Peranakan anak Melayu*. As noted in Chapter 7 in the discussion of the *Hikayat Seri Rama*'s scribe categorizing himself as *peranakan Selong*, in the Indonesian–Malay world the term "peranakan" referred broadly to those of mixed descent, most commonly the descendants of local Malay mothers and foreign fathers, be they of Indian, Chinese or Arab descent. The term's employment in Ceylon highlights the diverse and diasporic elements of the Malay community, with Burhan Lye's own family background of mixed Chinese and Javanese descent providing evidence.[42] Lye went on to elaborate further on himself, in unusual detail:

> As I am an orphan
> I lack good common sense,
> Like a ghost inhabiting [the world]
> With no place to call my own.
>
> Here is the sign that I am the author,
> A feeble body in a foreign land,
> Heart filled with regret and affliction,
> Unacknowledged at this time.
>
> May God not put me to shame.
> If there is lack may it be filled.
> The text is very much groping its way
> As my heart is exceedingly perplexed.[43]

The colophon reveals some details of Lye's life while giving rise to more questions. Why did he write of himself as living in a foreign land? Was the expression used metaphorically or did it mean, in conjunction with his identifying as peranakan, that he came from elsewhere or did not fully identify as a Malay? Be that as it may, the *Syair* feels more personal than most as it conveys an eyewitness account of a traumatic event encompassing military life, referencing the fear and pain of war, homecoming,

---

[41] Ibid., verses 69–71.
[42] According to Hussainmiya, citing the colophon of the *Syair Syaikh Fadlun*, Burhan Lye was of Chinese ancestry and his family hailed from Semarang (*Lost Cousins*, 112).
[43] Burhan Lye, *Syair Kisahnya*, MS PNM 1061, verses 57–59.

internal rivalries among the Malay soldiers, and tensions between differ-ent native groups serving in the British army. The *Syair* also offered an insiders' view of the Malays that was neither monolithic nor self-glorifying but spoke to the ambivalence in the community, the struggles it faced and the mechanisms of survival within the military and, more broadly, of living as a small diasporic Muslim community under colonial rule. The latter aspect emerged most clearly in the description of the Malays as easily provoked and tending toward volatility yet, when facing the British court, able to navigate their way and gain favor by apologizing, offering plausible justifications for their actions and generally bowing down before the higher authority. Concurrently, the *Syair* invited the Malays to praise all those rulers who were believers, i.e. Muslims – surely a call excluding the British – even while they acknowledged and served their European, Christian rulers. Furthermore, the *Syair* affords rare insight into Malay writing practices in Ceylon in the early nineteenth century, proving that knowledge of the genre, the conventions of author-ial apology and self-deprecation and orthographical codes formed part of a dynamic tradition that was not solely dependent on the copying of older texts. To this tradition, whether through authorship, scribal practice, choice of textual subject matter or audience formation, Regiment members and military life were key.

In considering military life in colonial Ceylon, the kingdom of Kandy and its relationship over time to the Portuguese, Dutch and British presence on the island was central. The last native kingdom to fall to European hands after a series of wars in the early nineteenth century, during the Dutch period and especially following the treaty of 1766 and the ceding of the entire coastline to the Dutch East India Company, Kandy was "a virtual prisoner of the Dutch but still far from a conquered state."[44] Situated in the rugged highlands, encircled by jungle and accessible only by a very few and narrow passes, Kandy was a natural fortress, its surrounding topography fit for guerrilla warfare, putting the Europeans aiming to reach it at a severe disadvantage. Beyond guerrilla tactics, another common strategy employed by the Kandyans against the

---

[44] Wickremesekere, *Kandy at War,* 41. However, Dutch dominance was not achieved immediately. The *Syair Hemop* (see Chapter 4) offers an early nineteenth-century perspective on early eighteenth-century Dutch relations with Kandy. The king of Kandy is depicted as a grand figure, wearing precious stones and ruling over a population that is as numerous as leaves in a forest, a sovereign toward whom the Dutch harbored feelings of *malu* (being intimidated, ashamed). See *Syair Hemop* (Rusconi, "Sja'ir"), 21.

foreign invaders was the subversion of non-Europeans who formed the majority of European armies invading Kandy.[45]

The Kandy Wars of the early nineteenth century constituted momentous episodes for the British as several centuries of European engagement with the inland kingdom were coming to their violent close. In 1803 Governor North initiated hostilities against the Kandyan king Sri Vikrama Rajasingha, wishing to replace him with his prime minister Muttusami. The king fled while the small British force left in Kandy with Muttusami was subject to attacks and disease. Major Adam Davie marched out of the kingdom on June 24, 1803, with what remained of the garrison, including 14 European officers, 20 British soldiers, 250 Malays, 150 gun lascars and Prince Muttusami. The latter was eventually handed over to the king on the promise of allowing safe passage to the troops and was executed; however, the rest of Davie's battalion had to surrender, and many were brutally killed.[46] In 1804, the British were able to reestablish a presence in Kandy, and in 1815 they brought its royal line to an end.

The capture of the last king of Kandy has been chronicled extensively, with many accounts accepting the colonial narrative of his brutality as justification for his fate while others strongly contradict and reject that narrative.[47] The Malays' position in this history was one of ambivalence, and there was no single "Malay position" across the series of conflicts.[48] The shifting allegiances of the Malays were nowhere more vividly clear

[45] Thus, the main Dutch force in 1765 comprised 900 Europeans, 800 Easterners and about 100 sepoys, while the Dutch garrison in Kandy that same year included approximately 550 Europeans and nearly 700 sepoys and Malays (Wickremesekere, *Kandy at War*, 133–134).

[46] On North's relationship with the kingdom, see U. C. Wickremeratne, "Lord North and the Kandyan Kingdom," *JRAS* 1 (1973): 30–42.

[47] See especially Gananath Obeyesekere, *The Doomed King: A Requiem for Śri Vikrama Rajasinha* (Colombo: Sailfish, 2017).

[48] On the Malays' positions as related to Kandy and depicted in contemporary colonial sources see, for example, Henry Marshall, *Ceylon: A General Description of the Island and its Inhabitants with An Historical Sketch of the Conquest of the Colony by the English* (London: William H. Allen and Co., 1846); H. W. Codrington (ed.), "Diary of Mr. John D'Oyly," *Journal of the Ceylon Branch of the Royal Asiatic Society* 25.69 (1917): iii–xvi, 1–269, repr. Navrang, 1995; Arthur Johnston, *Narrative of the operations of a detachment in an expedition to Candy, in the Island of Ceylon, in the year 1804* (Dublin: James McGlashan, 1854). The discussion focuses on Kandy in 1803–1805, but Malays also played important roles in the later Kandyan Wars and the 1818 Rebellion, which will not be discussed. The king was finally caught on February 18, 1815, as a result of collaboration between the British and Kandy aristocrats, and was exiled to Vellore in south India. Kandyan nobles ruled over several provinces until the 1818 uprising which brought the area under complete British control. The Malays' conflicting and complex affiliations continued throughout this period. According to Hussainmiya, the Malays took a more ambivalent stand in the 1803 war than in the other Kandyan wars, when

than in the episode of the "Noordeen brothers" as it was commemorated in both written and oral accounts.[49] The brothers, sons of the twenty-sixth sultan of Gowa, Fakhruddin Abdul Khair, who had been exiled by the Dutch from his south Sulawesi kingdom in 1767 on charges of conspiring with the British, served the two opposing sides in the war of 1803, and their story serves here in considering the wider question of the Malays' position in Ceylon's colonial conflicts.[50] One of the brothers, Karaeng Sangunglo, is said to have escaped from the Dutch and entered the service of the king of Kandy around 1800. Two other brothers, Karaeng Muhammad Noordeen and Karaeng Saifudeen, served as captains in the Malay Regiment of the British army dispatched to Kandy.[51]

The most readily available details on the Noordeen brothers in Kandy come from contemporary British sources. Cordiner, who lived in Ceylon from 1799 to 1804, serving as chaplain to the garrison in Colombo, wrote a detailed account of the 1803 events that was "compiled at Colombo from the information of the principal civil servants."[52] According to this narrative the king made ongoing attempts to seduce the Malays into desertion.[53] As part of these efforts, Captain Noordeen received a letter from his brother, "a Malay prince in the Candian service," soliciting him

their loyalty to the British was far more pronounced. For speculations on the causes of these developments, see Hussainmiya, *Orang Rejimen*, 67–68. On Malays bribed to assassinate the king of Kandy in 1806, see Marshall, *Ceylon: A General Description*, 133; on John D'Oyly reporting in his diary that it was Malays who provided him with detailed information of the king's movements in anticipation of the British conquest in 1813, see Obeyesekere, *The Doomed King*, 120; for a note on subsequent events, telling of Assan Captar, a very prominent officer in the king's Malay Regiment who fled from Kandy and entered the service of the British in 1811, who was of much help and was amply rewarded, then "negotiated with rebels" and fell out of favor, see *Jubilee Book*, 164.

[49] Although only one of the brothers was named Noordeen, this is the popular name by which the episodes to be discussed have come to be known and therefore it is employed throughout.

[50] On Sultan Fakhruddin and his family's exilic life in Ceylon, as reconstructed from a letter written by the sultan's widow Siti Hapipa to the governor-general in Batavia in 1807, see Suryadi, "Sepucuk Surat." For extended accounts of the war, see Geoffrey Powell, *The Kandyan Wars: The British Army in Ceylon 1803–1818* (London: Leo Cooper, 1973), and V. M. Methley, "The Ceylon Expedition of 1803," *Transactions of the Royal Historical Society* 1 (1918): 92–128. The emphasis here is on the Noordeen "dimension."

[51] Suryadi, "Sepucuk Surat," 15–16. Karaeng is a Makassarese nobility title.

[52] James Cordiner, *A Description of Ceylon, containing an account of the country, inhabitants, and natural products; with narratives of a tour round the island in 1800, the campaign in Candy in 1803, and a journey to Ramisseram in 1804*, 2 vols. (London: Longman, Hurst, Rees, and Orme, 1807), I: vi.

[53] Hussainmiya notes that, although desertions elicited by the Kandyan Malays' promises of security and rewards were quite common at the time, 250 of 700 Malays serving the British in Kandy remained loyal as the British prepared to leave the city (*Orang Rejimen*, 68).

to persuade "his countrymen to revolt and assassinate the British soldiers" in exchange for land and money that would be handsomely
provided by the king as reward.[54] Captain Noordeen immediately
informed his superior Major Davie and did what he could to prevent
desertion.[55]

When the British garrison that had been occupying the Kandy palace
since February 1803 was stormed on June 24 of that year, the attack was
led by Kandyan Malays headed by Sangunglo. He died in battle, but the
British could not hold out, and soon his brother Captain Noordeen and
Major Davie went out to offer their surrender.[56] An agreement was drafted
and signed, and the British troops left the city on the road to Trincomalee
while 120 of them who were ill and hospitalized remained and were
promised exit once recovered. The next few days were disastrous for the
British, led by Major Davie, as the Kandyan king gradually went back on
his word, ultimately demanding on pain of death that they lay down their
arms and march back to Kandy. As they walked back, accompanied by
Kandyan Malays, the troops suddenly found themselves surrounded.
The Malays serving the British were then separated from the European
troops and told to march on, with four officers and several servants among
them refusing to budge. The others were asked whether they would enter
into the king's service, again on pain of death, and most said they would.[57]

Upon the return to Kandy, Captain Noordeen and his brother, who
was also a native officer in the Malay Regiment, were called into the
king's presence. James Cordiner described the scene in which they were
brought to the palace at Hangaramketty:

On their arrival there the Adigar attempted to force them to prostrate themselves
before the King, according to the custom of the country; but they would not
condescend to perform an act of so much humiliation. They saluted the King
agreeably to their own rank and usage, telling him that they inherited royal blood,
and that their grandfather had been an independent monarch. Their conversation
did not displease the King: he spoke kindly to them, requested them to enter into
his service, and to take the command of all the Malays. Nouradeen replied, that
he could not accept of his Majesty's offer, without entailing upon himself
everlasting disgrace; that he had already sworn allegiance to the King of
England, and that he would live and die in his service.[58]

---

[54] Cordiner, *A Description*, II: 204.
[55] In a letter to Colombo, Major Davie reported that in an attempt to lure Noordeen,
Sangunglo offered him the income from fourteen districts and better pay than under the
British: cited in Wickremesekera, *Kandy at War*, 135.
[56] Cordiner, *A Description*, II: 209.
[57] Most of these Malays eventually escaped from Kandy and returned to British service
(ibid., 220).
[58] Ibid., 217.

The brothers were put in confinement, where they remained for several weeks, after which the king sent for them again, to ask if they would prefer death to entering his service. Again, the brothers maintained that they were willing to sacrifice their lives "in the service of the illustrious King of England." Enraged, the king ordered their immediate execution. The brothers' bodies were not offered burial but were dragged instead into the forest and left there, prey to wild beasts.[59] Another British account in 1817 praised Noordeen's "incorruptible integrity" and his resisting "the most flattering offers of the enemy." He and his brother, the report went on, "nobly preferred death to the violation of their oaths."[60] Several decades later, Henry Charles Sirr in his *Ceylon and the Cingalese* depicted Noordeen as an honorable man who refused to switch sides, contrasting him with Major Davie's despicable, cowardly behavior.[61] This contrast with Davie was also made in the earlier writings, if not always explicitly.

These colonial accounts consistently praised and commemorated the Noordeen brothers' loyalty and courage, all the more impressive when recalled against the backdrop of a devastating British debacle and the sense, palpable in contemporary accounts, that the British leadership, and above all Major Davie, had "in a moment of infatuated weakness, forgetting that it was their duty rather to face death, than to incur disgrace, submitted to the insolent and atrocious demands of the Candians, and consented to purchase a delusive security, by the sacrifice of all high and honourable sentiment."[62] The account of the Noordeen brothers, themselves not mere native soldiers but princes from a faraway land who were perceived as proud and noble yet devoted to the king of England and absolutely trustworthy to the end, offered an almost mythical model for the ideal British military man's desired actions. It is difficult to know precisely how reliable was the account of the palace scene (which may have been reported by a Malay servant who had escaped), but the account lived on regardless and was remembered by the British in subsequent reports of the war.[63]

[59] Ibid., 217–218.
[60] A. M. Philalethes, *History of Ceylon from the Earliest Period to the Year 1815* (London: n.p., 1817; repr. Cambridge: Cambridge University Press, 2012), 160, 167.
[61] Henry Charles Sirr, *Ceylon and the Cingalese. Their history, government and religion. The antiquities, institutions, produce, revenue and capabilities of the island with anecdotes illustrating the manners and customs of the people* (London: William Shoberl, 1850), 313–314.
[62] Philalethes, *History of Ceylon*, 164.
[63] Henry Marshall expressed regret that Cordiner "rarely mentions his authority on the facts he narrates" and assumed that it was probably a Malay servant who supplied the information on the Noordeens. Marshall himself gave a different account of events, based

The British were not alone in acknowledging the roles played by Malays in the conflicts between Europeans and Kandy in their historiography of the period, as Malays appeared also in contemporary Sinhala chronicles. Such was the case in the *Ingrīsi Haṭana* ("The English War"), composed in the well-known tradition of praise poetry (Sin. *praśasti*) that extolled a particular king and was likely composed by professional poets in the Kandy palace, to be recited and enacted before the king.[64] The poem, belonging to the category of *haṭana kavi*, "war poems," eulogized the Kandyan victory over the British in the war of 1803. It mentioned the king preparing for war and giving instructions to various ministers and officers. Among his troops was an "attachment called Ja," referring to the Malays by their Sinhala name, which was responsible for two areas in the city and the rural area of Maduge. The attachment, the poem recounted, was assigned to the minister Dehigama, who was a highly skilled fighter.[65]

Later in the account, the attack on the British garrison stationed in the palace was depicted. The king and his chief minister, the *adigar*, gave the command to charge toward the enemy and the first to rush forth was "the Captain of the Java regiment named Sangkilan," who was none other than Sangunglo, the leader of the Kandyan Malay troops and brother of Captain Noordeen. Having charged ahead, "standing in the middle of the great esplanade, [Sangkilan] began chopping the English soldiers with his sword."[66] In the final section of the poem, the author briefly

---

largely on Kandyan testimonies. According to this version, the British officers were asked to come meet the king after their return to Kandy, while the troops remained by the river. Noordeen voiced his opposition but Major Davie agreed. Upon arrival at the palace they were arrested. Noordeen resisted capture and died on the spot, "having been nearly cut to pieces," after which a Malay deserter was despatched to inform British troops that Davie had sent a message that they should give up their arms. In this instance Noordeen was still portrayed as exhibiting pride and courage but the account was much less dramatic and evocative. In this scene Malays again played crucial roles on both sides of the conflict (Marshall, *Ceylon: A General Description*, 99–101).

[64] Obeyesekere, *The Doomed King*, 345. The poem was translated into English by Udaya Prasanta Meddegama, and also appears in somewhat modified form ibid., 347–360. The available translation is partial. Verses 204–244, which contain a eulogy for the king and glorify his defeat of the British, are not included. Further study would reveal whether the Malay troops are mentioned in these verses and the extent to which they were credited with Kandy's victory. Recital of the poem could have meant dissemination of the Malays' battle feats.

[65] Meddegama (trans.), *The English War*, verse 109.

[66] Ibid., verses 134–135. Cordiner depicts the same scene thus: "Soon afterwards, about five o'clock a.m. a strong party of Candian Malays, headed by Sanguylo their chief, attempted to force the palace at the eastern barrier, where likewise one gun was posted. They were opposed by Lieutenant Blakeney, and a few men of the nineteenth regiment. Sanguylo crossed the stockade, and was immediately seized by the Lieutenant: they struggled, and fell both together; and while lying on the ground, Sanguylo gave a mortal

addressed the events of 1804 when the British reassembled an army and invaded Kandy. This time a Malay (Ja) captain, serving under Captain Arthur Johnston, was described as leading the enemy's army:

The foolish, idiotic English, having forgotten the beating they suffered in the war with our king, built up a large and powerful army under the Malay Captain called Jaan who was a man of mixed, *tuppahi* descent, saying, "these troops of ours are capable of even crushing Mt. Meru, we will take the Hill Country," and laughing to humiliate [the Sinhalese], set off from Batticaloa.[67]

The English War thus mentions two Malay captains, one fighting for the king – Sangkilan – and the other, Jaan, against him. The tension that was inherent in these circumstances was not explicitly addressed but the concern becomes evident when the poem is read within the context of the multiple voices of the period depicting the same events. Thus Captain Johnston in his own account described how the Kandyan troops he faced along with his Malay soldiers were led by Malay deserters from the British army, and how these Malays, now in the service of Kandy, "repeatedly addressed their countrymen in Captain Johnston's detachment, exhorting them to join the royal forces, by which they would escape danger, and be highly rewarded."[68] This was a scene of great physical proximity between Malay fighters on both sides, deep in the forests of the Hill Country, with the Kandyan Malays shouting out propositions and possibly threats as the battle was raging.

The representation of Malays within a Sinhala chronicle composed in Kandy is in part limited by the praśasti genre's parameters that, for example, "find it difficult to envisage surrender, defeat or retreat" of a glorified king.[69] This may explain why the famous episode of the brothers of Sangkilan/Sangunglo, Noordeen and Saifudeen, refusing to enter the king's service and preferring death to dishonor was not recorded. In addition, depicting Kandyan Malays in any aspect of their lives was clearly not a major goal of such poems. And yet exploring such

---

stab to his opponent with his creese. Lieutenant and Adjutant Plenderleath and a private of the nineteenth regiment ran two bayonets through the body of the Candian chief." See Cordiner, *A Description*, II: 208.

[67] Meddegama (trans.), *The English War*, verse 245. *Tuppahi* is a variation on *toepasser*; see above. The reference is to Mt. Meru, the cosmic mountain in Hindu belief. According to the poem the British were arrogant enough to believe themselves capable of conquering Mt. Meru and therefore taking Kandy's Hill Country by force seemed to them a trivial task. Obeyesekere believes that Jaan was probably the Javanese commander Captain Virgo under the British commander Johnston, who destroyed the king's palace in Mahiyangana (Obeyesekere, *The Doomed King*, 360). On the circumstances leading to Johnston's campaign, see Johnston, *Narrative*, 36–45.

[68] Johnston, *Narrative*, 75–76.   [69] Obeyesekere, *The Doomed King*, 364.

representations, however brief, contributes to understanding the history of the Kandy Wars and the place of the Malays in Ceylon's colonial society.

An exploration of the historiography of the 1803 Kandy War and the Malays' roles within it cannot be complete without asking: What of the Malay side? Contemporary Malay accounts depicting the war have not survived. A major Malay historical narrative written in the early twentieth century, the *Syair Faiḍ al-Abād*, was conspicuously silent on the Noordeen affair, as will be discussed in Chapter 9. Another Malay source in a volume listed as the *Kitab Panthong Suatu*, offered a very brief and general recounting:[70]

> *Thathakala Engrish de parang kandy de seetu*
> *suda de thangkap Regiment inni de Kandy itu*
> *barsama kapithan Nurdin samowanyah itu*
> *de bunu seeree Wikrama sagala dia de Layvallay itu*

> When the English fought the Kandy War
> The Regiment was captured in Kandy.
> Along with Captain Nurdin they were all
> Killed by Sri Wikrama at Layvallay.

> *Seeree Wikrama de minthakan dia*
> *sapaya manjadi soldadu de bawa karajaan dia*
> *kapithan Nurdin suda manduwakan dia*
> *Morgala Wikrama dan de bunu samuwanyah dia*

> Sri Wikrama requested that he
> Serve as a soldier of his kingdom.
> Captain Nurdin disobeyed
> Morgala Wikrama and was killed by him[71]

The Malay Cricket Club *Jubilee Book*, a commemorative volume written in English celebrating the Club's fiftieth anniversary in 1924, includes a section by F. E. Gooneratne on the war of 1803 that cites British sources which remain unnamed. The important point concerning this relatively late acknowledgment of the Malays' roles in 1803 within a Malay

[70] *Kitab Panthong Suatu*, n.d., Perpustakaan Negara Malaysia, Kuala Lumpur, MS PNM 431, verses 107–108. The volume contains several hikayats read from right to left, and on its other side (read from left to right) this romanized Malay poem. The original spelling has been maintained to show how significantly it had been adapted to the Ceylon variety of Malay by the early twentieth century. The poem is missing verses 1–39, but may be the *Panthong Temenggong dan 44 Raden Melayu* composed by Jumaron Tungku Usman in 1906 and mentioned briefly by Hussainmiya, *Orang Rejimen*, 142.
[71] Layvallay refers to Lewella, on the banks of the Mahaveli River, the place where the British troops tried to cross the swelling waters to safety during their retreat from Kandy, but failed. Morgala may refer to Moragolla, a village to the south of Kandy.

community publication is that it refers positively to Malays serving on both sides of the conflict. Regarding Noordeen, the depiction contains cultural dimensions of the episode which were not found in the earlier accounts: It is said that the king of Kandy's minister offered Noordeen and his brother rank and *nindagama* (a Sinhala term for an area of land or a village granted by the king to a nobleman in return for service) if they agreed to change sides. Once the brothers nobly refused, the author dramatically goes on, the king sent his executioner, dressed in black and decked with flowers which the Sinhalese call *wadha mal* ("torture flowers"), with orders for their execution.[72] As for Malays on the Kandyan side, the account contains praise for a senior advisor bearing the title Ja Muhandiram who was "a favourite of the king," "a popular man in the Kandy court," and who had once saved a great minister's life by navigating the complicated terrain of palace politics, proving that he was a "trusted advisor to the king yet very cunning and insightful in his guidance also to those who fell out of favour."[73]

The memory of the Malay brothers who participated in the Kandy War of 1803, often referred to in recent times as the "Noordeen brothers," lived on. The most remarkable telling collected situated the brothers' tombs within the grounds of the Sri Dalada Maligawa, the Temple of the Sacred Tooth Relic in Kandy where the Buddha's tooth is believed to be enshrined. According to this account, the brothers' valor was rewarded with burial within the sacred compound and in turn it was their supernatural powers, as local Malay "saints," that protected the Buddhist temple when it was attacked by the LTTE ("Tamil Tigers") in 1998 and, although damaged, its inner chambers and the tooth remained miraculously unharmed.[74] In this story many of the details appearing consistently in earlier tellings, like internal Malay divisions and the refusal to allow Noordeen burial, were left out or forgotten. What remained was the memory of the Malays' courage and honor, their image as faithfully serving Kandy and, in line with a broader belief in miracles and the supernatural attributes of heroes and holy men, the brothers' ongoing ability to affect events in the present.[75]

---

[72] *Jubilee Book*, 163.

[73] Ibid., 163–164. *Muhandiram* was an influential post in the system of native headmen in Ceylon. "Ja," as noted, was the word used for the Malays in Sinhala.

[74] Mr. Samad of Kandy, personal communication, October 11, 2009.

[75] The notion that the royal brothers' bodies, desecrated in the older tellings, found respectable burial in sacred shrines in the more recent narrative, resonates with the stories of earlier generations of royal men from the archipelago who were first buried in Ceylon but later re-reinterred in their proper place and with proper rites in Java, including Amangkurat III and Pangéran Arya Mangkunagara; see Chapters 4 and 5.

The different, at times contradictory, uses of the Noordeen story highlight questions central to Malay life in Ceylon in the nineteenth century,
chief among them the challenges of military life and divided loyalties. The
accounts convey a sense of fluid boundaries through which many Malays
chose to pass, whether as "deserters," "spies," "loyalists," "countrymen"
or "kin," depending on point of view. Proximity among Malays on different sides of colonial wars was palpable, and the accounts recreate scenes of
men shouting to each other, looking at each other, touching and walking
along the same paths, situations that must have created anxiety, doubt and
temptation.[76] This in-betweenness of the Malays, the liminal space they
occupied at least in potential if not in practice is evident in the sources that
project different, at times contrasting, qualities onto this martial group.

Still within the context of service but possessing a broader scope on
diasporic Malay life in Ceylon are additional extant writings, often in the
form of family diaries or notebooks.[77] The Weerabangsa family notes,
written largely in English, fit within this category.[78] Temporally, the notes
cover an extended period, in one section going back to the age of the gods
and several times to the family's arrival in Ceylon, yet they were put down in
writing in 1924 in Kurunegala by Mas Tuan Jury Weerabangsa (b. 1877 in
Kampung Katukelle, Kandy) and rewritten or revised in 1940. Despite the
uncertainty regarding their precise assemblage history and some historical
inaccuracies that they contain, the notes are important for the wealth of
information about events, beliefs and practices they offer as they relate to
Malay culture in Ceylon. Above all, the notes reflect a deep pride in the
Weerabangsa family's descent and in its royal and martial roots. The family's
founding ancestor, Pangéran Seenthakeerthy, was said to have been a king of
Aceh who went into the wilderness as a hermit for seven years. His son Ratu
Pagar Uyung also spent seven years in a hermitage, traveled to Mecca and
Baghdad, and was known to possess special powers. He went to Makassar

[76] For a rare account of a Malay soldier, Drum-Major Oodeen, who deserted from the
British to Kandyan forces in 1803, was captured, tried for treason and sentenced to
death in 1815, only to have his sentence commuted to transportation to New South
Wales, see Paul Thomas, "Oodeen, a Malay Interpreter on Australia's Frontier Lands,"
Indonesia and the Malay World 40.117 (2012): 122–142. As Thomas explains (ibid.,
126–128), Oudeen's reduced sentence was a result of British attentiveness to Malay
sentiments and their desire to maintain the Malay troops' loyalty.
[77] See, for example, *Saldin Family Records* (BL, EAP609/1/8), *Sinthaby Badulla Diary* (BL,
EAP609/15/1), *Doole-Cassim Tidbits* (BL, EAP609/28/1).
[78] The extant notebook is most likely a copy of an earlier original and is messy, with many
repetitions, including those of name lists and bits of family history, as well as arrows
sketched to link sections, added page references, numbers and lists. The family name is
spelled Weerabangsa in English but Weerawangsa in Malay, with such orthographic
differences common across scripts. See Mas Tuan Jury Weerabangsa, *Weerabangsa
Family Notes*, BL, EAP609/17/4.

and there ordained his son Yusuf as a spiritual guide and "termed him Mas sheikhul Islam i.e. a holy person who is capable of crowning kings with the help of the King of Kings." This claim ties the family to the most famous exile in the Dutch period, Sheikh Yusuf al-Makassari.[79] Although the Weerabangsa lineage is described several times throughout the notebook, it comes through with the most force and clarity in a document written in gundul on the occasion of the marriage of a young couple, Mas Muhamad Ghuice and Siti Jasmani, on September 30, 1897, which is worth quoting in full:

Marriage announcement, Kandy, 30.9.1897

The groom: Mas Muhamad Ghuice, known affectionately as Mas Tuan Jury Weerawangsa, son of Mas Tuan Anom, son of Tuan Captain Husain, son of the late Tuan Captain Weerawangsa

The bride: Siti Jasmani, daughter of Tuan Baba Zain, son of Tuan Baba Yunus Jailani, son of Tuan Luru Kajung, son of the late Tuan Captain Jurangpati

The origin of the youngsters is from the land of Java, the island of Madura.

The late Tuan Captain Weerawangsa was descended from Pangéran Sintakirti of Mangkasar; one of his sons named Bintara Sahut moved to Sumenep and lived in that kingdom in a house in Kampung Limabawang, and that was the place where Tuan Captain Weerawangsa was born to his parents. He came to Ceylon bringing people along during the time when the Dutch ruled Ceylon, on the command of his king the sultan of Sumenep.

Tuan Captain Jurangpati was descended from Pangéran Pali of Bangkalan. He too came to Ceylon upon the command of his king, the Panembahan of Madura.

They lived in the places mentioned above, i.e. Mangkasar, Bangkalan and Sumenep on the island of Madura.

The two have been matched by Allah and so we beseech Him that these two youngsters be guarded and protected [as] husband and wife

And may they prosper, amen O Lord of the Worlds.[80]

---

[79] Ibid., 8. Sheikh Yusuf's name appears occasionally in Malay manuscripts from Ceylon, attesting to a lasting awareness of his legacy; see for example the statement in the *Syair Ibadat* crediting him with the transmission of its teachings: "*Ya inilah risalah turun daripada sheikhmu sheikh kamil mukamil ya itu wali Allah yang 'arif billah ya itu sheikh Yusuf Mangkasari*" (*Syair Ibadat*, n.d., Perpustakaan Negara Malaysia, Kuala Lumpur, MS PNM 423, 123).

[80] The orthography is often different for romanized and gundul-script Malay. Punctuation was added to the translation. The *Notes* contain a copy of this letter:

Khabar kahawin di Nagari Kandy. 30.9.1897
Pengantin lanang Mas Muhamad Ghus timangannya Mas Tuan Juri Weerawangsa anaq Mas Tuan Anom ibn Tuan Kapitan Husain anaq kepada almarhum Tuan Kapitan Weerawangsa.
Pengantin wadon Siti Jasmani binti Tuan Baba Zain ibn Tuan Baba Yunus Jailani ibn Tuan Luru Kajung anak kepada almarhum Tuan Kapitan Jurangpati.

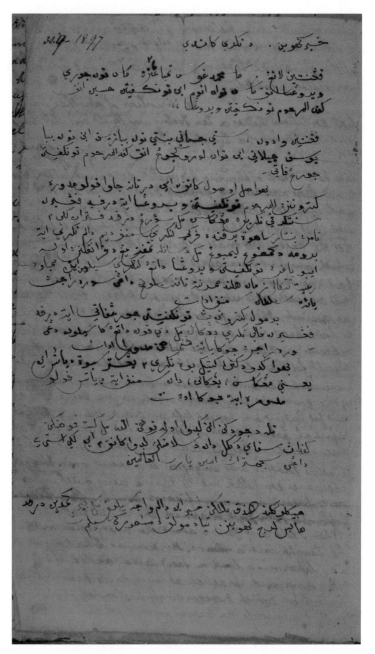

Figure 8.2 Marriage document from Kandy, 1897. *Weerabangsa Family Notes*, BL, EAP609/17/4, 44.
Courtesy M. J. Weerabangsa

The document presents the history of the two families in condensed form, spelling out their lineage and attachment to faraway places in the Indonesian Archipelago that are recalled at the *kampung* level, and provides evidence for an ongoing connection through marriage between such families with a common site of descent and shared martial positions of leadership in the Ceylon diaspora. The bride and groom were both grandchildren of captains from the island of Madura – from Sumenep and Bangkalan – serving the British in Ceylon. The two families, Weerabangsa and Jurangpati, were also central to Malay literary culture in the nineteenth century with scribes, manuscript owners and patrons of the Malay writing tradition among their members.

In their recounting of events big and small, the *Notes* touched upon objects and practices central to Malay life. Kerisses, important objects in both royal and martial contexts, appeared several times. Pangéran Seenthakeerthy, founder of the Weerabangsa lineage, followed the ancient practice of kings performing asceticism, and while spending seven years as a hermit discovered the *keris Majapahit*, the legendary dagger of Java's last Hindu–Buddhist kingdom;[81] many generations later, a relative, Captain Sawal, was said to have once been attacked by an elephant near Dambolla, when he used the same keris with its poisoned tip to instantly kill the brute. There was also the case of Captain Assen (d. 1858), second son of Mas Weerabangsa, who inherited Pangéran Seenthakeerthy's possessions, and while on a ship bound for Hong Kong was asked by a European officer why he carried the keris with him at all

---

Bahwa asal ada mula kanaq2 ia dari tanah Jawa pulau Madurah
keturunannya almarhum Tuan Kapitan Weerawangsa itu daripada Pangéran
Sintakirti nagarinya Mangkasar maka seorang daripada putranya laki2
namanya Bintara Sahut berpinda pergi kenagari Sumenep diam dalam nagari itu
beruma di kampung Limabawang maka disanalah tempat yang diperanaqannya oleh
ibu bapanya Tuan Kapitan Weerawangsa datang ke nagari Seylon itu membawa
ra'yat tatkala zaman Halanda memerintah tanah Selong dengan suruh rajanya
yaitu sultan Sumenep adanya.
Bermula keturunannya Tuan Kapitan Jurangpati itu daripada
Pangéran Pali Nagari Bangkalan maka dia pun datang ke Seylon dengan
suruh rajanya juga ya itu Panembahan Madura adanya.
Bahwa kedudukannya ketika buah nagari2 yang tersebut di atas ini
ya'ani Mangkasar, Bangkalan, dan Sumenep itu di atas pulau
Madurah itu juga adanya.
Telah dijodokan akan kedua oleh tuhan Allah maka kita pohonkan
kepadanya supaya dikekal dan diselamatkan kedua kanaq2 ini laki istri
dengan sejahteranya amin ya Rab al-'alamin (Weerabangsa, *Weerabangsa Family Notes*, BL, EAP609/17/4, 44).

[81] He is also said to have discovered the one-eyed coconut shell, with both objects still in the family's possession and believed to be potent. I was shown these objects by Mr. M. J. (Joe) Weerabangsa, January 3, 2014.

times. Taking the keris out of its scabbard, Captain Assen pointed it at a mat which immediately caught fire, astonishing the onlooker. When Captain Assen was on his deathbed only one son, Mas Anom, was there with him, and so he inherited the keris Majapahit, as well as several other sacred objects. Mas Jury Weerabangsa, Mas Anom's son and compiler of the *Notes*, recalled how his father in turn carried the keris on a night journey they took through rugged terrain where they faced danger but prevailed.[82]

The keris was an obvious object to embody sanctity, power and a connection to the past within the Malay community on account of its importance to their martial lifestyle, and its association with kingship and sacred heirlooms, including those of the walis. There were, however, other objects and forms of recitation that were infused with the supernatural. Incantations known as doas (also spelled *duva* and *donga*) or wasilans were discussed in Chapter 3. Mas Jury mentioned several such doas, some explicitly related to martial life, while others are depicted as offering protection or other benefits in noncombat circumstances. When writing about the recital of *Landa Landi*, Mas Jury noted that this doa was employed by his great-grandfather when facing the enemy during the British campaign at Panjaanam Kurichie in south India.[83] The *seerap* (from J. *sirep* – to go back to normal, be calm again; *nyirep*, put someone under a magic spell) was a spell he decided to practice in order to seek angelic protection.

Mas Jury also related a story of competing powers pitted against one another: Once, when Captain Assen was serving in Trincomalee, he had money at home where he had taken it the previous night for safeguarding. Some of the privates, knowing this was the case and coveting the money, cast a sleeping spell (*sirep aji*) on all the residents of the house, setting the scene for its theft. Captain Assen's daughter Mas Adaney woke up first, as she used to teach the children Qur'anic recital every morning, and was surprised when she opened the kitchen to find a man sitting on the floor deep in sleep. Others – all of them privates who had broken in – were found around the house in unexpected positions, one holding a rope and another digging into the wall while asleep. Captain Assen poured cold water over them and they awoke, fell at his feet and begged forgiveness. They explained that after entering the house they found themselves on a

---

[82] These references appear, respectively, in Weerabangsa, *Weerabangsa Family Notes*, BL, EAP609/17/4, 5, 17, 20, 23, 34. Majapahit is spelled Manjapahit, incorporating a nasalization common in current spoken Sri Lanka Malay.

[83] This campaign and its depiction in a Malay source are discussed in Chapter 9. The site of the campaign is conventionally spelled Panchalankurichi.

big ship, all topsy-turvy, and had to perform various tasks (for example, the man found with a rope was trying to tie the mast). Captain Assen intervened on their behalf, saying they had been divinely punished and that receiving the scorn of their own community was penalty enough. After this incident, the captain was respected and recognized as a holy man. In the competition between the soldiers' spell and Captain Assen's powers, he was no doubt the victor.[84]

Mas Jury reported his own interest in the charms and how during the time his father worked for the Matale police in 1884, as they walked home together, he saw a young Malay man rushing out of a house, cursing and rolling up his sleeves and going toward his father. He watched as his father uttered a doa and with his toe sketched a line in the dirt. Once the man crossed that line he fell to the ground senseless and had to be taken by others to his house while the elder Weerabangsa kept walking quietly on the road.[85] His utterance was none other than the *garis Laksamana*, the spell recalling the protective line that Laksmana sketched around Sita before leaving her in the forest hermitage. Subedar Musafar, a neighbor, came and asked Mr. Weerabangsa to awaken the villain. He said a prayer over some water and sprinkled it on him. The man awoke and later came with some relatives to ask forgiveness, bringing some fruit. The father thanked them and told them many things about proper behavior and ever since that day his son, Mas Jury, was very eager to learn the prayers and committed to his religious observances as he was told that, without religious practice, the doa would possess no efficacy. When he left for the Kurugama Estate, his father taught him that same garis Laksamana and another doa known as *sagentar alam,* which, if practiced properly, were said to be like food for the soul and to enrich the physical body with strength like that of twelve elephants.[86]

---

[84] Weerabangsa, *Weerabangsa Family Notes*, BL, EAP609/17/4, 22.   [85] Ibid., 29.

[86] Ibid., 29–30. Mas Jury's father further narrated an incident that happened to Mas Jury's great-grandfather's cousin named Juthabachana, who, when stationed in Colombo, faced an enemy and was able to sink a large vessel by pulling the rope of the mast and reciting the *sagentar alam*. Mas Jury was so impressed by this that he practiced the prayer often while working at the factory (ibid., 30). Additional doas are mentioned throughout the *Notes* as taught and practiced for particular purposes, sometimes accompanied by fasting; see for example ibid., 39–41. Mrs. Mas Naleera Rahim, Mas Jury's granddaughter (b. 1948), learned many doas from her late father M. M. G. Weerabangsa and possesses a notebook in which she has written some of them down, using the Sinhala, Tamil and romanized scripts so that they can be accessible to future generations (personal communication, July 15, 2015). For the notebook, see Mas Naleera Rahim, *Wasilan*, BL, EAP609/25/2.

Spells were of pervasive importance to a range of Malay life realms in late nineteenth-century Ceylon, one of which was forbidden love, as evident from an incident in 1897 just before Mas Jury was married. A Sinhalese co-worker on the tea estates spoke ill of him, and he was to be sent away. Therefore, the wedding had to take place quickly. The next morning, he went out in his groom's attire and was greeted by a cheering crowd thanks to his good looks. The mistress of the estate came too. When he got to his bungalow he found her on his verandah and greeted her with utmost respect, struck up a polite conversation and offered her refreshments "according to Malay custom." She told him she would try to cancel his dismissal. Later, the master came and said he could stay. The mistress stopped by to visit a few more times, including at night, and after three days offered him a large sum of money and all her belongings if he would "fall in love with her." Mas Jury was shocked and immediately refused. She insisted, but with the help of the doa he was able to avoid "falling into great sin."[87] He then told her he could never touch her unless she converted to Islam and married him after he got the consent of his wife and parents. The mistress decided to go to Kandy to speak with his family but had a change of heart and returned after talking to the wife and begged Mas Jury's forgiveness, later turning out to be a great asset whom he and his wife honored and respected even more than their own mothers. This story is immediately followed in the *Notes* by the statement: "Dear Children, this little bit of information is cited here just to show an instance of how youngsters should behave against the temptation of Satan to seek Allah's blessing,"[88] raising questions about whether the events took place, were exaggerated, or even invented for a didactic purpose. Clearly the *Notes* were written with the aim of informing future generations of the family's past and its contemporary values, but they also offer insight into issues on the writer's mind at the time, including acceptable and forbidden relationships across class, faith and race in the colony.

And so, the *Weerabangsa Family Notes*, by way of anecdotes, cautionary tales, genealogical lists and documents, invoke many themes of contemporary Malay culture. Noteworthy are the spells and mystical knowledge passed down in the family, only to the deserving, as danger loomed of such knowledge falling into the wrong hands, and the interdependence between Islamic practice and the doas' efficacy; the devotion to particular religious teachers, as evident by Mas Jury's identification as a follower of ʿAbd al-Qadir Jailani, and his claim that spiritual knowledge could not be

---

[87] Weerabangsa, *Weerabangsa Family Notes*, BL, EAP609/17/4, 46.   [88] Ibid., 47.

attained by study but required initiation and practical lessons from a
"competent and recognized spiritual guide [*peer*]"; the young woman
teaching children to recite the Qur'an; an esteem toward Regiment
soldiers and a deep sense of pride harbored by the Weerabangsa family –
as was true for additional families – in their royal and martial roots. In
addition to laying out a genealogy that spoke to place, travel, enlistment
and the bonds created among families originating in the archipelago in
the Ceylon diaspora, the *Notes* expanded a view of Malay life that went far
beyond the central hub of Colombo, encompassing Trincomalee,
Kandy, Hambantota, Kurunegala and Nawalapittiya; they spoke to occupations that were open to the Malays, many of which entailed serving the
British, whether in the army, police, infrastructure building or tea estates.
The multilingual character of the *Notes*, written primarily in English but
with bits of Sinhala, Arabic, Tamil and Malay, testified to an important
dimension of Malay society. Toward the end of the *Notes*, Mas Jury wrote
of how he received knowledge of his ancestor Dathu Dewa Seenthakeerthy from his spiritual sheikh, who said Seenthakeerthy was descended from the gods before the advent of the Prophet Muhammad
but as soon as he heard of the Prophet's birth in 570 CE he was "the
first to accept Islam in the East having seen many miracles,"[89] tying
together divine descent from the pre-Islamic gods, an early conversion
of a ruler to Islam and his playing a foundational role in the Islamization
of the region, a long-drawn-out process that via family, and circuits of
mobility and faith, led to Mas Jury's here and now.[90]

The strong ties between Mas Jury's present, and a personal and
collective past in the lands to the southeast of Ceylon, were epitomized
in a letter that Mas Anom Weerabangsa, Mas Jury's father, wrote to his
son on February 19, 1903, "in gundul characters of the Malay language"
when the young man was promoted to sergeant. In a letter that opened
with conventional phrases in Arabic and Malay praising God and the
Prophet Muhammad and asking for blessings, the father emphasized
repeatedly that the values leading one to a good life in this world and
rewards in the next were passed down in the family by Mas Jury's *kake
moyang* or *turun temurun* – ancestors – stretching back all the way to their
patriarch Dewa Seenthakeerthy.[91] The main lessons of, for example, not

---

[89] Ibid., 75.
[90] The claim of being a "first convert" in the region and of propagating Islam echoes with
the wali sanga stories but presents a non-Javanese account of the Islamization of the
archipelago. In many such accounts it is the king who was the first to convert, often after
an encounter with, or rumor of the Prophet; see Jones, "Ten Conversion Myths from
Indonesia."
[91] Weerabangsa, *Weerabangsa Family Notes*, BL, EAP609/17/4, 67–68.

behaving arrogantly, following the orders of one's superiors and treating the "little people" justly made for good advice for someone who had recently been accorded status (M. *martabat tinggi*) within the police but also echoed with broader concerns related to hierarchy within the Malay community and beyond it. Mas Jury added a signed note in 1925 to the effect that he had followed the advice offered with very positive results.[92]

Family notes and diaries convey much about certain aspects of Malay life in British Ceylon, while letters reveal others. Malay letters written in Ceylon, some of which were addressed to the authorities, made claims about descent, status, entitlement and place, expressing longing and frustration and making requests of various kinds. Other Malay letters, like the one written by Mas Anom Weerabangsa, were composed for relatives and friends. No longer written in Javanese like the letters translated into Dutch during Amangkurat III's time, and containing memories that were less direct and immediate, the thread of writing continued, with Malay and its writing practices becoming more dominant. Thus the letters present examples of the ongoing use of Malay letter-writing conventions carried to Ceylon, including typical letter headings complimenting the recipient (M. *puji-pujian*) and concluding statements (M. *termaktub*), greetings in Malay and Arabic, an attunement to hierarchy and etiquette expressed through the choice of personal pronouns, time-reckoning conventions, particular forms of script and the inclusion, when appropriate, of apologies for the author's or scribe's supposed dearth of knowledge, ignorance and poor use of Malay. Like the Javanese *Kidung* maintaining not just the language but also Javanese literary, poetic and metric sensibilities, so the modes of Malay letter writing from Ceylon exemplify a rich cultural tradition in concise form.[93]

In conclusion, the concept of mengamok (Eng. running amok) will serve to briefly pull closer the different strands of this chapter, which has explored the Malays' roles as a martial community and as cultivators of a literary tradition as well as overlaps between the two, and diverse perceptions of Malay life and experience in Ceylon. The practice of *amok*, and the motivations behind it, fascinated European observers and was much

---

[92] Ibid., 70. A note in red ink was also added, saying that "the letter can be translated into English if necessary." This suggests that Mas Jury, who intended that the *Notes* serve future family generations, was concerned that the Malay language and gundul writing would become less accessible with time.

[93] For a pioneering study of Malay letters, see Annabel Teh Gallop, *The Legacy of the Malay Letter: Warisan Warkah Melayu* (London: British Library, 1994). Ceylon was not included in this study.

debated in contemporary writings.[94] Although not exclusively related to military life (and associated also with criminality and mental illness), it was in the context of war that this trope, seen as an essential Malay tendency, received the most attention in colonial sources.[95] Amok was viewed as both a great asset and a dire threat, depending on whether the attacking Malays were on one's own side or against it. As North wrote in 1799, when describing the Malays' character (without explicitly mentioning amok):

These troops are cruel and dissolute and require a very strict discipline, neither are they much to be trusted at present, in case this place should be attacked by a Dutch force. But the terror with which they are beheld by the natives is such, as renders them the most effectual that we have for subduing insurrections. When they shall be officered in the manner I have recommended they will probably grow less dangerous to the police and more trustworthy than they can be considered at present.[96]

A more complex picture of amok emerges when it is viewed from the perspective of Malay writing. It was a practice that appeared consistently in Malay texts from Southeast Asia and also Ceylon and served as a thread linking these texts by a common cultural practice and its written depictions. In Malay literature it was not only humans who could men-gamok but also objects: In the *Hikayat Indera Quraishi*, a Malay work that is known only from Ceylon, Tuan Putri, daughter of the naga king, showed the hero Indera Quraishi a sword given to her by her father that could be commanded to run amok on its own. And, indeed, Indera Quraishi saved himself at the last minute from three jinn by instructing the sword to kill them.[97] A similar example is found in the *Hikayat Tuan Gusti*, which depicted how the king of Majapahit in Surabaya was furious upon hearing of Tuan Gusti's powers and his prohibition of idols. Led by the king's advisor, the people of Majapahit and many vassal kings

---

[94] For a brief survey and assessment of some of these debates, see Eduarto Ugarte, "Running Amok: The Demoniacal Impulse," *Asian Studies Review* 16.1 (1992): 182–189; Manuel L. Saint Martin, "Running Amok: A Modern Perspective on a Culture-Bound Syndrome," *Journal of Clinical Psychiatry* 1.3 (1999): 66–70.

[95] Ekama cites the only amok case to appear in Ceylon court records; see Kate Ekama, "Slavery in Dutch Colombo: A Social History," unpublished MA thesis, University of Leiden (2012), 68–74.

[96] SLNA 55/1, North to Court of Directors, February 26, 1799. Percival depicted amok as an indiscriminate, ferocious, cruel and violent rush toward the enemy, which often caused severe injury and death to anyone on the attacker's path. He also tied amok to the use of opium; see Percival, *An Account*, 157–160.

[97] *Hikayat Indera Quraishi*, MS PNM 431, 90–168. The references are on 33, 45. This *Hikayat* was transliterated and published with an introduction by Monique Zaini-Lajoubert, *Hikayat Indera Quraisyin: Satu Kajian* (Kuala Lumpur: Perpustakaan Negara Malaysia, 1998).

marched on Giri, the multitudes frightening the people of Giri, who ran to find their leader. With God's grace, a huge swarm of bees appeared and ran amok among the people of Majapahit; and Tuan Gusti took a Qur'an and pen and the pen flew away, attacking the enemy along with six other pens. Many were injured and killed. Meanwhile, Tuan Gusti's two sons encountered the enemy and ran amok, attacking and killing in a burst of violence. Radèn Fabulah, one of the sons, met his father and told him of these developments, whereby Tuan Gusti informed him that since he had run amok without his father's permission he was destined to die. Soon afterwards a man came and struck his flank and he fell to the ground, but the keris he held in his hand could not be released.[98] This latter *Hikayat*, including its scenes of amok, constitutes part of the wali tradition as maintained in Ceylon.

In these instances, the European and Malay understandings of amok did overlap in the centrality of the practice to warfare and its overpowering ruthlessness, blind determination and courage. However, whereas in colonial writings this was often the main and even singular prism through which amok was considered, the Malay materials are complex. The relationship of certain material objects such as swords or pens to the practice and the possibility of commanding them to action show the powers inherent in such objects and tie in with the notions of the pusaka and wasilan. They also blur the boundaries between material objects and humans, as the limits between humans and the animal kingdom, as well as the world of subtle, invisible beings, become ambiguous when the practice of amok is seen as shared across species. Amok in the literature appeared in a range of emotional contexts beyond courage or sacrifice, including grief, envy, helplessness, love and desire, connecting with multiple dimensions of being. As the Malays in Ceylon were more than just colonial troops or fanatical and unpredictable subjects for whom British rule would prove a much-needed corrective, so amok in Malay writing possessed a semantic field and range of associations that went beyond its narrow meaning in British administrative documents and period memoirs.

The chapter has also explored how pivotal episodes in Ceylon's history, like the transition between colonial empires or the Kandy Wars might be viewed differently, or at least with more subtlety, if a Malay vantage point were integrated into the historical inquiry. For one thing, the chapter has suggested the relevance of considering the complexity of the Malay presence in Ceylon and the internal diversity of this group, and

---

[98] Mursit, *Hikayat Tuan Gusti*, MF 182. The events are depicted on 86 and 113–114.

their shifting roles as both insiders and outsiders, best exemplified by the Noordeen brothers' episode and its various incarnations. These included tellings as diverse as those idealizing the brothers as British heroes and as the saviors of Buddhism's most sacred temple on the island, offering unconventional views on the dynamics of ruler and ruled, Islam and Buddhism, the meanings of conquest, defeat, valor and power, in a multi-ethnic and multireligious society. The juxtaposition of sources in English, Sinhala and Malay to examine depictions of events in Kandy in 1803 highlights different perspectives on and imaginings of events. In addition, comparing Malay and Sinhala chronicles exposes links between the literary cultures of textual communities that may not have been as mutually exclusive as often imagined and casts light on their views and memories of shared events and broader histories. As discussed in Chapter 7, the Ramayana provided a rich pool of signifiers for Malay authors as they depicted righteous kings, villains and battle scenes. *The English War* poem in Sinhala similarly likened Sri Vikrama Rajasingha to Rama and the war between the Kandyans and British to that fought between Rama and Rawana.[99] The poem also contained very graphic depictions of the Kandyan army and its commanders wounding, humiliating and killing the British troops, reminiscent in these portrayals of brutal fighting appearing in the *Syair Kishanya Orang Wolenter Benggali*. These two examples draw a connection between Malay and Sinhala literary conventions at the time in Ceylon and suggest that authors writing in both languages drew on common literary and devotional tropes across languages and religions, inviting a reconsideration of boundaries and a method to better understand Ceylon's nuanced colonial history and the Malays' place within it.

---

[99] For examples of the king as likened to Rama, see Meddegama (trans.), *The English War*, verses 18, 39, 40. For the battle comparison, see verse 191. It is noteworthy that an epic now considered Hindu provided inspiration to Muslim-majority and Buddhist-majority literary cultures. Exploring Tamil and Malay literature from Ceylon comparatively is another practically untouched endeavor.

9   Malay Writing in Ceylon: Roots and Routes

This final chapter expands further on the documentation of the Malay experience in Ceylon and the forms of writing it took. It asks how the Malay presence in Ceylon was made sense of, remembered and consolidated into a meaningful experience that would be passed down through the generations; it considers the always-complex diasporic condition and the gaps and silences inherent in its archives, viewing Malay diasporic life and writing as loosely forming a vernacular frontier of language, culture and religion. That frontier was not a stable, static physical edge but an unfolding and expanding geographical and metaphorical sphere in which Malay expressiveness and the concerns, beliefs and imaginings of its speakers endured far from the "mainstream" of the Malay world. The chapter also returns to the issue of nomenclature, employed throughout this book as a lens through which to consider shifting identities and affiliations over time, attachments to place and particular temporal understandings. I suggest that the discussion of the Malays' role in the military and of their place in Ceylon's society, as well as the book as a whole, brings the Malays "back" into Sri Lankan history – in which nationalist tendencies have prioritized a past divided along Sinhalese and Tamil lines – and offers a destabilizing perspective on this history "from the margins." By providing this view of the Malays in Ceylon, the book also returns them, concurrently, into the history of modern Indonesia where they have for the most part been entirely absent.

The chapter explores these themes – Malay writing, literary culture, nomenclature, diasporic life, "Malayness" and identity, and historical salience – primarily via the biography and writing of Baba Ounus Saldin (1832–1906), a central presence in the Malay community as author, publisher, editor and religious leader. Two of his major works are read in tandem, one a history of the community explicitly aimed at telling a younger generation about the experiences, challenges and accomplishments of the past (the *Syair Faiḍ al-Abād*) and the other containing his personal and family memories (the *Kitab Segala Peringatan*).[1]

Baba Ounus Saldin's grandfather went to Ceylon from Sumenep on the island of Madura, Indonesia, around 1800, recruited by the British government, which was engaged at the time in war in south India and incorporating soldiers from the Dutch East Indies into its forces. Baba Ounus Saldin was born in Colombo in 1832 and, as was common for his generation, was made to enter the Ceylon Rifle Regiment at the age of sixteen. He was employed for many years as a shopkeeper and clerk for various European agency houses and made a good living by the standards of the time. Concurrently, he was one of the pioneers of the lithographic printing industry in Ceylon, printing not only Malay books but also many Arabu-Tamil ones on behalf of the Tamil-Muslim community. Baba Ounus Saldin wrote booklets on Malay poetry and grammar, copied manuscripts and assembled a large collection of books over his lifetime. He was a religious scholar initiated into the Qadiriyyah Sufi order, a businessman and entrepreneur, among other things importing books from Singapore and Malaya. He was also the founder, editor and publisher of *Alamat Langkapuri*, one of the world's first Malay newspapers, published in Colombo in 1869, and of a second newspaper, *Wajah Selong*, in 1895, and a leader who invested much time and effort in the improvement of the social and economic conditions of his community.

Saldin's two texts, taken together, constitute important sources on the Malays. The *Syair* and the *Kitab* provide representations, in different genres, of many of the same events and sensibilities, offering a panoramic yet nuanced view of family life, mystical tendencies, cultural practices, diasporic connections and everyday life. The centrality of the military to Saldin's accounts comes through in his discussions of the Poligar Wars of the late eighteenth century in south India, the first and second Kandy Wars of the early nineteenth century, life in the Malay Regiment, and the Matale rebellion, all reflecting a wider culture of enlistment and deployment of the Malays under colonial rule – as shown in Chapter 8. The differences in depiction and emphasis are not, however, only between the *Syair* and the *Kitab*: Each is a hybrid text in its own right, combining topics and genres, and so both intra- and intertextual connections come to the fore.

---

[1] The *Syair* was mentioned in earlier chapters: Baba Ounus Saldin, *Kitab Segala Peringatan*, Dewan Bahasa and Pustaka Library, Kuala Lumpur, MS 137. This is a facsimile copy. I was unable to access the original. I thank Mr. Tony Saldin for giving me a partial transliteration of the text before I was able to locate the fuller copy in Kuala Lumpur.

The *Syair Faiḍ al-Abād* ("Bounty of the Ages") was published by Saldin's press in Colombo in 1905 (1322 AH), just a year prior to his death. The *Syair*'s forty-six pages are divided into three main sections and contain a combination of historical data pertaining to the Malays' past in colonial Ceylon, religious teachings titled *'Ilmu Maʿaripat* ("The Science of Mystical Knowledge") and, toward the end, a few pages that recount well-known stories of the prophets Adam, Noah and Moses, bearing the title *Ceritra sedikit daripada nabi-nabi* ("A Few Stories of the Prophets").[2] Taken together, the *Syair* suggests a pattern of Malay identity in late nineteenth-century Ceylon that combined strong Islamic sentiments with pride in the Malays' contribution to imperial wars. Whereas the two latter sections of the *Syair*, on mysticism and the prophets, are quite typical of Malay writing in Ceylon, the former, on military history, is not. It is that initial section of the *Syair* dealing with Malay history and war that will be highlighted here, and connected to the themes of vernacular writing, Islamic identity and frontiers. A focus on the depictions of military campaigns, associated with political, colonial and military frontiers, suggests a way to think also of Islamic and diasporic frontiers.[3]

Saldin explained that he had written a history of the Malays following a request from friends and that he wished his book to offer knowledge of the past to the younger generation. He referred to Malay as their mother tongue (M. *bahasa ibu*) and to the Malays as *bangsa* (from Sanskrit *vaṃśa*), a term that in modern Malay and Indonesian has come to refer primarily to the nation, but at the time of writing connoted more broadly family, race, descent group or community.[4] After this introduction Saldin recounted very briefly, in a section discussed in Chapter 6, Ceylon's history prior to the British conquest, beginning with Adam who was banished by God to the island, at the time known as Sarandib. The *Syair* then noted that the island was further named Ceylon on account of the riches of its sea and land, then immediately events moved forward to the Portuguese conquest. The Portuguese, according to the *Syair*, defeated the king of the Sinhalese people and built forts and towns. The Dutch then heard of the island's wealth and came by sea with

---

[2] These titles open the above-mentioned sections; however, they are somewhat altered on the *Syair*'s title page. See Figure 6.2.

[3] Despite the resonance of the concept of frontier in the history of Islam, where the world has often been viewed as divided into Islamic and non-Islamic realms (A. *dār al-Islām* and *dār al-ḥarb*), that particular understanding of a border or frontier was hardly relevant in the context of colonial Ceylon.

[4] William Marsden, *A Dictionary of the Malayan Language, to which is prefixed a grammar with an introduction and praxis* (London: Cox and Batlis, 1812), 41.

thousands of soldiers, ready to conquer. The entire Portuguese and Dutch periods were covered in just a few lines before Saldin moved on to the British period, likely reflecting his greater familiarity with it, based on the experiences of his own lifetime and those of his immediate ancestors.

Then followed a chapter on the British military fighting a war in south India, part of the Poligar Wars of 1799–1805. Malay soldiers from Ceylon played an important role in the battles described, those against the legendary anti-British leader Virapandiyan Kattabomman of Panchalankurichi.[5] In this section, Saldin provided much greater detail than he did for the entire Dutch period, expanding on the origins of soldiers brought from the Indonesian Archipelago and Malay Peninsula for the purpose of fighting on the British side. He explained that the British had brought 500 men from Java along with their commanders, then noted that the men were from Sumenep on the island of Madura. This was precisely the place where Saldin's own family originated, with the timing corresponding to his grandfather's arrival in Ceylon; thus it is likely that Saldin had heard of this campaign at first hand. In addition to the Sumenep men, others – all described as courageous and daring – were brought from Semarang, Bugis, Betawi, Palembang, Surabaya, Bogor and Singasari. Royal persons were mentioned among their leaders, their arrival in Ceylon and India echoing that of their forefathers, high-status men and women banished throughout the eighteenth century. They were depicted as exceptionally brave – men whose skin could withstand even bullets – the trope of courage appearing repeatedly in Saldin's account and resonating with the Malays' image as ferocious, loyal and determined warriors leading the troops and willing to fight to the end.

The enemy was also depicted in detail: large, fearsome, mean-looking men who spoke a local language (M. *bahasa waduwu*) mixed with Malabar (Tamil). The battle was decided on the tenth day of Muḥarram, known as ʿAshura, a significant date to which tradition ascribes many important events in Islamic history including nabi Nuh (Noah) and his ark reaching land, and nabi Musa (Moses) being saved from the pharaoh's troops. It is also a day of commemoration for Hussein, the Prophet's grandson, who died a martyr's death at Karbala (61/680).

---

[5] The Polygar chieftain Virapandiya Kattabomman ruled Panchalankurichi in Tirunelveli district from 1790 to 1799. He was one of the first to oppose British rule in the region before being captured and hanged in 1799. His brother Umaidurai was arrested, escaped and continued to fight until captured in 1801, when the fort was razed and the site plowed over. See Nicholas B. Dirks, *The Hollow Crown: Ethnohistory of an Indian Kingdom* (Cambridge: Cambridge University Press, 1988), 22.

Although at present viewed as mainly a Shiite affair, this latter event was widely and often grandly commemorated by South and Southeast Asian Muslims of various affiliations in the nineteenth century, including in Ceylon. In addition to its mention in the *Syair*, ʿAshura has also emerged in other accounts of Muslim native soldiers' lives in the British army, as in the sepoys' uprising at the Bolarum cantonment outside Hyderabad in 1855.[6] The mention of such a significant date, with its heightened resonance, is one of the few instances in this section of the *Syair* where an Islamic referent is explicitly inserted, yet it is a reminder of the broader mindset of the author retelling the events and the temporal and historical framework within which the Malay soldiers were operating. By connecting the tenth of Muḥarram with the soldiers' own actions and achievements, the poem located them as one more link in the long chain of prophets and heroes of the Islamic past and as current reincarnations of those earlier illustrious men. In this decisive battle, the Javanese fighters grasped both guns and kerisses, the traditional, spiritually potent Javanese daggers, and ran amok, "resembling male lions."[7]

Two more episodes discussed by Baba Ounus Saldin and related to military service are of note. The first is an account of the Kandyan Wars. Saldin depicted one of several attacks that took place against Kandy during the war of 1803–1805, mentioning the Kandyans' cruelty toward prisoners and the difficulty of gaining ground in a territory that was well known to one side but a mystery to the other. The *Syair* is filled with intriguing details: Saldin depicted the suffering in the Kandyan prison and the orders to slit the white prisoners' throats, then leave them to be devoured by beasts; he recounted the Kandyan prime minister's defection to the British because the king lusted after his wife. Chapter 8 highlighted the competing patronage systems, opportunities and risks of the martial lifestyle led by many of the Ceylon Malays and the conflicting loyalties within their society. But despite the fact that Malays played important roles on both sides of the Kandy conflict, this complicated aspect of Malay life – serving two opposing powers (for both of whom the Malays were considred outsiders) – is not mentioned in the *Syair*. Its silence on these complex matters, including the Noordeen episode, is suggestive, perhaps wishing to avoid retroactive controversy and ambivalence and to emphasize themes of unity and strength. It may be that it was in this same vein that it noted, again, the origins of the Malay soldiers, recruited in multitudes to fight once more on the side of

---

[6] Nile Green, *Islam and the Army in Colonial India: Sepoy Religion in the Service of Empire* (Cambridge: Cambridge University Press, 2009), 62–70.

[7] *Beramuknya Jawa seperti singa jantan* (Saldin, *Syair*, 7).

the British and representing, in their very mixed origins, a "unity in diversity" ethos:

> *Dikirimnya orang ke tanah sabrang dari Betawi Bugis Semarang*
> *Banten Ternate Petani Palembang Tuban Padang Periaman Kelantan*
> *Pulau Penang*

This brief passage conjured an entire region, with its seas, islands and coasts: men were sent overseas from Betawi (Jakarta), Bugis (South Sulawesi), Semarang, Banten and Tuban (Java's north coast), the island of Ternate in the eastern archipelago, Patani (southern Thailand), Palembang (south Sumatra), Padang and Pariaman (west Sumatra), Kelantan and the island of Penang, the latter two now located in peninsular Malaysia. It offered a truly accurate Malay-world representation, from present-day southern Thailand through Malaysia and Indonesia. The diverse geographical and linguistic backgrounds of these men coalesced in the passage into a more unified identity through their joint recruitment and service, as well as via writing in a common vernacular that became the vehicle for expressing literary and religious ideas and sentiments, and the parlance of everyday life. A text like the *Syair* could only be written in the vernacular, the significance of which Saldin was fully aware, as he mentioned his choice to write in Malay explicitly in the initial lines of the *Syair*. It was by writing in the Malay language and in keeping with one of its most popular generic styles that a particular tradition – at once religious, historical and cultural, whose roots in the wider Indonesian–Malay world were represented in the brief passage but whose branches spread over the island of Ceylon – could be kept alive into the future.[8]

Finally, a third major episode discussed by Saldin is that of the Ceylon Rifle Regiment's dispatch to "Cina," referring to Hong Kong and Taiwan.[9] A potential and often-feared aspect of army life was assignment overseas. Soldiers from the Ceylon Rifle Regiment were sent to Malabar, Madras, Singapore, Labuan and Hong Kong throughout the nineteenth century. Such travel sometimes entailed separation from loved ones for extended periods, alongside the risks of battle, disease and storms at sea. Saldin's account of soldiers departing revealed an aspect of military life

---

[8] Interestingly, the *Syair* recorded British attempts to teach the foreign soldiers English, probably so they could better communicate with their superiors but also, perhaps, to speak among themselves, testifying indirectly to the fact that Malay was not a universally known language to these men from across the archipelago.

[9] There is yet another episode of conflict narrated in the *Syair*: the anti-British Matale rebellion of 1848 which the Malays played a key part in quelling; see Saldin, *Syair*, 16–20. The year corresponded to that of young Saldin's enlistment at the age of sixteen.

not often exposed in writing, one that was more private, personal and emotional. The text included moving descriptions of the young men about to go overseas, with their beards barely grown, looking longingly at their homes; it mentioned how unsettling the news of this departure was for soldiers and families, with "Cina" perhaps the furthest away they had ever been, outside their regular routes of travel and service in south India and Southeast Asia; and it portrayed the day of departure when all lost their composure and wept as a slow tune was played. When soldiers began sending home their wages, families were content and grateful, but not for long, as this peaceful period was followed by the news of a terrible disease that caused many deaths among the troops, highlighting the dependency of those who remained behind on the shifting fates of recruited relatives and the opportunities and dangers of colonial enlistment.[10] A similar episode of disease spreading among Malay soldiers from Ceylon stationed in Labuan was reported in an 1870 issue of *Alamat Langkapuri*.[11]

Assignments overseas also meant that Malays from Ceylon were likely to meet "other Malays," not just in the context of manuscript copying in barracks, as depicted in Salimudeen's case in Chapter 8, but also on British ships, in colonies other than their own and on military expeditions. Travel by ship could be dangerous due to weather and epidemics, but also because outbreaks of violence were not rare and ships often carried – along with goods and soldiers – mutineers or convicts sentenced to transportation. An unremarkable court case from Hong Kong, which received much coverage because of an idiosyncratic sentence, reveals such an instance. In 1852 two Malay men were convicted of murdering John Pateson, the chief mate of the British brig *Corsyra*, which had left Singapore bound for Hong Kong. The file contains the testimony of the two men, Booray and Baba Seeleem, as well as that of several other Malays present but acquitted, and the ship's captain, who

---

[10] Ibid., 14–16.

[11] *Alamat Langkapuri* issue 28, June 26, 1870. The troops' sorry state was noted also in Governor John Pope Hennessy's speech of late August 1870: "I have observed with extreme regret, an extraordinary mortality for the last twelve months among the Ceylon Rifles stationed here. Every thing that the Military and the Civil authorities could do to ascertain its nature and to check it appears to have been done. The disease has now been ascertained to be that which is described in the books as 'Beri Beri, or the Bad sickness of Ceylon'" (*The Strait Times*, August 27, 1870; National Library Board, Singapore; eresources.nlb.gov.sg/newspapers/). In the 1840s the previously uninhabited island of Labuan (off the north coast of Borneo, currently part of eastern Malaysia) was proposed as a base for British operations against piracy in the South China Sea. In 1846, the sultan of Brunei, Omar Ali Saifuddin II, signed a treaty and ceded Labuan to Britain in the same year.

heard the victim's testimony before he died after being stabbed with a long knife and suffering multiple wounds.[12] It is not clear if the Malay men were from Ceylon or elsewhere, although Ceylon was a likely place of origin as six companies of the Ceylon Rifle Regiment served in Hong Kong between 1847 and 1854. What the documents do reveal are glimpses of life as a Malay man in British service: The captain of the *Corsyra* did not speak Malay and potential misunderstandings were rife; Malay convicts on board were heard by at least one witness plotting to steer the brig to Aceh and to kill any Malays on the ship who refused to join them. Additional cases from those years in Hong Kong point to the intersections of Malays from various places including Java, Singapore, Celebes and Penang. It is not far-fetched to imagine contacts between Malays from different places crossing paths during enlistment, and to consider military life in colonial armies as a form of exile, at times temporary, at times final as for those who died of illness or in battle, which entailed longing, adjustment and resilience. Saldin's depiction of departure makes it abundantly clear that those present – going or remaining – felt a deep uncertainty about whether they would meet again.

Anxiety about surviving life in the military, above all in war, was often assuaged through the recitation of prayers and charms geared toward protection as well as through the use of talismanic objects that recalled the pusakas.[13] In another of Saldin's writings, a small booklet titled the *Kitab Awrad* (Sin. *wirid*, recitations chanted after the obligatory prayers) dated 1905, he included various Arabic prayers and verses from the Qurʾan to be recited on particular occasions, the latter elaborated upon in Malay. Among them was the *Doa Angkasa* ("Prayer to the Heavens"), a prayer that was said to be potent in a range of circumstances; however, Saldin opened his framing comments by stating its potency in combat: "Here is outlined the procedure for, and benefits of, the *Doa Angkasa*. It

---

[12] The case, which was not unusual, was debated at several levels of government because the judge had given the two Malays a death sentence, which was not to be executed but rather commuted to transportation for life. This, the judge argued, was in line with an earlier case in which the punishment of nine Chinese men convicted of piracy and stabbing was commuted without consulting the judge, and he believed that capital punishment for those who killed a European (as in the *Corsyra* case) but not for those who killed natives (as in the earlier case) would send a dangerous message. For testimonies from the *Corsyra* case and related correspondence and newspaper articles, see Hong Kong Public Record Office, Reference C.O. 129/39 and C.O. 129/41.

[13] One such object was a "one-eyed" coconut shell that was tied by a string around a soldier's waist and said to offer protection from bullets, mentioned in the *Weerabangsa Family Notes* (see Chapter 8) and inherited by Mr. M. J. (Joe) Weerabangsa (personal communication, January 3, 2014).

was first put to the test by our elders at the time they served in the ranks of the British Crown's army. They created amulets with the *Doa Angkasa*, then they participated in several battles and returned home safe and sound guarded by Almighty God against all misfortune. And at that time [the *Doa*] was famed among the Javanese for its gains and miracles, both of which [were granted] without fail."[14] The *Doa* was linked by Saldin to places of origin and the wisdom of prior generations whose members were likely among the troops depicted in the *Syair*, their doctrines of protection and potency recited and trusted by subsequent generations.[15]

The three episodes depicted in the *Syair* – war in south India, war in Kandy and recruitment to East Asia – underscore the martial lifestyle of the Malays in nineteenth-century Ceylon. They expose the entanglements of colonizer and colonized in settings where great differences in status were contrasted with the egalitarianism of vulnerability to illness or the cruelty of battle and, from Baba Ounus Saldin's early twentieth-century perspective, seemed to have demanded a glorification of military life which may have served to justify the many challenges and sacrifices endured by the Malays.

The question of how the *Syair* might be classified as vernacular and Islamic, and positioned along a frontier, requires some definition of these aspects of the literature. Here vernacular literature is defined as a literature that is not only written in a vernacular language but, in the term's broader sense of "common," "local," "idiomatic," engages with and depicts places and events and people in a way that was distinctly tied to Malay diasporic life in Ceylon and extending to the coasts of the Indian Ocean. It is also a literature that explores the movement across and among these people and sites, as well as the kinds of dynamics that

---

[14] *Inilah tersebut kipit dan kebijakannya Doa Angkasa itu, bermula sudah dicobahinya oleh orang2 tuah kami pada masa mereka itu ada didalam barisan kerajaan Inggeris telah merekaitu dibuat 'azimat akan Doa Angkasa itu lalu mereka itu didalam beberapa peperangan pula ia pulang dengan 'apit selamat dijagahkan Allah Ta'ala daripada segala bencana celaka dan pada masa itu telah mashur antara bangsa Jawa daripada manfa'atnya dan mu'jizatnya duanya tiada sia2* (Baba Ounus Saldin, *Kitab Awrad*, Safar 1323/April 1905). I thank Mrs. Warnishiya Dole for showing me the *Kitab*.

[15] Another example is found in the *Angkatan Menulis Ism* which mentions a *Kidung bab Rasa* that was transmitted (M. *diturunkan*) by Tuan Kapitan Jurangpati. Reciting this *Kidung* a thousand times for forty days, if well received by God, will grant the reciter immunity from bullets so that he may not be quickly swallowed by the earth (*ampat puluh hari amalkan 1000 kidung ini ansha allah ta'ala jadi kabul sajati tida makan tubu kita peluru tida sampai jika kita lulur kabumi*). The prayer was said to have been written in the language of Sumenep (*bahasa Sumenep*). It was inscribed by Mas Murat ibn Mas Juri ibn Mas Anom Weerabangsa in August 1949, over what seems like much older writing. See *Angkatan Menulis Ism*, BL, EAP609/17/3.

emerged from lives lived in the region. Since being Malay and Muslim in Ceylon were intertwined aspects of identity, much of what can be understood as vernacular is also Islamic, although at times in subtle and implicit ways.

The *Syair Faiḍ al-Abād* presents instances of these trends: Considering geography, the spatiality covered in the text recalls Tamil lands in India's southern parts; Ceylon; many islands of the Indonesian Archipelago, including Java, Sumatra, Sulawesi, Ternate and others; and coastal towns of the Indonesian–Malay world, including Semarang, Padang, Banten and Penang. Also central are the links across the Indian Ocean to European ports in Portugal, the Netherlands and Britain, and the Arab lands figured in the ancient stories of the prophets that appear in the *Syair*'s third and final section. Many different groups and communities play a part in the *Syair*, and all are among those with whom the Malays interacted and who contributed to Malay identification and differentiation: villagers in south India who fought against the British imposition of taxes; the Sinhalese and Tamils of Ceylon; Javanese, Bugis and people from Penang, Semarang and Madura; Portuguese and Dutch officers; and British military men, administrators and politicians.

Movement across the ocean is palpable in a range of ways: in the depiction of conquering Portuguese ships arriving on Ceylon's shores and Dutch ships that dock at those same shores a century and a half later, some of which had brought soldiers from the archipelago to assist in the conquest; in sailing across the sea to distant Hong Kong and Taiwan by way of unfamiliar oceanic routes only to return in greatly diminished numbers; in the recruitment of soldiers from the farthest reaches of the Indonesian Archipelago and from the Malay Peninsula and in their travels to Ceylon and India; in memories of earlier exile and recruitments that echo with those depicted by Saldin, in families parting, soldiers deployed, even salaries sent home from afar. Movement is also apparent in texts and stories circulating across the Indian Ocean from and to Arabia, India, Ceylon and Southeast Asia, some as ancient as Adam's fall to earth and others as recent as the chronicling of Ceylon's political and military history in colonial times.

When considering the *Syair* as Islamic, this particular dimension is most evident, beyond the *Syair*'s framing by Adam's ancient banishment from Paradise, in the two sections mentioned but not elaborated upon in this chapter, namely the tract titled ʿIlmu Maʿaripat – based for the most part on the writings of prominent Muslim philosopher, theologian and jurist al-Ghazālī (d. 1111) – and the tales of the prophets. It is noteworthy how different in tone and content these two sections are from the *Syair*'s historical chapters. Even so, the latter occasionally hint at what might be termed broadly an "Islamic ethos," as when blessings are incurred on all those who read the section on military history, in this world and the next. A more pronounced and powerful view in terms of the *Syair*'s Islamic character, however, appears from a holistic look at the complete volume rather than at its parts: the Arabic title – "Bounty of the Ages" – that resonates with all the depth and sanctity of Muslim history from its very beginning to the time of writing; the employment of the Arabic script with its divine echoes; the author, well known to his readership for his accomplishments as an important figure in the Muslim community and especially for his contributions to Muslim learning and publishing; and the significant part of the *Syair*'s content, encompassing twenty-four pages out of forty-six, that engages with religious ideas, stories and morals.

The inclusion of the three sections in a single volume must have been viewed as appropriate, showing at the very least that Baba Ounus Saldin was engaged with all these topics at once and did not view them as requiring separate publications, title pages or introductions. To a contemporary reader, it is somewhat striking that there is no explanation or justification whatsoever for the combining of ancient traditions about Adam and Moses, a treatise on mystical knowledge and the recounting of recent military campaigns. Within the volume, if read in sequence as it was apparently meant to be, there is a nonchronological, nonthematic yet organic thread that weaves the three together. It is also possible to read the sequence as possessing a nonlinear, circular chronology that begins with Adam (falling to earth in Sarandib), "fast-forwards" to the recent past, only to return to Adam and his fall, as well as other ancient prophets, in closing. Considering Gérard Genette's important insights concerning paratexts, with introductions, conclusions and framing devices chief among them, the history encased between the two "prophetic references" in the *Syair* becomes subordinate to these brief, subtle yet deeply resonant signposts.[16]

Frontiers, as they relate to the *Syair*, can be addressed in their physical and metaphorical senses. From an authorial, personal perspective, the *Syair* was written on the frontier, or edge, of Baba Ounus Saldin's life,

---

[16] The reference to Adam's descent to Sarandib toward the end of the *Syair* is on p. 44:

> *Kemudian daripada dimakan buah khuldi/digoda Iblis kedua laki istri*
> *Demi diturunkan kedalam dunia ini/dalam pulau nama Sarandib*
> *Malam dan siang tiap2 bertangis/mengingatkan celaka nasib*

> Then having eaten the khuldi fruit/tempted by Iblis the two, man and wife
> Were sent down into this world/to an island called Sarandib
> Night and day they never stopped crying/recalling their miserable fate.

just a year before his passing. In its closing lines, he seemed to acknowledge his approaching death by going beyond the typical apologies for the dearth of his knowledge and style, asking specifically for God's compassion and the Prophet's intervention on Judgment Day and expressing hope that God would ease his path upon his death.[17]

The *Syair* and Malay writing in Ceylon more generally were produced in a region that was a frontier of Indonesian–Malay Islam, of the Malay language as well as additional vernacular languages of the Indonesian Archipelago, and of multiple genres of Malay-Islamic writing. Saldin's retelling of Malay history and of soldiers dispatched to the front underscores the frontiers of colonial power, which were transformed in the telling also into frontiers of a Malay-Muslim presence on the stage of contemporary world events. The Malays as a group (as opposed, for example, to the Sinhalese) were selected to be sent to war along the frontier for their boldness and bravery. In the *Syair*, their excellence in battle and their sacrifice are carried out for Empire's sake.

These different perspectives on the trope of the frontier – personal, religious, linguistic, military – show how the frontier, albeit constituting a spatial category or metaphor, does not convey a rigid, nor a stable, idea of place. While, as in the cases of the Malay language, Islamic traditions and Malay warriors, it can evoke the front, progression and an expansive directionality, it can also signal, as in the life stage of the elderly Saldin's writing, an edge, a limit, a proximity to a boundary, an end. This fluidity allows a consideration of Malay diasporic life in Ceylon as extending the limits – of Malayness, of the Malays' language and their Islamic and literary traditions – toward new horizons while simultaneously residing at the edge, the margin, the farthest limit of the wider Malay world. In this way, diasporic life itself signals the emergence of new frontiers that extend previous places and ways of life and uses of language outward, and mark new – always porous – boundaries.

The *Syair Faiḍ al-Abād* offers a way to consider the frontiers of Southeast Asian Islam, of the Malay language and its poetic genres, and of colonial war and expansion by conveying to its readers a sense of geographical, cultural and religious frontiers. It did so by means of its content, including its historical narrative and descriptions of space; through its choice of language and genre, as well as by its employment of alternative temporalities that combined ancient with contemporary, European with Islamic, human with divine; and by telling both of man's military might and of the path to knowing God, underscoring the

---

[17] Ibid., 48.

different forms of knowledge available to Malay Muslims and the choices and consequences inherent in each.

The second major work authored by Saldin, the *Kitab Segala Peringatan*, was written in the form of a diary containing a mix of very personal family history, developments in Ceylon and the world, and reports of religious visions. First and foremost, it documented various events in the life of Baba Ounus Saldin and his family, in particular births, marriages and deaths.[18] It began with early memories and wove its way to the end of Saldin's life, covering many years and multiple events that shaped personal lives as well as those of the community, the colony and, to a lesser degree, the world. From reading the *Kitab* one also gains, beyond faint glimpses of particular individuals' lives, a sense of Malay culture in nineteenth-century Ceylon, in its Islamic dimensions as well as the way military service formed a constant thread of the Malays' livelihood and identity. Entries were arranged chronologically, with dates given according to the Hijri, Gregorian and Javanese years or a combination of these time-reckoning systems, at varying levels of detail which included, beyond the year, also the month, day of the week, astrological body (M. *bintang*) ascribed to the day and the specific hour at which an event took place. Whereas the *Syair* opened with Adam, father of mankind, and his primordial banishment by God to Sarandib, the *Kitab* commenced with Sheikh Yusuf al-Makassari, a "patriarch" for the Malays in Ceylon, the first major political and religious figure to be banished by the Dutch.[19] Although the historical facts regarding Sheikh Yusuf presented in the *Kitab* are inaccurate, it is the invocation of this foundational figure in the *Kitab*'s initial lines that is significant and that produced an echo between the two texts. Also evocative is the way both texts' titles speak to time and its passage through the words *abad* (age, century) and *peringatan* (memory).

The *Kitab*'s first personal entry offered details of the death of Saldin's father and mother and of his subsequent enlistment after being orphaned at age sixteen. His father died in Kampung Kertel, Colombo, at six o'clock in the evening, the hour of the Maghrib prayer, on Wednesday, July 4, 1848/ Sha'abān 25, 1264, and was buried in the grounds of Wekande mosque. His mother, Saldin added, had died earlier in the same neighborhood of

---

[18] The facsimile copy cited does not include page numbers. I have numbered the pages beginning with the first page written in Baba Ounus Saldin's hand.

[19] The first page includes the title of the *Kitab* and a note on the tuans, kings, tumenggungs, ministers and Sheikh Yusuf al-Mangkasari who left Colombo by ship to Betawi on March 9, 1831/Dhu al-Ḥijjah 10, 1246. The two dates do not correspond exactly but are approximately two months apart. Sheikh Yusuf in fact left Colombo by ship for the Cape in 1694.

ombo, but since he was a small child at the time he did not know the precise date, although he believed it was 1837, i.e. when he was five years old.[20]

On September 4, 1848, two months after his father's death, his uncle (*uwa*) Tuan Ajidan Miskin enlisted Saldin and his older brother Baba Halaludeen as soldiers (M. *dimasukkan dalam seldadu*) and they joined the British army's Second Company. In 1850 they were sent to Kandy, where they spent four years, returning to Colombo in 1853. During those years Saldin attained the rank of lance corporal and moved to Company Six. In 1854, he reported leaving the Regiment by paying £8 to release himself from duty, after which he worked building bridges in Peradeniya and Gampolla.[21] In between these brief entries about his time in the military and his release are interwoven the dates of family events, including Baba Halaludeen's marriage and the birth of his daughter, his death and the death of Saldin's grandmother and uncle. Thus, the *Kitab* introduces two of its major themes right from the start: genealogy and military service.

Service in the British army, especially in the Regiment, appears throughout the *Kitab*, although never in the detailed manner found in the *Syair*, which documented campaigns, battles and the textures of the soldiers' and their families' lives. The *Kitab* mentioned particular events and figures related to the Regiment: Several members of the Regiment were sent to London to appear before the queen on January 1, 1863, as she "wished to see the soldiers of the Ceylon Rifle and to watch the troops conduct their drills," the entry demonstrating that the Malays constituted an integral element of the military in British Ceylon;[22] an 1864 cholera epidemic struck the Regiment soldiers hard and many died; a note on the disbandment of the Regiment appeared in September 1873.[23] Despite the brevity and laconic tone when referring to this watershed event, as late as 1889 men were still noted by Saldin along with their former military ranks of letnan, sarjen, koperal, ajidan and kapitan; the cemetery by the mosque had a special section for the *orang pensiun*, Regiment retirees.[24] It was only in the final pages of the *Kitab*, when Saldin reiterated his genealogy – employing the Arabic term "silsilah," "chain" of descent or initiation – that he expanded on the foundational role played by service in the colonial army in his personal, familial and community biographies. It is in this section, too, that one of the clearest links between the *Syair* and the *Kitab* was implicitly established:

[20] Saldin, *Kitab*, 2.   [21] Ibid., 5.
[22] Ibid., 6: *Ratu Inggris hendaq melihat seldadunya Seilon Raifel beserta membala berderil.*
[23] Ibid., 13.   [24] Ibid., 40.

Our[25] history and genealogy are as follows: My grandfather Enci Pantasih came from Sumenep in the land of Java when the English government brought five hundred men, all from Sumenep and Mandura, to attack Raja Kaku and fight the war in Kochi. The English had heard from the Dutch that the people of Sumenep and Mandura were exceedingly brave and determined of heart and that they would enter battle with hand-held weapons. After winning both campaigns, they remained in Kochi for a time and while there my grandfather Enci Pantasih was married in Kochi. He then came to the island of Ceylon, to Colombo, and lived in several places on this island. My grandfather had three sons: The first was my father Captain Saldin, the second my uncle [*bapa mudahku*] Tuan Corperal ʿAbadeen, and the third my uncle Enci Sadu. My grandfather Pantasih passed away [*pulang ke rahmatullah ta ʿala*, literally "returned to exalted God's mercy"] in the Maldives and my grandmother passed away in Colombo, likely in 1841.[26]

A few details were added to this statement by Saldin in the final pages of the *Kitab* which seem somewhat repetitive and perhaps confused, written very close to Saldin's own death. His father Captain Saldin or Salahudeen was born in Colombo in 1796 and was recruited into the Regiment in Trincomalee in 1811. He was employed in the Regiment for thirty years and seventy-four days, retired in Colombo on July 30, 1847, and passed away at age fifty-four on July 4, 1848, the same date that appeared in the *Kitab*'s opening entry; Saldin's mother Dainikar was the daughter of the scribe (*juru tulis*) Burhan from Sumenep; Saldin's parents had four sons and two daughters, of which he was the fourth child. The name of his grandmother, the Kochi woman married to Pantasih, was not recorded, but in a more general entry that repeated the episode of recruitment by the British, Saldin noted that "the majority [of the recruits from Sumenep and Mandura] were young and had not yet reached the age of marriage. Those married among them were three or four of their leaders [*penghulu*] who brought their wives along. Some of the men, while living in Kochi, married Muslim women [*perempuan Islam*]. It was during that time that my grandfather took a wife [*diambil bini*] in Kochi."[27]

Several central themes developed in the *Syair* are evident in these passages: the Malays' famed courage, which formed a core incentive for their recruitment, first by the Dutch, then the British; the young age at which men, or rather boys, were called up and sent to war; marriages that transpired during overseas campaigns and the centrality of family, even during campaigns and as an accompaniment to military life despite its

---

[25] Malay uses two plural first-person pronouns (personal and possessive), *kita* ("we" or "our," inclusive) and *kami* ("we" or "our," exclusive). The one employed here is *kita*.

[26] Saldin, *Kitab*, 58. Encik Pantasih was mentioned in Chapter 2 as an ancestor of B. D. K. Saldin, the late owner of the *Malay Compendium*.

[27] Saldin, *Kitab*, 51.

Figure 9.1 An anonymous tombstone inscribed in Malay at the Jawatte
Cemetery, Colombo, stating the date and age at death (*11 Juli 1888, pada
umur 52 tahun*).
Photo: Tuan Younis Ahmed Hannan

frequent transitions; and travel through enlistment and war, followed by
settlement in Ceylon that signaled the beginning of yet another phase
in Malay history there, this time not grounded in political exile by a
European power but in a commitment made to that very power.[28]
Reading the *Kitab* highlights how these themes were, for Saldin, not only
part of a broader history he wished to bequeath to the young, but also
very personal ones, glimpses of his biography.

   Whereas the *Syair* occasionally depicted death in battle, or due to
captivity and epidemics striking the troops, death constituted a major
force in the *Kitab*, showing clearly its proximity and immediacy to the
living, above all through the high mortality rates of babies and children,
but also those of young women giving birth and among victims of disease
of all ages, including those dying from fever, colic and cholera. Saldin

---

[28] The marriage of Malay soldiers in south India is also mentioned in the *Weerabangsa
Family Notes*: A native captain by the name of Pangeran Goonawijaya was said to have
taken a third wife who was a "coast Moor lady from Panjaanam Kurichi," the site of
battles depicted in the *Syair* (Weerabangsa, *Weerabangsa Family Notes*, BL, EAP609/17/
4, 13).

noted a cause for each reported death, as well as the precise details of when it occurred, including time of day, date and burial site, always in a mosque's grounds or in the adjoining cemeteries of Wekande, Kampung Jawa, Maradana and, as time went by, Jawatte.

Religious life and conviction pervaded both texts, as did Malay customs, the former and latter often inextricably linked. According to the *Kitab*, when daughters married the husband's family was given a dowry (*mas kawin* or *maher*); the names given to children were almost always Arabic ones, such as Muhammad, Khalid, Safiyah, Kamil, Ahmad and Jurairah, while many Malay titles were used, either embedded within names or affixed to them, including *tuan, nyonya, baba, enci, siti* and *dain*; circumcisions were entered, as were Islamic marriages performed in the presence of a *katib* and witnesses as required. The importance of an Islamic-mystical dimension in Saldin's life is apparent in the *Syair*'s full chapter dedicated to *'Ilmu Ma'aripat*; yet, once again, this element too is expressed more personally and directly in the *Kitab*, coming across most powerfully through Saldin's depiction of his visions of, or encounters with, the Prophet Muhammad. The first such encounter, defined by Saldin with the Sufi concept *mushāhadah* by which a devotee attains a certainty unattainable by intellectual means, took place on the night of the Prophet's Ascension to the Heavens (M. *malam mi'raj*) in the year 1290/1873, just after the death of Saldin's brother Halaludeen from a fever and his burial at the Wekande Mosque cemetery. As Saldin was walking that night, he heard that the Prophet was about to return from the *mi'raj*, his nocturnal ascension to the heavens from the Temple Mount (A. *Bayt al-Maqdis*) in Jerusalem, which is commemorated on Rajab 27. Along the road, Saldin saw a beautiful palace surrounded by walls and when he approached its gate he found a man standing guard. He asked the man politely when the Prophet would arrive and was told that he had just entered the palace, but that Saldin could remain there for a while. Then the guard asked whether Saldin recognized him, and he replied that he did not. The guard introduced himself as the Prophet's son-in-law (M. *mantunya Rasulullah*), whereby Saldin touched his hands in reverence and kissed them repeatedly. Then a balcony of sorts appeared and Saldin saw clearly, with his own eyes, the Prophet, "intercessor on behalf of sinners" (A. *shāfi' al-mudhnibīn*), glowing with a radiance like no other he had ever encountered in this world. 'Ali, now mentioned by name, then explained that the Prophet had just descended from *jinan* (from A. garden, the Garden of Eden) and Saldin treasured the word in his mind lest he forget it. Turning his head, he found his recently departed brother Baba Halaludeen standing beside him, having come to see the Prophet too. Returning to the name *jinan* he mentioned finding its meaning as *sorga*, Paradise. He ended this long and striking entry with a note on glimpsing the Prophet's beard which was long and gray.[29]

The next encounter, to which Saldin again gave the title *mushāhadah bagi Muhammad SAW*, transpired in February 1875. Standing right in front of his house while carrying his small son, Saldin smelled a fragrant scent and wondered aloud what it might be. Someone answered that it was musk (M. *kasturi*), and Saldin understood this to indicate that the Prophet was close by. Following the scent, he walked until he saw a mosque at the foot of a hill. At the door he met Katib Tuan Guru Baru and Shaykh Qabar Sahib and the former told him to quickly approach the Prophet's feet. He hurried in and heard the Prophet calling to him "Yunus," to which he replied *"labayka ya Rasulullah"* (A. "Here I am at your service, O Messenger of God") as he put his son down. The Prophet reached out to take both of Saldin's hands, asking about the little boy and his name. When he heard the boy was named Muhammad Khalid he was pleased that Saldin gave his name and that of his Companion (M. *sahabat*) to his son.[30] The Prophet continued speaking but Saldin was awakened from sleep, only to weep bitterly for his misfortune at not gaining more from this auspicious occasion.[31]

Saldin's third and final such encounter as depicted in the *Kitab* took place when Saldin met the Prophet on *malam 'arafah*, the second day of the hajj rituals when pilgrims congregate at the foot of Mt. 'Arafah, celebrated on Dhū al-Ḥijjah 9. Saldin heard that the Prophet was in one of the houses. He went there to visit and held the Prophet's hands requesting his intercession. The Prophet answered that, God willing, he would obtain it. Saldin then asked to take leave. Muhammad granted him permission and touched him with his revered hands before he went home.[32] The encounters with the Prophet are depicted as infused with sensual experiences of sight, hearing and smell and above all coming into physical contact, touching the Prophet's hands or feet and being touched by him, recalling similar encounters in early conversion stories from the archipelago and the blessed healing touch of the walis and other holy men.

The next entry in the diary stated that Saldin's daughter Nyonyai Dahmani gave birth to twin boys in February 1884, which could have been taken as a direct result of the encounter and the Prophet's promised

---

[29] Saldin, *Kitab*, 13–14.
[30] Khālid ibn Walīd was a Companion of the Prophet and a commander famed for his military prowess.
[31] Saldin, *Kitab*, 13.   [32] Ibid., 19.

intercession. Another similar episode involved the great Muslim and Sufi sheikh ʿAbd al-Qadir Jailani, whom Saldin referred to as "our master" (M. *tuan kami*)[33] and also as Sheikh Muhideen, the epithet by which he was popularly known in south India and Ceylon, where he is said to have meditated for twelve years after paying his respects to Adam's footprint on the mountain.[34] Jailani was seen walking along with another unnamed "pillar of Islam" followed by many disciples, and he was said to have entered Saldin's home briefly. A final event of this nature was noted on July 9, 1888, when Saldin witnessed the gates of the heavens parting.[35]

Saldin was initiated into the Shatariyyah tarekat by Sheikh Muhammad Tambi Hasan Tambi, together with his close relatives Nurul ʿAyn Hasan, Ahmad Sabar and Muhammad Sabar. Saldin's sheikh Tuan Sheikh Luwana Marakkaiyar ibn Ahmad Labbai passed away on September 20, 1881, and was buried in Maliyawatte.[36] These entries point to Saldin's Sufi leanings and learning and a connection to a tarekat which was widely followed in both Ceylon and the Malay world to the southeast. They also provide evidence of the close contacts between the Malay community and the Tamil-Muslim one, as indicated by the Tamil terms *tambi* ("younger brother"), *labbai* (name of a south Indian Muslim community) and *Marakaiyar* (a south Indian Muslim trader community of Arab descent).[37] These contacts were based on a shared faith, common textual and interpretive traditions, tarekat affiliations and guru–disciple relationships. Explicit contacts with non-Muslims were limited in the *Kitab* to mention of Sinhalese (M. *Cinggala*) midwives who assisted in the births of several of Saldin's children.

The outside world filtered in to the *Kitab*, complementing entries on family members and mystical visions with those on politics, scientific innovation and climate. The appearance of gaslights in Colombo in 1871, the Turkish sultan's decision to go to war with Russia in 1876 and his defeat two years later, the first train from Colombo to

---

[33] Here Saldin employed the Malay exclusive first-person plural pronoun *kami*, indicating the nature of attachment between the master and his disciples.

[34] The cave where Jailani is said to have meditated, Daftar Jailani, is situated approximately 70 km from Adam's Peak, and draws thousands for an annual commemorative festival. See Dennis McGilvray, "Jailani: A Sufi Shrine in Sri Lanka," in Imtiaz Ahmad and Helmut Reifeld (eds.), *Lived Islam in South Asia: Adaptation, Accommodation and Conflict* (Delhi: Social Science Press, 2004), 273–289; M. L. M. Aboosally, *Dafther Jailany: A Historical Account of the Dafther Jailany Rock Cave Mosque* (Colombo: Sharm Aboosally, 2002).

[35] Saldin, *Kitab*, 34.

[36] For both events, the initiation and burial, Saldin noted the Javanese years (*tahun Alif* and *Jim*, respectively).

[37] The name *labbai* or *lebai* was incorporated into Indonesian languages and has come to mean "an Islamic scholar."

Moratuwa in 1877, the completion of the railway to Matale in 1880, and news of floods and the catastrophic eruption of Krakatau in west Java in 1883, the echoes of which could be heard all the way to Ceylon, were all noted by Saldin. In this dimension, the *Kitab* was linked less to the *Syair* and more to the *Alamat Langkapuri* and *Wajah Selong* newspapers published by Saldin, which covered domestic and international events while being rooted in Malay community affairs and published in the Malay language. For example, the *Kitab* contained an entry on the duke of Edinburgh's visit to Colombo on March 30, 1870. It described the noise and excitement, the decorations and preparations along the streets, and the extravagant sum of £30,000 spent on the brief visit. The same event was reported at length in the *Alamat Langkapuri*.[38]

Especially noteworthy in the context of this chapter are references in the *Kitab* to what can be broadly defined as "Malayness." In addition to the customs already noted, Saldin documented his writing and publishing of two books on the Malay language meant for children's education: The first, titled *Mirātul Ghulam* (A. "Mirror for a Young Boy") and published in 1891, was geared toward teaching children Malay. Three hundred copies were printed. The second book, printed in 250 copies around the same time, was also written for children and dealt with aspects of Malay grammar (untitled, but described as *sebuah kitab nahu dan saraf Melayu*, "a book on Malay grammar").[39] The book's title page expanded, in Arabic and Malay: *Inilah kitāb al-sirr al-jāwā fi ta'līm al-naḥw al-jāwī kebantuan kepada kanak-kanak mengajar rahsia dalam nahu bahasa jawi* ("This is a book on the secrets of jawi [revealed] through the study of jawi grammar, an aid to children instructed in the secrets of jawi grammar").[40]

Not long afterward, Saldin reported the establishment of an Islamic school (*madrasah*), founded by Abu Saleh Wahid, a Regiment retiree, for both girls and boys under the age of ten. The school received government approval and funding to hire three teachers in August 1892. At the madrasah, children were taught the Qur'an, Arabic and Malay, referred to (as in the title of Saldin's grammar for children) as *bahasa Jawi* (and not as Melayu or gundul).[41] In the *Alamat Langkapuri*,"jawi" was used

---

[38] Saldin, *Kitab*, 12; *Alamat Langkapuri*, issue 22, April 3, 1870, and issue 24, May 1, 1870.

[39] Saldin used two Arabic-derived terms, *nahu* (grammar) and *saraf* (grammatical inflexion). "Kitab" was often used in the sense of religious text, or a text of religious instruction.

[40] The first part of the statement gave the Arabic title of the book: *Kitāb al-sirr al-jāwī fi ta'līm al-naḥw al-jāwī*, followed by an explication in Malay. Here Saldin used "Jawi" to name the Malay language (*Kitab*, 37).

[41] Ibid., 38.

occasionally to refer to a Malay person (*seorang anak jawi, seorang pensiun jawi*) or as a verb referring to translation into Malay (*menjawikan*), but "Melayu" was employed much more dominantly to refer to people (*seorang Melayu, anak Melayu*), the Malay lands (*tanah Melayu*) and above all the Malay language, *bahasa Melayu*. The publication of Malay newspapers in Ceylon was itself a significant step in the preservation and circulation of written Malay, and the *Syair* was a synthesis of many of the themes and sentiments expressed in those earlier manifestations of Saldin's writing. While in the *Kitab* and *Alamat Langkapuri* the emphasis was on Malay as a unifying language, the *Syair*, especially in its depictions of the early military campaigns, returned to the soldiers' diversity which was made abundantly clear, only to emphasize Malay as a mother tongue and a group identity of its readership, implicitly declaring the extent of the transformation from multiple roots to a collective language and affiliation.

An example of the personal dimension of Saldin's writing in the *Kitab* is found in the entries relating to his daughter Nyonya Johari. In 1857 Saldin married Nyonya Nurani. Their firstborn son, Muhammad Amin, born in 1859, died at the age of one week; their second baby, a daughter born in 1861, died after nine days; the third child, Nyonya Johari, was born in 1862. Four more children were born to the couple in the coming years, one of whom died at a young age, while Nyonya Johari survived the precarious childhood years; Saldin's entry of July 5, 1878, when she was sixteen years old, announced that she had reached adulthood (M. *telah ia baligh*), an indication of her first menstruation and the sexual maturity it signaled. A year later, in 1879, she married Baba Nur ibn Jain Busu and Saldin noted the names of the katib and witnesses at the wedding; in October 1880 she gave birth to a baby girl; soon after Nyonya Johari fell sick with colic and on the twenty-third of that month, a Saturday, she succumbed to the illness. The entry also included the site of her burial in Jawatte and the fact that she was nineteen years old at the time of her death. Saldin referred to her as his darling (M. *jantung hatiku*, literally "my heart and liver," my life), and added the traditional Arabic words uttered in grief and resignation, "we belong to Allah and to Him we shall return." Although many deaths of close relatives, as well as friends and teachers were noted in the *Kitab*, it is only for Nyonya Johari and Saldin's beloved sister Katima that this phrase was added.[42] With so many of his children dying, she, who had reached young adulthood, seems to have been especially dear to him. The documentation of her life in the

[42] Katima's death is chronicled ibid., 41.

Kitab, albeit containing more gaps than information, reveals a thread of palpable emotion. The death of his first child to survive the first weeks, then years, of life, and to provide hope for the future by marrying and having a child of her own, left Saldin heartbroken. Further entries show how her memory lived on: Her daughter Nyonya Hafsah died on May 2, 1881, just seven months after birth, and was buried in Jawatte beside her mother; when Saldin's brother Tuan Ajidan Jumat died in September of that year he was buried in the same cemetery, with his feet in the direction of Nyonya Johari's grave; in June 1881, a year after Saldin married his second wife Nyonya Nun binti Encik Kamdin ibn Tamurtu in Matale, they named their firstborn, a daughter, Nyonya Johari; in 1886 at the age of five this second Nyonya Johari fell sick but recovered; in 1899 she married Kamaludeen Lye, to whom Saldin paid two hundred rupiah as *maher*; in 1903 she bore a second child and in 1905 a fourth (the first and third are not mentioned); finally, in the *Kitab*'s concluding pages, Saldin again mentioned the death of the first Nyonya Johari who had been married to Baba Nur.

The *Kitab* and the *Syair* taken together provide important information and insights on the Malays in nineteenth-century Ceylon. The texts resonate with and complement one another, connected by joint authorship but capturing different moments, moods and particularities of experience. The many details of Saldin's family history in the *Kitab* add a personal touch to depictions in the *Syair*, the knowledge that among those going to war were Saldin's own relatives framing the scenes anew. Reading the section on the path to inner, intuitive truth in the *Syair* sheds light on the visions and direct encounters with the Prophet and ʿAbd al-Qadir Jailani described in the *Kitab*. Reminiscent of the way Yasadipura's different works speaking of Selong, Langka and Sarandib in eighteenth-century Java offered clues to how the island was imagined in nomenclature-dependent ways, considering the works of Saldin comparatively complicates and expands an understanding of Malay life and its multiple dimensions, as well as of Malay writing practices, on that same island.

The *Syair*, as noted, opens with Adam while the *Kitab* begins with Sheikh Yusuf, the texts juxtaposing these two father figures, two "firsts" in Malay genealogy in Sarandib and colonial Ceylon, respectively. Saldin also associated himself with Sheikh Yusuf as author: Yusuf's title *Nafḥat al-Sailāniyyah*, "Whiff of Ceylon," conjured the island's proximity to the fragrances and beauties of Paradise, the same image of closeness and continuity between Paradise and Sarandib appearing in the *Syair*'s opening lines in the depiction of Adam's descent to earth. Both texts associated the names Ceylon and Sarandib: Sheikh Yusuf framed his work with those heavenly scents and employed Ceylon in his title, while his depiction of exilic desolation referred to Sarandib, speaking more directly to Adam's plight after banishment. Saldin dedicated four lines of verse each to Sarandib and Ceylon in the opening section of the *Syair* and conveyed a more positive impression of the island as a site of procreation and abundance. This may be attributed to Saldin's sense of appreciation of his forefathers' return to a most significant Islamic site, his own distance from lived experiences of exile, a need to justify the price paid in defending the island through military service, and his perspective from the brink of a long and full life about to come to a close.

The genres of syair and kitab in Malay literature are broad. Syairs, especially, have been composed on nearly any conceivable topic from war to daily life, love, travel, politics, genealogy and legend. Even with this fluidity in mind, the *Syair Faiḍ al-Abād* and the *Kitab Segala Peringatan* are somewhat unusual in their employment of these terms. The *Syair* incorporated under its title what was essentially a compendium, briefer than the *Malay Compendium* discussed in Chapter 2 but resembling it in its hybridity.[43] The category of kitab, most often used for religious books, was employed by Saldin for a family diary yet its incorporation of many deeply religious experiences and its framing by the arrival of the great sheikh and *'alim* Yusuf may have caused him to employ more religiously charged terminology. Whatever the motivations for the choice of generic titles, the two texts are clearly hybrid. Incorporating intra- and intertextual connections, they partook of a Malay literary culture that drew on, and continued to engage with, wider Islamic models of writing, commemorating and explicating, including the silsilah (genealogy), *ceritra nabi* or *anbiya* (tales of the prophets) and *'ilmu tasawuf* (Sufi knowledge). Concurrently, Saldin's works also overlapped with non-Malay writing in Ceylon: his military history with poems like the Sinhala *English War* and British reports and memoirs; his mystical verses, stories of prophets and experiences of initiation into a Sufi tarekat with the rich literary corpus produced in Arabu-Tamil.[44]

---

[43] It may be that if not for the demands of the print industry and the need for a book to bear a title, the term "syair" would have referred only to the initial poem on the wars rather than the entire work.

[44] On tales of the prophets and sufi literature composed in Arabu-Tamil in south India and Ceylon, see 'Ālim, *Arabic, Arwi and Persian*, 226–228 and 406–409 respectively, and *passim*. Such Arabu-Tamil literature was also incorporated occasionally into Malay manuscripts (as discussed in Chapter 2), or as part of collections owned by Malay families. See, for example, the *khotba* volume, a manuscript containing sermons presented at the Wekande Mosque on Slave Island, Colombo, by Muhammad Tajudin Tamim Ameer (1904–1972) now in the possession of his grandson, the

Saldin's works, as well as additional ones written in Malay in nineteenth-century Ceylon, should be considered within the framework of diasporic writing. The three elements central to a diasporic imaginary in literature according to Quayson's formulation, i.e. place, nostalgia and genealogical accounting, are evident in Saldin's texts.[45] The colophon of one of his manuscripts, completed in Kandy in April 1856 and containing maulud recitations and sections of *furudh* (obligatory religious duties) reads as follows: "this book belongs to Baba Ounus Saldin, son of Captain Saldin, son of Enci Pantasi of bangsa Sumenep."[46] As in other works discussed, the name of Sumenep appears as a place of origin and as a marker of belonging, the word "bangsa" connoting at the time racial distinction and a descent group, especially in the sense of noble descent.[47] Writing half a century after his grandfather's arrival in Ceylon, Saldin was making a clear statement about his ancestor's homeland and people. Names of places in the Indonesian–Malay Archipelago pepper Malay texts from Ceylon, yet none appear as consistently as Sumenep, Madura, Makassar and Jawa, names that seem to overlap and merge, having in time become more symbolic of faraway and by now blurry islands, regions, kingdoms and homes than of geographically verifiable sites. And so place related to diasporic identity becomes not so much a concrete site whence one's ancestors arrived but, to borrow Salman Rushdie's phrase, an "imaginary homeland."[48] In a reverse variation on Massey's formulation about space as always constituted by a multiplicity of events, people and perspectives, a "simultaneity of stories-so-far," in the Malays' recollections the same events unfolded, and the same

---

current katib, Mr. Muznee Ameer, BL, EAP609/9/1; an Arabu-Tamil book of prayers and recitations inherited by Maas Maureen Weerabangsa, BL, EAP609/18/2; the *Arabu-Tamil Compendium*, containing many tales of the prophets and Qur'anic explication, inherited by Maas Syrni Sookoor from her mother Radèn Jawi Cuttilan, BL, EAP609/10/1.

[45] Quayson, "Postcolonialism and the Diasporic Imaginary," 148–150.

[46] *Bahwa kitab ini yang ampunya Baba Ounus ibn Kapitan Saldin ibn Enci Pantasyang bangsa Sumenep. Kandy bulan April 1856.* A note beneath this colophon explains that the current owner was gifted the volume by "Tuan Leuian Baba Jalaludeen Candianom ibn Tuan Ajidan Miskin Candianom," the rank designations (Lieutenant, Adjutant) once more highlighting the military element in Malay writing culture (*Subhana Mauludum Afurudhum*, BL, EAP609/5/5). A note at the end gives a different date, perhaps that of the original inscription: Ramadan 22, 1266/August 1, 1850. The title used the Tamil connective particle "um" to join the maulud and afurudh texts. The manuscript has several sections written in Arabic, but for the most part comprises sections alternating between Arabic and Arabu-Tamil, many of which are dedicated to ʿAbd al-Qadir Jailani.

[47] Wilkinson, *Malay–English Dictionary*, 100. Later in the twentieth century the word would come to primarily connote "nation."

[48] Salman Rushdie, *Imaginary Homelands: Essays and Criticism 1981–1992* (London: Penguin, 1992), 7–21.

individuals appeared, in multiple spaces that had merged indistinctly in their imagination.

Nostalgia, which in this model overlaps with the concept of place as it often entails a sense of displacement, comes through in Saldin's statement in the *Syair Faiḍ al-Abād*, in his desire to tell Malay youth at the turn of the twentieth century about their past, including its glorious moments in battle, a shared ethos of courage and faith. It is not about longing to return to a site of origin, but more of a temporal nostalgia to an earlier time that was, in his depiction, characterized by cohesion and purpose. Genealogical accounting, which provides an individual or a community with a distinctive past and addresses the history of present circumstances, is palpable in the opening section of the *Syair Faiḍ al-Abād* that addressed the question of "how did we get here" in two ways: The first referred to Adam's fall from Paradise to Sarandib, offering a universally human but also specifically Muslim genealogy, which can be read as viewing all humans as exiles from heaven, diasporics on earth; the second presented the much later narrative of Malay participation in colonial military expansion which brought them to Ceylon. Through this dual genealogy, Saldin condensed space and time, portraying the Malays as the earliest inhabitants of Ceylon and thus entirely at home there, and as recent newcomers, a community with roots and pasts elsewhere, whose particular historical trajectory brought it to a new home.

Saldin, a prominent individual of his generation, was a diasporic figure rooted in Ceylon, whose "homing desire"– a longing to feel at home in a diasporic's adopted land – was most likely fulfilled, also possessed, concurrently, a strong sense of pride and connection to places and people elsewhere.[49] His repertoire of Malay writing – both original and via translation and transmission – was vast, and included not only the genres of syair and kitab, anbiya and tasawuf but also those of doa, maulud, furudh, along with writing grammar books for schoolchildren and establishing newspapers, all of which were encompassed within Malay diasporic writing. In many of these instances, Saldin's Muslim and Malay senses of belonging merged indistinctly. And while the process of becoming a diaspora was initially linked with Adam's banishment, for Saldin and others living generations after the early exiles and more recent recruitments, their history may have also produced additional echoes: Like the seminal migration of the Prophet and a small group of followers from Mecca to Medina in 622 CE to avoid persecution, the Malays'

[49] On the idea of a "homing desire," which is not the same thing as a desire for a "homeland," and its relation to diaspora, see Avtar Brah, *Cartographies of Diaspora: Contesting Identities* (London and New York: Routledge, 1996) 180, 192–195.

history contained episodes of forced mobility, which ultimately produced positive results in the creation of a new community of Muslims who had overcome many challenges and could look back with dignity on what they had achieved in a new land.

In diasporic writing time can stand still or slow down significantly, as distant events and places are kept alive in words and the imagination. The *Syair* presented different temporal frames through which to consider exile and diaspora, with Adam's banishment, mentioned in its opening lines, framing the work in a manner that put the colonial period in perspective within a divinely designed chronology. The return to Adam, as well as to Nuh and Musa in the concluding section on the lives of the prophets, expanded this theme further. Adam appeared first, with his banishment from Paradise to "an island called Sarandib" and his subsequent misery retold briefly.[50] Then the story of the prophet Nuh was presented, also briefly, centered on the building of the ark and surviving the flood. Finally, with a bit more detail, the *Syair* depicted the life of Musa since infancy, when he was placed by his mother in a basket to avoid capture and death, through his time in the pharaoh's palace, to his ascent to Mt. Sinai and loss of consciousness as he stood before God. The latter scene was articulated in mystical terms of secrecy, hidden truths and initiation, again linking this aspect of Saldin's own practice and writing to the foundational biblical episode. Although the three prophets are no doubt important figures in Islamic tradition, their exclusive inclusion by Saldin invites an explanation. It is noteworthy that the biographies of all three contain episodes of banishment: Adam from Paradise, Nuh from his stubborn, infidel community and away from civilization into the raging flood, and Musa from his parents and people. Of the three, Adam's exile alone remained a permanent state; however, all three exemplified, through their life stories – only hinted at in the *Syair* but well known to its audience – models of banishment, its challenges and potentialities. The stories of the three prophets echo most powerfully with the plight of the early exiles: The destruction of Nuh's previous life and world, Adam's lost Paradise and, for Musa, the inability to reach the promised land all conjure the hardships of the first generation of the banished. Despite the brevity of the stories, water plays an important part in each: Adam's tears that "flowed ceaselessly," Noah who faced the flood waters that made the world "resemble a scene of the Final Day" and Moses who was placed by his mother "on the river Nile." The fluidity of water, its dangers and life-giving capacities resonate with exilic

---

[50] Saldin, *Syair*, 44.

and diasporic conditions, while the ark and small basket recall islands in the sea, like the Sarandib where Adam, and the Malays, found themselves and rebuilt their lives.[51]

And so, reading the *Syair*, the *Kitab* and additional Malay works at present, as literary and historical works from a world unknown to us temporally and culturally, they resonate with familiar themes such as colonialism and diaspora, yet conjure them anew through the particularities of the perspective, genre and language employed. They provide ways to consider how diasporic life can alter understandings of space, boundaries, frontiers, and individual and collective imaginations. Reading these works invites a consideration of the Malays' movement "forward" from being people of mixed, diverse backgrounds toward becoming "Malay," but also "backwards," through their writing, to those multiple roots and routes.

★ ★ ★

In closing I return to nomenclature, a theme that weaves through this book and frames it. Cases were presented of employing place names for self-identification (*bangsa Sumenep*, *peranakan Selong*, *orang dari nagari Makassar*) and as a means for defining the group now known as the "Sri Lankan Malays" from without. This final section draws on and expands the discussions of nomenclature as it refers to both place and people.

Considering social categorizations, in the Dutch period although the broad term "Easterners" was common, people arriving from the Indonesian Archipelago were classified for the most part based on their place of origin, with "place" typically referring to a particular island: Java, Bali, Madura, Ternate, Tidore or Ambon. Sometimes the designation spoke to more specific sites such as Sumenep, Banten or Makassar, or to an ethnic group such as the Malays or Bugis. The British takeover of the late eighteenth century signaled a flattening of the earlier nomenclature diversity, with the bureaucracy and military functioning as catalysts for the widespread adoption of the term "Malay." The influence of this administrative process was clearly evident in the pages of the pioneering Malay newspaper *Alamat Langkapuri*, edited and published by Baba Ounus Saldin, where the designation *Melayu* is used almost exclusively for the community and its language. Nonetheless, this was by no means a

---

[51] *Malam dan siang tiap-tiap bertangis* (Adam), *dikata setengah qiyamat dunia 'alam* (Nuh) and *dilantar pada sungai Nila* (Musa) (ibid., 44–45). Although not explicitly mentioned for Nuh in the *Syair*, the three are also associated with mountains: Nuh with Mt. Ararat, Musa with Mt. Sinai (M. *Tursina*) and Adam with the Peak (M. *Bukit Sarandib*).

straightforward or linear progression from many names to one but a convoluted path, or rather, several diverging paths. Throughout the nineteenth century and into the twentieth, different names and meanings continued to be invoked, as is evident in the titles of Malay poems, songs, documents and newspapers, as well as in books written about the Malays or mentioning them in passing. Thomas Skinner, in his memoir of fifty years spent in Ceylon, wrote of the Bugis native troops he saw in Batavia that "they are undoubtedly the finest of all the Malay tribes, and it is said of them that the word of a Bugis man is more to be depended on than the oath of any other man."[52] In this passage, the category of "Malay," and especially that of the courageous, trustworthy "Malay soldier," is unpacked to reveal its internal diversity and a hierarchy of loyalty and reliability in which Bugis men occupied the top rung.

The case of the two Malay newspapers published by Saldin in the latter decades of the nineteenth century is interesting for the choice of their titles, each putting forth a different name for the island, with its echoes and associations. The first newspaper, the already mentioned *Alamat Langkapuri*, which focused primarily on local news and the dynamics of Malay life including much that belonged to the religious sphere, bore the old Sanskritic name of Langka. The later publication was called *Wajah Selong* ("Views of Ceylon"), perhaps a title seen as appropriate for the disseminating of its more outward-looking, international news and meant for distribution also beyond the domestic market in Batavia and Singapore, major centers of the colonial world in which Selong was rooted.

This association between Lanka and Ceylon in Saldin's nomenclature choices was later followed in his *Syair*'s opening with the linking of Sarandib and Ceylon. In another example from the mid to late nineteenth century, a brief and anonymous poem, an association between Selong and Jawa was put forth:[53]

Muntiara di tana Seylong	Pearls in the land of Selong,
Emas biduri kitab Jawa	Gold [and] opal the books of Java,
Hamba inila anaq Seylong	This humble servant, a child of Selong,
Tida lupandia bahasa Jawa	Has not forgotten the tongue of Java.

---

[52] Skinner, *Fifty Years*, 139.
[53] Hussainmiya Collection, Department of National Archives, Sri Lanka, MF 182. The poem was microfilmed among different texts and textual fragments that appear in no particular order, and it is difficult, therefore, to know of which larger manuscript it formed a part.

Although the context in which this poem was composed is unclear, its author was stating, in the condensed form of the pantun, a relationship between the beautiful pearls of Ceylon and precious Javanese books, likely religious books (kitabs), and between himself as one born on that island, belonging to it as a child does to his family, yet deeply tied also to Java, if not through physical presence than by remembering its language. The pantun's rhyme scheme was such that in the first and third lines, the land of Ceylon and the child of that land were mentioned (*tana Seylong, anaq Seylong*), while in the second and fourth lines are found two references to Javanese: books, standing for an entire writing tradition, and the language (*kitab Jawa, bahasa Jawa*), still kept alive by the generations born in Ceylon. The poem thus suggested a symmetry between the two, Ceylon and Java, each appearing twice and in alternating order, creating in the listeners' mind a back-and-forth movement between the places, between a site of birth and home and the memory of elsewhere, between two spheres of beauty and richness. While Ceylon was represented as a concrete site, a stretch of land on which people were born and lived, Java, a land spatially and temporally distant for one raised in Ceylon, was kept alive in the author's diasporic consciousness through an ongoing association with its language and literary tradition.[54]

Additional, later cases could be cited, among them A. H. Greasy's collection of poems titled *Dendang Sayang Pantun Selong* ("Love Poem of Ceylon") and B. D. K. Saldin's *Pujian kepada Sri Lanka* ("Praise for Sri Lanka").[55] While the names Ceylon and Lanka seem to have gained

---

[54] It is possible that the author was invoking not Javanese but Malay, which was commonly referred to as jawi across Southeast Asia. If that was the case, it would not significantly change the point made about a diasporic consciousness that was maintained in Ceylon primarily through linguistic and literary means. The use of Jawa, not jawi, strengthens the case for translating it as "Javanese," but, as part of the broader discussion of nomenclature it has already been pointed out that Ja and Jawa were (and are) employed to refer to the Malays. A twentieth-century pantun, titled *Orang Ja*, can also be cited as evidence:

Hey Orang Java	Hey you Javanese [or Malays],
Saribu tahon suda	By now for a thousand years
Dato moyang kita	Our ancestors
Suda pegang Lanka	have had a hold on Lanka.

The pantun from which this verse is cited was composed in Sri Lankan Malay by the late Mr. M. I. Haniz; see BL, EAP609/7/2. Mr. Haniz offered pantun classes to children (in the 1970s?) (personal communication, Kartini Mohamed, May 27, 2013).

[55] A. H. Greasy, *Dendang Sayang Pantun Selong* (Colombo: A. H. Greasy, n.d.), BL, EAP609/7/1. The booklet was published prior to 1953. *Dendang sayang* is a traditional genre of love songs, possibly originating from the fifteenth-century Malacca court, which are typically sung as a duet of pantuns between a man and a woman, accompanied by musical instruments. For *Pujian kepada Sri Lanka*, see Saldin, *Portrait of a Sri Lankan Malay*, 120.

Figure 9.2 Malay Street sign, Slave Island, Colombo.
Photo by author

prominence among the Malays in the late nineteenth century and beyond, Sarandib was favored by non-Malay Muslim writers whose works centered on Islam and Muslims on the island, including Asiff Hussein's *Sarandib: An Ethnological Study of the Muslims of Sri Lanka*[56] and Tayka Shuʿayb ʿĀlim's *Arabic, Arwi and Persian in Sarandib and Tamil Nadu*.[57]

The questions regarding Malayness, the use of Ja/Java and Melayu and other forgotten, ignored or potential names that speak to alternative pasts and futures, played out not only in manuscript pages and other written and spoken Malay words but also spatially, in the built environment of a range of sites. Signs across Colombo testify to an earlier geography of the city, especially in the Slave Island area where Malays formed a majority in the nineteenth century and until recently accounted for a large share of inhabitants. In Colombo one comes across Jawatte ("Ja Compound") Road, Jawatte Street, Jawatte Mosque and Jawatte cemetery, as well as signs that declare the presence of Malay Street (Figure 9.2), the Malay Cricket Club and Sri Lanka Malay Association, the latter two located at

---

[56] Hussein, *Sarandib*.

[57] ʿĀlim, *Arwi, Arabic and Persian*. The designation "Sarandib," as discussed in Chapter 6, was favored by Tamil Muslim poets. However, M. A. M. Shukri's classic volume is titled *Muslims of Sri Lanka: Avenues to Antiquity* (Beruwala: Jamiah Naleemia, 1986).

Figure 9.3 Jawa Jummah Mosque sign, Kinniya, northeastern Sri Lanka.
Photo by author

the compound known as Padang ("field," referring to the playing field where cricket matches took place). Perhaps most evocative, especially in light of the discussions in this chapter and the preceding one, is the old, whitewashed building of the Malay Military Mosque standing on the small, winding Java Lane. Mosques known locally as "the Malay Mosque" were erected in towns across Ceylon, often in the context of regimental life, including in Badulla, Kurunegala, Kandy, Trincomalee and Hambantota. The mosque in Kinniya, on the island's northeast shore, boasts a trilingual sign asserting its resonant name: "The Jawa Jummah Mosque" (Figure 9.3).

In what may be a mirror image of these memorializations of Java and the Malay world in Ceylon and Sri Lanka, there are sites in Indonesia that, I believe, carry the memories of the small island and the mythic and human memories encapsulated in its names. Gunung Srandil (Mt. Srandil) near Cilacap on central Java's southern coast bears the Javanized form of the name Sarandib. Recalling through its name and topography Adam's fall on another, distant mountain, it is, fittingly, a site of spiritual and religious importance where many perform pilgrimages (M. *berziarah*), praying at the nearby sacred tombs and meditating in the caves situated on the mountain's slopes.[58] Sunan Kuning is said to be interred in one of the tombs and, even if historically inaccurate or referring to another man with the same epithet, this reference recalls the young Javanese prince Radèn Mas Garendi who was born in Ceylon, taken to Java where his grandfather Amangkurat III was reburied in the royal cemetery, then exiled again in 1743 as Sunan Kuning, having been briefly elevated to the throne in Kartasura during the Chinese War. Nearby is Gunung Selok (Mt. Selok, which could be a misrepresentation of Selong), also a site of Javanese ascetic practices that is associated with foundational figures of the Mataram lineage. On the island of Lombok, east of Java, Bukit Selong (Selong Hill) towers majestically over the rice fields. It too may have been linked to traditions of Adam and the mountain, with the names Sarandib and Selong with time viewed as interchangeable, perhaps due to stories told by exiles returning from Ceylon. Such intertwinings of names, stories, images and the imagination across the sea between Ceylon and Java were highlighted in several chapters by way of their textual and visual manifestations. The image of a tree, appearing in an 1814 dynastic diagram of Java's rulers and adorning this book's cover,[59] is a case in point. Like a map both spatial and temporal, it charts the history of Javanese royalty from Adam, whose name appears prominently at the bottom of the trunk, all the way to the exiled king Amangkurat III, referred to as "Amangkurat Selong" on a treetop leaf. The towering tree with its somewhat twisted yet sturdy trunk thus visually suggests a dynastic continuity between Adam's original expulsion to earth as humanity's progenitor and the much later, but linked, exile of Javanese royals, and affirms both banishment and belonging, with the king still associated with the foliage sprouting from the living tree, rooted in Java, despite his fate of being "Ceyloned." The *Syair Hemop*, for example, which depicted Ceylon's geography, its highland kingdom of Kandy, its riches, customs and internal politics from Java, can be viewed as a text that is in conversation, albeit indirectly, with one like the *Hikayat Tuan Gusti* that retold Javanese history, and imagined Javanese life in detail, from the shores of Ceylon.

Reading the *Hikayat* and other Sri Lankan Malay texts in the present invites us to rethink the boundaries of the "Malay world." It also provides clear evidence for ties, circulations and exchanges across the Indonesian

---

[58] Among the pilgrims have been two of modern Indonesia's presidents: Sukarno and Suharto. On the traditions associated with the mountain and its role as a site of spiritual and religious rituals, especially for the country's leaders, see Sidik Purnama Negara, *Gunung Srandil dan Selok. Tempat Olah dan Laku Spiritual Kejawen Para Pemimpin Indonesia* (Yogyakarta: Penerbit Narasi, 2010).

[59] British Library Board Or 15932, f. 72. See Figure 4.1.

Archipelago, port cities in peninsular Malaysia, Singapore, Sri Lanka, south India and beyond, and displays an important dimension of such transregional contact across Islamic societies – participation in literary networks – that has been central to the Malay community's sense of identity for at least two centuries. Gaining an expanded view of an already vast and diverse Malay world is one part of the story. Another is thinking about the history and writings of the Malays, a minority within Sri Lanka's Muslim minority, through the particular prism of nomenclature which means, in part, considering practices of naming as sites of contestation where the less powerful often lose out but, concurrently, suggests how recovered names – like Sarandib – can reorient our vision and offer alternative, competing chronologies and spatial interpretations that are different than those promoted by "the center."

For Sri Lanka's history, thinking in terms of "Sarandib" provides a way to connect the island to other places and to Muslims across space and time because of the religious and historical importance of this designation and its appearance in multiple stories and textual traditions. Sarandib as a land reminiscent of Paradise in its riches and beauty, a gateway, an entry point to the world as Adam first saw it. And later (with this history as backdrop) – an island favored by Muslim traders traversing the Indian Ocean as well as many a pilgrim ship from Southeast Asia making its way to Arabia. Thus, invoking the name "Sarandib" offers inroads to considering the experiences and worldviews of the minority community of Malays, who are often marginalized in official histories and grand narratives of the island. And it also suggests going beyond the boundaries of colonial and national histories to assess Sri Lanka's place in competing and overlapping narratives of the past in the region and further afield. In this vein, a more nuanced history of Sri Lanka would contribute also to complicating Indonesian and Indian Ocean histories and historiographies.

Names – Sarandib, Lanka, Ceylon – bearing long histories and laden with particular sensibilities and associations afforded a point of departure. Related to names are additional words and their etymologies: The name "Ceylon" transformed into a Malay and Javanese verb connoting banishment (M. *disailankan*; J. *dipunsélongaken*) while "Sarandib" inspired "serendipity," associated with searching, finding the new and unexpected. These two words deriving from the island's names and speaking respectively to displacement and discovery, exile and fortuitous encounters encompass the Malays' history and the ways it was remembered, retold and imagined.

Glossary

Adipati Anom	Javanese crown prince
alun alun	a broad field in front of a Javanese palace or regent's residence where rituals, tournaments and other events took place
baba	a term of address and honorific, typically used in the Indonesian–Malay world to refer to men of Chinese descent
babad	a Javanese chronicle, typically written in verse
bupati	a regent, a high official in the court or the countryside
dain	from *daeng*, a nobility title of the Bugis of south Sulawesi
encik	a polite Malay term of address for a male or female
gundul	a name used in Ceylon/Sri Lanka to refer to Malay written in Arabic script; in Java (spelled *gundhul*) it refers to the writing of Javanese in unvocalized Arabic script
hikayat	a story; also a popular genre of Malay prose writing
jawi	a name used across Southeast Asia to refer to Malay written in the Arabic script; known in Ceylon/Sri Lanka as *gundul*
katib	a writer or scribe; a preacher or official at the mosque
kyai	a male title of respect, often used for Muslim scholars; can also be applied to a revered heirloom
lebai	a Tamil term for a learned elder; a Muslim religious official or scholar

Mas	a Javanese title of lower nobility; among Malays in Ceylon/Sri Lanka it was given as part of a proper name (as was the title Tuan)
muhandiram	an influential post in the system of native headmen in Ceylon
nyonya	a term for a married woman, typically of Chinese descent; counterpart of *baba*
Pangéran	a Javanese prince
pantun	a popular Malay genre of four-lined poems with internal assonance, often improvised and sung; known in Ceylon/Sri Lanka as *pantong*
Patih	a prime minister, chief councilor or administrative officer to a Javanese king or regent
pendhapa	a large square pavilion or hall in a Javanese house or palace featuring a raised floor, open sides and an elaborate roof and used for receptions and performances
pusaka	an heirloom, especially a royal heirloom with supernatural powers, often in the form of a gong, saddle or keris
Radèn	a Javanese title applied to male royal descendants of middle rank
Radèn Ayu	a Javanese title for a married female of noble descent
Radèn Ngabèhi	a Javanese title for a married male or female of noble descent
Susuhunan, Susunan, Sunan	titles of the kings of Kartasura and Surakarta; Sunan is also used for the early propagators of Islam in Java, known as the *wali sanga*
syair	a form of traditional Malay verse, consisting of four-line verses with each line containing four words; among the most popular of genres across Muslim Southeast Asia
Tuan	a Malay title of respect; among Malays in Ceylon/Sri Lanka was given as part of a proper name (as was the title Mas)
Tumenggung	a high Javanese administrative rank; title applied to a regent
wasilan	a mantra-like talismanic text, also known as a *doa*; recited for personal gain, success and

| | prosperity, as well as for the purposes of recovery from illness, overcoming danger in travel, childbirth and war, and seeking blessings for marriage and old age |
| *zikir* | from Arabic "remembrance"; ceremonially reciting the names of God |

Bibliography

Malay and Javanese Primary Sources: Manuscripts and Print

Angkatan Menulis Ism. BL, EAP609/17/3.

Anonymous poem. Hussainmiya Collection, Department of National Archives, Sri Lanka. MF182.

Arabu-Tamil Compendium. BL, EAP609/10/1.

Babad [untitled]. Inscribed Semarang, 1834. John Rylands Collection, University of Manchester Library. Javanese MS 18.

Babad Jawi Kartasura. vol. 4. Transliterated by Sri Soehartini. Jakarta: Departemen Pendidikan dan Kebudayaan Proyek Penerbitan Buku Sastra Indonesia dan Daerah, 1987.

Babad Kartasura. Inscribed Surakarta, n.d., Reksa Pustaka Library, Kadipatèn Mangkunagaran. MS MN 199. Transliterated as B21d by Mulyo Hutomo, n.d.

Babad Kartasura. Inscribed Surakarta, 1844, Reksa Pustaka Library, Kadipatèn Mangkunagaran. MS MN 200. Transliterated as B21c by Mulyo Hutomo, n.d.

Babad Tanah Jawi, 21 vols. Betawi Sentrum: Bale Pustaka, 1940.

Burhan Lye. *Syair Kisahnya Kabar Wolenter Benggali.* Inscribed Ceylon, 1861, Perpustakaan Negara Malaysia, Kuala Lumpur. MS PNM 1061.

Cabaton, Antoine. "Raden Paku, Sunan de Giri (légende musulmane javanaise). Texte malais, traduction française et notes." *Revue de l'histoire des religions* 54 (1906): 374–400.

Citrasantana. *Babad ing Mangkunagaran.* Inscribed Surakarta, 1918, Reksa Pustaka Library, Kadipatèn Mangkunagaran. MS MN 208B.

Doole-Cassim Tidbits. BL, EAP609/28/1.

Encik Hakim. *Hikayat Seri Rama.* Inscribed Trincomalee, 1859, Perpustakaan Negara Malaysia, Kuala Lumpur. MS PNM 1055.

Greasy, A. H. *Dendang Sayang Pantun Selong.* Colombo: A. H. Greasy, n.d. (BL, EAP609/7/1).

Hatmowasito, S. *Babad Giyanti dumugi Prayut: Gancaran.* Inscribed Surakarta, 1977, Reksa Pustaka Library, Kadipatèn Mangkunagaran. MN 693 (c).

Hikayat Indera Quraishi. Inscribed Colombo, 1881, Perpustakaan Negara Malaysia, Kuala Lumpur. MS PNM 431.

Hikayat Seri Rama. Inscribed Colombo, 1865, Perpustakaan Negara Malaysia, Kuala Lumpur. MS PNM 1056.

Jurangpati, Muhammad Yusuf Jailani. *Hikayat Amir Hamzah.* Inscribed Kandy, c. 1870–1880, Perpustakaan Negara Malaysia, Kuala Lumpur. MS PMN 1056.

Kitab Panthong Suatu. Inscribed Ceylon, n.d., Perpustakaan Negara Malaysia, Kuala Lumpur. MS PNM 431.

Letter from Cucunda Radèn Tumenggung Wira Kushuma ibn Mas Kreti to the governor-general and Council of the Indies. Colombo, 1806. Leiden University Library, MS LOr 2241-I (24).

Letter from Descendants of Sultan Bacan Muhammad Sah al-Din to the governor-general and Council of the Indies. Colombo, 1792. Leiden University Library, MS Cod. Or. 2241-Ia (11).

Letter from Pangéran Mas Adipati Mangkurat to the governor-general and Council of the Indies. Colombo, 1806. Leiden University Library, MS LOr 2241-I (23).

al-Makassari, Yusuf. *al-Nafḥat al-Sailāniyyah fi manḥat al-Raḥmāniyyah,* in *'Ilm at-Taṣawwuf.* Composed Ceylon, n.d., Perpustakaan Nasional Republik Indonesia, Jakarta. MS PNRI A 101.

Malay Compendium. BL, EAP450/1/2.

Mangkunagara I. *Serat Babad Pakunegaran.* Composed Surakarta c. 1757, inscribed 1779. British Library, Add. MS 12318.

Mas Ngabéhi Rongga Panambangan III. *Babad Kartasura.* Inscribed Surakarta, 1852, Reksa Pustaka Library, Kadipatèn Mangkunagaran. MS MN 185. Transliterated as MN 185 TT (B21i) by Hatmo Wasito, 1981.

Morset. *Hikayat Muhammad Hanafiyah.* Inscribed Colombo, 1894, Perpustakaan Negara Malaysia, Kuala Lumpur. MS PNM 453.

Mursit. *Syair Sultan Abdul Muluk.* Inscribed Colombo, n.d., Perpustakaan Negara Malaysia, Kuala Lumpur. MS PNM 450.

Hikayat Ahmad Muhammad. Inscribed Kampung Wekande, Colombo, 1890, Perpustakaan Negara Malaysia, Kuala Lumpur. MS PNM 1058.

Hikayat Tuan Gusti. Inscribed Ceylon, 1897. Hussainmiya Collection, Department of National Archives, Sri Lanka. MF 182.

Rahim, Mas Naleera. *Wasilan.* BL, EAP609/25/2.

Rahim, Noor R. "Reminiscence of Our Proud Malay Heritage." Unpublished manuscript, June 2015.

Ronggawarsita. *Babad Itih IV: Kartasura.* Composed Surakarta mid-nineteenth century, inscribed mid- to late nineteenth century, Reksa Pustaka Library, Kadipatèn Mangkunagaran. Transliterated as MN 88 TT by Djajeng Susarno, n.d.

Saldin, Baba Ounus. *Kitab Segala Peringatan.* Inscribed Ceylon, n.d., Dewan Bahasa and Pustaka Library, Kuala Lumpur. MS 137.

Subhana Mauludum Afurudhum. Inscribed Kandy, 1856. BL, EAP609/5/5.

Kitab Awrad. Inscribed Ceylon, 1905. Private Collection of Warnishiya Dole.

Syair Faiḍ al-Abād. Colombo: Alamat Langkapuri, 1905.

Saldin Family Records. BL, EAP609/1/8.

Saliman ibn Asmara. *Hikayat Nabi Berperang dengan Raja Kaibar.* Inscribed Ceylon, 1861, Perpustakaan Negara Malaysia, Kuala Lumpur. MS PNM 1061.

Salimudeen. *Hikayat Qobad Shah.* Inscribed Colombo, 1865, Perpustakaan Negara Malaysia, Kuala Lumpur. MS PNM 1063.

Hikayat Indera Putra. Inscribed Colombo, 1866, Perpustakaan Negara Malaysia, Kuala Lumpur. MS PNM 1063.

Hikayat Isma Yatim. Inscribed Colombo, 1871, Perpustakaan Negara Malaysia, Kuala Lumpur. MS PNM 1063.

Samsudeen ibn al-Taif. *Hikayat Ahmad Muhammad.* Inscribed Malapingi, 1867, Perpustakaan Negara Malaysia, Kuala Lumpur. MS PNM 1063.

Samud. N.d., Leiden University Library. MS LOr 4001.

Serat Samud. Inscribed Yogyakarta, 1884, Pura Pakualaman Library. MS PP St. 80.

Sinthaby Badulla Diary. BL, EAP609/15/1.

Sunan Bonang Fragment. Inscribed Ceylon, n.d., Hussainmiya Collection, Department of National Archives, Sri Lanka. MF 178.

Syair Ibadat. Inscribed Ceylon, n.d., Perpustakaan Negara Malaysia, Kuala Lumpur. MS PNM 423.

Tales of the Prophets and miscellaneous. BL, EAP450/2/1.

Tuan ibn Cenci. *Hikayat Shah Kobad.* Inscribed Agrapatni, 1892, Perpustakaan Negara Malaysia, Kuala Lumpur. MS PNM 446.

Weerabangsa, Mas Anom. *Pelbagai Catatan.* Inscribed Ceylon, n.d., Perpustakaan Negara Malaysia, Kuala Lumpur. MS PNM 1062.

Weerabangsa, Mas Muhammad Ghais. *Hikayat Seri Rama.* Inscribed Trincomalee, n.d., Hussainmiya Collection, Department of National Archives, Sri Lanka. MF 176.

Weerabangsa, Mas Tuan Jury. *Weerabangsa Family Notes.* BL, EAP609/17/4.

Weerabangsa, Tuan Jury ibn Husain. *Hikayat Nabi Musa Munajat.* Inscribed Kandy, 1892, Perpustakaan Negara Malaysia, Kuala Lumpur. MS PNM 430.

Yasadipura I. *Babad Giyanti.* Surakarta: Budi Utama, 1917.

Babad Giyanti. 21 vols. Betawi Sentrum: Bale Pustaka, 1937–1939.

Babad Giyanti dumugi Prayut. Composed Surakarta, late eighteenth century, inscribed 1976, Reksa Pustaka Library, Kadipatèn Mangkunagaran. MS MN 692.

Babad Prayut. Composed Surakarta, late eighteenth century, inscribed 1854, Reksa Pustaka Library, Kadipatèn Mangkunagaran. MS MN 212. Transcribed as MN 212 TT by Suroso, 1980.

Babad Prayut. Composed Surakarta, late eighteenth century, inscribed 1857, Reksa Pustaka Library, Kadipatèn Mangkunagaran. MS MN 211. Transcribed as MN 211 TT by Mulyo Hartono and M. Husodo, n.d.

Ménak Serandhil. Betawi Sentrum: Bale Pustaka, 1933.

Serat Rama. Weltevreden: Bale Pustaka, 1925.

Other Primary Sources

Printed Sources

Ahmad, S. Maqbul (ed. and trans.). *India and the Neighbouring Territories in the Kitāb nuzhat al-mushtāq fī 'khtirāq al-'āfāq of al-Sharīf al-Idrīsī: A Translation, with Commentary, of the Passages Relating to India, Pakistan, Ceylon, Parts of Afghanistan, and the Andaman, Nicobar, and Maldive Islands, etc.* Leiden: Brill, 1960.

Brohier, Pieter (trans.). "Phillipus Baldaeus: A True and Exact Description of the Great Island of Ceylon," *Ceylon Historical Journal* 8.1–4 (1958–1959): 1–403.

Capper, John. *Old Ceylon: Sketches of Ceylon Life in the Olden Time.* Colombo: Ceylon Times Press, 1877. Repr. University of California Libraries.

Codrington, H. W. (ed.). "Diary of Mr. John D'Oyly," *Journal of the Ceylon Branch of the Royal Asiatic Society* 25.69 (1917): iii–xvi, 1–269. Repr. Navrang, 1995.

Cordiner, James. *A Description of Ceylon, containing an account of the country, inhabitants, and natural products; with narratives of a tour round the island in 1800, the campaign in Candy in 1803, and a journey to Ramisseram in 1804.* 2 vols. London: Longman, Hurst, Rees, and Orme, 1807.

Cummings, William (trans. and ed.). *The Makassar Annals.* Leiden: KITLV, 2011.

Ibn Kathīr. *Stories of the Prophets*, trans. Mohammed Hilmi al-Ahmed. Beirut: DKI, 2013.

Johnston, Arthur. *Narrative of the operations of a detachment in an expedition to Candy, in the Island of Ceylon, in the year 1804.* Dublin: James McGlashan, 1854.

Jones, Russell. "One of the Oldest Malay Manuscripts Extant: The Laud Or. 291 Manuscript of the *Hikayat Seri Rama*," *Indonesia Circle*, November 1986 (41): 49–53.

Jubilee Book of the Malay Cricket Club. Colombo: Ceylon Malay Cricket Club, 1924.

Lee, Samuel (trans.). *Travels of Ibn Batuta; Translated from the Abridged Arabic Manuscript Copies, preserved in the Public Library of Cambridge.* London: Oriental Translation Committee, 1829.

Marshall, Henry. *Ceylon: A General Description of the Island and its Inhabitants with An Historical Sketch of the Conquest of the Colony by the English.* London: William H. Allen and Co., 1846.

al-Masʿūdī, ʿAlī b. al-Ḥusayn. *Murūj al-dhahab wa-maʿādin al-jawāhir: les prairies d'or*, ed. and trans. C. Barbier de Meynard and Pavet de Courteille. Paris: L'Imprimerie Impériale, 1861.

Meddegama, Udaya Prasanta (trans.). *Ingrīsi Haṭana.* Unpublished translation, [Peradeniya, 2010].

Millie, Julian (trans.). *Celebration of the Desires through the Narration of the Deeds (Manaqib) of the Crown of Saints and the Convincing Beacon among Allah's Beloved Friends; Sheikh Abdul Qadir al-Jaelani*. Queenscliff: Joseph Helmi, 2003.

Paranavitana, K. D. (trans. and ed.). *Memoir of Librecht Hooreman commander of Jaffna 1748 for his successor Jacob de Jong*. Colombo: Department of National Archives, Sri Lanka, 2009.

Percival, Robert. *An Account of the Island of Ceylon: containing its history, geography, natural history, with the manner and customs of its various inhabitants: to which is added, the journal of an embassy to the court of Kandy*. London: C. and R. Baldwin, 1803.

Philalethes, A. M. *History of Ceylon from the Earliest Period to the Year 1815*. London: n.p., 1817. Repr. Cambridge: Cambridge University Press, 2012.

Rosenthal, Franz (trans. and annot.). *The History of al-Ṭabarī. Vol. I: General Introduction and From the Creation to the Flood*. Albany: State University of New York Press, 1989.

Rumpf, Isaac Augustus. *Travel Diary of Isaac Augustus Rumpf, the Dutch Governor of Ceylon (1716–1723)*, trans. and ed. K. D. Paranavitana. Colombo: Department of National Archives, Sri Lanka, 2015.

Sachau, Edward C. (ed.). *Alberuni's India. An account of the religion, philosophy, literature, geography, chronology, astronomy, customs, laws and astrology of India about AD 1030*. London: Kegan Paul, Trench, Trubner and Co., 1910.

Sirr, Henry Charles. *Ceylon and the Cingalese. Their history, government and religion. The antiquities, institutions, produce, revenue and capabilities of the island with anecdotes illustrating the manners and customs of the people*. London: William Shoberl, 1850.

Skinner, Thomas. *Fifty Years in Ceylon: An Autobiography*, ed. Annie Skinner. London: W. H. Allen & Co. 1891.

Togan, A. Zeki Validi (ed.). *Memoirs of the Archeological Survey of India No. 53: Biruni's Picture of the World*. Delhi: Latifi Press, 1937.

Archives

Department of National Archives, Sri Lanka

Lot 1 (VOC Archive)

SLNA 1/23, Political Council Minutes, July 18, 1691.
SLNA 1/51, Political Council Minutes, January 1717 (no day noted).
SLNA 1/61B, Political Council Minutes, June 13, 1727.
SLNA 1/69, Political Council Minutes, November 14, 1733.
SLNA 1/73, Political Council Minutes, August 30, 1736.
SLNA 1/95, Political Council Minutes, May 5 and August 24, 1745.
SLNA 1/109, Political Council Minutes, April 28, 1750.
SLNA 1/122, Political Council Minutes, October 5, 1757.
SLNA 1/173, Political Council Minutes, December 5, 1776.
SLNA 1/176, Political Council Minutes, June 19, 1778.

SLNA 1/181, Political Council Minutes, 1780.
SLNA 1/183, Political Council Minutes, November 30, 1781.
SLNA 1/200, Political Council Minutes, March 8, 1788.
SLNA 1/218, Political Council Minutes, May 19, 1792.
SLNA 1/225, Political Council Minutes, January 9, 1794.
SLNA 1/232, Political Council Minutes, November 24, 1795.
SLNA 1/3956, List of Dutch State Exiles in Ceylon, 1788.
SLNA 1/4722, Political Council Minutes, May 23, 1791.

British Ceylon Archival Documents
(Catalogues of the British government in Sri Lanka are unpublished but available
in typescript in Mottau, Index to the Dispatches of the Governors (1798–1822),
Department of National Archives, Sri Lanka

SLNA 5/7, Brownrigg to Bathurst, August 17, 1814.
SLNA 5/78, Maitland to Windham, February 28, 1807.
SLNA 55/1, North to Court of Directors, February 26, 1799.

Hong Kong Public Record Office

Reference C.O. 129/39.
Reference C.O. 129/41.

National Archives, The Hague

Hague letters NL-HaNA, VOC, 1.04.02, inv. nr. 8939. Tommengung
    Surapati to his mother, wives and children, Ceylon to Batavia, July
    11, 1724.
Hague letters NL-HaNa, VOC, 1.04.02 inv. nr. 8942. Pangéran Pur-
    baya to his wife Ratu Purbaya, Ceylon to Batavia, December
    31, 1725.
VOC 2787, Overgek. Brieven & Papieren 1752, Pakubuwana III to
    Batavia, 1751.
VOC 2825, Overgek. Brieven & Papieren 1754, van Hohendorff to
    Batavia, May 24, 1753.

Newspapers

Alamat Langkapuri
The Ceylon Observer
Java Government Gazette
Kajawèn
The Strait Times

Secondary Sources

Aboosally, M. L. M. *Dafther Jailany: A Historical Account of the Dafther Jailany Rock Cave Mosque*. Colombo: Sharm Aboosally, 2002.

Abu Amar, H. Imron. *Sunan Kalijaga Kadilangu Demak*. Kudus: Menara Kudus, 1992.

Abu Hamid. *Syekh Yusuf Makassar. Seorang Ulama, Sufi, dan Penjuang*. Jakarta: Yayasan Obor Indonesia, 1994.

Aldrich, Robert. "The Return of the Throne: The Repatriation of the Kandyan Regalia to Ceylon," in Robert Aldrich and Cindy McCreery (eds.), *Crowns and Colonies: European Monarchies and Overseas Empires*. Manchester: Manchester University Press, 2016, 139–162.

ʿĀlim, Tayka Shuʿayb. *Arabic, Arwi and Persian in Sarandib and Tamil Nadu*. Madras: Imāmul ʿArūs Trust, 1993.

Amrith, Sunil S. *Migration and Diaspora in Modern Asia*. Cambridge: Cambridge University Press, 2011.

Anthonisz, R. G. *Digest of Resolutions of the Dutch Political Council Colombo, 1644–1796*. Colombo: Department of National Archives, Sri Lanka, 2012.

Arps, Bernard. "The Song Guarding at Night: Grounds for Cogency in a Javanese Incantation," in Stephen C. Headley (ed.), *Towards an Anthropology of Prayer: Javanese Ethnolinguistic Studies/Vers une anthropologie de la prière: études ethnolinguistiques javanaises*. Aix-en-Provence: Publications de l'Université de Provence, 1996, 47–113.

Arps, Bernard and Annabel Teh Gallop. *Golden Letters: Writing Traditions of Indonesia/Surat Emas: Budaya Tulis Di Indonesia*. London: British Library, 1991.

Axel, Brian Keith. "The Diasporic Imaginary." *Public Culture* 14.2 (2002): 411–428.

Azra, Azyumardi. *Jaringan Ulama: Timur Tengah dan Kepulauan Nusantara Abad XVII dan XVIII*. Bandung: Mizan, 1999.

Barnard, Timothy P. (ed.). *Contesting Malayness: Malay Identity across Boundaries*. Singapore: NUS Press, 2014.

Becker, A. L. "Silence across Languages," in A. L. Becker, *Beyond Translation. Essays toward a Modern Philology*. Ann Arbor: University of Michigan Press, 1995, 283–294.

Biedermann, Zoltan and Alan Strathern (eds.). *Sri Lanka at the Crossroads of History*. London: UCL Press, 2017.

Brah, Avtar. *Cartographies of Diaspora: Contesting Identities*. London and New York: Routledge, 1996.

Brakel, L. F. "Two Indian Epics in Malay." *Archipel* 20 (1980): 143–160.

Bruinessen, Martin van. "Kitab Kuning: Books in Arabic Script Used in the Pesantren Milieu." *BKI* 146 (1990): 226–269.

Burah, Tuan Arifin. *Saga of the Exiled Royal Javanese Unearthed*. Dehiwala: Tuan Arifin Burah, 2006.

Carey, Peter. *The Power of Prophecy: Prince Dipanagara and the End of an Old Order in Java, 1785–1855*. Leiden: KITLV, 2008.

Carey, Peter and Vincent Houben, "Spirited Srikandhis and Sly Sumbadras: The Social, Political and Economic Role of Women at the Central Javanese

Courts in the Eighteenth and Early Nineteenth Centuries," in Elsbeth Locher-Scholten and Anke Borkent-Niehof (eds.), *Indonesian Women in Focus: Past and Present Notions* (Leiden: KITLV, 1987), 12–42.

Day, Tony. "The Drama of Bangun Tapa's Exile in Ambon," in L. Gesick (ed.), *Centers, Symbols, and Hierarchies: Essays on the Classical States of Southeast Asia.* New Haven: Yale, 1983, 125–193.

Deckard, Sharae Grace. "Exploited Edens: Paradise Discourse in Colonial and Postcolonial Literature." Unpublished Ph.D. dissertation. University of Warwick, 2007.

de Silva, K. M. *A History of Sri Lanka.* Berkeley: University of California Press, 1981.

Dirks, Nicholas B. *The Hollow Crown: Ethnohistory of an Indian Kingdom.* Cambridge: Cambridge University Press, 1988.

Drewes, G. W. J. *Directions for Travellers on the Mystic Path: Zakariyya Al-Ansari's Kitāb Fatḥ Al-Raḥmān and Its Indonesian Adaptations.* Verhandelingen van het Koninklijk Instituut Voor Taal-, Land- en Volkenkunde, vol. 81. The Hague: Martinus Nijhoff, 1977.

Ekadjati, Edi S. dan Undang A. Darsa (eds.). *Katalog Induk Naskah-Naskah Nusantara. Jawa Barat: Koleksi Lima Lembaga.* Jakarta: Yayasan Obor Indonesia, 1999.

Ekama, Kate. "Slavery in Dutch Colombo: A Social History." Unpublished MA thesis. University of Leiden, 2012.

Elsner, John. "Hagiographic Geography: Travel and Allegory in the Life of Apollonius of Tyana." *Journal of Hellenic Studies* 117 (1997): 22–37.

Ernst, Carl W. *Refractions of Islam in India: Situating Sufism and Yoga.* New Delhi: Sage, 2016.

Fang, Liaw Yock. *A History of Classical Malay Literature.* Trans. Razif Bahari and Harry Aveling. Singapore: ISEAS, 2013.

Florida, Nancy K. *Javanese Literature in Surakarta Manuscripts: Introduction and Manuscripts of the Karaton Surakarta*, vol. I. Ithaca: Cornell University Press, 1993.

Writing the Past, Inscribing the Future: History as Prophecy in Colonial Java. Durham: Duke University Press, 1995.

Javanese Literature in Surakarta Manuscripts: Manuscripts of the Mangkunagaran Palace, vol. II. Ithaca: Cornell University Press, 2000.

Javanese Literature in Surakarta Manuscripts: Manuscripts of the Radya Pustaka Museum and the Hardjonagaran Library, vol. III. Ithaca: Cornell University Press, 2012.

Fontein, Jan. "The Abduction of Sita: Notes on a Stone Relief from Eastern Java." *Boston Museum Bulletin*, 71 (1973): 21–35.

Francisco, Jaun R. "The Ramayana in the Philippines," in K. Krishnamoorthy and Jithendra Nath (eds.), *A Critical Inventory of Ramayana Studies in the World: Foreign Languages.* New Delhi: Sahitya Akademi, 1993, 119–145.

Godakumbura, C. E. "Ramayana in Sri Lanka and Lanka in the Ramayana," in K. Krishnamoorthy and Jithendra Nath (eds.), *A Critical Inventory of Ramayana Studies in the World: Foreign Languages.* New Delhi: Sahitya Akademi, 1993, 95–118.

Green, Nile. *Islam and the Army in Colonial India: Sepoy Religion in the Service of Empire*. Cambridge: Cambridge University Press, 2009.

Griffiths, Arlo. "Imagine Laṅkapura at Prambanan," in Andrea Acri, Helen Creese and Arlo Griffiths (eds.), *From Laṅkā Eastwards: The Rāmāyaṇa in the Literature and Visual Arts of Indonesia*. Leiden: KITLV, 2011, 133–148.

Guruge, Ananda W. P. "Sri Lankan Attitude to the Ramayana: A Historical Analysis." *Indologica Taurinensia* 19–20 (1993–1994): 131–146.

Hamid, Ismail. *Kesusasteraan Melayu Lama dari Warisan Peradaban Islam*. Kuala Lumpur: Penerbit Fajar Bakti, 1983.

The Malay Islamic Hikayat. Bangi: Universiti Kebangsaan Malaysia, 1983.

"Islam dalam Sejarah dan Masyarakat Melayu Sri Lanka." *Sari* 9 (1991): 25–41.

Hariwijaya. *Kisah Para Wali*. Yogyakarta: Nirwana, 2003.

Harun Mat Piah. "Tradisi Kesusasteraan Melayu Sri Lanka dalam Konteks Kesusasteraan Melayu Tradisional Nusantara: Satu Tinjauan Ringkas." *Sari* 4.2 (1986): 63–82.

Hijjas, Mulaika. *Victorious Wives: The Disguised Heroine in Nineteenth-Century Malay Syair*. Singapore: NUS Press, 2011.

Hodgson, Marshall G. *The Venture of Islam*, 3 vols. Chicago: University of Chicago Press, 1974.

Holt, John Clifford (ed.). *The Sri Lanka Reader: History, Culture, Politics*. Durham and London: Duke University Press, 2011.

Hooykaas, C. "The Paradise on Earth in Lenka (Old-Javanese Ramayana XXIV. 87–126)." *BKI* 114.3 (1958): 265–291.

Hussainmiya, B. A. "'Melayu Bahasa': Some Preliminary Observations on the Malay Creole of Sri Lanka." *Sari* 4.1 (1986): 19–30.

Lost Cousins: The Malays of Sri Lanka. Bangi: Universiti Kebangsaan Malaysia, 1987.

Orang Rejimen: The Malays of the Ceylon Rifle Regiment. Bangi: Universiti Kebangsaan Malaysia, 1990.

Hussein, Asiff. *Sarandib: An Ethnological Study of the Muslims of Sri Lanka*. Dehiwala: Asiff Hussein, 2007.

Ikram, Achadiati. *Hikayat Sri Rama: suntingan naskah disertai telaah amanat dan struktur*. Jakarta: Universitas Indonesia, 1980.

Jappie, Saarah. "Jawi dari Jauh." *Indonesia and the Malay World* 40.117 (2012): 143–159.

Jones, Russell. "Ten Conversion Myths from Indonesia," in Nehemia Levtzion (ed.), *Conversion to Islam*. New York and London: Holmes and Meier, 1979, 129–158.

Juynboll, H. H. "Eene Episode uit het Oudindische Ramayana Vergeleken met de Javaansche en Maleische Bewerkingen." *BKI* 50.1 (1899): 59–66.

"Eene Episode uit het Oudindische Ramayana Vergeleken met de Javaansche en Maleische Bewerkingen." *BKI* 54.1 (1902): 501–565.

Kahn, Joel. *Other Malays: Nationalism and Cosmopolitanism in the Modern Malay World*. Singapore: NUS Press, 2006.

Kern, W. "Aantekeningen op de Sja'ir Hémop (Sja'ir Kompeni Welanda berperang dengan Tjina)." *Tijdschrift voor Indische Taal-, Land- en Volkenkunde*
82.2 (1948): 211–257.

Kevin, Kenny. *Diaspora: A Very Short Introduction.* New York: Oxford University
Press, 2014.

Khair, Tabish. "African and Asian Travel Texts in the Light of Europe:
An Introduction," in Tabish Khair, Martin Leer, Justin D. Edwards and
H. Ziadeh (eds.), *Other Routes: 1500 Years of African and Asian Travel
Writing.* Oxford: Signal Books, 2006, 1–27.

Kumar, Ann. *Surapati: Man and Legend.* Leiden: E. J. Brill, 1976.

Maier, Hendrik M. J. *We Are Playing Relatives: A Survey of Malay Writing.*
Leiden: KITLV Press, 2004.

Margana, Sri. "Caught between Empires: *Babad Mangkudiningratan* and the
Exile of Sultan Hamengkubuwana II of Yogyakarta, 1813–1826," in Ricci
(ed.), *Exile in Colonial Asia*, 117–138.

Marsden, William. *A Dictionary of the Malayan Language, to which is prefixed a
grammar with an introduction and praxis.* London: Cox and Batlis, 1812.

Massey, Doreen. *For Space.* London: Sage, 2005.

McDonald, Barbara. "Kawi and Kawi Miring: Old Javanese Literature in
Eighteenth-Century Java." Unpublished Ph.D. dissertation. Australian
National University, 1983.

McGilvray, Dennis. "Jailani: A Sufi Shrine in Sri Lanka," in Imtiaz Ahmad and
Helmut Reifeld (eds.), *Lived Islam in South Asia: Adaptation, Accommodation
and Conflict.* Delhi: Social Science Press, 2004, 273–289.

McLoughlin, Sean. "Religion, Religions, and Diaspora," in Ato Quayson and
Girish Daswani (eds.), *A Companion to Diaspora and Transnationalism.*
Oxford: Wiley-Blackwell, 2013, 125–138.

Methley, V. M. "The Ceylon Expedition of 1803." *Transactions of the Royal
Historical Society* 1 (1918): 92–128.

Miller, Kevin C. "Beyond Exile: The Ramayana as a Living Narrative among
Indo-Fijians in Fiji and New Zealand," in Farzana Gounder (ed.), *Narrative
and Identity Construction in the Pacific Islands.* Amsterdam: John Benjamins,
2015, 225–241.

Millie, Julian. "Supplicating, Naming, Offering: *Tawassul* in West Java," *Journal
of Southeast Asian Studies* 39.1 (2008): 107–122.

Milner, Anthony. *The Malays.* Oxford: Wiley-Blackwell, 2008.

Mohamad, Maznah and Syed Muhd Khairudin Aljunied (eds.). *Melayu: The
Politics, Poetics and Paradoxes of Malayness.* Singapore: NUS Press, 2011.

Mohammad, Afsar. *The Festival of Pīrs: Popular Islam and Shared Devotion in
South India.* New York: Oxford University Press, 2013.

Negara, Sidik Purnama. *Gunung Srandil dan Selok. Tempat Olah dan Laku Spiritual
Kejawen Para Pemimpin Indonesia.* Yogyakarta: Penerbit Narasi, 2010.

Noertjahajo, A. M. *Cerita Rakyat Sekitar Wali Sanga.* Jakarta: Pradnya Paramita,
1974.

Nordhoff, Sebastian (ed.). *The Genesis of Sri Lanka Malay: A Case of Extreme
Language Contact.* Leiden: Brill, 2012.

Obeyesekere, Gananath. *The Doomed King: A Requiem for Śri Vikrama Rajasinha*. Colombo: Sailfish, 2017.

Overbeck, H. "*Hikayat Maharaja Rawana.*" *JRAS Malayan Branch* 11.2 (1933): 111–132.

Paranavitana, K. D. "Dutch Political Council Minutes: An Introduction," in Anthonisz, *Digest*, 9–20.

Pigeaud, Theodore G. T. *Literature of Java*, 3 vols. The Hague: Martinus Nijhoff, 1967–1970.

Poerwadarminta, W. J. S. *Kamus Bausastra Jawa*. Groningen and Batavia: J. B. Wolters, 1939.

Powell, Geoffrey. *The Kandyan Wars: The British Army in Ceylon 1803–1818*. London: Leo Cooper, 1973.

Proudfoot, Ian. "From Recital to Sight Reading: The Silencing of Texts in Malaysia." *Indonesia and the Malay World* 30.87 (2002): 117–144.

Qadhiri, Shaik Hasan Sahib S. A. *The Divine Light of Nagore*. Nagore: Habeen & Fahira Publishers, 1998.

Quayson, Ato. "Postcolonialism and the Diasporic Imaginary," in Ato Quayson and Girish Daswani (eds.), *A Companion to Diaspora and Transnationalism*. Oxford: Wiley-Blackwell, 2013, 139–160.

Raben, Remco. "Batavia and Colombo: The Ethnic and Spatial Order of Two Colonial Cities, 1600–1800." Unpublished Ph.D. dissertation, Leiden University, 1996.

Rahim, Noor R. *Malay Culinary Delights*. Kotikawatta: Kumpulan Melayu Kotikawatta, 2015.

Rahimsyah, M. B. *Biografi dan Legenda Wali Sanga dan Para Ulama Penerus Perjuangannya*. Surabaya: Penerbit Indah, 1997.

Ramanujan, A. K. "Three Hundred Ramayanas: Five Examples and Three Thoughts on Translation," in Paula Richman (ed.), *Many Ramayanas: The Diversity of a Narrative Tradition in South Asia*. Berkeley: University of California Press, 1991, 22–48.

Remmelink, Willem G. J. *The Chinese War and the Collapse of the Javanese State 1725–1743*. Leiden: KITLV, 1994.

Ricci, Ronit. *Islam Translated: Literature, Conversion, and the Arabic Cosmopolis of South and Southeast Asia*. Chicago: University of Chicago Press, 2011.

"The Discovery of Javanese Writing in a Sri Lankan Malay Manuscript." *BKI* 168.4 (2012): 511–518.

"Remembering Java's Islamization: A View from Sri Lanka," in Nile Green and James Gelvin (eds.), *Global Muslims in the Age of Steam and Print*. Los Angeles: University of California Press, 2013, 185–203.

"Asian and Islamic Crossings: Malay Writing in Nineteenth-Century Sri Lanka." *South Asian History and Culture* 5.2 (2014): 179–194.

"Story, Sentence, Single Word: Translation Paradigms in Javanese and Malay Islamic Literature," in Sandra Bermann and Catherine Porter (eds.), *A Companion to Translation Studies*. Hoboken, NJ: Wiley-Blackwell, 2014, 543–556.

(ed.). *Exile in Colonial Asia: Kings, Convicts, Commemoration*. Honolulu: University of Hawai'i Press, 2016.

"From Java to Jaffna: Exile and Return in Dutch Asia in the Eighteenth Century," in Ricci (ed.), *Exile in Colonial Asia*, 94–116.

"Introduction," in Ricci (ed.), *Exile in Colonial Asia*, 1–19.

"Jawa, Melayu, Malay or Otherwise? The Shifting Nomenclature of the Sri Lankan Malays." *Indonesia and the Malay World* 44.130 (2016): 409–423.

"Reading between the Lines: A World of Interlinear Translation." *Journal of World Literature* 1.1 (2016): 68–80.

"Along the Frontiers of Religion, Language and War: Baba Ounus Saldin's *Syair Faid al-Abad*," in May Hawas (ed.), *The Routledge Companion to World Literature and World History*. London: Routledge, 2018, 82–92.

Ricklefs, Merle C. *Jogjakarta under Sultan Mangkubumi 1749–1792: A History of the Division of Java*. London: Oxford University Press, 1974.

Modern Javanese Historical Tradition: A Study of an Original Kartasura Chronicle and Related Materials. London: School of Oriental and African Studies, 1978.

"The Missing Pusakas of Kartasura, 1705–1737," in Sulastin Sutrisno, Darusuprapta and Sudaryanto (eds.), *Bahasa, Sastra, Budaya*. Yogyakarta: Gadjah Mada University Press, 1985, 601–630.

War, Culture and Economy in Java, 1677–1726: Asian and European Imperialism in the Early Kartasura Period. Sydney: Asian Studies Association of Australia, 1993.

The Seen and Unseen Worlds in Java, 1726–1749: History, Literature and Islam in the Court of Pakubuwana II. Honolulu: University of Hawai'i Press, 1998.

Mystic Synthesis in Java: A History of Islamization from the Fourteenth to the Early Nineteenth Centuries. Norwalk, CT: EastBridge, 2006.

A History of Modern Indonesia since c. 1200, 4th ed. Stanford: Stanford University Press, 2008.

"*Babad Giyanti*: sumber sejarah dan karya agung sastra Jawa," *Jumantara: Jurnal Manuskrip Nusantara* 5.2 (2014): 11–25.

Soul Catcher: Java's Fiery Prince Mangkunagaran I, 1726–1795. ASAA Southeast Asia Publications Series. Honolulu: University of Hawai'i, 2018.

Ricklefs, Merle C., P. Voorhoeve and Annabel Teh Gallop (eds.). *Indonesian Manuscripts in Great Britain: A Catalogue of Manuscripts in Indonesian Languages in British Public Collections*. Jakarta: EFEO and Yayasan Pustaka Obor Indonesia, 2014.

Rinkes, D. A. *Nine Saints of Java*, trans. H. M. Froger. Kuala Lumpur: Malaysian Sociological Research Institute, 1996.

Ronkel, Ph. S. van. *De Roman van Amir Hamza*. Leiden: E. J. Brill, 1895.

Mengenai Pengaruh Tatakalimat Arab Terhadap Tatakalimat Melayu, trans. A. Ikram. Jakarta: Bhratara, 1977. First published as "Over de Invloed der Arabische Syntaxis op de Maleische," *Tijdschrift voor Indische Taal-, Land- en Volkenkunde* 41 (1899): 498–528.

"Aanteekeningen op een Ouden Maleischen Ramajana-Tekst," *BKI* 75.1 (1919): 379–383.

Roorda van Eysinga, P. P. *Geschidenis van Sri Rama, beroemd Indisch Heroisch Dichtstuk, oorspronkelijk van Valmic en naar eene Maleische vertaling daarvan uitgegeven*. Amsterdam: L. van Bakkenes, 1843.

Rusconi, J. "Sja'ir Kompeni Welanda Berperang dengan Tjina." Academic dissertation; Utrecht: Wageningen Veenman, 1935.

Rushdie, Salman. *Imaginary Homelands: Essays and Criticism 1981–1992.* London: Penguin, 1992.

Saint Martin, Manuel L. "Running Amok: A Modern Perspective on a Culture-Bound Syndrome." *Journal of Clinical Psychiatry* 1.3 (1999): 66–70.

Saldin, B. D. K. *The Sri Lankan Malays and Their Language/Orang Melayu Sri Lanka dan Bahasanya.* Kurunegala: B. D. K. Saldin, 1996.

Portrait of a Sri Lankan Malay. Dehiwala: B. D. K. Saldin, 2003.

Saldin, M. D. "Constable Tuan Saban's Shootout with Saradiel." *Sunday Island,* March 16, 2003.

"The Keris – Malay Weapon, Social Symbol and Talisman." *The Sunday Times,* August 7, 2011.

Samaraweera, Vijaya. "Aspects of the Muslim Revivalist Movement in Late Nineteenth Century Sri Lanka," in M. A. M. Shukri (ed.), *Muslims of Sri Lanka: Avenues to Antiquity.* Beruwala: Jamiah Naleemia Institute, 1986, 363–383.

Sankalia, H. D. *Ramayana: Myth or Reality?* New Delhi: People's Publishing House, 1973.

Sariffo'deen, B. G. N. *The Story of My Life.* B. G. N. Sariffo'deen, n.d.

Schomburg, Susan Elizabeth. "'Reviving Religion': The Qadiri Sufi Order, Popular Devotion to Sufi Saint Muhyiuddin 'Abdul Qadir Al-Gilani, and Processes of 'Islamization' in Tamil." Unpublished Ph.D. thesis, Harvard University, 2003.

Schrikker, Alicia. *Dutch and British Colonial Intervention in Sri Lanka, 1780–1815: Expansion and Reform.* Leiden: Brill, 2007.

"Caught between Empires: VOC Families in Sri Lanka after the British Takeover, 1806–1808." *Annales de Démographie Historique* 2 (2011): 127–147.

Sears, Laurie J. "Epic Voyages: The Transmission of the Epics from India to Java," in Stephanie Morgan and Laurie J. Sears (eds.), *Aesthetic Tradition and Cultural Transmission in Java and Bali.* Madison: University of Wisconsin Press, 1984, 1–30.

Shellabear, W. G. "Hikayat Sri Rama: Introduction to the MS in the Bodleian Library at Oxford." *Journal of the Straits Branch of the Royal Asiatic Society* 70 (1917): 181–207.

Shukri, M. A. M. *Muslims of Sri Lanka: Avenues to Antiquity.* Beruwala: Jamiah Naleemia, 1986.

Singaravelu, S. "A Comparative Study of the Sanskrit, Tamil, Thai and Malay Versions of the Story of Rama, with Special Reference to the Process of Acculturation in the Southeast Asian Versions." *Journal of the Siam Society* 56.2 (July 1968): 137–185.

Skeen, William. *Adam's Peak: Legendary Traditional and Historic Notices of the Samanala and Sri Pada with a Descriptive Account of the Pilgrims' Route from Colombo to the Sacred Foot Print.* Colombo: W. L. H. Skeen & Co., 1870.

Skinner, Cyril. "The Influence of Arabic on Modern Malay (with Particular Reference to Spoken Malay)," in Justin Corfield (ed.), *Cyril Skinner*

(1924–1986): Orientalist, Linguist, Historian, Scholar. A Collection of Essays and Reviews. Clayton: Monash Asia Institute, 1996, 3–20.

Sourjah, M. A. *The Sri Lankan Malay Heritage in Brief.* Battaramulla: M. Wazir Sourjah, 2005.

Suryadi. "Sepucuk Surat dari Seorang Bangsawan Gowa di Tanah Pembuangan (Ceylon)." *Wacana: Jurnal ilmu Pengetahuan Budaya* 10.2 (2008): 214–245.

Taylor, Jean Gelman. "Belongings and Belonging: Indonesian Histories in Inventories from the Cape of Good Hope," in Ricci (ed.), *Exile in Colonial Asia*, 165–192.

Teh Gallop, Annabel. *The Legacy of the Malay Letter: Warisan Warkah Melayu.* London: British Library, 1994.

Teh Gallop, Annabel, et al. "A Jawi Sourcebook for the Study of Malay Palaeography and Orthography." *Indonesia and the Malay World* 43.125 (2015): 13–171.

Thomas, Paul. "Oodeen, a Malay Interpreter on Australia's Frontier Lands." *Indonesia and the Malay World* 40.117 (2012): 122–142.

Ugarte, Eduarto. "Running Amok: The Demoniacal Impulse." *Asian Studies Review* 16.1 (1992): 182–189.

Umam, Saiful. "God's Mercy Is Not Limited to Arabic Speakers: Reading Intellectual Biography of Muhammad Salih Darat and His Pegon Islamic Texts." *Studia Islamika* 20.2 (2013): 243–274.

Ward, Kerry. *Networks of Empire: Forced Migration in the Dutch East India Company.* Cambridge: Cambridge University Press, 2009.

Wheeler, Brannon M. *Prophets in the Quran: An Introduction to the Quran and Muslim Exegesis.* London and New York: Continuum, 2002.

Wickramasinghe, Nira. *Sri Lanka in the Modern Age: A History.* London: Hurst, 2014.

Wickremeratne, U. C. "Lord North and the Kandyan Kingdom." *JRAS* 1 (1973): 30–42.

Wickremesekere, Channa. *Kandy at War: Indigenous Military Resistance to European Expansion in Sri Lanka 1594–1818.* Colombo: Vijitha Yapa, 2004.

Widjojo, Muridan. *The Revolt of Prince Nuku: Cross-Cultural Alliance-making in Maluku, c. 1780–1810.* Leiden: Brill, 2008.

Wieringa, Edwin P. "Dotting the Dal and Penetrating the Letters: The Javanese Origin of the Syair Seribu Masalah and Its Bantenese Spelling," *BKI* 159.4 (2003): 499–518.

Wilkinson, R. J. *A Malay–English Dictionary*, 2 vols. Singapore: Kelly and Walsh, 1901; London: Macmillan & Co., 1959 (repr.).

Windstedt, Richard O. "An Undescribed Malay Version of the Ramayana." *JRAS* 76.1–2 (1944): 62–73.

An Unabridged Malay–English Dictionary. Kuala Lumpur and Singapore: Marican and Sons, 1967.

A History of Classical Malay Literature. Oxford: Oxford University Press, 1969.

Yang, Anand. "Bandits and Kings: Moral Authority and Resistance in Early Modern India." *Journal of Asian Studies* 66.4 (2007): 881–896.

Zainalfattah. *Sedjarah Tjaranja Pemerintahan di Daerah-daerah di Kepulauan Madura dengan Hubungannja.* Pamekasan: Paragon, 1951.

Zaini-Lajoubert, Monique. *Hikayat Indera Quraisyin: Satu Kajian*. Kuala Lumpur: Perpustakaan Negara Malaysia, 1998.

Zameer Careem, Tuan M. *Persaudaraan: Malay Life in Sri Lanka*. Colombo: S. Godage and Brothers, 2016.

Zieseniss, Alexander. *The Rama Saga in Malaysia: Its Origin and Development*. Trans. P. W. Burch with an introduction by C. Hooykaas. Singapore: Malaysian Sociological Research Institute, 1963.

Zoetmulder, P. J. *Pantheism and Monism in Javanese Suluk Literature*, trans. and ed. Merle C. Ricklefs. Leiden: KITLV, 1995 [1935].

Websites

Anonymous. "Pegang Keris Sunan Giri, Prabowo Bakal Jadi Wapres?" *Kompas*, June 24, 2009, www.kompas.com

Babad Tanah Jawi. Balai Pustaka 1939–1941, sastra.org/kisah-cerita-dan-kroni kal/69-babad-tanah-jawi/1027-babad-tanah-jawi-balai-pustaka-1938-41-1024-jilid-18

Bruinessen, Martin van. "Gunungjati, Sunan," in *Encyclopaedia of Islam*, THREE, Part 2014-3, 148–150, dx.doi.org/10.1163/1573-3912_ei3_COM_27552.

Menocal, Maria Rosa."The Culture of Translation." *Words without Borders* (October 2003), www.wordswithoutborders.org/article/the-culture-of-translation.

Index

'Abd al-Qādir al-Jīlānī ('Abd al-Qadir
   Jailani), 29, 212–213, 236, 239. *See also*
   Sheikh Muhiddin
Abraham. *See* Ibrahim (Abraham)
   Adam: in *Babad Tanah Jawi*, 153; clothes
      made by, 129, 135; connection with
      Sita stories, 179; death and burial of,
      138; directionality and traditions of,
      178; etymology of name of, 148, 176;
      expulsion from Paradise, 125–126,
      130, 134–135, 161, 249; falls to earth
      in Sri Lanka (Sarandib), 2, 9, 125,
      126–133, 138, 140, 143, 144–147,
      175, 177, 178, 242, 243, 244, 250; in
      Hikayat Seri Rama, 149, 161, 162–163,
      164, 178; Javanese exiles link their fate
      to that of, 133, 134–135, 138–148;
      Malay Compendium on, 26, 130–131;
      paradigmatic exile of, 125, 145,
      147–148; in Paradise, *128*; pilgrimage
      of, 136; returns to Sarandib, 137–138,
      144, 159; in Saldin's *Syair Faiḍ al-*
      *Abā*d, *140*,
      144–145, 220, 227, 230, 239, 242, 243;
      Surapati on, 146; *Tales of the Prophets*
      and miscellaneous on, 136–139; weeps at
      being in this world, 144; in Yasadipura
      I's *Serat Ménak Serandhil*, 142,
      143–144, 177
Adam's Bridge (Rama's Bridge), 150,
   178–179
Adam's Peak, 131–133; al-Bīrūnī on, 127;
   as exilic, 148; in *Hikayat Seri Rama*,
   162, 163, 175; Ibn Baṭṭūṭa on, 135; as
   pilgrimage site, 178; *Tales of the*
   Prophets and miscellaneous on, 138, 139;
   in Yasadipura I's *Serat Ménak*
   Serandhil, 143, 144
Adiwijaya, Pangéran, 94n57
Agung, Sultan, 3n3, 131
Alamat Langkapuri (newspaper), 168–172,
   173, 219, 224, 237–238, 244–245

Ālim, Tayka Shu'ayb, 130, 247
Alit, Ratu, 112
Amangkurat III of Mataram: as
   Amangkurat Selong, *89*, 249;
   correspondence with Suradilaga,
   50–56, *51*, 70, 75; death and return of
   body to Java, 88–93, 98, 111, 249;
   descendants and body repatriated, 4, 20,
   74; descendants' claim to throne,
   111–117, 123; distant descendants
   appeal to lineage of, 120–121; on
   dynastic tree-diagram, *89*, 249; exile
   of, 2, 76, 79–80; letter regarding his
   illness and imminent death, 118;
   missing *pusaka*s of Kartasura and,
   64–65, 72, 74, 80, 90, 144; sons of, 53,
   90–91; treatment in exile, 118–119
Amir Hamzah. *See* Ménak Amir Ambyah
   (Amir Hamzah)
Ampel, Sunan, 65
Angelbeek, Johan Gerard van, 170, 184
Anggakusuma, 112
Angkatan Menulis Ism, 73
al-Anṣārī, Zakariyyā, 28
apologies, 169, 196, 197, 229
Arabic language: in Abu Saleh Wahid's
   madrasah, 237; in *Hikayat Tuan Gusti*,
   68; interlinear translation for teaching,
   44; in Islamization, 39, 48; stories of
   the prophets in, 130; in *Weerabangsa*
   Family Notes, 213
Arabic script: for Javanese language, 6n8,
   15, 35, 39, 48; in *Malay Compendium*,
   39; for Malay language, 6, 15, 39, 48,
   187; soldiers receive education in, 187;
   in Sri Lankan Malay manuscripts, 1;
   for Tamil (Arabu-Tamil) language, 15,
   30, 35, 39, 48
Arabu-Tamil (*arwi*), 6n10, 30, 130, 240
Aroetekoe, Prince, 14
artinya/tegesé, 37–38, 136
arwi. See Arabu-Tamil (*arwi*)

272   Index